The Complete Poetry and Translations

CLARK ASHTON SMITH

The Complete Poetry and Translations

Volume 2: *The Wine of Summer*

Edited by S. T. Joshi and David E. Schultz

Hippocampus Press

New York

Works by Clark Ashton Smith copyright © 2012 by Arkham House Publishers, Inc., and CASiana Literary Enterprises, Inc. This edition copyright © 2012 by Hippocampus Press. Introduction and editorial matter copyright © 2012 by S. T. Joshi and David E. Schultz.

The photograph of Clark Ashton Smith on page 2 is used by permission of Alan H. Teague and The Literary Estate of Emil Petaja.

Cover photograph © 2012 by Anastasia Damianakos.
Cover Design by Barbara Briggs Silbert.
Hippocampus Press logo designed by Anastasia Damianakos.

Published by Hippocampus Press
P.O. Box 641, New York, NY 10156
www.hippocampuspress.com

The Library of Congress has cataloged the hardcover edition as follows:

Smith, Clark Ashton, 1893-1961.
  [Poems]
  The complete poetry and translations / Clark Ashton Smith ; edited by S. T. Joshi and David E. Schultz. -- 1st ed.
      p. cm.
  Includes bibliographical references and index.
  ISBN-13: 978-0-9771734-0-2 (v. 3)
  I. Joshi, S. T., 1958- II. Schultz, David E., 1952- III. Title.
  PS3537.M335A6 2007
  811'.52--dc22
                          2006039390

First Paperback Edition, 2012
1 3 5 7 9 8 6 4 2

ISBN 978-1-61498-046-9 (Volume 2)
ISBN 978-1-61498-048-3 (3 Volume Set)

Contents

Spectral Life

1927–1929

Les Violons

J'entends vibrer en moi des violons mystiques,
Envenimés longtemps de rêves maléfiques:
Ils parlent les mots je ne pas savoirais
Souvent ils maudissent, ils vagissent jamais,
Comme ils sourdent du sein des fosses sataniques.   5

J'entends vibrer en moi des violons mystiques
Emmiellés longuement de rêves séraphiques.
Ils parlent tous les mots je ne pas oublierais,
Souvent ils benissent, ils chantent pour jamais,
Comme ils sourdent du sein des trônes angéliques.   10

Au bord du Léthé

Les pétals des vieux pavots,
Et les boutons des lys perdus,
Au bord du Léthé sont déchus
Pour joncher le fleuve sans flots.

Là se fanent des anémones,   5
Des lys tigrés, et des muguets;
Leurs pâles fleurs, leurs fruits violets,
Là tombent prés des belladones.

Et là gisent les floraisons
D'automne, sous les vents sans trames;   10
Et là, des funestes jusquiames
Mêlent aux pensées leurs fleurons. . . .

Et tous mes amours, tous mes mots,
Et tous mes rêves, disparus,
Au bord du Léthé sont déchus   15
Pour joncher le fleuve sans flots.

The Nevermore-to-Be

Lady, be the chatelaine
Of my vagrant dreams and vain:
Knowing naught is true and fair
Save the love that is despair,
In thy heart's withholden visne   5
Share with me the might-have-been,

Weave with me the sorcery
Of the nevermore-to-be.

Lady, let us pluck delight
Only from a forfeit night,   10
From the bedded myrtles strewn
'Neath a never-risen moon.
From the coil of years made free
In the climes of reverie,
Flee we to the phantom Troy   15
Of a time-forbidden joy.

Lady, be the chatelaine
Of my vagrant dreams and vain:
Be thou true and be thou kind
To the love we shall not find—   20
Sweet as aught the sirens sang:
Time shall bring no dearer pang
Nor a mightier sorcery
Than the nevermore-to-be.

Fantaisie d'antan

Lost and alien lie the leas,
Purfled all with euphrasies,
Where the lunar unicorn
Breasts an amber-pouring morn
Risen from hesperian seas   5
Of a main that has no bourn.
Only things impossible
There in deathless glamor dwell:
Pegasus and sagittary,
Trotting, part the ferns of faery,   10
Succubi and seraphim
Tryst among the cedars dim;
Where the beaded waters brim,
White limoniads arise,
Interlacing arms and tresses   15
With the sun-dark satyresses;
There, on Aquilonian skies,
Gryphons, questing to and fro
For the gold of long ago,
Find at eve an aureate star   20

In the gulf crepuscular;
There the Hyperboreans,
Pale with wisdom more than man's,
Tell the wileful centauresses
Half their holocryptic lore;   25
There, at noon, the tritonesses,
All bemused with mandragore,
Mate with satyrs of the shore.

Love, could we have only found
The forgotten road that runs   30
Under all the sunken suns
To that time-estrangèd ground,
Surely, love were proven there
More than long and lone despair;
Holden and felicitous,   35
Love were fortunate to us;
And we too might ever dwell,
Deathless and impossible,
In those amber-litten leas,
Circled all with euphrasies.   40

Canticle

In my heart a wizard book,
Only love shall ever look:
Darling, when thou readest there,
Wisely falter and forbear
Ere thou turn'st the pages olden,   5
Deeply writ and deeply folden,
Where the legends of lost moons
Lie in chill unchanging runes.
Trifle not with charm or spell,
Heptagram or pentacle,   10
Leave in silence, long unsaid,
All the words that wake the dead.

Darling, in my heart withholden,
Letters rubrical and golden
Tell the secret of our love   15
And the philtred spells thereof;
There, my memories of thee,
Half of all the gramarie,

Are a firm unfading lore:
Read but these . . . and read no more. . . .   20
Shall it profit thee to find
Loves that went with snow and wind?
Leave in silence, long unsaid,
All the words that wake the dead.

A Fable

O lords and gods that are! the assigning tide, upon
Some prowless beach where a forgotten fisher dwells,
At last will leave the sea-flung jars of Solomon;

And he, the fisher, fumbling 'mid the weeds and shells,
Shall find them, and shall rive the rusted seals, and free   5
The djinns that shall tread down thy towering iron hells

And turn to homeless rack thy walled Reality;
That shall remould thy monuments and mountains flown,
And lift Atlantis on their shoulders from the sea

To flaunt her kraken-fouled necropoles unknown;   10
And raise from realm-deep ice the boreal cities pale
With towers that man has neither built nor overthrown. . . .

O lords and gods that are! I tell a future tale.

De Consolation

Tout n'est que rien, ma triste amante:
Rêver est le meilleur oubli;
Ne pleure pas la chair absente—
La chair, elle est un rêve aussi.

Tiens-toi toujours le Souvenir: 5
Il est la volupté mystique,
Et le passé est l'avenir
En son éternité féerique.

De Consolation

All things are nothing, my sad heart;
To dream is the best oblivion.
Weep not the absent flesh—
The flesh is also a dream.

*   *   *

Keep always the Memory—
It is the most mystical delight.
All things that pass become the future
In its magical eternity.

Simile

Ah! chide me not for silence, or that I,
Who lack not love, have wanted oftentime
Brave words wherewith to love you: as a lake,
Lulled in to sombre crystal by sad pines
Doth hold the moon made perfect in its heart   5
So have I held your image perfected
In this my sombre soul, nor troubled it
With the vain wind of words.

Trope

Deem me not dull or cold
For love not always told.

For when the lake at even
Is lorn of wind and air,
The moon lies perfect there   5
As in another heaven.

In sombre crystal holden,
In silence exquisite,
No ripple shadows it
Nor blurs the rondure golden.   10

Deem me not dull or cold
For love not always told.

Venus

Since I have seen her luster low and near
And warm and intimate within thine eyes,
Far Venus in her skies
Is fair as any star of Paradise.

But now thou hast departed, many a tear   5
Bedims her glory when she goes upon

The ways where thou art gone—
Westward and autumnward in silence drawn.

One Evening

We lay at twilight on the hill
And saw the citron gold of sunset drain,
Delicate as the sunsets of Cocaigne,
From heavens green and still.

Till fallen Venus burned to rose   5
We lay, and round us lay the lapsing world,
Low vales and hills in dusky velvet furled
That rimmed us with repose.

Above, was naught except the night
And all the stars, like pulses of white fire;   10
And our dark veins, fulfilled of long desire,
Pulsed with the pulsing light.

Tristan to Iseult

My thirst is as the thirst of light
On gardens long foredrained of dew:
A longing goes from me to you
Not all your sweetness shall requite,
And all my blood is wind-blown fire. . . .   5
Ah, in the desert of desire,
The fleeting fountains of delight!

Long hopeless, long forlorn of peace,
My lips are burning with your name,
Your kisses fall like flame on flame   10
And in your flesh is no release:
Ever I hear, in heart and vein,
The tumult of a surging main,
The unturning tides that never cease.

Far off, for others, slumber lies   15
A valley-land of leaf and bloom
The still, unfallen stars illume:
My sleep is made of flaring skies
And meads where running flame has been,
Where ashen blossoms crumble, in   20
A sere and blasted paradise.

Somewhere, on rose and rosemary,
On lotus red and lotus wan,
Distill the dews of Acheron:
Not yet, not yet, for you and me   25
To find the placid fields of death
And spend our sighs upon the breath
Of poppies of Persephone.

My thirst is as the thirst of light
On gardens long foredrained of dew: 30
A longing goes from me to you
Not all your sweetness shall requite
And all my blood is wind-blown fire. . . .
Ah, in the desert of desire
The fleeting fountains of delight!   35

Souvenance

Jazel, amber, opal, jet,
Planets low in summer skies,
Pool of noon and sunset mere—
One and all I shall forget
Sooner than your wistful eyes,   5
Brown as brook-water and clear.

Musk, amomum, frangipane,
Orange-scent and scent of fern,
And the spice of flowering cresses:
All are memories vague and vain—   10
None so swiftly shall return
As the perfume of your tresses.

To Antares

Antares, star of memory,
Her name I whisper unto thee;
Be thou tonight my messenger
And featly bear my love to her,
When she, as I, with like desire,   5
Gazes upon thy sanguine fire,
Dreaming of all thou sawest of old,
Things not to be forgot or told,
And borne beyond all others' knowing

By tongueless Lethe in its flowing: 10
Till, gazing thus, in one same thought
Our hearts shall be together brought,
And each insuperable mile
Forfeit its triumph, for awhile.

Song

I am grown tired of suffering,
Grief is a trite and tasteless thing,
And the dark Tyrian I have worn
Against the wind of ways forlorn,
Is faded in this deeper morn. 5

Ah! give me joy, to-day, tomorrow,
For I am surfeited with sorrow:
Be thou the source of memory,
And let thy bosom shut from me
All days and ways unshared with thee. 10

Amor Autumnalis

My love is the flame of an unfading autumn,
It is the flare of unconsuming leaves
In an ecstasy of halcyonian space and light;
It is the lingering of tall, untended flowers
And winds that bear the balsams of flown summer 5
In a valley-land, oblivious and secluded,
Where you shall come and wander tranquilly,
Forgetful of the roseless gardens—
In a quiet valley-land
Where vine to sanguine-colored vine shall lead you on, 10
Where golden woods and hills shall fold you in,
And you shall peer on pools of lucid bronze
And of black opal;
On vistas of the climbing pine,
And amber willows burning 15
Against the dreamful mauve of mountains floating vaguely
Within the skies' faint fringes.

Warning

Hast heard the voices of the fen,
That softly sing a lethal rune
Where reeds have caught the fallen moon—
A song more sweet than conium is,
Or honey-blended cannabis,   5
To draw the dreaming feet of men
On ways where none goes forth again?

Beneath the closely woven grass,
The coiling syrt, more soft and deep
Than some divan where lovers sleep,   10
Is fain of all who wander there;
And arms that glimmer, vague and bare,
Beckon within the lone morass
Where only dead things dwell and pass.

Beware! the voices float and fall   15
Half-heard, and haply sweet to thee
As are the runes of memory
And murmurs of a voice foreknown
In days when love dwelt not alone:
Beware! for where the voices call,   20
Slow waters weave thy charnel pall.

Temporality

Minutes and hours and days and months and years
As life-blood flowing from a lethal wound!
Let knee to knee and breast to breast be bound,
And still awhile the tremors of our fears.

Ah! deep in love's oblivion withdrawn,   5
As in some far and faery place to dwell,
Nor hear the sinister metallic knell
Of pendulums at moonset or at dawn.

Though time runs on, and star nor sun may stay,
Your bosom is the maze of my delight,   10
Where I can lose the minutes in their flight
And know not when to-day is yesterday.

Chansonette

Mon coeur n'a trouvé point de valeur, par delà
La borne enchantée de tes bras;
Entre tes pieds et tes cheveux, mystiques,
Se trouvent les rivages des royaumes féeriques;
Et celui qui erre en avant   5
Venira aux vallées de l'île d'Avilion.

Je ne sais pas du nord et du sud, que le chemin
Que font des genoux aux lèvres ma bouche et mes mains,
Ton sein qui s'arronde, à demi caché,
Sera encor mon horizon cherché,   10
Mon rêve plus vaillant est un oiseau qui vole
Dans le ciel de tes yeux frivoles.

Un parfum vient de toi, mollement,
Comme l'été de l'Arabie, mené par le vent;
O royaume de tout relâche, où l'amour   15
Veut demeurer, veut parcourir toujours!
Les îles plus belles et plus lointaines des Etres Heureux
Sont les îles qui surgissent de ton sein amoureux.

Chansonette

Little of worth my heart has found
Beyond thine arms' enchanted bound:
Between the feet and hair of thee
Lie all the shores of Faëry,
And he that wanders there has won   5
To the island-vales of Avalon.

My kisses' road from knees to mouth
Is all I know of north and south,
Thy rounding bosom endlessly
Shall still my sought horizon be,   10
My bravest dream a bird that flies
In the warm heaven of thine eyes.

A subtle perfume flows from thee
Like summer borne from Araby.
O realm of all delight, where love   15
Is fain to dwell, is fain to rove!
The fairest Islands of the Blest
Are those that rise upon thy breast.

Credo

Two things alone are good: to love, and to forget
All else but love and love's divine forgetfulness.
Vain is the world, and vain is all thine old distress,
All tears but love's are idle, idle is all regret.

There are no other sins than these: to put love by,   5
Or let the world be lord and arbiter of love:
Give me thy lips, thy heart, and all the sweets thereof—
And we shall drain the draught of Lethe ere we die.

The Autumn Lake

O sapphire lake amid autumnal mountains,
With fire of aspens round about you burning,
I would my love and I were now returning,
Perchance to leave you never—

To dwell with you, and know the mountain seasons,   5
The fleeing cloud, the cliff and pine eternal,
The fall of leaf and snow and blossom vernal
Upon your placid waters.

Le Lac d'automne

Lac de saphir, parmi d'automnales montagnes,
Avec le tremblaie rouge autour de toi brûlant,
Je veux que mon amour et moi, là retournant,
Te laisserions jamais:—

Que nous en demeurions, sachant les mois montagnards,   5
Le rocher éternel, et la fuyante nue;
Et la feuille, et la neige, et la fleur, y déchues
Sur tes tranquilles eaux.

On a Chinese Vase

Lovely as on the boughs of spring
Beneath the fallen suns of Ming,
There bloom the flowers of the plum
Where bloomless autumn shall not come
That came for all the years of Ming.   5

And here the flower-white herons peer
Unmoving on a waveless mere;
And ever, past the green bamboo,
The halcyon flies toward the blue
From waters where the herons peer.   10

Enchanted realm of porcelain
Whereon the sunken suns remain,
Wherein the perished blossoms bloom!
An ancient spring defers its doom
Within this land of porcelain.   15

November

Unshaken still, through wind and rain,
Red autumn rears her blazonry.
But, ah! the barren grief and pain
Of loveliness unshared with thee!
Ah! weariness of leaves and rain.   5

Wanting thy hand within my hand,
The heart of life eludes my will,
And dimly, through a doubtful land,
The moth of beauty flees me still,
And flutters from my lonely hand.   10

Until thy mouth be wed to mine,
A secret wound shall bleed in me.
And vain is all the season's wine
And vain her crimson blazonry
Until thy mouth be wed to mine.   15

Chanson de Novembre

Les cimes blasonnées et superbes du bois
Susurrent longuement au vent du morne mois:
Embrunies, safranées, empourprées ou vermeilles,
Chaque arbre faut épandre enfin ses feuilles vieilles,
Qui s'arrêtent sur l'onde, ou parmi les roseaux,   5
Ou dans l'ombrage vert des sapins automnaux.

Pour moi, leur son se mêle aux soupirs des ramées
Des arbres dans mon coeur aux feuilles safranées,
Embrunies, empourprées, et vermeilles, qui font

La magique forêt de mon amour profond: 10
Mais dans mon coeur toujours ces feuillages demeurent,
Ils ne décherront pas des rameaux qui susurrent.

Chanson de Novembre

The blazoned and superb tops of the wood
Whisper long while in the wind of the mournful month:
Or brown or saffron or purple or crimson,
At length each tree must cast afar its olden leaves,
That come to rest on the water, or among the reeds,   5
Or in the green shade of the autumnal firs.

For me, their sound immingles with the sigh of branches
Of trees in mine own heart, with saffron leaves,
Or purple or brown or crimson leaves, which make
The magic forest of my love profound . . .   10
But always in my heart these foliages remain—
They shall not ever fall from the whispering boughs.

Exorcism

Like ghosts returning stealthily
From those grey lands
Palled with funereal ashes falling
After the burnt-out sunset,
The mists of the valley reach with wavering, slow,   5
Malignant arms from pine to pine, and climb the hill
As fatal memories climb
To assail some heart benighted and bewitched. . . .

And once they would have crept
Around me in resistless long beleaguerment,   10
To lay their death-bleak fingers on my heart:
But now
My memories are of you and of the many graces
And tender, immortal, mad beatitudes of love;
And every chill and death-born phantom,   15
Made harmless now and dim,
Must pass to haunt the inane, unpassioned air;
And only living ghosts
Of raptures gone or ecstasies to be,
May touch me and attain within the circle   20
Your arms have set about me.

Winter Moonlight

After our fond, reiterate farewells
In the shadow of the wall, between the lamplight and the moon,
I left you, and returned, and, torn from you once more,
Departed loath and laggardly
Into the icy, luminous, immense white night.   5
But, though mine every step was a gulf dividing us
On ways forlorn and chill,
I was not cold nor sorrowful nor alone,
Nor friended by regret:
For love went with me like the warmth of a hearth-lit room   10
And soft enfolding arms;
And the widening space between us
Was somehow one with love,
And evermore I knew
That your heart and my heart were islanded   15
In the same full-tided sea of happiness and light,
And washed by the same waves of vibrant memory,
Like shores of halcyon summer
Where halcyon perfumes mount beneath a burning moon.

Connaissance

Only through the senses have I known you,
But you are nearer than the things of sense—
Nearer than is the daylight in mine eyes,
And nearer
Than scent of orchard blossoms in the dark,   5
Or touch of mountain wind or water flowing,
Or long belovèd music heard once more
Among belovèd faces.
The sense of you is more than sight or audience,
The thought of you lies deeper   10
Than the clear springs of recollection,
The shallow tarns of dreaming.
You flow a stronger blood within my blood,
Poured from a heart whose pulses
Suffuse the veins of centaurs and of gods.   15
You are a thought encompassing all other thoughts,
Even as the sea enfolds the kelp and coral
And the sea-flowers and sea-monsters
And the domes of deep unsunned Atlantis.

Harmony

Black pines above an opal tarn,
And the grey cliff above the pines,
And the clouds above the cliff,
Rose-hued with a hidden sunset.

O longed-for place beyond the world!   5
Let love be beautiful and tranquil
And high and everlasting
And perfect as thou art.

Moon-Sight

We wandered in your garden
When the broad magnolia-flowers
Took on a stranger pallor from the moon
And the rose gave up the half of all its redness.
I turned to you,   5
And your face was the long-expected vision,
Far-sought, but never found,
In the dark bafflement of many a dreamland maze,
Through sunless, moonless woods
And beside unflowing waters   10
In the twain deserts of the waking world
And of the worlds of sleep.
I saw you then,
Supremely fair, incomparably dear,
Till seeing was become a greater ecstasy   15
Than others know in all possession—
Till the whole of love and life was in your face
And the whole world's loveliness,
And memory was no more
Than an arabesque of shadows swept away in light,   20
And time and space were phantoms
Forgotten and dispersing
To leave this ever-during instant,
This luminous parterre
Bearing the one momentous flower of your face.   25

Sonnet

Empress with eyes more sad and aureate
Than sunset ebbing on a summer coast,
What gold chimera lovest thou the most—
What gryphon with emblazoned wings elate,
Or dragon straying from the dim estate   5
Of kings that sway the continents uttermost
Of old Saturnus? Or what god, or ghost,
Or spacial demon for thy spirit's mate
Art fain to choose? Howbeit, in thy heart,
Though void as now to vision and desire   10
The days and years deny thee, shall abide
The passion of the impossible, the pride
Of lust immortal for the monstrous ire
And pain of love in scarlet worlds apart.

Similitudes

My love for you is tender
As flowers after snow
Amid a mountain fir-wood
Where mountain waters flow.
My love for you is tender   5
As flowers after snow.

My love for you is deeper
Than a mountain tarn at noon,
That lulls the ledge-flung torrents
To frame the shadowy moon.   10
My love for you is deeper
Than a mountain tarn at noon.

My love for you is lasting
As pines amid the spring,
As pines that bore no transient   15
Autumnal blazoning.
My love for you is lasting
As pines amid the spring.

Calendar

To find with you the earliest
Willow-buds before their silver turns to gold,
And the first previous buttercup and cyclamen that blossom
Ere the leaflets of the vernal trees unfold;
To lie with you in June   5
Beneath a broad magnolia-scented moon,
And under stars and meteors of late summer;
To see with you
The goldenrod become an ashen ghost
And the rose of autumn crumble   10
And the leaf put on the splendor of the rose,
And the last leaf fall upon the wintry blue
In a wind from the lofty snows;
To sit with you beside the murmuring fire
When a stifled sunset dies,   15
And watch through misty panes
The boughs that toss upon a winter-driven sky
And the swift eternal slanting of dark rains:

These are my seasons,
This is my calendar,   20
Where love appoints the course of many a sun and star;
And, wanting you, I should not care nor know
If it were the time of falling jasmine-petals
Or the time of falling snow.

February

Gossamer-frail, the moon
Goes down the skies of day;
Vague winds are on the noon,
Blown from the wandering vales of cloudland far away.

They come, and hardly stir   5
The dell-grown grasses high:
But in the pine and fir,
As in my musing heart, I hear a tender sigh.

Fragile as dreams, afloat
Between the earth and skies,   10
Beyond serene, remote,
Blue-folded hills the fair and moon-white mountains rise.

In woodland shadows deep
The firstling flowers blow;
And in my heart I keep   15
A love that also came after the frost and snow.

Variations

Love is a rift of azure
Within the sombre ceiling of the storm.

Love is a rainbow,
Whereof one burning end is at our feet
And the other   5
Is lost amid the purple flowers and castles
And clouds of Faërie.

Love is a heaven
Where myrrh and cassia rise from summer lands
For an incense to the summer sun.   10

Sufficiency

To house our happy love
We long for an alcove
Curtained against the dawn in Ispahan,
Or some Algerian roof, whereon
At eventide to lie   5
And watch the fiery passing of the sky;
Till morning takes the last star, ere it set
Beyond the parapet.

And yet,
In this one little room, this homely place,   10
Have we not known enough of time and space?
With mouths together drawn,
Have we not prayed the night to linger on,
And found as much of glamor manifold,
Of happiness and pleasure,   15
As our four hands can measure
And our two hearts can hold?

Lichens

Pale-green and black and bronze and grey,
In broken arabesque and foliate star,
They cling, so closely grown
Upon the sombre stone
That one would deem they are   5
As much a part thereof as the design
Is part of some porcelain from Cathay—
Some vase of Tang or Ming
Patterned with blossoms intricate and fine
And leaves of alien spring   10
Exempt forever from the year's decay.
Old too they seem and with the stones coeval—
Fraught with the stillness and the mystery
Of time not known to man;
Like runes and pentacles of a primeval   15
Unhuman wizardry
That none may use nor scan.

Vaticinations

I heard the leaves of the willow whisper
As they fell at morn on the gusty mere:
"You shall be torn and blown as we are,
In a wind that bears the crumbling year."

I heard the boulders murmur mutely   5
In the noontide sun on the windless hill:
"Sometime you shall be calm as we are
And as tranquil and as still."

Nyctalops

Ye that see in darkness
When the moon is drowned
In the coiling fen-mist
Far along the ground—
Ye that see in darkness,   5
Say, what have ye found?

—We have seen strange atoms
Trysting on the air—
The dust of vanished lovers
Long parted in despair,   10
And dust of flowers that withered
In worlds of otherwhere.

We have seen the nightmares
Winging down the sky,
Bat-like and silent,   15
To where the sleepers lie;
We have seen the bosoms
Of the succubi.

We have seen the crystal
Of dead Medusa's tears.   20
We have watched the undines
That wane in stagnant weirs,
And mandrakes madly dancing
By black, blood-swollen meres.

We have seen the satyrs   25
Their ancient loves renew
With moon-white nymphs of cypress,
Pale dryads of the yew,
In the tall grass of graveyards
Weighed down with evening's dew.   30

We have seen the darkness
Where charnel things decay,
Where atom moves with atom
In shining swift array,
Like ordered constellations   35
On some sidereal way.

We have seen fair colors
That dwell not in the light—
Intenser gold and iris
Occult and recondite;   40
We have seen the black suns
Pouring forth the night.

The Hill-Top

Alone upon my hill-top,
After the ravelled rains,
I see the cloudy mountains,
I see the misty plains.

Fair is my hill, and rugged,   5
Where silken grasses grow,
And the drifted clouds go by me
More soft than woven snow.

The pale fantastic lichens
Make patterns on the stone,   10
And the oaks are old and dwarfèd,
With golden mosses grown.

Beneath the ancient boulders
There dwells the shadowy fern;
And here the twisted pine-trees   15
To shapes of beauty turn.

I wander through the seasons
With thoughts of love and grief
That fall with the flowers of springtime
Or blow with the autumn leaf.   20

Between the plains and mountains,
Between the clouds and grass,
I find the dreams that linger,
And the fairer dreams that pass.

L'Amour suprême

Parmi des grands ennuis, des grands voeux mis en cendre,
Un seul amour en moi flamme éternellement:
Tel est un vieux volcan, altier, au feu moutant,
Dans un monde envieilli où la nuit vient descendre:

Autrement, tout est mort, tout est noir et glacé;   5
Mais, à ce fier flambeau magistral et suprême,
On voit des bois flétris, qu'assombrit le ciel blême,
Et des murs foudroyés du royaume enfoncé.

O mes rêves errant comme des vieux nomades,
Au long d'un vain séjour, déroutés, maussades, 10
Cherchant les champs fanés, les puits évanouis,

Que cette flamme sous un ciel final vous mène
Au vallon encore vert, où toute fleur est pleine
De la pluie et du miel de nos premières nuits.

L'Amour suprême

Among the great ennuis, and great longings laid in ashes,
One only love flames evermore in me.
Such an old volcano, with ever-mounting fire,
In an aging world whereon the night descends:

Otherwise, all is dead, all is grown dark and frore; 5
But, by this proud flambeau, magistral and supreme,
One sees the withered woods, clear-lined on a pale heaven,
And the thunder-blasted walls of a sunken kingdom.

O my dreams wandering like old nomads
The length of a vain way, sullen and baffled, 10
Seeking the faded fields, the vanished wells,

Let this flame lead you under a final sky
To the valley verdant still, where every flower is full
Of the honey-mingled rain of your first nights.

Alexandrins

Sachant l'ennui du jour, de la nuit, et des rêves,
La lourde vanité des joies et des douleurs;
Le frêle amour, laissant ses immenses langueurs,
Les désespoirs si longs, et les délices brèves;

Sachant que le ver, dans les sots cerveaux qu'il teint, 5
A prospéré, est mort joint à sa grise amante;
Sachant que pour jamais une ombre croupissante
Reste dans le tombeau la nuit et le matin;

Sachant la feuille qui vacille, et flambé, et tombe,
La douce mort des fleurs et des soirs étoilés— 10
Oui, sachant tout cela, les coeurs trop désolés
Ont soif du seul sommeil qui remplit toute tombe.

Absence

En ton départ, ma déité,
Ma vie aussi s'en est allée,
Ainsi que l'hirondelle ailée
Qui suit la fuite de l'été.

Et quand de la mienne ton âme   5
Recule et s'enfuit quelquefois,
Mon rêve, dans un morne bois,
Cherche un trésor qu'il ne réclame.

Une Vie spectrale

Je fus longtemps un vieux fantôme,
Flottant léger comme un arôme
Autour de mes tombeaux détruits,
Et dans mes salles écroulantes
Que soutenaient des lourds atlantes   5
Aux dos de métaux inouïs.

J'ai rencontré des reines pâles
Et des naïades trop spectrales
Que je baisais au bien antan
Plus loin que les sphères lointaines;   10
J'ai respiré les spectres vaines
Des roses mortes pour maint an.

J'ai demeuré sur une terre
Qui n'était que cendre et poussière;
Cherchant des floraisons flétris   15
Dans des ténèbres croupissantes,
J'ai flairé, faibles et stagnantes,
Les puanteurs des dieux pourris.

Mes nuits étaient des nuits passées
Où luisaient des lunes glacées,   20
Des noirs hiers étaient mes jours;
Des choses longuement perdues,
Des souvenances disparues,
M'apparaissaient dans ces séjours.

Je n'écoutais que des voix grêles,   25
Je ne touchais que des seins frêles
Des succubes plus exsanguins;

Je ne sentais qu'une détresse
Trop languissante, une tristesse
Sans goûts, sans parfums, et sans teints.   30

Je m'ennuyais dans cette vie,
Et les mortels m'ont fait envie:
Ainsi me voilà maintenant
Soulevant un corps comme d'autres,
Portant un coeur comme les vôtres,   35
Un très tangible revenant.

Spectral Life

I was long-while an ancient phantom,
Floating light as an aroma
Around mine ancient tombs
And over mausoleums
Upborne by wingèd women   5
On their backs of strange mineral.

I have met pale queens
And nymphs a little spectral
Whom I have known in some antiquity
Remoter than the far-off stars;
I have breathed the spectres vain
Of roses dead for many a year.   10

I have dwelt upon an earth
That was no more than ashes and dust;
With the flowers of withered autumns,
Amid the unflowing shadows,
I have known, exiguous and stagnant,
The stench of gods decayed.   15

My nights were nights long overpast,
Were nights with frosted moons,
And my days were all dark yesterdays;
The things long lost,
And remembrances confused,
Appeared to me in these sojourns.   20

Hearing the fragile speech,
The wailings of shrill voices
Of vampires wholly bloodless,
I have found no more than a distress

Feeble and dim, a sadness
That had nor taste nor perfume nor colour.   25

And of this life I have grown weary,
And I have envied the living;
Therefore behold me now
Supporting a body like others,
Bearing a heart like yours,
A very tangible phantom.   30

Seins

J'aime vos seins, petits mais très venustes
Dont je me plaît plus que des seins robustes;
Ils sont pour moi des mondes neufs encor,
Remplis toujours d'ineffable trésor.
Et nulle fleur de rêve n'est plus douce   5
Que chaque bout comme un fère rousse, du vin inépuisé
Où j'ai teté
Mêlant la joie du jour et du passé
L'oubli suprême, et l'ultime paresse,
Dans un baiser, dans une caresse.   10

Les Marées

Mon coeur se désemplit d'une immense rancune
Qui retire sa mer sous quelque occulte lune,
Sous quelque lune noire, au lointain de l'esprit:
Aux sables trop laves, les eaux d'amour on tri,
Et les nymphes de l'onde, oubliant l'amère mer   5
Sourient lentement dans une molle écume.

O lune du bonheur, ne t'éloigne jamais,
Soulève incessament tes lames désormais:
Reveille en moi la mer pour chanter des louanges,
Pour crier un cher nom aux côtes plus étranges,   10
Pour cacher doucement les recifs froids et nus.
Laissant renaître aussi l'éternelle Vénus:
Maintiens ta douce mer à sa pleine mare
Pour baigner les piedes blancs de ma belle adorée.

Paysage païen

Je songe à cette terre ancienne
Où des couchants longtemps déchus
Dorent des grands cygnes perdus
Pagayant dans une eau païenne
Au pied des rochers blancs et roux;   5
Où les vents somnolents et doux
Ne sèment pas à l'onde oisive
Les frêles fleurs des myrtes verts
Qui poussent pardessus les mers
Aux bois habités d'un dive.   10

C'est un pays d'où les vieux dieux
N'ont pas volés vers d'autres cieux;
Où des helléniques lamies
Nous leurrent au couvert caché;
Où des dryades endormies   15
Gisent dans l'ombrage taché
D'un soleil d'or par la saulaie;
Où la sirène dans la baie
Du glauque golfe approfondi
Nage indolemment à midi.   20

Il n'est pas des châsses croulées,
Il n'est pas des lauriers cassés:
On trouve ici les jours passés
Et les nuits longtemps écoulées.
Pour nous qui venons, plus tardifs   25
A ses vallons, à ses massifs,
Ce pays reste impérissable,
Sommeillant chimériquement
Et baigné par l'enchantement
De sa jaune aube intarissable.   30

Le Souvenir

Quand mon âme vient rappeler
Ta mémoire à sa nuit malsaine,
Un soleil fortuné m'amène
Dans un domaine ensorcelé:

Car toujours ta face m'éclaire 5
Parmi de souvenirs chéris:
C'est un rayon de soirs mûris
Qui teint un opulent parterre.

Je sens la superbe chaleur
Dont mon amour de toi m'allume, 10
Comme un verger qui se consume
Sous fort Septembre en sa ferveur.

La roideur de la nuit frileuse
Me lâche encor, facilement,
Dans mon heureux tâtonnement 15
Autour du corps d'une amoureuse.

Rêvasserie

Au vert du vieux bocage
Le monde est un mirage
Plus terne et plus blafard
Que l'étang qui refléte
Dans une autre planète 5
Le blanc du nénufar.

Je me souviens à peine,
Je méconnais ma peine:
De ce vert demi-jour
Je vois partir, futiles 10
Sous leurs masques mobiles,
La mort avec l'amour.

Pardelà ma feuillée,
La mare ensoleillée
M'endort l'oeil ébloui, 15
Comme un cristal d'où passe
La flamme d'une extase
Au mage évanoui.

L'oubliance incroyable
M'accroche, inenarrable, 20
Du fond de son abri;
Je me perds, et je frôle
La chose qui s'envole,
Trop vaste pour l'esprit.

Je ne sais si le chêne   25
Soupire à mon haleine,
Ni si j'y tire l'air;
Parfois je suis l'oeillette,
Et parfois la massette
Qui s'égrène au flot clair.   30

Pour moi, toute pensée
Est feuillue et boisée,
Et se mêle aux sureaux:
A la sève écoulié,
Elle mûrit la boie   35
Et s'épand aux rameaux.

La Mare

La lune décroissante
Se couche au noir dédale
D'une aunaie automnale
Dans la nuit sans luisance.

Je me perds et m'égare   5
Au bord des eaux profondes,
Ténébreuses, immondes,
D'une funeste mare.

Les loques de l'automne,
Comme elles s'en envolent,   10
Dans leur chute me frôlent:
Je tremble et je frissonne,

Et ma rêvasserie
S'effeuille à l'eau prochaine
Au feuillage du frêne,—   15
Pareillement flétrie.

Le Miroir des blanches fleurs

Rappelez-vous l'étang dont l'eau nous attirait
Dans d'estivaux matins,
Voyez-vous notre étang, ceint de buissons alpins,
Où de mignonnes fleurs la blancheur se mirait
Au vert fond assombri par l'ombre des sapins.   5

C'était un lieu de fée, une scène enchantée
Par des charmes antiques:
L'on aurait cru y voir sortir des bois féeriques,
Des forêts des romans, une reine montée
Sur un palefroi pâle aux harnais mirifiques.　　　　　10

Les hauts rochers au loin, les hauts arbres prochains,
Le silence des eaux
Et le silence noir pesant sur les rameaux,
Tous semblaient apportés des espaces lointains
Qu'endormait un sort blanc aux temps des fabliaux.　　15

Oh! dans quelle chronique, oh! dans quelle légende
Dérobée à cet âge,
Était ce lieu dépeint? . . . Fleurs du petit rivage,
Qui fleurissaient au bord des eaux de l'ancien monde,
Pourquoi donc venez-vous dans ce nouveau parage? . . .　　20

Nous y traînaient, dans nos esprit le sentiment
D'autres temps, d'autres lieux:
Le charme était si fort et si prestigieux,
Que nul roi des lutins, venant plus vaillament,
N'eût étonné nos coeurs avec son cor mielleux.　　25

—Et toi, dont l'oeil aimé doublait ce paysage,
De quelle dame altière
As-tu porté un peu la pâleur légendaire?
Et moi, de quel trouvère errant au vieux bocage
Ai-je connu l'amour, les chants, et la chimère?　　30

Le Miroir des blanches fleurs

Remember thou the tarn whose water once allured us
In happy mornings,
See thou the tarn, encinct with mountain bushes,
Where the whiteness of the tiny flowers was mirrored
In a green depth darkened by the shadow of the fire.　　5

It was a faery place, a place enchanted
By the charms of olden time;
Here one had thought to see, from the elfin wood,
From the forest of romaunts, a queen emerge
Mounted on a pale palfray with mirific trappings.　　10

The lofty rocks afar, the lofty trees nearby,
The silence of the waters
And the dark silence weighing down the branches,
All seemed as if brought over from far spaces
Endrowsed by a white spell in the time of ballads.   15

Oh! in what chronicle, oh! in what legend
Long hidden from our age,
Was this place haply pictured? . . . Flowers of the little shore,
Have you not bloomed about the old-world waters?
How are you transported to this new latitude? . . .   20

We lingered there, in our souls the sentiment
Of other times, of other scenes:
The charm so potent was, and magical,
That an elfin king, coming full valorously,
Had not surprised our hearts with his sweet horn.   25

—And thou, in whose loved eye the landscape was redoubled,
Of what high and stately dame
Hast thou borne for a little while the legendary pallor?
And of what troubadour, far-roaming in the boscage,
Have I known the love, the songs, and the chimera?   30

The Dragon-Fly

By the clear green river,
One afternoon in early autumn,
A dragon-fly with crimson wings alit
On the white thigh of my belovèd;
And, ever since it flew,   5
More fully have I known the loveliness
And the transiency of days;
And love and beauty burn within me
Like the piled leaves of blood and amber
That burn at autumn's ending.   10

September

Slumberously burns the sun
Over slopes adust and dun,
Leaning southward through September. . . .
I forget and I remember,
Life is half oblivion. . . .   5
Somnolently burns the sun.

Close and dim the horizons creep,
Earthward lapse the heavens in sleep;
Woodlands faint with azure air
Seem but bourns of Otherwhere: 10
Swooning with ensorcelled sleep,
Close and dim the horizons creep.

Embers from a dreamland hearth,
Glow the leaves in croft and garth;
Vines within the willows drawn   15
Relume the gold of visions gone;
Darkly burn, in croft and garth,
Embers from a dreamland hearth.

Sleepy like an airless fire,
Smoulders my supreme desire: 20
Throeless, in the tranquil sun,
Hearts could melt and merge as one
In forgetful soft desire
Drowsy like an airless fire.

Shadows

Thy shadow falls on the fount,
On the fount with the marble wall. . . .
And in alien time and space
On the towns of a doomèd race
The shadows of glaciers mount;   5
And patchouli-shadows crawl
On the mottling of boas that bask
In the fire of a moon fantasque;
And the light shades of bamboo
Flutter and ruffle and lift,   10
In the silver dawn they sift
On the meadows of Xanadu. . . .

They shall fall, till the light be done,
By moon and cresset and sun,
From gnomon and fir-tree and throne,   15
And the vine-caught monoliths leaning
In the woods of a world far-flown;
They shall pass on the dim star-dials
By the peoples of Pluto wrought;
They shall follow the shifted vials   20

Of a sorceress of Fomalhaut;
They shall move on the primal plains
In the broken thunder and rains;
They shall haply reel and soar
Where the red volcanoes roar   25
From the peaks of a blackening sun;
They shall haply float and run
From the tails of the lyre-birds preening
On the palms of a magic mead;
And their mystery none shall read,   30
And none shall have known their meaning
Ere night and the shadows are one.

Evanescence

Where the golden rose
Of autumn goes,
Love shall go:
How the petals pass
In the snow-lost grass,   5
No man shall know.

But heed not thou
The barren bough
And the ravening wind,
Though the flower be blown   10
And the leaf be flown
And the sun grow blind.

For the rose that is gone
Forgotten and wan
In the death-wan snows,   15
Another flower
In an alien hour
Oblivious blows.

Fellowship

O ye that follow the sun,
O ye that follow the light
Of the fen-fire through the night,
Are your ways in the end not one?

Ye shall know but the single doom,   5
Ye shall sleep the self-same sleep,
And the trench of the trooper is deep
As the vault of an emperor's tomb.

Though dolor be yours, and dearth,
And the noon be darkness above,   10
Or ye know delight and love
In the pleasant places of earth,

Though your mouths be mirthful or dumb,
When the worm has eaten them thin
Ye shall grin with the same white grin   15
At the death whereto ye are come.

Ougabalys

In billow-lost Poseidonis
I was the god Ougabalys:
    My three horns were of similor
Above my double diadem,
My one eye was a moon-wan gem   5
    Found in a monstrous meteor.

Incredible far peoples came,
Called by the thunders of my fame,
    And fleetly passed my terraced throne,
Where titan pards and lions stood,   10
As pours a never-lapsing flood
    Before the wind of winter blown.

Before me, many a chorister
Made offering of alien myrrh,
    And copper-bearded sailors brought,   15
From isles of ever-foaming seas,
Enormous lumps of ambergris
    And corals intricately wrought.

Below my glooming architraves,
One brown eternal file of slaves   20
    Came in from mines of chalcedon,
And camels from the long plateaux
Laid down their sard and peridoz,
    Their incense and their cinnamon.

But now, within my sunken walls,   25
The slow blind ocean-serpent crawls,
    And sea-worms are my ministers;
And wondering fishes pass me now,
Or press before mine eyeless brow
    As once the thronging worshippers.   30

Ineffability

Thy deepest dolor shalt thou tell,
But nevermore thy happiness:
Unworded still and utterless,
The incredible dark raptures dwell.

Too readily our lips repine   5
For splendor lost and beauty flown:
Our speech is made of earthly moan
And not the praise of things divine.

Ah, facile are the songs we sing
To dulcimers that sorrows mute: 10
But joy requires a stronger lute
Of high unshatterable string.

The Nightmare Tarn

I sat beside the moonless tarn alone,
In darkness where a mumbling air was blown—
A moulded air, insufferably fraught
With dust of plundered charnels: there was naught
In this my dream but darkness and the wind,   5
The blowing dust, the stagnant waters blind,
And sombre boughs of pine or cypress old
Wherefrom a rain of ashes dark and cold
At whiles fell on me, or was driven by
To feed the tongueless tarn; within the sky   10
The stars were like a failing phosphor wan
In gutted tombs from which the worms have gone.
But though the dust and ashes in one cloud
Blinded and stifled me as might a shroud,
And though the foul putrescent waters gave   15
Upon my face the fetors of the grave,

Though all was black corruption and despair,
I could not stir, like mandrake rooted there,
And with mine every breath I seemed to raise
The burden of some charnel of old days,   20
Where, tier on tier, the leaden coffins lie.

While sluggish black eternities went by
I waited; on the darkness of my dream
There fell nor lantern-flame nor lightning-gleam,
Nor gleam of moon or meteor; the wind   25
Withdrawn as in some sighing tomb, declined,
And all the dust was fallen; the waters drear
Lay still as blood of corpses. Loud and near
The cry of one who drowned in her despair
Came to me from the filthy tarn; the air   30
Shuddered thereat, and all my heart was grown
A place of fears the nether hell might own,
And prey to monstrous wings and beaks malign:
For, lo! the voice, O dearest love, was thine!
And I—I could not stir: the dreadful weight   35
Of tomb on ancient tomb accumulate
Lay on my limbs and stifled all my breath,
And when I strove to cry, the dust of death
Had filled my mouth, nor any whisper came
To answer thee, who called upon my name!   40

Cumuli

They seem the enfolding mountains of some fairer land
That lies beyond the world,
With vales of purpling rose in hills eburnean furled
And halcyonian flowers unplucked of any hand.

I deem their creamy crags look distantly on meres   5
Where misty torrents fall
Sleepily through the silver dimness covering all,
Vague as the magic air of half-remembered years.

Below their sun-bright passes, leading palely down
To meadows never seen,   10
Are fruits that star with shadowy gold the strange demesne,
The purple realms of peace that bear no tower nor town.

And though they change and pass, with toppling peaks unstable,
To leave the land we know,
This fantasy is mine from long and long ago,   15
A dream unproven still, and still inviolable.

Refuge

Though winter come with cleaving rain, with bonds of rime,
It shall not sever us, the dreamers calm and wise,
From succor and solace of our pagan paradise:

For in your cypress-bole, still standing from the prime,
Dear hamadryad, you and I shall drowse content,   5
Bosom to bosom, till the evil term be spent.

And, though the wrackful storm on seas and headlands climb,
Another dreamer has found a long-abiding home,
Save in the nereid's cavern, far beneath the foam.

Some Older Bourn

1930–1938

Answer

The brief and piteous loves of yore—
Canst not forget them, or forgive?
All that I have to give, I give;
Ask not if it be less or more
For glad or mournful loves of yore.   5

The blood in all my veins is thine;
My pouring pulses flow to thee
As vernal torrents tow'rd the sea.
Love is the winepress and the wine:
The blood in all my veins is thine.   10

Content thee; for I find or lose
No breast but thine in any dream;
I hear thy name at night's extreme—
'Tis mine own whisper; dawn renews
No other love to find or lose.   15

I make this love my calendar;
Thine arms, thy lips, are termini
To mete the bourn of memory:
All else is doubtful, dim, and far.
I make this love my calendar.   20

If others loved me ill or well,
It was as in a legend old;
Their love is now a story told,
And ours alone remains to tell:
Therefore, be wise! and love me well.   25

Song at Evenfall

I have no silver gifts for thee,
No scented words nor frankincense:
Only this love, that burns in me
Like a vain fire in valleys whence
The sun has flown beyond the sea.   5

Though moon and dawn alike delay,
Let love the mobled ways illume,
As once, on evening roads, the ray
Of Venus thrilled athwart the gloom
And led us home from far away.   10

Jungle Twilight

From teak and tamarind and palm
The heavy sun goes down unseen;
The jungle drowns in duskier green;
And quickening perfumes vespertine
Alone assail the sluggish calm.   5

Narcotic silence, opiate gloom:
The painted parakeets are gone,
The blazoned butterflies withdrawn.
Nocturnal blossoms, weird and wan,
Like phantom wings and faces bloom.   10

In the high trees the darkness grows,
And, rising, overbrims the sky.
Like a black serpent gliding by
'Neath woven creepers covertly,
Unknown and near, the river flows;   15

Where deeplier in oblivion's tide
The dateless, fair pagodas fall,
And, winding on the toppled wall
Where carven gods hold carnival,
The cobra couples with his bride.   20

Madrigal of Evanescence

Dear, can we endure to know
How these jasmine-girdled hours
Shall become the long ago?
Love, can we endure to know
How our longing and our woe   5
Fall like autumn-loosened flowers
Down the gulf of days foredone
On unstelled oblivion?

Love, can we endure to prove
How no longest pang or pleasure   10
Lengthens out the lot of love?
Dear, can we endure to prove
How the sharpening moons will measure
Our permitted joys, and pass
Autumnward on withered grass?   15

Solicitation

Are you to blame, or I, if round you twine
The wanton tendrils of the heart's wild vine?
Ah, suffer them to live, and in your heart
Permit the scioned love to mount with mine.

Vainly I strove against it, half afraid   5
Of the mad cast that destiny had made:
Vainly I strove . . . and must I love in vain
When two might share the arbor's clustered shade?

Purer and sweeter than any poet's rhyme,
From out the clement Cytherean clime,   10
The lyric voice of Cypris calls to us
Across the dismal dissonance of time.

Harken, and heed, and let the hateful din
Fail to an insect's fretting far and thin.
Though others prate of shame and wrong, we shall   15
Maintain the pagan purity of sin.

Oh, heed, and follow: in autumn forests lone,
Again the immemorial doves make moan,
And flashing waters beckon like white hands
Where all the wings of all the loves have flown.   20

An Old Theme

Harder is this to bear than love's own pain—
That love and even pain alike shall pass
Nor haply come again.
Ah, can we seize the moonlight on the grass,
Or bid the shadow stay   5
Beneath the growing day?
Give me thy mouth to kiss,
Give me thy breasts to hold
Ere love's desire and love's delight grow old
And the last sun go down upon the last abyss.   10
Ah, share thy body and its joy with me,
So, if the moments pass,
At least they shall not pass too emptily.

Psalm

I have sealed my desire upon thee
With the red seal of kisses,
Of innumerable kisses red as flame:
On mouth, and cheeks, and arms, and throat and shoulders,
And between thy breasts,   5
Whose buds are like the buds of pomegranate-flowers,
I have sealed my desire with the red seal of kisses.

I have bound my love about thee
With close embraces, the embraces of naked arms,
That burned thy flesh to a lingering rose: 10
About thy slender flanks,
And about thy bosom that swelleth gently
With its two breasts that are like the halves of a white apple,
And about thy hips and thighs
With their solemn curves like the curve of an antique lyre,   15
I have bound my love with close embraces, the embraces of naked arms.

I have set my delight upon thee
With caresses slow and gentle as meandering waters,
With caresses hot and rapid as a running fire;
Upon thy hair that is black as nocturnal clouds   20
Or the moon in eclipse,
And beneath thine arms,
And between thy fingers and between thy knees,
And upon the secret places of thy flesh,
I have set my delight with caresses slow and gentle as winding waters,   25
With caresses hot and rapid as leaping fire.

Ah, hide my love
And hide my desire
And keep my delight
As attar in the white rose of thy limbs,   30
As honey in the red lotus of thy heart
And the deep and hidden blossom thy body hath,
The blossom that is sweeter than all blossoms
But nameless.

The Pool

The decrescent moon
Sets in the black maze
Of an autumnal alder-wood
In the night with no bright star.

I lose myself, I stray   5
On the verge of the deep waters,
Dark and unclean,
Of a melancholy pool.

The tatters of autumn,
As they take flight,   10
Touch me in their fall:
I tremble and shiver,

And my reverie
Sheds itself on the near water
With the ash-tree's foliage—   15
Similarly withered.

Revenant

I am the spectre who returns
Unto some desolate world in ruin borne afar
On the black flowing of Lethean skies:
Ever I search, in cryptic galleries,
The void sarcophagi, the broken urns   5
Of many a vanished avatar;
Or haunt the gloom of crumbling pylons vast
In temples that enshrine the shadowy past.
Viewless, impalpable, and fleet,
I roam stupendous avenues, and greet   10
Familiar sphinxes carved from everlasting stone,
Or the fair, brittle gods of long ago,
Decayed and fallen low.
And there I mark the tall clepsammiae
That time has overthrown,   15
And empty clepsydrae,
And dials drowned in umbrage never-lifting;
And there, on rusty parapegms,
I read the ephemerides
Of antique stars and elder planets drifting   20

Oblivionward in night;
And there, with purples of the tomb bedight
And crowned with funeral gems,
I hold awhile the throne
Whereon mine immemorial selves have sate,   25
Canopied by the triple-tinted glory
Of the three suns forever paled and flown.

I am the spectre who returns
And dwells content with his forlorn estate
In mansions lost and hoary   30
Where no lamp burns;
Who trysts within the sepulchre,
And finds the ancient shadows lovelier
Than gardens all emblazed with sevenfold noon,
Or topaz-builded towers   35
That throng below some iris-pouring moon.
Exiled and homeless in the younger stars,
Henceforth I shall inhabit that grey clime
Whose days belong to primal calendars;
Nor would I come again   40
Back to the garish terrene hours:
For I am free of vaults unfathomable
And treasures lost from time:
With bat and vampire there
I flit through sombre skies immeasurable   45
Or fly adown the unending subterranes;
Mummied and ceremented,
I sit in councils of the kingly dead,
And oftentimes for vestiture I wear
The granite of great idols looming darkly   50
In atlantean fanes;
Or closely now and starkly
I cling as clings the attenuating air
About the ruins bare.

A Dream of the Abyss

I seemed at the sheer end:
Albeit mine eyes, in mystery and night
Shrouded as with the close deep caul of death,
Or as if underneath Lethean lentors drowned,
Saw never lamp nor star nor dead star's wraith of light,   5

Yet seemed I at the world's sheer end;
And fearfully and slowly I drew breath
From silent gulfs of all uncertainty and dread,
Precipitate to nadir from around;
Nor trusted I on any side to tread   10
One pace, lest I should overstep the brink,
And infinitely and forever sink
Past eye-shot of the Cyclopean sun
When from the bulwark of the world, adown oblivion,
He on the morrow should stare after me.   15

Swift from infinity,
The enormous Fear that lives between the stars
Clutched with the cold great darkness at my heart;
Then from the gulf arose a whispering,
And rustle as of silence on the wing   20
To stay and stand
Anear at my right hand:
What powers abysmal, born of the blind air,
What nameless demons of the nether deep
That 'scape the sun and from the moonlight live apart, 25
Came and conspired against me there,
I heard not, ere the whispering
Ceased, and a heavier darkness seemed to spring
Upon me, and I felt the silence leap
And clasp me closer, and the sweep   30
Of all the abyss reach up and drag
Body and feet from the crumbling uttermost crag
To the emptiness unknown;
Nor knew I, plunging through those nadir firmaments,
If Azrael or Abbadon bore me thence,   35
Or if I fell alone.

In Slumber

The stench of stagnant waters broke my dream,
Where through had run, with living murmur and gleam,
The Rivers four of the Earthly Paradise:
From the azured flame of those effulgent skies
And valleys lifting censers of vast bloom,   5
I was drawn down into a deathlier gloom
Than lies on Styx's fountain. By such light
As shows the newly damned their dolorous plight,

I trod the shuddering soil of that demesne
Whence larvae swarmed, malignant and obscene,   10
Like writhen mists from some Maremma reeking:
Through the gross air, fell incubi went seeking
Their prey that slumbered helpless; at my knee
There clung the python-bodied succubi;
I heard the wail of them that walked apart,   15
Each with a suckling vampire at his heart;
And, as I stumbled loathly on, the ground
Was rent with noiseless thunder all around
To pits that teemed with direr prodigies:
Grey, headless coils, and worm-shaped infamies   20
Unmeasured, rose above the sun that rotted
Black as a corpse in heavens thick and clotted;
The rusty clang and shaken soot of wings
Deafened and stifled me; from pestilent springs
Slime-mantled horrors boiled with fume and hiss   25
To plunge in frothing fury down the abyss.
Then, from an outmost circle of that hell,
The tumbling harpies came, detestable,
With beaks that in long tatters tore my breast
And wove from these their crimson, wattled nest.   30

Necromancy

My heart is made a necromancer's glass,
Where homeless forms and exile phantoms teem,
Where faces of forgotten sorrows gleam
And dead despairs archaic peer and pass.
Grey longings of some weary heart that was   5
Possess me, and the multiple, supreme
Unwildered hope and star-emblazoned dream
Of questing armies . . . Ancient queen and lass,
Risen vampire-like from out the wormy mould,
Deep in the magic mirror of my heart   10
Behold their perished beauty, and depart.
And now, from black aphelions far and cold,
Swimming in deathly light on charnel skies,
The enormous ghosts of bygone worlds arise.

Outlanders

By desert-deepened wells and chasmed ways,
And noon-high passes of the crumbling nome
Where the fell sphinx and martichoras roam;
Over black mountains lit by meteor-blaze,
Through darkness ending not in solar days,   5
Beauty, the centauress, has brought us home
To shores where chaos climbs in starry foam,
And the white horses of Polaris graze.

We gather, upon those gulfward beaches rolled,
Driftage of worlds not shown by any chart;   10
And pluck the fabled moly from wild scaurs:
Though these are scorned by human wharf and mart—
And scorned alike the red, primeval gold
For which we fight the griffins in strange wars.

Dominion

Empress of all my life, it is not known to thee
What hidden world thou holdest evermore in fee;
What muffled levies rise, from mist and Lethe drawn,

Waging some goblin war at thy forgotten whim;
What travelers in lone Cimmeria, drear and dim,   5
Follow the rumor of thy face toward the dawn.

Plain are those nearer lands whereon thou lookest forth,
Thy fields upon the south, thy cities in the north;
But vaster is that sealed and subterraneous realm.

High towers are built for thee with hushed demonian toil   10
In dayless lands, and furrows drawn through a dark soil,
And sable oceans crossed by many an unstarred helm.

Though unto thee is sent a tribute of fine gold
By them that delve therefor, never shalt thou behold
How the ore is digged in mines too near to Erebus;   15

Though strange Sabean myrrh within thy censers fume,
Thou shalt not ever guess the Afrit-haunted gloom
Whence the rich balm was won with labor perilous.

Occulted still from thee, thy power is on lost things,
On alien seraphim that seek with desperate wings,   20
Flown from their dying orb, the confines of thy heaven;

Yea, still thy whisper moves, and magically stirs
To life the shapeless dust in shattered sepulchers;
And in dark bread and wine thou art the untold leaven.

But never shalt thou dream how in some far abysm   25
Thy lightly spoken word has been an exorcism
Driving foul spirits from a wanderer bewrayed;

With eyes fulfilled of noon, haply thou shalt not see
How, in a land illumed by suns of ebony,
Beneath thy breath the fiery shadows flame and fade.   30

In Thessaly

When I lay dead in Thessaly,
The land was rife with sorcery:
Fair witches howled to Hecate,
Pouring the blood of rams by night
With many a necromantic rite   5
To draw me back for their delight. . . .

But I lay dead in Thessaly
With all my lust and wizardry:
Somewhere the Golden Ass went by
To munch the rose and find again   10
The shape and manlihead of men:
But in my grave I stirred not then,

And the black lote in Thessaly
Its juices dripped unceasingly
Above the rotting mouth of me;   15
And worm and mould and graveyard must
And roots of cypress, darkly thrust,
Transformed the dead to utter dust.

The Phoenix

I, I alone have seen the Phoenix fail,
His regal wings their vibrant glories vail
In gyres of baffled crimson, flagging gold
Below the heaven of his conquests old.
I, I alone have seen the Phoenix build   5
His pyre with bitter myrrh and spices filled
Amid the ardent waste; and none but I

Has known his death and immortality,
Has watched the yellowy teeth of flame consume
Shell-tinted beak and heaven-painted plume,   10
Has heard the fatal anguish of his cries
And felt the fierce despair with which he dies
Oblivious of that rebirth to be.
Nor shall another know the mystery
Of flames that turn to plumes, and ashes stirred   15
To yield once more the fiery-crested bird
With beating rainbow pinions that arise
And take again the lost Sabean skies.

The Outer Land

I

From the close valleys of thy love,
Where flowers of white and coral are,
And the soft gloom of cave and grove,
How have I wandered, spent and far,
By fell and mountain thence forbanned,
Into this lamia-haunted land?

I could not know the coiling path,
Pebbled with sard and lazuli,
Would lead me to the desert's wrath,
The rancor of the glaring sky,   10
The tarns that like stirred serpents hiss,
The den of drake and cockatrice.

I roam a limbo long abhorred,
Whose dread horizons flame and flow
Like iron from a furnace poured: 15
A bournless realm of sterile woe,
Where made mirages fill the dawn
With roses lost and fountains gone.

O land where dolent monsters mate!
I know the lusts that howl and run   20
When the red stones reverberate
The red, intolerable sun;
The soot-black lecheries that wail
From Hinnom to the moons of bale.

What desert naiads, amorous,   25
Have drawn me to their sunken strand!
How many a desert succubus
Has clasped me on her couch of sand!
What liches foul, with breast nor face,
Have seemed to bear thy beauty's grace!   30

What voices have besought me there
With sweet illusion of thine own,
Luring me, rapt and unaware,
To pits where dying demons moan!
What marble limbs have gleamed as thine—   35
Slow-sinking into sand or brine!

Briefly, in desert hermitages,
I have lain down in my despair,
Dreaming to sleep as slept the sages:
But unseen lust oppressed the air,   40
And crimson dreams of incubi,
And thirst of anthropophagi.

II

Entire, from mountains scaled at noon,
I scan the realm of my duress:
Deep-cloven plain and nippled dune,   45
Like to some sleeping giantess,
Pale and supine, by gods desired
With hearts deliriously fired.

Still without respite, I must follow
Where the faint, exile rills bequeath   50
Their bitterness to gulf and hollow.
Still the blown dusts of ruin breathe,
Fretting my face. My feet return
By salt-bright shores that blind and burn.

Silence immeasurable creeps   55
Across my path. . . . My sharpened ears
Are dinned with tumult from the deeps,
Are frayed by whispers of the spheres;
And darkly, in the sepulchre,
I hear the strident dead confer.   60

Gnawed by unceasing solitude,
The secret veils of sight grow thin:
High Domes that dazzle and elude,
Columns of darkling god and djinn
Appear; and things forbidden seem   65
Unsealed as in some awful dream.

My heart, consumed yet unconsuming,
Burns like a dreadful, ardent sun,
The horror of strange nights illuming:
Shall yet I find the ways foregone,   70
And speak, before the heart of thee,
The still-remembered Sesame?

Day-Dream

Here, in the olden wood,
The world is a mirage
More wan and dim
Than the pool wherein is mirrored
In the profound of another sphere   5
The strange nenuphar.

Scarcely I remember,
I forget my pain:
From this verdant twilight,
I see depart, alike futile   10
Beneath their varying masks,
Both love and death.

Athwart the foliage,
The sunlit lake
Drowses my dazzled eye   15
Like a crystal from which passes
The flame of an ecstasy
To the swooning mage.

The incredible oblivion
Plucks at me, ineffable,   20
From the depth of its lurking-place.
I lose myself, I brush
The thing that takes flight
Too vast of the spirit.

I know not if the oak 25
Suspires with my breath
Or if I draw air therein;
Sometimes I am the poppy,
And sometimes the mace-reed
Whose down is scattered on the clear stream. 30

For me, all thought
Is leafed and woodlike,
And mingles itself with the elders:
It flows with the sap,
It ripens the berry, 35
And spreads out with the branches.

Contra Mortem

Death is the eternal tedious platitude
With which all tales invariably end.
Deviceless seems the scurvy Demiurge
Who can invent no other doom, but must
Repeat, as puerile penny-a-liners do, 5
This horror staled by time-long usage. Why,
For variation's sake, if for naught else,
Not dower with immortality one rose,
One seer, one star, one duad of blest lovers? . . .
O, bestial, dumb submission! Will no voice 10
Cry out against this cosmic abatoir
Where God the butcher drives us one by one
Into the slaughter-pen and slits our throats?
In lieu of prayer or incense, let us proffer
A protest and a taunt, deriding Him 15
Who is corruption's pimp, and caterer
To pampered maggots. . . .

The Cycle

O love, long known and revenant forever!
How vast the ways wherein our footsteps fall,
The ways that meet and sever;
And yet how few withal
The fleeting yesternights that we remember. 5
These things are past surprise:

What fiery moons have died
To feed our ancient passion,
Leaving no shard nor ember,
What suns gone dark and ashen   10
Lighting strange lands for our extinguished eyes.

Kin

As you lie below in darkness and in duress,
    And you hear the young Spring call,
There shall come to you far lonelier than loneliness—
    The pity of it all.

And your eyes shall see their confines ere they darken   5
    But your heart must have no dread,
For across the lonely spaces you shall hearken,
    The dead men call their dead.

Sanctuary

Ah! love, to find for thee and me
A little space, alone,
Some vale of love and reverie
Where time unknowing and unknown
Shall pass, but not for thee and me.   5

Ah! love, in lands of Otherwhere,
To prove the afternoon
Of suns that cede the myrtled air
To Venus and the semilune!
Ah, love, in lands of Otherwhere.   10

Simile

Truth is a soundless gong
By an altar black and cold;
Life is a tale half-told,
Love is a broken song;
Beauty, besought so long,   5
Is a legend lost and old.

Le Refuge

À Benjamin DeCasseres

J'ai bâti moi-même un palais dans l'oubli,
Loin de l'étonnement ou du rire du foule;
Un couchant d'autrefois sur mes fiers murs s'écoule,
Rallumant tout blason rembruni ou pâli.

De trésor oublié, perdu des rois anciens,   5
Dort un sommeil de flamme en mes cryptes profondes;
L'anneau de Salomon est relevé des ondes
Pour semer sur mon or ses rayons orients.

De mon trône de jais, de bijoux et d'albâtres,
Je vois, par mes vitraux violet et verdâtres,   10
La fuite de tout rêve, ou d'ailes de flamant

Ou d'ailes de corneille; et, par mes sorts mystiques,
Je fais sortir encor les splendeurs plus antiques
Des soleils anuités, sombrant en le Néant.

Le Refuge

I have built for myself a palace in oblivion,
Far from the wonder or the laughter of the throng.
A sunset of olden time glows on my haughty walls,
Enkindling all my pale or tarnished blazonries.

Forgotten treasure that none has regathered,   5
Sleeps a flaming slumber in my deep vaults.
The ring of Solomon is re-risen from the waters
To cast upon my gold its reflected gleams.

Upon my throne of jet, of jewels and alabasters,
I see, through green and violet windows,   10
The flight of every dream, or with flamingo wings

Or raven wings. And my word evokes,
By its flaming spell the fantastic memories
Of blackened universes that founder in nothingness.

La Forteresse

À Benjamin DeCasseres

Loin du tumulte, et loin du braîment de la foule,
J'ai bâti pour moi-même un donjon dans l'oubli:
Embrasant tout pennon rembruni ou pâli,
Un couchant d'autrefois sur mes fiers murs s'écoule.

De trésor oublié, ravi des fois anciens,   5
Dort son sommeil de flame en mes voûtes profondes;
L'anneau de Salomon se relève des ondes
Pour semer sur mon or ses reflets orients.

Du siege fait de jais, de bijoux ed d'albâtres,
Je vois par mes vitraux violets et verdâtres   10
La fuite de tout rêve, ou d'ailes de flamant

Ou d'ailes de corneille; et parfois mes magies
Font s'élever encore d'aurores inouïes
Des univers noircis qui sombraient en néant.

The Fortress

Far from the tumult, far from the braying of the throng,
I have built for myself a keep in oblivion:
Enkindling every paled or darkened pennon,
A sunset of old time flows past on my proud walls.

Forgotten treasure, ravished from ancient kings,   5
Sleeps its flaming slumber in my deep vaults;
The ring of Solomon arises from the billows
To sow upon my gold its orient reflections.

From the seat of jade, of jewels and alabasters,
I see through violet and greenish windows   10
The flight of every dream, or with flamingo wings

Or raven wings; and sometimes my enchantments
Make rise again the unheard-of dawns
Of blackened universes that foundered in nothingness.

Sonnet

Slowly, sweetly, from the fear that folds or breaks,
Deliver the soul; listen to the many secrets avowed
In silence, like one caressed by raven hair;
Watch for the sweetness flowing on the breeze

In the dusk, in an evening of storm with the flesh electrised,   5
Let golden fingers wander on the keyboard;
Minorate the voice; calm the ardor of fire;
Exalt the colour of grey with the colour of rose.

Essay the accord of words mysterious
Harmonious like the eyelid kissing the eye;   10
Make undulate the flesh of gold pale in the mist,

And, in the soul an immense sigh inflates,
Leave, in going, the memory
Of a great swan of snow with long, long plumes.

Ennui

Thou art immured in some sad garden sown with dust
Of fruit of Sodom that bedims the summer ground,
And burdenously bows the lilies many-crowned,
Or fills the pale and ebon mouths of sleepy lust
The poppies raise. And, falling there imponderously,   5
Dull ashes emptied from the urns of all the dead
Have stilled the fountain and have sealed the fountain-head
And pall-wise draped the pine and flowering myrtle-tree.

Thou art becalmed upon the slothful ancient main
Where Styx and Lethe fall; where skies of stagnant grey   10
With the grey stagnant waters meet and merge as one:
How tardily thy torpid heart remembers pain,
And love itself, as aureate islands far away
On seas refulgent with the incredible red sun.

Adjuration

O ghostly loves that come and go
In this fantasmal autumn vale
Where stones and trees and hills remain
Unreal, and ghostly leaves are blown:—

Bright wraiths of yestereve, and pale   5
Ghosts of the darkling farther past
That mingle in ambiguous dance,
Haunting again the hollow day.

Depart, depart, nor vex in vain
With shadowy lips the lips of drouth,   10
Nor fill my arms with shifting cloud.
But linger awhile, O fair and face,

My youngest and my latest love,
And press your cheek against my cheek
To blend the substance with the dream   15
In the dry cup of Tantalus.

Song of the Necromancer

I will repeat a subtle rune—
And thronging suns of Otherwhere
Shall blaze upon the blinded air,
And spectres terrible and fair
Shall walk the riven world at noon.   5

The star that was mine empery
Is dust upon unwinnowed skies:
But primal dreams have made me wise,
And soon the shattered years shall rise
To my remembered sorcery.   10

To mantic mutterings, brief and low,
My palaces shall lift amain,
My bowers bloom; I will regain
The lips whereon my lips have lain
In rose-red twilights long ago.   15

Before my murmured exorcism
The world, a wispy wraith, shall flee:
A stranger earth, a weirder sea,
Peopled with shapes of Faëry,
Shall swell upon the waste abysm.   20

The pantheons of darkened stars
Shall file athwart the crocus dawn;
Goddess and Gorgon, Lar and faun,
Shall tread the amaranthine lawn,
And giants fight their thunderous wars.   25

Like graven mountains of basalt,
Dark idols of my demons there
Shall tower through bright zones of air,
Fronting the sun with level stare;
And hell shall pave my deepest vault.   30

Phantom and fiend and sorcerer
Shall serve me . . . till my term shall pass,
And I become no more, alas,
Than a frail shadow on the glass
Before some latter conjurer.   35

Rêves printaniers

Bien loin des fleurs et des feuilles décloses,
Mes rêves vont dans les jardins secrets,
Mes rêves vont, clandestins et discrets,
Pour chercher du renouveau les vraies roses.

Hélas! ils vont tout seuls, et vainement,   5
Dans ces jardins, où mes mains et mes lèvres
Allaient jadis pour adoucir leurs fièvres,
Pour cueillir, comme un tendre effeuillement,

Les douceurs de tes seins et leurs dictames.
—Fleurs enivrantes comme des bergames   10
Et les nocturnes fleurs des abricots!

Sous quel croissant qui couche, ou dans l'aurore
De quelle lune s'affaiblant encore,
Reprendrai-je ces ravissants pavots?

Rêves printaniers

Far, far from the unfolded leaves and flowers,
My dreams go wandering in thy secret gardens,
My dreams go wandering, clandestine and discreet,
To seek the living roses of the spring.

Alas! for all alone and vainly do they go,   5
Within these gardens where my lips and hands
Aforetime went to mollify their fevers,
To cull, as in a tender unleafing,

The sweetness of thy breasts and all their balsams . . .
Flowers that have made me drunk, like bergamots,   10
Or the nocturnal flowers of apricots!

Beneath what falling crescent, or in the dawn
Of what moon that wanes anew,
Shall I possess again these ravishing poppies?

Amour bizarre

Sur les gazons ratatinés du sec automne,
Une blanche sorcière à moi son amour donne:
Son ventre a la pâleur
Volée au lune morte, et sa douce froideur
Est pénetrante et bonne.   5

Dans ses cheveux où dort un or blafard et lourd,
Je cache moi jamais, muet, aveugle, sourd;
Entre ses seins glacés,
Je prends mortellement des plaisirs affilés
En frissonnant amour.   10

Comme l'ermite fou, dans les jours d'autrefois,
Qui serrait un pilier de neige à brûlants bras,
Je l'embrasse, et je tire
Des chaudes voluptés de ce pâle vampire,
De quoi l'enfer est las.   15

. . . . .

Je suis ensorcelé sous la lune tombante:
Je m'éveille, et ne trouve point ma belle amante—
Mais, dans sa place vide,
Je vois un vieux tombeau qui gît, brisé, livide,
Dessous l'aube sanglante.   20

L'Ensorcellement

Les phalènes s'envolent trop étrangement,
Ce soir jaune: on croirait que par enchantement
Leurs ailes s'agitaient. Quelle occulte sorcière
Envoie chacune en vol de laurier à cyprière?
De quel sorcier ont-elles vu l'envoûtement?   5

Quelles fumées affublent tout le marécage,
Nées de chaudrons noircis?—C'est la broués, qui nage
De l'eau vers l'if enraciné dans un charnier,
Et qui traîne comme un feston à l'amandier
Où sort la lune ainsi qu'un vermoulu visage.   10

Quel poison a rempli ce pays plus rêveur,
Ce vent plus indolent?—Ce n'est rien qu'une odeur
Montant du marécage et des saulées pourries.
—Mais, née de mes amours noires et envieillies,
Quelque noire magie m'envenime le coeur.   15

Le Fabliau d'un dieu

Dans un beau monde évanoui,
Dessous un ciel longtemps détruit,
Je fus le blanc dieu de la nuit.

Mes deux faces en noir voilées,
J'avais des races oubliées   5
Devant mes bleus autels pliées.

Mon trône était de froids métaux;
Dans mes châsses et mes caveaux
J'avais de chaleureux joyaux.

Respirant la myrrhe étrangère,   10
La louange inouie, altière,
Je fus le maître de la terre.

De mes vieux avatars les os
Remplissaient maints divins tombeaux
J'étais dans tous les fabliaux.   15

Sombrant, les rameurs de galères
Parlaient aux côtés des chimères
Mon nom en leurs suprêmes prières.

Durant mille ans de mon séjour,
J'aimais d'un vaste et vain amour   20
La verte déesse du jour.

Des flammes du matin, des ailes,
L'orage avec des pleurs plus belles,
Nageaient dans ses larges prunelles.

Ses seins étaient plus saveureux   25
Que le brugnon qui pend, heureux,
Au bord d'un Léthé paresseux.

Orgueil

À Benjamin de Casseres

L'orgueil des tous les dieux et démons plus hautains
Habete dans mon coeur; je porte un front d'airain
Dans les parades et l'enfer;
Malgré les vers
De tous mes morts, malgré es gouffres du léthé,   5
Je maintiens aujourd'hui mon ancienne fierté,
Et je maintiendrai—le demain.

J'ai trouve un poison dans le miellat du l'amour,
J'ai bu d'une amertune à les fleuves d'oubli;
Les chemins longs ou courts   10
Les mondes plus lointains,
Ne cachaient point pour moi que le premier ennui.

Sea-Memory

Since I have seen the refluent glory of the sea,
My dreams are made of azure, emerald and gold:
Tumultuous topaz, flowing sapphire manifold,
Have turned my slumber to a deep and splendid sea.

My memories are vibrant gold, sonorous green: 5
My brain is like a palace built from chrysolite,
Where lines of long-resounding columns infinite
For ever glimmer through a twilight gold and green.

Farewell to Eros

Lord of the many pangs, the single ecstasy!
From all my rose-red temple builded in thy name,
Pass dawnward with no blasphemies of praise or blame,
No whine of suppliant or moan of psaltery.

Not now the weary god deserts the worshipper,   5
The worshipper the god . . . but in some cryptic room
A tocsin tells with arras-deadened tones of doom
That hour which veils the shrine and stills the chorister.

Others will make libation, chant thy litanies . . .
But, when the glamored moons on inmost Stygia glare   10
And quenchlessly the demon-calling altars flare,
I shall go forth to madder gods and mysteries.

And through Zothique and primal Thule wandering,
A pilgrim to the shrines where elder Shadows dwell,
Perhaps I shall behold such lusters visible   15
As turn to ash the living opal of thy wing.

Haply those islands where the sunsets sink in rest
Will yield, O Love, the slumber that thou hast not given;
Or the broad-bosomed flowers of some vermilion heaven
Will make my senses fail as on no mortal breast.   20

Perchance the wind, on Aquilonian marches blowing
From the low mountains isled in seas of russet grass,
Will make among the reeds a sweeter shuddering pass
Than tremors through the chorded flesh of women flowing.

Perchance the fountains of the dolorous rivers four   25
In Dis, will quench the thirst thy wine assuages never;
And in my veins will mount a twice-infuriate fever
When the black, burning noons upon Cimmeria pour.

Yea, in those ultimate lands that will outlast the earth,
Being but dream and fable, myth and fantasy,   30
I shall forget . . . or find some image reared of thee,
Dreadful and radiant, far from death, remote from birth.

Indian Summer

Surely these muted days are one with days remembered,
This necromantic sun is an evocation
Of suns whereunder we have walked before:
For when I see the peach-trees
Flame-colored and far off   5
Where the blueness of the air has crept among them,
The love I feel today
Somehow resumes the bygone flames and shadows,
The vanished incommunicable moods
And fugitive lost colors   10
Of the love I felt for you in autumns past.

Mystery

To me, who have but known
The senses' doubtful lore,
Thy soul is evermore
Mysterious as mine own.

With ears I strive to hear   5
A song that is not sound,
With eyes, to pierce the bound
Of things unseen and dear.

But in delectable
Dark ways, and wordless speech,   10
Our hearts throb each to each
The tale we cannot tell.

The flesh unto the flesh
Utters deliciously
Desire and ecstasy   15
Through all its subtle mesh.

In a swift glance, or in
The close and eyeless night,
As light that meets with light,
My soul has seemed to win   20

Communion clear with thine,
Has found the oblivion deep
Which is not death nor sleep
But ampler life divine.

Touch

In touching you
My hands have known the savor of delight
As the mouth knows the savor of sweet fruit;
And in your flesh my hands have seemed to hear
A melody that pulsed and pulsed   5
Even as the melody of dulcimers—
Yea, to my hands
Your flesh has breathed the perfume of its being,
Has sighed a secret essence,
Has given forth its immanent mystery   10
To mingle with the mystery of mine.

To Howard Phillips Lovecraft

Lover of hills and fields and towns antique,
How hast thou wandered hence
On ways not found before,
Beyond the dawnward spires of Providence?
Hast thou gone forth to seek   5
Some older bourn than these—
Some Arkham of the prime and central wizardries?
Or, with familiar felidae,
Dost now some new and secret wood explore,
A little past the senses' farther wall—   10
Where spring and sunset charm the eternal path
From Earth to ether in dimensions nemoral?
Or has the Silver Key
Opened perchance for thee
Wonders and dreams and worlds ulterior?   15
Hast thou gone home to Ulthar or to Pnath?
Has the high king who reigns in dim Kadath
Called back his courtly, sage ambassador?
Or darkling Cthulhu sent
The sign which makes thee now a councilor   20
Within that foundered fortress of the deep
Where the Old Ones stir in sleep
Till mighty temblors shake their slumbering continent?

Lo! in this little interim of days
How far thy feet are sped   25
Upon the fabulous and mooted ways
Where walk the mythic dead!
For us the grief, for us the mystery. . . .
And yet thou art not gone
Nor given wholly unto dream and dust: 30
For, even upon
This lonely western hill of Averoigne
Thy flesh had never visited,
I meet some wise and sentient wraith of thee,
Some undeparting presence, gracious and august.   35
More luminous for thee the vernal grass,
More magically dark the Druid stone,
And in the mind thou art forever shown
As in a magic glass;
And from the spirit's page thy runes can never pass.   40

The Prophet Speaks

City forbanned by seer and god and devil!
In glory less than Tyre or fabled Ys,
But more than they in mere, surpassing evil!

Yea, black Atlantis, fallen beneath dim seas
For sinful lore and rites to demons done,   5
Bore not the weight of such iniquities.

Your altars with a primal foulness run,
Where the worm hears the thousand-throated hymn . . .
And all the sunsets write your malison,

And all the stars unrolled from heaven's rim   10
Declare the doom which I alone may read
In moving ciphers numberless and dim.

O city consecrate to crime and greed!
O scorner of the Muses' messenger!
Within your heart the hidden maggots breed.   15

Against your piers the nether seas confer;
Against your towers the typhons in their slumber
In sealed abysms darkly mutter and stir;

They dream the day when earth shall disencumber
Her bosom of your sprawled and beetling piles;   20
When tides that bore your vessels without number

Shall turn your hills to foam-enshrouded isles,
And, ebbing, leave but slime and desolation,
Ruin and rust, through all your riven miles.

On you shall fall a starker devastation   25
Than came upon Tuloom and Tarshish old,
In you shall dwell the last abomination.

The dust of all your mansions and the mould
Shall move in changing mounds and clouds disparted
About the wingless air, the footless wold.   30

The sea, withdrawn from littorals desert-hearted,
Shall leave you to the silence of the sky—
A place fordone, forlorn, unnamed, uncharted,

Where naught molests the sluggish crotali.

Desert Dweller

There is no room in any town (he said)
To house the towering hugeness of my dream.
It straitens me to sleep in any bed

Whose foot is nearer than the night's extreme.
There is too much of solitude in crowds   5
For one who has been where constellations teem,

Where boulders meet with boulders, and the clouds
And hills convene; who has talked at evening
With mountains clad in many-colored shrouds.

Men pity me for the scant gold I bring: 10
Unguessed within my heart the solar glare
On monstrous gems that lit my journeying.

They deem the desert flowerless and bare,
Who have not seen above their heads unfold
The vast, inverted lotus of blue air;   15

Nor know what Hanging Gardens I behold
With half-shut eyes between the earth and moon
In topless iridescent tiers unrolled.

For them, the planted fields, their veriest boon;
For me, the verdure of inviolate grass   20
In far mirages vanishing at noon.

For them, the mellowed strings, the strident brass,
The cry of love, the clangor of great horns,
The thunder-burdened ways where thousands pass.

For me, the silence welling from dark urns,   25
From fountains past the utmost world and sun . . .
To overflow some day the desert bourns . . .

And take the sounding cities one by one.

Requiescat

Whither, on soft and soundless feet,
With careful pace and air discreet,
O grey companion, art thou gone,
Quietly, like a shade withdrawn?

Too strange, in each beloved spot   5
To peer once more, and meet thee not;
To pass, amid the desolate rooms,
Among the garden's lonely blooms.

Still shall we seek and never find,
Save in the chambers of the mind,   10
And in the deepening heart's demesne,
Thy furry presence, bland, serene.

O wise and tender! calm and sweet!
Slumber, in peace for aye replete;
Gently as thou upon its breast,   15
Let the kind earth above thee rest.

Wizard's Love

O perfect love, unhoped-for, past despair!
I had not thought to find
Your face betwixt the terrene earth and air:
But deemed you lost in fabulous old lands
And rose-lit years to darkness long resigned.   5
O child, you cannot know
What magic and what miracles you bring
Within your tender hands;
What griefs are lulled to blissful slumbering,
Cushioned upon your deep and fragrant hair;   10
What gall-black bitterness of long ago,
Within my bosom sealed,
Ebbs gradually as might some desert well
Under your beauty's heaven, warm and fair,
And the green suns of your vertumnal eyes.   15

O beauty wrought of rapture and surprise,
Too dear for heart to know, or tongue to tell!
Now more and more you seem
Fantasy turned to flesh, incarnate dream.
Surely I called you with consummate spell   20
In desperate, forgotten wizardries,
With signs and sigils of dead goeties,
And evocations born of blood and pain
But deemed for ever vain.
Surely you came to me of yore, among   25

The teeming specters amorous
With faces veiled and splendid bosoms bare
That turned my sleep to fever and delight
In ever-desolate years when love was young.
Or I, perchance,   30
Begot you on some golden succubus
Amid the madness of the Sabbat's night
In earlier lives forevowed to Satanry
And sorcerous dark romance.
For all your heart and flesh are sib to me,   35
And in my soul's profound
Your face, an irrecoverable pearl,
Is ultimately drowned.
So thus, delicious girl!
Whether love's destiny be weal or woe,   40
I hold you now, and shall not let you go.

The Last and Utmost Land

1939–1947

From Arcady

To you, that went from Arcady
To follow after worldy shows,
My songs shall bring unfailingly
The scent of bay and forest rose.

To follow after worldy shows   5
You left our laurel-sheltered bourn. . . .
The scent of bay and forest rose
Too heavy lies on hearts forlorn.

You left our laurel-sheltered bourn,
Our love must wander desolate: 10
Too heavy lies on hearts forlorn
The fallen, faded petals' weight.

Our love must wander desolate,
Weaving in pain, to one wild dirge,
The fallen, faded petals' weight,   15
The rolling of a roted surge;

Weaving in pain, to one wild dirge,
The ancient, deep, forgone delight. . . .
The rolling of a roted surge
Returns around a pagan height.   20

The ancient, deep, forgone delight
Wakens the pastoral pipes again,
Returns around a pagan height
To call, nor always call in vain—

Wakens the pastoral pipes again   25
My songs shall bring unfailingly,
To call, nor always call in vain
To you, that went from Arcady.

Ode

O young and dear and tender sorceress!
Your delicate, slim hands
Reweave the glamors of Hellenic lands
To enchant the noon or night—
With many a soft caress   5
Restore the lost and lyrical delight.

The limbs of maenads flown
Have given you their grace,
And immemorial Aprils haunt your face.
All that was not, but should have been, mine own,   10
Your gentle beauty brings
Till the heart finds again its forfeit wings.
The young, Favonian loves
That passed aversely, darkling and unknown,
About your bosom dwell like coted doves.   15
Long-fallen fruits by necromancy burn
Upon your lips; and perished planets rise
Into the beryl evening of your eyes;
And the lost autumns in your hair return.

In you each yesterday   20
Shall past tomorrow stay;
And love would linger here,
Letting your pulses tell his destined time
Through all the clement year:
Yea, having known your fair, Arcadian heart,   25
He would not thence depart:
Harsher it were than death
To face again the lonesome rain and rime,
And draw reluctant breath
From the grey rigors of an alien clime.   30

Sestet

I have no heart to give you: long ago
Exceeding love has found and left me blind
To lesser loves. You are no more to me
Than some chance tavern with its doors aglow,
Proffering warmth and hospitality   5
On a strange road beset with night and wind.

Bacchante

Men say the gods have flown;
The Golden Age is but a fading story,
And Greece was transitory:
Yet on this hill hesperian we have known
The ancient madness and the ancient glory.   5

Under the thyrse upholden,
We have felt the thrilling presence of the god,
And you, Bacchante, shod
With moonfire, and with moonfire all enfolden,
Have danced upon the mystery-haunted sod.   10

With every autumn blossom,
And with the brown and verdant leaves of vine,
We have filled your hair divine;
From the cupped hollow of your delicious bosom,
We have drunk wine, Bacchante, purple wine.   15

About us now the night
Grows mystical with gleams and shadows cast
By moons for ever past;
And in your steps, O dancer of our delight,
Wild phantoms move, invisible and fast.   20

Behind, before us sweep
Maenad and Bassarid in spectral rout
With many an unheard shout;
Cithaeron looms with every festal steep
Over this hill resolved to dream and doubt.   25

What Power flows through us,
And makes the old delirium mount amain,
And brims each ardent vein
With passion and with rapture perilous?
Dancer, of whom our votive hearts are fain,   30

You are that magic urn
Wherefrom is poured the pagan gramarie;
Until, accordantly,
Within our bardic blood and spirit burn
The dreams and fevers of antiquity.   35

Resurrection

Sorceress and sorcerer,
Risen from the sepulcher,
From the deep, unhallowed ground,
We have found and we have bound
Each the other, as before,   5
With the fatal spells of yore,
With Sabbatic sign, and word
That Thessalian moons have heard.

Sorcerer and sorceress,
Hold we still our heathenness—   10
Loving without sin or shame—
As in years of stake and flame.
Share we now the witches' madness,
Wake the Hecatean gladness,
Call the demon named Delight   15
From his lair of burning night.

Love that was, and love to be,
Dwell within this wizardry:
Lay your arm my head beneath
As upon some nighted heath   20
Where we slumbered all alone
When the Sabbat's rout was flown;
Let me drink your dulcet breath
As in evenings after death.

Witch belovèd from of old,   25
When upon Atlantis rolled
All the dire and wrathful deep,
You had kissed mine eyes asleep.
On my lids shall fall your lips
In the final sun's eclipse;   30
And your hand shall take my hand
In the last and utmost land.

Witch-Dance

Between the windy, swirling fire
And all the stillness of the moon,
Sweet witch, you danced at my desire,
Turning some weird and lovely rune
To paces like the swirling fire.   5

As in the Sabbat's ancient round
With strange and subtle steps you went;
And toward the heavens and toward the ground
Your steeple-shapen hat was bent
As in the Sabbat's ancient round.   10

Upon the earth your paces wrought
A circle such as magians made . . .
And still some hidden thing you sought
With hands desirous, half afraid,
Beyond the ring your paces wrought.   15

Your supple youth and loveliness
A glamor left upon the air:
Whether to curse, whether to bless,
You wrought a stronger magic there
With your lithe youth and loveliness.   20

Your fingers, on the smoke and flame,
Moved in mysterious conjuring;
You seemed to call a silent Name,
And lifted like an outstretched wing
Your somber gown against the flame.   25

What darkling and demonian Lord,
In fear or triumph, did you call?
Ah! was it then that you implored,
With secret signs equivocal,
The coming of the covens' Lord?   30

Sweet witch, you conjured forth my heart
To follow always at your will!
Like Merlin in some place apart,
It lies enthralled and captive still:
Sweet witch, you conjured thus my heart!   35

Song of the Bacchic Bards

O crown us with laurels, unbung the barrels,
Though the stars decline
We'll souse like devils in Plutonian revels
Till two moons shine.

Oh, let not the chorus of satyrs outroar us,   5
Vaunting the vine,
While, shedding their panties, the shameless Bacchantes
Get tanked on our wine.

May the pale water-drinker, the Puritan stinker
With snoot cyanine,   10
Be filled through a funnel with a ceaseless runnel
Of green sea-brine.

May Bacchus his pards devour the bards
Of a tuneless line,
The foals of wild asses who fart on Parnassus   15
At the Muses nine.

By Rabelais' bottle, we'll hang and we'll throttle
With the grape's tough twine,
The horse's katitty who sings a dumb ditty
Called Sweet Adeline.   20

Then bring us fresh laurels, unbung new barrels,
Though the world decline,
We'll souse like demons with Plutonian lemans
Till two suns shine.

Anteros

What voice, O vengeful Anteros,
Has called thee from the seedless weald?—
Dark sower of the tares of loss
Amid the foison of love's field!
What mouth, O mournful Anteros,   5
Must eat the grain the seasons yield?

Thy touch, O mortal Anteros,
Has turned the sapphic laurel sere,
Thy wings have cast their night across
The dial of our Saturnian year,   10
The cypress, O sad Anteros,
Grew darker when thou drewest near.

O lover, thy black prayer unsay,
Who called on baleful Anteros!
Crown thee with nettles, kneel, and lay   15
Thy brows upon love's altar close,
To the departing Eros pray
Against the wrath of Anteros.

Lamia

Out of the desert lair the lamia came,
A lovely serpent, shaped as women are.
Meeting me there, she hailed me by the name

Beloved lips had used in days afar;
And when the lamia sang, it seemed I heard   5
The voice of love in some old avatar.

Her lethal beauty like a philtre stirred
Through all my blood and filled my heart with light:
I wedded her with ardor undeterred

By the strange mottlings of her body white,   10
By the things that crept across us in her den
And the dead who lay beside us through the night.

Colder her flesh than serpents of the fen,
Yet on her breast I lost mine ancient woe
And found the joy forbid to living men.   15

But, ah, it was a thousand years ago
I took the lovely lamia for bride . . .
And nevermore shall they that meet me know

It is a thousand years since I have died.

Interim

Darling, how near we lay
To Lethe on that day
When, wandering far amid the wreathed fog
And through the veiling verdure spring had drawn
On slopes where fire had ravened years agone,   5
We paused awhile, and made our bed between
The mounting bushes green
And the black, fallen log. . . .
Closely, more closely ever,
Like flames that meet and mingle in blown air,   10
Mouth drew to mouth, bosom to bosom there
In the long kiss that could not sever.
Sequestered and apart,
In death-grey mist and silence deeplier furled,
While faded the wan world   15
In ghostliness and mystery retreating,
We felt the answering throb of heart to heart
Like one warm pulse amid oblivion beating.
And our love seemed a solitary flame
Soaring from lands of pallid nothingness   20
That had no bound nor name;
Where all hours that had been
And days to be
Were part of some abolished calendar;
Where all things fell away, and ebbed afar   25
As if dissolved within
The wavering vapors thin:
Yea, the pale mists, and life and memory

And all things passed before our ecstasy
Like alien phantoms, furtive and unknown,   30
To their dim tombs returning . . .

O love unquenchable and stilly burning!
The peace at thy white core was made our own . . .
A little, and we too had surely passed
With incorporeal ease   35
Upon the voidness vast—
Going with those frail vapors like a breath,
Drifting from mortal ecstasy to death
Among the ghostly trees.

Sonnet

How shall our hearts, those fragile shrines of thee,
Forefend the siege of wrackful circumstance?
Or this thy brittle, earth-wrought beauty be
The unshaken ultimate fortress of romance?
How shall the Golden Age thy bosom brings—   5
That home of dreams unharbored otherwhere—
Not fall before this brazen press of things,
Till we too fade like morning phantoms there?
How shall one rose from out our seasons done
Rear to the rune of any necromant? . . .   10
When all is over, let the cindered sun
Go down in night no memory shall haunt—
Yea, let full-fountained Lethe rise and flow
As on the loves of lovers long ago.

To One Absent

Return, to save me still from her,
The false and barren comforter,
Who wears in vain thy spectral mien
Amid the desert of my dearth—
That ancient empress of the earth,   5
That lethal and immortal queen.

Return, to take this empty hand
And lead me in that longed-for land
Where still the years of Saturn roam;
Where satyrs rob the purpling vine   10

And the green-fruited laurels shine
Against the siren-cloven foam.

Return, with all the ancient loves,
Like Venus and her circling doves,
With Cyprian cinctures to unweave,   15
And snatches of some Lesbian air
To lighten this my long despair
Upon a saffron-bordered eve.

Return, to be the Muse of old
In songs and paeans manifold;   20
The sorceress of a secret garth
Distilling balms and philtres sweet;
Bacchante, dancing on wild feet;
And goddess of the glowing hearth.

Silent Hour

In this drear interim
Of days disconsolate, remote from thee,
Surely it were enough of happiness
To sit once more beside thee, and to see
Thy patient fingers press   5
The clay whereon, still inchoate and dim,
Wavers the face of some fair satyress,
Or dancer's form, or goddess revenant
From deep antiquity;
To watch throughout the sunned or lamplit hour   10
Thy tireless toil intent—
Speaking no word, while on my heart again
Full-tided love draws back in every vein
Like a dark sea through caverns refluent;
But deepens still the fountains of its power.   15

Thus, thus to wait, with eyes
That love thy drooping hair, thy bended brow,
Till the hour becomes an everlasting Now;
Till all the silence opens into flower—
Till some great rose of wonder and surprise   20
In secret, sudden bloom
With magic fragrance overbrims the room.

Grecian Yesterday

To the loved days we shared alone,
Leda, beyond the moons and miles
The swan of my desire has flown.

Again you stand, as once you stood,
Naked, with sun-ignited hair,   5
Before the dark Hellenic wood

That hangs beside that halcyon sea:
And all my heart is turned to love,
And love fulfills the veins of me.

No Syrinx flees, no satyr sallies   10
From the still oaks and brooding bays:
In us their ancient rapture rallies

That sweeps away the world, and brings
Once more the many-flowered prime
After an age of flowerless things.   15

To the loved days we shared alone,
Leda, beyond the moons and miles
The swan of my desire has flown.

But Grant, O Venus

Though love had dreamt of soft eternities
For never-flagging pulses still to mete,
Those minutes of our bliss were few and fleet.
Breast-pillowed in their aftermath of ease,
She said to me at midnight: "Memories   5
Are all we have in the end." Ah, bitter-sweet
The doom that tolling bells of thought repeat—
This verity of solemn verities
Wherein the sorrowful senses find despair
And the heart an iridescence on dark tears. . . . 10
But grant, O Venus of the hidden hill,
That many a rose-lit eve remain to share,
And midnights in the unascended years,
And starry memories unbegotten still.

Bond

By the red seal redoubled of that kiss
When thy lips parted softly to my own
Ere the sun sank from doomed Poseidonis;

By nights of searing ecstasy and moan;
The wine-wet bosoms in Pompeii bared,   5
And the pale breasts and limbs in Lesbos known;

By dreams and deities and dolors shared
Before the Olympian glory passed from Greece;
By sharp and secret raptures that we dared

In Druid towers of ocean-founded Ys;   10
By every cup of wine in Naishapur
We drank by turns even to the purple lees;

By the dark Sabbats, vowed to Lucifer,
Making us one before his muffled throne
In rites of sorceress and sorcerer;   15

By the sealed ways no prophet has foreshown,
Whereon our lips shall meet, our footsteps go:—
By these, by these I claim thee for mine own . . .

Even as I have claimed thee long ago.

Madrigal of Memory

To my remote abandonment
Your deep and lustrous hair has lent
How many an autumn-colored dream;
Your eyes bring many an April gleam
To this my place of uncontent.   5

Like torchy fires your footsteps leap
Where covens of lost dreamers keep
Their sabbat and their bacchanal;
Your breasts are moons that mount and fall
Through the dim, turbulent climes of sleep.   10

Among the rondured hills that merge
Into the prone horizon-verge,
My haunted eyes have seen, have felt,
Your mobile hips at twilight melt,
Your supple bosom lift and surge.   15

In dryad ways not understood
You stir and whisper through the wood.
Far off the throbbing waters flow
Against a sanguine afterglow
Like the sweet pulses of your blood.   20

At morning, from the cloudy south,
Your tresses sweep athwart my drouth.
Night bears amid its magic bower
Your body's many-scented flower
And bud and blossom of your mouth.   25

"That Last Infirmity"

Fame is the passing of a fitful wind—
A shouting of the tempest, and the sigh
That lingers in the sunset-ending sky,
To stillness and the alien stars resigned.

The Thralls of Circe Climb Parnassus

Between the mountain meadow and the pines
In one still wave the flowered azaleas clomb—
A billow laced and crested with pale foam
Unscattered by the balsam-bearing winds.

High-rearing on their miry haunches, where   5
Some grassy-bottomed tarn had sunk and died,
A black hog and his mate stood side by side,
Sniffing those elfin blossoms cool and fair.

Straying in new-found freedom, hungry still,
They had gone forth beneath the immaculate sky   10
Through fir-set fells beyond their broken sty

And lofty valleys, wild and aspen-grown . . .
As those who haply seek for husks and swill
Amid the flowers upon Parnassus blown.

Dialogue

One said: "I have seen, from cliffs of doom,
The seven hells flame up in flower
Like a million upas trees that tower,
Massing their realms of poisonous bloom.

I have gone down where dragons writhe,   5
Mating within the nadir slime;
I have caressed in some made clime
The Gorgon's ringlets, long and lithe."

Another answered: "I have known
The undated hour of agony   10
When sightless terror leers and crawls

Out of mere soil and simple stone;
When horror seeps from out four walls
And trickles from the unclouded sky."

The Mime of Sleep

My dreams are turned to some disordered mime:
A plot that pandemonian shadows feign
Ravels half told; and dead loves live again
In settings of distorted place and time:
A broken drama, puerile or sublime,   5
Whose riddled meaning I must guess in vain;
A masque, whose grey grotesques of mirth and pain
Move randomly through an occulted clime.

But though they pass, and slumber blot them all,
Your beauty's burning shade more slowly dims—   10
Where, dancing like Salome, you let fall,
In splendid sequence under a sad sky,
The seven veils of fantasy that I
Have wound about your young, delightful limbs.

The Old Water-Wheel

Often, on homeward ways, I come
To a deserted orchard, old and lone,
Unplowed, untrod, with wilding grasses grown
Through rows of pear and plum.

There, in a never-ceasing round,   5
In the slow stream, by noon, by night, by dawn,
An ancient, hidden water-wheel turns on
With a sad, reiterant sound.

Most eerily it comes and dies,
And comes again, when on the horizon's breast   10

The ruby of Antares seems to rest,
Fallen from star-fraught skies:

A dolent, drear, complaining note
Whose all-monotonous cadence haunts the air
Like the recurrent moan of a despair   15
Some heart has learned by rote;

Heavy, and ill to hear, for one
Within whose breast, today, tonight, tomorrow,
Like the slow wheel, an ancient, darkling sorrow
Turns and is never done.   20

Fragment

This I remember clearly: from stone to stepping-stone
I bore you in my arms across the quiet stream. . . .
And yet I know not where nor when; nor whether in dream
It was, or in some former land, or land foreknown.

Willows there were, and leaves and flowers of arrowhead,   5
And the tall reeds that lifted up their bronzy maces. . . .
Yet in what place among the long-forgotten places?
Or in what untold year, or year of ages sped?

What chanceful magic brings this moment back to me,
Or calls it from the murk and mist of worlds unborn?—   10
A burst of sun on Lethe boundless and forlorn,
A narrow circle of noon where else is mystery.

This I remember only, beloved, that it was you
I held with tender care and loving arms that yearned:
Your breasts were light upon my heart; your tresses burned   15
Between the nameless heavens and nameless waters blue.

Yerba Buena

The fragrant leaf and small white flower!
The fragile wreath my fingers twined
Amid your fleece in some lost hour
Flown seaward with the summer wind.

The fragile wreath my fingers twined   5
Still wafts a perfume wild and sweet
Flown seaward with the summer wind
Within that place where laurels meet—

Still wafts a perfume wild and sweet—
Crushed by the limbs and breasts of love   10
Within that place where laurels meet
Amid the ocean-fronting grove.

Crushed by the limbs and breasts of love,
Ever it mounts from bygone days
Amid the ocean-fronting grove   15
Where summer comes but never stays.

Ever it mounts from bygone days,
The wild sweet memory we share,
Where summer comes but never stays,
Drunk with a philtre-laden air.   20

The wild sweet memory we share!
Amid your fleece in some lost hour
Drunk with a philtre-laden air,
The fragrant leaf and small white flower!

Consummation

Musing upon our strange close trinity,
On all the golden gramaries of our days,
And the bleak sadness found in sundered ways,
I dream a strange sweet ending for us three
That shall illume the future's legendry,   5
Till poets, crowned with late, hesperian bays,
Shall chant for us their elegies and lays
Upon the sapphic headlands of our sea;

Telling of old, idyllic things that were;
Of how two lovers laid their brows and lips   10
Down on their love's warm bosom, and with her
Drew rapture and oblivion in one breath,
And found with her, in that divine eclipse,
The indissoluble unity of death.

Humors of Love

Our love has grown a thing too deep and grave
For touch and speech of trivial gallantries:
For we have wrought consummate sorceries
From which no lifted sign nor prayer may save:

To seize the perilous hour we have been brave;   5
And passion, past all fleshly ecstasies,
Has flung us into stilled eternities
Where the moment hung like some unfalling wave.

Yet, though our love outsoar the exalted clay
To stand in firmamental station fixed,   10
We find, with some enchanted memory mixed,
The laughters heard in Swift and Rabelais;
And, blended with the rapture and the woe,
Are drolleries of blithe Boccaccio.

Town Lights

For him who wanders up and down
Its long-familiar streets in autumn nights,
With melancholy meaning shine the lights
Of the small, scattered town.

Often, where lamp-bright windows cast   5
Their homely splendor forth on tree and lawn,
Strange moths of dream and memory are drawn,
Flown from the ghostly past.

And kisses faint as falling mist
Await the wanderer at some old door,   10
And sorrowful voices crying Nevermore
From bygone lips he left unkissed.

What panes illumed by love's own lamp
Are darkened now, or lit by alien hands;
Where friendship sat before the rose-red brands   15
Comes in the invasive cold and damp,

Or strangers make oblivious cheer:
Till he that watches dimly from without
Feels as a leaf blown in the autumn's rout
From desolate trees foredoomed and sere.   20

But still he turns, and marks again
Some aureate lamp that friends have lit afar;
Some radiance, with love for inner star,
That burns behind a trellised pane;

Knowing if it were not for these,   25
His vagrant soul would haunt a vaster night

Lit only by the inalienable light
Of all the quenchless galaxies.

The Sorcerer to His Love

Within your arms I will forget
The horror that Zimimar brings
Between his vast and vampire wings
From out his frozen oubliette.

The terror born of ultimate space   5
That gnaws with icy fang and fell,
The sucklings of the hag of hell,
Shall flee the enchantment of your face.

Ah, more than all my wizard art
The circle our delight has drawn: 10
What evil phantoms thence have gone,
What dreadful presences depart!

Your arms are white, your arms are warm
To hold me from the haunted air,
And you alone are firm and fair   15
Amid the darkly whirling storm.

To George Sterling

And I too found the seaward way.
                              —*Venus Letalis.*

Deep are the chasmal years and lustrums long
Since, following that dark Venus of thy dream,
Thou camest to the lulling foam's extreme. . . .
But, safely builded beyond change and wrong,
And past "the fleeting plaudits of the throng,"   5
With blazons blown on some ethereal stream
In crystal and in haliotis gleam,
Crag-founded, thine aeolian domes of song.

Yet, ah! the vanished voice we shall not hear!
Alas! thy footsteps ending on the sand   10
By doubtful seas and skies not understood. . . .
Strange shells are found along that silent strand:
Thou too hast often held them to thine ear
And heard the baffled murmur of thy blood.

L'Espoir du néant

(à George Sterling)

La douceur du dernier anéantissement!
O! l'hydromel des morts nous boirons lentement,
Comme des enivrés qui buvotent leur vin!
Profond comme l'abîme, et plus inépuisable,
Il nous accordera la paix incomparable,   5
Le sommeil, qui renferme un univers sans fin,
Et qui fait le bonheur des anges moins divins;
Mais il n'aura jamais de maléfiques rêves
Pour offrit à nos nuits leurs plus sinistres dons—
Pour restaurer dans notre oubli les trahisons   10
Et les travaux du temps: une grande trêve
Il sera dans la guerre immortelle des dieux
Aux fourmis en la terre, aux aigles dans les cieux.

Bientôt nous le boirons, d'étain, d'or ou de verre,
Bientôt nous trouverons pour lit et pour suaire   15
Son léthé qui s'écoule à travers l'infini:
Avec les vieux soleils, nous dormirons la nuit.
Bientôt, comme une mer aux plus énormes ondes,
Sa nuit avalera les astres et les mondes,
Et bientôt ce sera du sommeil apaisant   20
Pour Jésus et Satan, enivrés du néant.

Amor Hesternalis

Our blood is swayed by sunken moons
And lulled by midnights long foredone;
We waken to a foundered sun
In Atlantean afternoons:
Our blood is swayed by sunken moons.   5

In gardens of another age,
For us, the Grecian roses fall,
The gold figs ripen by the wall;
And your pale breasts my love assuage—
In gardens of another age.   10

Our lot is with the lost and old:
We live, as in some fabulous
Fair idyl of Theocritus
Or tale by Heliodorus told—
Our home is with the lost and old.   15

Unmuted still, our pain abides,
Part of the lyre that Sappho smote,
And in the songs Catullus wrote
Our rapture and our grief resides.
Unmuted still, our pain abides.   20

A lamp in realms of night and death,
Our love reveals a tidal shore;
And still we follow, still implore
The sunken horns of Ashtoreth
In lands where all is night and death.   25

We are the specters of past years:
But soon Atlantis from the main
Shall lift; and Sappho bring again,
Risen from ancient brine and tears,
The living Lesbos of past years.   30

"All Is Dross That Is Not Helena"

What wistful lover has not mused upon
The waste of years that never knew his love!
And, wanting her once more, the seasons prove
But dearth and draff to feed oblivion.

I deem that all is empty, in my turn,   5
Beyond your tender arms, your tender heart:
Void and deviceless are the nets of art,
And song and silence are of one concern.

Dearer than Paphos' joy, or Lethe's peace!
In you alone are solace and surcease   10
Of antenatal dolor, ancient wrong.

You are the supreme boon, the only good
To one, who finds despair in solitude,
And weariness of heart amid the throng.

Future Pastoral

Dearest, today I found
A lonely spot, such as we two have loved,
Where two might lie upon Favonian ground
Peering to faint horizons far-removed:

A green and gentle fell   5
That steepens to a rugged canyon's rim,
Where voices of vague waters fall and swell
And pines far down in sky-blue dimness swim.

Toward the sunset lands,
A leafless tree, from tender slopes of spring,   10
Holds out its empty boughs like empty hands
That vainly seek some distance-hidden thing.

Strange, that my wandering feet,
In all the years, had never known this place,
Where beauty, with a glamor wild and sweet,   15
Awaits the final witchcraft of your face.

Upon this secret hill
I gave my dark bereavement to the sun,
My sorrow to the flowing air . . . until
Your tresses and the grass were somehow one,   20

And in my prescient dream I seemed to find
An unborn joy, a future memory
Of you, and love, and sunlight and the wind
On the same grass, beneath the selfsame tree.

Wine of Summer

From the deep azure chalice of the sky,
Inverted on the vale
And hot horizons pale,
The philtered wine of summer drains away. . . .
It was but yesterday   5
We drank that draft together, you and I.

Here in the grove the fallen needles bear,
Broken and disarrayed,
The print our presence made. . . .
O! haunted hollow left by your sweet form!   10
How the swift tears are warm
In eyes that seek and cannot find you there.

It seems the selfsame wind is in the pine
That sighed or sank above
Our ecstasy and love. . . .   15

But now no dryad face, no dryad voice
Shall make my heart rejoice,
No dear Bacchante wear the wilding vine.

O love! no other lips than ours have known
How sweet the wine, how sweet   20
With honey and soft heat
Mingling within that blissful magistral . . .
And yet how sadly fall
The slow, slow drops for him that drinks alone.

In Another August

How often must my steps retrieve
The lonely and memorial way
Of that receding yesterday!
While flesh and spirit darkly grieve
For loveliness that could not stay.   5

Why is it that you are not here
In the loved place where you have lain?
How can your beauty disappear
Out of the still-returning sphere
That brings again the stars and rain?   10

That brings again the tawny grass,
The summer sky, the summer tree,
And makes the pines' long shadow pass
Adown the hill, as once, alas!
Upon the loves of you and me.   15

Though suns return, and love delay,
Here in the wood my spirit waits,
In faithful trysting fain to stay
Till cyclic time restore the day
Alone allotted by the Fates.   20

Nocturne: Grant Avenue

The city's towers were limned in fire
When, down the long, the hill-descending street,
We rode as down some cataract of stars:
Our hearts replete
With that rebirth of wonder and desire,   5
We seemed to overpass the night's effulgent bars.

Quoting those lines of Baudelaire
On what delight the Town's old lovers seek,
I saw your face by subtler dreams illumed,
And heard you speak   10
Of how, amid that multifold parterre,
Beauty and mystery and evil softly bloomed.

Through us, in throbbing unison,
Strange pulses ran and secret powers thrilled
From all the thronging darkness hazardous: 15
We twain were one
As in remembered noons by rapture stilled
When all the forest fountains sang unheard of us.

And yet . . . how far from Arcady
And from the shores and dales of sylvan love!   20
And yet . . . what ghostly train of nymph and Pan,
Goddess and dove,
Through the walled mazes followed you and me
From out that halcyon world in which our love began;

And, through the city's glare and sound,   25
What ghosts of faint hesternal flowers blew
And freshness borne from woodlands far away:
Until, anew,
At parting in your long, deep kiss I found
The savor of sweet balm and spiced immortal bay.   30

Classic Epigram

Sweet Lesbia, when our love is done,
Leave no reproachful shade or blot,
No least reproof, on all or aught
That made us twain, that made us one:

Say only, Love has lived his hour   5
Blameless as any rose's bloom,
And faultless now his final doom
As is the dying of the flower.

Twilight Song

O heart, be sad, be still!
She that we love is far,
Veiling her face with folded plain and hill
Below the vesper star.

Breathe only one wild sigh   5
On winds of sunset gone—
Flown like the exile, brief, October cry
Of oread and faun.

Mute evening wanes in mist. . . .
Our feet have lost the way   10
Leading to that inviolable tryst
In dells of yesterday.

O night! upon thy stream
Obliviously to float
And haply find in westward-flowing dream   15
Her place and face remote.

Supplication

Be clement still, and steep
Thy breasts in mandragore,
And let thy hands a poppied vintage pour
Whenas we turn, idolatrous,
Fain of thy yielded bliss and given sleep   5
In nights calamitous.

Tender thou art, and kind:
Unto thy place we came
Through dolorous realms by roads of dust and flame:
Our eyes, in twilight sweetly lost,   10
Are shut like poppy-buds against the wind
From heavens of holocaust.

Before our feet depart,
With hemlock fill the cup
Our hands unto thy laden urn hold up;   15
With deadliest dwale bedew thy kiss
To leave a Stygian stillness in the heart
That begs no later bliss.

Erato

Ah, suffer that my song
To thee alone belong:
No dearer happiness my heart would choose
Than thus to cast, O sweet,
Each measured scroll before thy perfect feet,   5
Having no other muse.

O wistful love! how well
All that my lips would tell,
All that the lyre's revibrant strings attest,
Was writ upon thy breast   10
With kisses keen and slow . . .
So long, so long ago.

What tears are confluent
From springs and summers spent,
Feeding the fount of this our Helicon;   15
And wine forlornly poured,
Or spilt for thee, O maenad most adored,
In feasts of moon or sun.

Let now some interval
Of lyric silence fall;   20
Like heavy garlands let thy hair be shed
About by brow and head,
While songs unsung and sweet
Within our pulses beat.

Anodyne of Autumn

Full-ripened on the bough,
Pends the bright apple now,
And the lees fall from out the unclouded wine.
These memories that return
Pour from their mellowing urn   5
A dreamful and delicious anodyne.

O love! thy face, thy hands,
Long lost in sadder lands,
Somewhere amid this golden dale remain:
All that was flown and dear   10
Lies somehow warm and near—
Nothing is gone but loneliness and pain.

All day I follow still,
On western wold or hill,
The dream redreamed, the enchantment wrought once more: 15
Tomorrow brings at last
All blisses of the past
For him that drinks of autumn's mandragore.

No bitter winds awake
In reedy tarn or brake;   20
The citron sunset leaves an orange moon.
Before my senses float
Thy breasts, thy lips, thy throat
Like fruit of Hesperus in a poppy-swoon.

The Hill of Dionysus

This is enchanted ground
Whereto the nymphs are bound;
Where the hoar oaks maintain,
While seasons mount or wane,
Their ghostly satyrs, dim and undispelled.   5
It is a place fulfilled and circled round
With fabled years and presences of Eld.

These things have been before,
And these are things forevermore to be;
And he and I and she,   10
Inseparate as of yore,
Are celebrants of some old mystery.

Under the warm blue skies
The flickering butterflies,
Dancing with their frail shadows, poise and pass.   15
Now, with the earth for board,
The bread is eaten and the wine is poured;
While she, the twice-adored,
Between us lies on the pale autumn grass.

Thus has she lain before,   20
And thus we two have watched her reverently;
More beautiful, and more
Mysterious for her body's nudity.

Full-burdened with the culminating year,
The heavens and earth are mute;   25

Till on a fitful wind we seem to hear
Some fainting murmur of a broken flute.
Adown the hillside steep and sere
The laurels bear their ancient leaves and fruit.

These things have happened even thus of yore,   30
These things are part of all futurity;
And she and I and he,
Returning as before,
Participate in some unfinished mystery.

Her hair, between my shoulder and the sun,   35
Is turned to iridescent fire and gold:
A witch's web, whereon
Wild memories are spun,
And magical delight and sleep unfold
Beyond the world where Anteros is lord.   40

It is the hour of mystical accord,
Of respite, and release
From all that hampers us, from all that frets,
And from the vanity of all regrets.
Where grape and laurel twine,   45
Once more we drink the Dionysian wine,
Ringed with the last horizon that is Greece.

Before Dawn

Bleak is the night and long
While slumber waits apart,
Refusing this lone heart,
These lips forlorn of song.

Deep is the night and slow   5
Whose gulf obscurely swarms
Mad, somber, faceless forms,
Blind masks of bale and woe.

The moon's late-risen ray
Through paling panes is shed. . . .   10
From dreams uncomforted
I rouse before the day.

Now, ere the morning break,
Would that my head found rest
Upon thy halcyon breast   15
To sleep, and not to wake.

Amor

This is the fire of Hestia's careful hearth;
The flame that fed on many-towered Troy;
Selene's light about the Latmian boy;
The all-consuming ardor of Melkarth.

This is the peregrine star that will return,   5
Faithful to the olden ephemerides;
The torch of corybantic mysteries;
The spark still burning in the stoppered urn.

This is the lamp ancestral hands have lit
Deep in the doorless crypts of blood and bone. . . .   10
For you and me, it is a witch-fire blown

Where secret airs and obscure pinions flit,
That has outburned Walpurgis and the moon
And lifts in quenchless rose to a cloudy noon.

Interval

Ah! silent is my love
For stress of all the words can never say,
Of all that lovers prove
Only with endless kisses, or delay
Of some supreme caress before the day.   5

No more of speech or song,
No more of music now: my lips are mute,
Wanting your lips too long:
For what the lute-player without the lute?
The flutist, vainly seeking his lost flute?   10

On ways not yet forgot.
Return, O nimble feet that stray too far:
If April brings you not,
Black are the days and false the calendar. . . .
I wait you as the twilight waits the star.   15

Postlude

Hearkening now the voices of the crowd,
Have you forgot the faint Parnassian music
We heard between the bracken and the cloud?

What have you found amid the many faces?
Nothing remains for me, save the spent echoes   5
Of words we said in falcon-hovered places.

O tryst too long delayed, too long denied!
I meet on changing paths a faceless phantom
Exile and chill as wisps of eventide.

Empty the forest now, empty the stream;   10
Your naked body on the noonlit hill
Has gone with the cloudy lovers lost in dream.

Strange Girl

What bond was this, or life or doom,
That swiftly drew your eyes to mine
Beyond the drinkers and the wine,
Across the crowded, garish room?

Beauty was yours, but beauty lost,   5
Bringing to that familiar bar
The lustre of a fallen star
On strands of night and chaos tossed.

O yours were soft, unhappy lips,
O yours were hard, unhappy eyes   10
Like agates under glacial skies
Laden with tempest and eclipse.

Upon the delicate chin you turned
Venus had set her cloven sign.
Like embers seen through darkest wine   15
Your unextinguished tresses burned.

Your gown revealed that gracious form
Tanagra's sculptors loved to mould
In clay immortal from of old,
With limbs for ever sweet and warm.   20

Or what we spoke, it matters not:
For in your wistful voice I heard

What hidden things that found no word—
Broken, half-dreamed or half-forgot.

Girlishly, half maternally,   25
You chid me for the fault we shared:
Your voice was sweet . . . your eyes despaired. . . .
It was your eyes that wounded me,

So bleak they were, so wan and chill,
Like eyes that meet the Gorgon's gaze   30
Amid the untraversable maze
Of all-reverting shame and ill.

But when you leaned to kiss me there,
It seemed some fragile moth of night
Had softly touched my lips in flight,   35
Swerving athwart the untroubled air.

Sister you seemed to all the woe
My heart has known but never sung. . . .
Was it for this your fingers clung
To mine, as loath to let me go?   40

De Profundis

Too long, alas, too long
My patient heart endures
This deep and desperate wrong—
To walk on fallen ways afar from yours.

O pain that loses not   5
Its sharp and ancient sting!
O rapture unforgot
Whereof some dark tomorrow yet shall sing!

O spirit, blood and bone
Whose deepening voices cry   10
She is mine own, mine own,
Though earth and all the ascendant spheres deny:

For her I have arisen
From many a broken tomb,
From out the darkling prison   15
Of sunken worlds and avatars of doom.

For her I bear the Flame
Replenished from of yore—
Unquenchably the same
Like the great fire within the planet's core.   20

O Flame that shall not fail
In voids of time and space,
At last you shall avail
To light my feet to her abiding-place.

Midnight Beach

In starlight, by the ghostly sea,
We ran, we loitered, hand in hand,
Along the lone, unending strand;
Where, flowing in the surf-wet sand,
The wan stars raced or paused as we.   5

Aloof we seemed, from time and change,
Like runes a magian might unroll
Upon some old unfading scroll,
Or phantoms loosed from earthly dole
In starry freedom, high and strange.   10

Some great, unspoken gramarie
Had exorcised that incubus,
The world, that fell away from us. . . .
Reborn, and dear, and perilous,
The past arose beside the sea.   15

Returning in that mystic hour,
Above us hovered many a night
That had your eyes alone for light:
Full-petaled, past all worldly blight,
Love bloomed an amaranthine flower.   20

In starlight, by the ghostly sea,
I caught and kissed you as of yore;
We ran, we tarried, as before;
Where, flowing on the surf-wet shore,
The wan stars raced or paused as we.   25

Illumination

Musing upon the mysteries of the flesh,
I am as some hierophant of old
For whom the temple's hidden valves unfold.
Remembering now your tresses' heavy mesh
A little harsh beneath my pillowed face;　　　　　　　　5
The savor of your bosom and the scent;
Your warmth, a blissful essence immanent,
Flooding my veins in the long unstirred embrace;

Your eyes, beheld so close their glory seemed
One strange great orb; your laughter's gentle fall:—　　　10
Remembering these, I know the mystical
Round lotos ripening, locked in garths of night,
And sighing of those live fountains that have streamed
In Edens of a seven-sensed delight.

Omniety

I am the master of strange spells
Whereby the past is made tomorrow,
And April blows in fields long fallow,
And Dis unseals Hyblaean wells.

From out the house of incarnation　　　　　　　　5
I pass with ether or with air,
In climes and times of otherwhere
Resume my destiny and station.

Loosed from the coils of space and number,
I am the shadowy self who stands　　　　　　　　10
Kissing your lips, holding your hands,
Warding your labor and your slumber.

Dream not to escape me, day or night,
Even in the passionate arms of others,
For I am one with all your lovers,　　　　　　　　15
Sharing their pain and their delight.

Even in Slumber

This separation cleaveth to the core. . . .
Even in slumber I am fated
To seek thee in vast throngs and dreamlands desolated—
And find thee nevermore.

* * *

Bewildering phantoms rise between, and ways   5
Where demons claim their olden debt;
The rote of sullen streets and streams; the spume and fret
Of planet-blinding sprays.

Moly

Who are ye that always wander
Up and down and here and yonder?

—We are they that ever seek,
Over fen and fell and peak,
Down the desert-straitened creek,   5
Through dank forests darkening wholly
Tarns remote and melancholy,
For the flower known as moly,
Flower that wards the flesh and heart
From beguileful Circe's art.   10

Seek no more! seek no more!
Not on mountain, moor or shore,
Not by noon, nor under moon,
Blows the plant of magic boon,
Not with eyes shall any find it   15
Nor with fingers pluck and wind it:
From the dust of limbs and heart
Shall the roots of moly start,
Over thy forgetful grave
Shall the flower of moly wave.   20

Cambion

I am that spawn of witch and demon
By time's mad prophets long foretold:
The unnamed fear of king and freeman,
I roam the lawless outland wold,
Couching amid the weeds and mould   5
With dire Alecto for my leman.

I am that hidden piper, playing
The Panlike strains of malefice
That lure the lonely wanderer, straying
Upon the crumbling precipice: 10

To filmed morass or blind abyss
His feet must follow, never staying.

I am that swart, unseen pursuer
Whose lust begets a changeling breed:
All women know me for their wooer: 15
Mine is the whisper maidens heed
At twilight; mine the spells that lead
The matron to the nighted moor.

I am that messenger whose call
Convenes dark mage and banished lord   20
And branded witch and whip-flayed thrall,
To plot, amid the madness poured
On the black Sabbat's frothing horde,
The bale of realms, the planet's fall.

The Knoll

All rimmed around with halcyon skies,
Filled with blue air and butterflies,
Mightily arched and intervalled,
And leaved with solemn emerald,
The century-lichened oaks arise   5

From this high knoll against the brine
Like those about Dodona's shrine:
For here Apollo still is god
And living dryads tread the sod
And love is Grecian and divine.   10

Not hidden with sad dreams of ill
Where Venus holds her vaulted hill,
For us the two, for us the three,
Here dwells the fair antiquity
Glad and august and pagan still.   15

And here how often has the sun
Brightened on breast and hair of One . . .
But never has the sun or shade
Amply and long enough delayed
For love that dreads oblivion. . . .   20

What shall the sealed horizons hold
For us, on future hills, untold—
The three, the two, that tarried here
Through azure mornings, hushed and dear,
And afternoons of forfeit gold? 25

Haply, by some dark ocean-stream,
These days shall dawn again in dream;
Through films of distance and of tears
We shall behold, in wintered years,
These butterflies that flit and gleam. 30

For an Antique Lyre

Still wanting you, perchance
How vainly love had waited,
An autumn faun belated
For whom the leaves like spectral dryads dance.

And time perhaps had run 5
A somber, songless river
Whence no nymph rises ever
With limbs that flash to lotus in the sun.

And happiness had been
A siren singing only 10
On shores unsought and lonely
Where Vesper falls to some untraveled visne.

And joy had tarried still,
A sleeping Venus hidden
In sunless halls forbidden 15
Within her undiscovered hollow hill.

On Trying to Read *Four Quartets*

There is a bard named T. S. Eliot
(Perhaps the British call him Heliot).
To one like me, like mind ingenuous
His poems seem too fine and ten[uous.]
In fact, the stuff's so dessicated [*sic*] 5
I half suspect he's constipated.
Methinks the beggar needs a _____
I find more pleasure in Ella's _____.

Greek Epigram

There is a bard named T. S. Eliot
(Perhaps the British call him Heliot).
He writes a tough untoothsome line,
I'd rather read a Valentine.

Lines on a Picture

O face upturned to alien splendors!
Sybil, what visions have you seen
In haunted worlds? what music hearkened
In Edens hushed and vespertine?

The far is near, the near is distant   5
For you that swell in dreams untold. . . .
And yet . . . and yet . . . perchance not wholly
Their riddled meaning lies unrolled.

Perchance your mouth is strangely wistful
For hidden things you know not of: 10
Your eyes forget, your lips remember
Some lost and Atlantean love.

Alternative

Who turns him from his earthly love
Must other lovers meet and prove;
Through plunging lands careened from light
Into the crimson-starred abyss,
He goes by sunken stairs, to kiss   5
The coal-hot lips of Baaltis
And Lilith in the nether night.

Or else, on mountains noonward-piled,
He climbs the planished walls, beguiled
By wispy, wavering spectres born   10
Of snow and sun; till, starkly mad,
In some delirium strange and glad,
He clasps an ice-limbed oread
Upon the slippery silver horn.

Hymn

For Puliakamon

Thou art both the yonic altar and the goddess,
And I am thine acolyte,
The bearer of the lingham.

Thou hast become the Muse—
Sweet, bawdy, sacred, pagan and profane.   5

I invoke thee,
Yet know not wholly that which I invoke.

I have brought thee earthly gifts as well as divine gifts:
For in earthliness there is also a sanctity and a sublimity.

The sound of thy laughter and mine has mingled with the sound of
    tabors in the adytum,   10
And the echoes thereof shall not be silenced,
And sidereal ears shall harken
And sidereal lips repeat the laughter.

I have poured into thee my seed,
And of that seed love shall be the progeny,   15
Since love was the father;
And generations of dreams and eons and divinities shall be born;
And the Mystic Rose shall spring thereof,
Unfolding in gardens tilled by seraphim,
And breathing on all the paths an attar of sevenfold delight.   20

Thou hast lain wholly naked in my embrace,
Nearer to me than my soul—
And yet thou standest on the flaming apex of the Star,
And cradlest in thine arms the fate that has not yet descended into flesh.

The Sorcerer Departs

I pass . . . but in this lone and crumbling tower,
Builded against the burrowing seas of chaos,
My volumes and my philtres shall abide:
Poisons more dear than any mithridate,
And spells far sweeter than the speech of love . . .   5

Half-shapen dooms shall slumber in my vaults,
And in my volumes cryptic runes that shall
Outblast the pestilence, outgnaw the worm

When loosed by alien wizards on strange years
Under the blackened moon and paling sun.   10

Surréalist Sonnet

The lyrebird giblets in the frying-pan
cheep crisply to the sibilant blue gas.
A Congo mouth gulps a blond demitasse,
then spews on the flowered rug from Ispahan.
Rome's red flamingo feathers wave their fan   5
while stilt-legged craw and stomach sac alas
march down beneath aforetime's blear morass
bannered with mildewed naperies of man.

But brandished over stale antiquities
still rise the verdant bones of gluttonies   10
flying the parchments of new horoscopes.
The sage arachnidan from Regulus
amid its souvenirs on raddled ropes
will haply hang some dried esophagus.

Paean

You are the golden guerdon
Of all the iron days:
Hereafter song shall praise
Only your pagan breasts, and have for burden
Your wine-sweet lips, your blithe, delicious ways.   5

Hereafter with wild glory
Engarlanding your head,
Wreathing your name unsaid,
Song yet shall leave untold a fairer story
Than fabled loves and passions legended.   10

Song shall repeat hereafter
No sigh from love forlorn
Importunately torn:
For love has known how tender is your laughter
In hours between the moonfall and the morn.   15

Do You Forget, Enchantress?

The Muses all are silent for your sake:
While night and distance take
The hamadryad's hill, the naiad's vale,
Low droops the hippocentaur's golden tail,
And sleep has whelmed the satyrs in the brake.   5

Unplucked, the laurels stand as long ago;
The balms of Eros blow
Rose-red and secret in the cedars' pall . . .
Do you forget, enchantress, or recall
The world you fashioned once, and now forgo?   10

Where, Venus-like from Lethe and the abyss,
Might rise the abandoned bliss;
Where the mute Muses bide your summoning word;
Where darkling faun and daemon drowse unstirred,
Waiting the invocation of your kiss.   15

The Horologe

O clock, your long and solemn tones,
That now resound the knell of time,
Are like some hammer's iron chime
That rings on broken tombs and thrones.

Parnassus à la Mode

Erato and Melpomene stumble in the stews
Through purblind alleys where a soused Apollo falls;
And bards pour out upon the altars of the Muse
A sacrifice from cuspidors and urinals.

Sea Cycle

Below the cliff, before the granite stair,
The foam-crests curl and feather in blue air,
Numberless as the helmet-plumes of hosts
Resurgent from millennium-foundered coasts.
The billows, wreathed with sea-weed and sea-flower,   5
Mount landward from the mermaid's plundered bower,
And shells and pebbles, torn from sunken strands,
Shift idly on the rainbow-haunted sands.

The slow tide stirs, amid the nether main,
The sluggish treasure-galleons of Spain; 10
And surely, if we wait and watch awhile,
The spars of galleys cast on the Sirens' isle,
Or broken on Saturnia's iron keys,
Will swirl before us from the cyclic seas. . . .

Dear, shall I pray the gulf's great deity, 15
Nodens, to bring once more for you and me
Some love-relinquished hour we could not save
That westered all too swiftly to the wave,
Ebbing between the cypress and the grass?
Though prayer be vain, this thing shall come to pass, 20
For still the solemn cycles wane and flow,
Bringing again the lost and long ago.
All that the sea has taken, the sea restores:
Somehow, somewhere, on ocean-winnowed shores,
Again we two shall wander, and shall not stay, 25
Finding the golden wrack of yesterday.

Dancer

O dancer with the dove-swift feet and hands,
So palely swaying
Against the moon's replenished rondure,
Thou treadest not this autumn ground alone:
But in my heart, as in some high-piled press, 5
Dancing, thou crushest out with thy wan feet
A vintage strong, a wine sanguinolent
That shall restore the summer.

Nevermore

Ah, let me not remember
The leaves of brown November
'Neath boughs renewed with May;
Let me forget the flowers
Of blown Aprilian bowers, 5
When autumn shades and showers
Besiege the flowerless day.

Ah, never, nevermore,
Beauty that burned of yore

As a great lamp of gold,   10
Must I recall thy grace,
Nor dream thy phantom face
In any lonely place
The moonless mists enfold.

Reverie in August

The heat is like some drowsy drug
Laden with honey-foundered dreams. . . .
Again the pagan forest seems
To couch and roof our pagan love.

Alone I wait . . . but not alone: 5
For something of you lingers yet,
Something returns, and subtly tells
Of all the beauty made our own.

Across the days that intervene
I breathe the fragrance of your hair,   10
One with the pine-embalsamed air:
Its warm oblivion covers me.

Again some gently murmured word
Lights the great fire in my blood;
Till rapture like a singing sun   15
Is in the riven spirit stirred.

And leaning thirstily and fain
On earth and air that burn with drouth,
I find again your pagan mouth—
Half-palpable, like dreams that fade.   20

Tin Can on the Mountain-Top

Tomato-can, of thee I sing:
bright beacon of liberty and civilization,
harbinger of progress
left by the picnicker
among the millennial junipers and glacier-moulded granites   5
on Donner's peak.
Insouciantly you lean, with label already peeling
in gaudy green and crimson décolletage
to reveal your rondure, dimpled slightly here and there by dents
but otherwise perfect

and suggesting with futuristic provocation   10
the cylindrical breast-form of a strip-teasing robot.
The wind, that ancient lecher, plays with the label
and it falls away like a slip
from around your dazzling flanks.
Profulgently you glitter, like the wings of planes   15
over Hispania or China,
or like the Coit tower
on a fogless morning.
In you we behold the ultimate avatar
of stellar slag and neutrons long dissolved   20
into nebulous vapor;
in you the transgalactic goal
of atom endlessly broken and re-alchemized
in the dark laboratory of time and space
by the demiurge who wears the night for mask.   25
In you the mystic ore
immured by subterranean gloom of aeons,
and carried obscurely by the womb of worlds
as they wandered on through gulfs and light-years,
in you the oft-remolten and star-pregnant metal   30
briefly gleams, refracting all the solar rays,
and batting back the electrons from the sun-spots,
and riddled by all the cosmic and ultra-cosmic and infra-cosmic and
other-cosmic radiations.
But soon, too soon, your glory tarnishes,
and the spots and mottlings and zones of stannic oxide   35
will damascene you with their rufous arabesques,
with their brownish nacarat and ruddled umber;
until you lapse in Huysmanesque corrosion,
colored and surfaced like the planet Mars.

Some Blind Eidolon

Longer ago than Eden's oldest morn,
Ere beast or man was born,
I chose for mine
The love whereto some ancient evil clings,
With sombre spectra barring still the wings   5
That wear the irised flame of suns divine—
The love whereto some ancient evil clings.

Down all the planet-paven ways of time,
Lengthening from the prime
A shadow falls—   10
A thing that climbs the pharos-guarded gates,
Or by the wizard's dying brazier waits,
Or lairs amid the many-tapered halls—
A thing that climbs the pharos-guarded gates.

Have we not known, O witch, O queen, O maid,   15
The stain that creeps unstayed
In love's alloy?
The fretful moth that frays the bed of lust?
The wingless and unweariable disgust
That overtakes the philtre-goaded joy—   20
The fretful moth that frays the bed of lust?

Though proud as gardened Babylon our bliss,
Mortal corruption is
The seed self-sown
Amid the rampant flowers and the founts. . . .   25
The laughter of some blind eidolon mounts
Where the self-deluded mourner sobs alone
Amid the ruined flowers and the founts.

Dark loves of all the vanished avatars,
What candor-heated stars,   30
What crimson hells,
Consumed us long ago but cleansed us not,
Nor could absolve us of the sombre blot!
Yea, all the Moloch-hearted suns and hells
Consumed us long ago but cleansed us not!   35

Where limbos of unfathomed ice immure,
Shall yet we couch secure
Our sundered clay?
What sea wherein the unshapen planets sleep
Shall make us one in its potential deep—   40
Washing the lethal dross of self away—
What sea wherein the unshapen planets sleep?

The Pursuer

Climbing from out what nadir-fountained sea,
From nether incarnations none may sound—
Sealed with the night of suns, forever bound
With frozen systems—comest thou to me,
Despair, whose darker name in memory   5
I know not, bringing from the dead profound,
With cerements and sepulchral purples wound,
The foulness of thine immortality?

O shape of loathlier horrors, here untold,
Have I not climbed secure from their abyss,   10
Those lower spheres, those limbos dire and old?
Thou tearest me beyond the hells of this,
Down chasms dreadful for the light of tears
Where worm-like terror crawls in the undead years!

To Bacchante

There was a place, belovèd,
Wherein we drank of beauty and of tears
Before the days had closed their iron circle,
Before the sullen lassitude of years.
(But who shall break the circle,   5
And drink again of beauty and of tears?)

Take thy war-shafts, O Cypris, and go at thy leisure to some
other target; for I have not even space left for a wound.
                              —The Greek Anthology.

Calenture

Rathe summer had sered the grass in which he lay
Under the little shade
The live-oak made,
While things remembered and foregone,
Loves from the drouth of other summers drawn,   5
Like rootless windlestrae
Went past him on
The hot and lucid flowing of the day.
The wine-flask at his side
Shone empty: he had spilled   10

The last drops for oblation on the dried
Pale rootlets dead with May
Of the small-seeded oats no man had tilled.
He thought: their death is clean,
This tawny change that overtakes the green   15
And makes the unnumbered fragile skeletons
Yet yields no mortal fetor to the suns.
Their death is clean . . . but ours
Is not the death of grasses and of flowers. . . .

He thought: they die and live and die again   20
With little travail, none or little pain:
But love, though brief as these,
With endless agonies
Of bitter and relucting breath,
Accepts, refuses, and receives its death. . . .   25
And here it was,
On grass that bore the seed of the same grass
On which I now recline,
That my mouth drank the wine
Of dregless love and beauty from the cup   30
Of the pagan flesh in fulness offered up.
To him that keeps, forlorn,
From morn to vacant morn
The vigil of the seasons, shall there come
Ever again the timeless, tall delirium?   35

In the afternoon with burning silence filled,
Cicada-like, a fever sang and shrilled,
Harrying anew his passion-wearied blood
Through veins oppressed by heat and hebetude.
Indifferently he watched the westering day   40
Like spreading fire consume
The thin last shrunken shade in which he lay.
He closed his dazzled eyes; in the red gloom
Behind the sun-confronting lids he saw
A faceless and colossal woman loom: 45
One moment in his eyes,
Ere the dislimning vision could withdraw,
The breasts were large and dim as daylight moons,
The hips, on scarlet skies,
Glimmered with arch of evening semilunes,   50
The shadowy shell curved down between vast thighs.

Copyist

I write the poems down
Line by line from old anthologies
Printed on the air and ether,
Shelved amid the leaves of trees,
Between the stars, or under stones   5
And mouldered bones.

Love and Death

Lying on the tiger-skin
In the secret, safe boudoir,
Lovers eat
The spicy luncheon-meat
Brought by several relays   5
From the abattoir.

Quintrains

Essence

Though the roses
Wreathe no more the garden
And the garden-dial,
Intenser grows the essence
In the vial.

Epitaph for an Astronomer

Shall he find
Novae in the darkness blind?
Or phantom of a farther sun?
These follow him not nor shall forerun
Where the night and stars are one.

The Heron

Entranced, unstirring,
Stands the heron
By the river's rippled gleam:
Fishes twinkle in the stream
And in his dream.

Bird of Long Ago

All that I remember
From a dim and verdant spring
Long dead
Is, that one bright mouche of red
Patched a blackbird's wing.

Late November Evening

Startled, I heard the clack and clatter
Of the stiff plane-leaves, blown abroad
Upon the paven road:
The noise of cymbals clashed by night
In autumn's flight.

Mithridates

Life the toxicologist
Proffers all the magistrals
Of death:
I chose love,
And I draw immortal breath.

Mummy of the Flower

Stiff and brown and dusty-
Coffined in the drawer,
I found the oleander-flower:
The love that in your tresses died,
Mummified.

Nightmare of the Lilliputian

I was a midge
With broken wing,
Crawling some colossal ridge
Underneath the world
At the roots of Ygdrasil.

Passing of an Elder God

In some Titan city, bells
Gigantically clangorous,
Endless, monotonous,
Ring for dead Enceladus
Monstrous knells.

Poets in Hades

At an inn called the Sign
Of the Acherontic Pump,
Two poets drank their ebon wine
In memory of the rose and amber
Essence of the vine.

Quiddity

When harbored in the stone,
With its stillness being one,
All its essence was our own:
Incarnate now, we abdicate
What kingdoms of the inanimate!

Someone

An orphaned baby
Fallen from its crib
On the floor
Crawls and gropes for a lost nipple
Evermore.

Dying Prospector

With my shovel, pick and bar,
I shall dig
The shining placers of the moon
And the star-
Loded mines.

Experiments in Haiku

1947

Strange Miniatures

Unicorn

Over fern, over thorn,
Rose the banded moonbow horn
Of the unicorn.

Untold Arabian Fable

Balkis feeds
Topaz grain and ruby seeds
To an uncouth fledgling roc.

A Hunter Meets the Martichoras

Through his three rows of teeth
The martichoras roared
Against my broken sword.

The Limniad

The pool's green lymph
Whitens with the floating nymph
Who rises algae-fleeced.

The Sciapod

Shaded by his palmy feet,
The sciapod
Roots his tresses in the sod.

The Monacle

He has one foot, one leg,
To bear him here and yonder
In lands of wonder.

Feast of St. Anthony

Birds of fable,
Phoenix, roc and simorg-anka,
Pecked my phantom-fruited table.

Paphnutius

From my Stylitean throne,
The crag turned to cloud,
The cloud returned to stone.

Philtre

Drunken with a thirsty spell,
Pygmies and giants warred
For the desert well.

Borderland

One cactus-column rears alone
Before the forest
Where the trees are stone.

Lethe

From the nameless dark distilled,
Lethe flows
Through the night that no man knows.

Empusa Waylays a Traveller

In my mule's long shadow
On the moon-wan waste,
Hung Empusa, horror-faced.

Perseus and Medusa

I met her mirrored stare:
The cycles of stone glories
Locked in the Gorgon's glare.

Odysseus in Eternity

Oblivion
Swells our sails and bears us on
To the seas beyond the sun.

The Ghost of Theseus

Where nights are one with days
I roam the empty stony maze
That stalled the Minotaur.

Distillations

Fence and Wall

Old, with scattered blocks,
Low-fallen beside the wire fence
Lies the wall of rocks.

Growth of Lichen

Over the rock the lichen
Stars the way whereon
Ten thousand suns have gone.

Cats in Winter Sunlight

In the slanted ray,
Huddling closely, my three cats
Slept the winter day.

Abandoned Plum-Orchard

Lichen, mistletoe, aloft
In the dying croft,
Leaf the winter trees.

Harvest Evening

Barnward come the cows
In the squash-hued sunset
Raddled by the buckeye boughs.

Willow-Cutting in Autumn

When I felled the willow,
From it flew a thousand
Slender wings of yellow.

Declining Moon

Close above the snow-scene,
Blue, purple, yellow-green
Clouds ring the moon.

Late Pear-Pruner

When I pruned the pear-trees,
Buds and blossoms falling
Strewed the path of spring.

Nocturnal Pines

From my door the pines,
To Polaris pointing,
Spoke the turning Signs.

Phallus Impudica

Through the rotting leaves,
Autumn fungi thrust:
Pale similitudes of lust.

Stormy Afterglow

In the east at sunfall
Lightning tore the clouds' tall
Rose and violet scarps.

Geese in the Spring Night

My lone heart afar
Trails the geese no longer heard
Below the northern star.

Foggy Night

Hastening I strode
Past the drunkard lying
Beside the moonless road.

Reigning Empress

From thy beauty
And thy lovers' ardent wars
Time shall make his metaphors.

The Sparrow's Nest

I found the sparrow's nest
Where the thorned blackberries reach
Boughs of unpruned peach.

The Last Apricot

When I came to pluck it,
Fallen, splashed in rot
Was the last apricot.

Mushroom-Gatherers

When our pails were brimmed,
Mushrooms white and brown
Clustered where the slope went down.

Spring Nunnery

Before the nunnery's cold
Walls the poplar-leaves unfold,
Plums are flowering.

Nuns Walking in the Orchard

Sable-robed, at noon,
They passed beneath red cherries
Ripening with June.

Improbable Dream

In my dream a nun,
Proudly bosomed, lunar-pale,
Danced naked in the sun.

Crows in Spring

Glossy-backed, the crows
Ward the garden-rows:
One turns to watch the farmer.

High Mountain Juniper

Far above pine and fir,
Mortised in granite aeons,
Stands the juniper.

Storm's End

At the storm's decline,
A vulture seeks its nest
In the bolt-cloven pine.

Pool at Lobos

Anemones yawn,
Shells walk, peaked and whorled,
In a still crystal world.

Poet in a Barroom

Faces of the four seasons
Throng the bar:
One peers from a time-lost star.

Fallen Grape-Leaf

From the fallen leaf
And from my deciduous heart
Fades the scarlet.

Gopher-Hole in Orchard

Again, from the gopher-hole
I plugged with straw and stones,
Bubbling, the water runs.

Basin in Boulder

In the boulder's top
The time-hollowed basin
Fills with rain, drop by drop.

Indian Acorn-Mortar

In the granite pits
Crumbling oak-leaves nestle;
Lichens asterick the pestle.

Old Limestone Kiln

In the crumbling topless kiln
Pines have taken root,
Oaks drop their fruit.

Love in Dreams

I saw you not nor heard,
Knowing your presence as one knows
The night-found rose.

Night of Miletus

When I saw you dance,
Milesian roses swayed in the wind
Of a lost romance.

Tryst at Lobos

I would meet you where
Summer vaults of cypress
Keep the balsams of the past.

Mountain Trail

In the steepest mile,
Climbing the mountain path,
You held my hand awhile.

Future Meeting

By what digit of the moon
Shall I question, late or soon,
Your shoal-green eyes?

Classic Reminiscence

The herd of goats for us
Turns the hillside to a scene
From Theocritus.

Goats and Manzanita-Boughs

To the gathered boughs we hold
Flock the goats
From the close-eaten wold.

Bed of Mint

Fragrant were the embraces
That I shared with you
Where the wild mint grew.

Chainless Captive

Beauty is the prisoner
None can hold,
Though all have captured her.

California Winter

Still, in January,
Hang a few yellowed leaves
On the naked willow.

January Willow

Far-separate, a few
Leaves illumed with perished autumn
Space the boughs against the blue.

Snowfall on Acacia

I

Drooping low,
Acacia-branches bear their double
Burden of flowers and snow.

II

Humped with snow, the golden
Sprays careen, lifting free
Suddenly.

Flight of the Yellow-Hammer

A flame of orange ashen-flecked
In a wavering line
Takes wing from pine to pine.

Sunset over Farm-Land

Over fields newly ploughed,
Pools of golden leaf-green
Broaden in the mallow cloud.

Flora

Spring came down the mountain-side,
Gentian-eyed,
From the snow-rimmed fountains.

Windows at Lamplighting Time

Black houses set
With little squares of golden dawn
Life where the sunset darkens.

Old Hydraulic Diggings

I

From the bedrock bottom
Dolomites upbear
Pines with roots that reach in air.

II

Roots of gnarled manzanitas
Tortuously coil,
Clutching the cobbled soil.

III

On the graveled slide
A log that ancient fires have charred
Lies, petrified.

IV

The reflex of stark rufous walls
Into milky waters green
Unfathomably falls.

Hearth on Old Cabin-Site

In the ruined fire-place
Grows the summer-brown fern,
And a few poppies burn.

Builder of Deserted Hearth

In what winter shrewd, morose,
Did he cower close
To the manzanita-blaze?

Aftermath of Mining Days

Monotonously rolled
On the hills the broom
Spreads its many-acred gold.

River-Canyon

I

Moss-cup oaks, broadly sprawled,
Clench the path, with sapling laurels
Intervalled.

II

Ledge-thinned waters
Falling, divide and ravel
Over ferns and cress and gravel.

III

Arbors of the wild grape
Climb from alder-tops
To the cliff-grown copse.

IV

Columbine and Indian pink
Light the vine-fringed pool
Where the foxes drink.

V

High above
In their azure-walled estate
Shrills the red hawk to his mate.

VI

Far down the gorge steepens
Where inch by centuried inch the channel
Deepens.

VII

By the grape's long root
We clamber from the last ledge
To the river's edge.

VIII

With bronze and silver stippled
Runs the shallow-rippled
River over stones.

IX

Pebbles and driftwood
High-lodged amid the willows
Mark the winter-widened flood.

X

Ouzels dart, swiftly gone,
Past the heron standing
Stirless and alone.

Childhood

School-Room Pastime

With pencils on scratch-paper
We drew grotesques
And passed them underneath our desks.

Boys Telling Bawdy Tales

Half-ignorant ribaldries,
Outrageous drolleries
Of infant Rabelais.

Fight on the Play-Ground

Agonists with bloody noses,
How we slugged and mauled,
Swore and squalled.

Water-Fight

Heaving rocks into the stream,
Each rival team
Splashed the other with glad cries.

Boys Rob a Yellow-Hammer's Nest

Porcelain-white, the flicker's eggs
Lined he bottom of the hole
In the pine's dead bole.

Nest of the Screech-Owl

When I groped eagerly
In the hollow tree,
The screech-owl nipped my hand.

Grammar-School Vixen

I went homeward by the willowed
Stream-bed, knowing
That she waited on the road.

Girl of Six

You cuddled me and kissed me,
Mussed my hair, and smiled:
The woman in the child.

Mortal Essences

Snake, Owl, Cat or Hawk

Who
Will heed the downy nestlings
Of the dove the hunter slew?

Slaughter-House in Spring

Burning hair, flesh, bones,
Taint the south wind blowing
Over flowers and mossy stones.

Cattle Salute the Psychopomp

Penned beside the abatoir,
Stridently they moo and bellow
To the night-bringing star.

Slaughter-House Pasture

Horned skulls and boned hooves
Litter the field
Together with the fallen leaves.

Field Behind the Abatoir

Where the mantled bones lie low,
Monstrous weeds and grasses lush
Thicklier grow.

Plague from the Abatoir

On the window-sill
Fall the blow-flies that I kill:
Dozens buzz and blunder still.

La Mort des amants

One bullet, dark and hard,
Stilled the coupling cats that yowled
In the yard.

Vultures Come to the Ambarvalia

Funereal and austere,
Their downward spiral narrows
On the fallen deer.

For the Dance of Death

In the stirless brake
Click the faint castanets
Of the rattlesnake.

Berries of the Deadly Nightshade

Black are the berries
Laden with slumber
Of nights that have no number.

Water-Hemlock

To the south wind's breath
Lean the stately stalks and umbrels
Rooted with death.

Felo-de-se of the Parasite

Dead and leafless too
Clings the clustered mistletoe
On the oak it slew.

Pagans Old and New

Initiate of Dionysus

Pagan shadows fill the eyes
Of one who shares
Even once the Mysteries.

Bacchic Orgy

Still, beneath the gibbous moon,
Bacchus-led, the maenad crew
Drank and danced and slew.

Abstainer

Pentheus, come not here
Where the thyrsi rear
And the maenads' frenzy mounts.

Picture by Piero di Cosimo

On the pagan down
Blithesome, naked, brown
Satyrs loot the bee-tree.

Bacchants and Bacchante

From the Chinese cymbal
Whereon we banged by fire-light
Clangors ranged the night.

Garden of Priapus

With lowered lids, you nod:
Somewhere in the garden
Lurks the garden-god.

Morning Star of the Mountains

Wakeful in the sleeping bag,
I met the stare
Of Venus, risen on your hair.

Bygone Interlude

I waited on the hot bank:
Naked and cool,
You floated in the river-pool.

Prisoner in Vain

About your wrists I bound
Fetters of water-grass
Where the streamlet wound.

Epitaphs

Braggart

His tales in hell make all the heads
[. . .]

Slaughtered Cattle

Through brief sarcophagi they pass
[. . .]

The Earth

Where countless constellations sparkle
[. . .]

Miscellaneous Haiku

Illuminatus

He draws empyreal breath
Who buys no potion
From the pharmacy of death.

Limestone Cavern

Grotesques leaning,
Hued with verdigris and cream,
Buttress the chambered gloom.

Maternal Prostitute

On the stranger at her breast
Patiently she smiled:
A mother with her child.

Ocean Twilight

Grey gulls on a grey sea:
Out of the sunset-glow
A wind blows bleak and keen.

Radio

When I heard the singer bawl
I thought he had swallowed his cocktail-cherries
Tooth-picks and all.

Tule-Mists

Where tules grow
The fumes of cauldrons chill
Engulf the sanguine afternoon.

If Winter Remain

1948–1950

Hellenic Sequel

I

Skies of verd-antique
Domed the murex-tinted peak
In the dreamland where I found
Flowering grape that clasped and crowned
One fluted column still unbroken,   5
Lovely, old and Greek.

II

Near the column,
In the stream that flowed
From the sunset mountain-spring,
I heard the lonely naiad sing,   10
Praising the weedy bowers of her abode.
Sweeter than silence was her song,
Sweeter than sleep her answer
When I spoke:
Quickly then her cold arms wound me   15
In the water, and they drowned me
Ere I woke.

No Stranger Dream

One rapid gesture of a supple arm
Has made your beauty strange and fabulous:
Mystery folds you and reveals you, thus
Weaving anew the seven-circled charm.

Love needs no stranger dream: your face calls back   5
The feet that flying Lemures have drawn
To years beyond the darkness and the dawn;
And thrusts afar the impending Zodiac.

He that has been the pilgrim of dark shrines,
And sued the silver wraith of Baaltis,   10
Would ask no wonder more arcane than this:—

To watch, in a place of summer grass and pines,
The spangled spectrum somnolently spun
In your deep hair by the seaward-turning sun.

On the Mount of Stone

In rock-bound Arabia
Grows the myrrh and cassia
Lost altars burned to Alilat,
And spices that
The phoenix gathered for his pyre.   5

Laurel-leaves and laurel-blooms,
Dreams, and blood, and flowers
Dropped by Hermes-footed hours,
Feed the fire
Wherein my love consumes   10
On the mount of stone, and springs
Renewed with young auroral wings.

Only to One Returned

Often, before the mortal mouth has known
What fruit the vagrant phoenixes devour
In Melusina's or Armida's bower,
Not fully savored are the apples grown
In charmless orchards closed about with stone: 5
Only to one returned, in some late hour,
From shores of lote where guardian Scyllas glower,
The sweetness of the fruits of earth is shown.

Thus, turning from translunar seasons bleak,
Or borderlands of Endor, ill to seek,   10
Where necromancy's wandering wisps grow dim
And Lilith and her night-bound daughters dwell,
Love finds again some fleshly citadel,
Safe-walled, with many a pleasance sweet to him.

Sonnet for the Psychoanalysts

When sleep dissolved that super-Freudian dream
where featherless harpies mated while they fed,
I could not find my body: but a thread
of blood on fabled stairs, through mist and steam,
led to a hall of legend. There, in the gleam   5
of classic lamps, my table-seated head
in gem-bright goblets lazuline and red
saw essences Falernian fall and cream,

self-poured, with cans of seething beer. Beyond,
in balconies that craned on vacant skies,   10
one booted leg went striding sentry-wise.
It was my own. It guarded with strict care
my heart, a sanguine, ice-girt diamond
imprisoned in some crystal frigidaire.

Avowal

Whatever alien fruits and changeling faces
And pleasances of mutable perfume
The flambeaux of the senses shall illume
Amid the night-furled labyrinthine spaces,
In lives to be, in unestablished places,   5
All, all were vain as the rock-raveled spume
If no strange close restore the Paphian bloom,
No path return the moon-shod maenad's paces.

Yea, for the lover of lost pagan things,
No vintage grown in islands unascended   10
Shall quite supplant the old Bacchantic urn,
No mouth that new, Canopic suns make splendid
Content the mouth of sealed rememberings
Where still the nymph's uncleaving kisses burn.

Tolometh

In billow-lost Poseidonis
I was the black god of the abyss:
My three horns were of similor
Above my double diadem;
My one eye was a moon-bright gem   5
Found in a monstrous meteor.

Incredible far peoples came,
Called by the thunders of my fame,
And passed before my terraced throne
Where titan pards and lions stood,   10
As pours a never-lapsing flood
Before the wind of winter blown.

Below my glooming architraves
One brown eternal file of slaves
Came in from mines of chalcedon,   15

And camels from the long plateaus
Laid down their sard and peridoz,
Their incense and their cinnamon.

The star-born evil that I brought
Through all that ancient land was wrought: 20
All women took my yoke of shame;
I reared, through sumless centuries,
The thrones of hell-black wizardries,
The hecatombs of blood and flame.

But now, within my sunken walls,   25
The slow blind ocean-serpent crawls,
And sea-worms are my ministers,
And wandering fishes pass me now
Or press before mine eyeless brow
As once the thronging worshippers. . . .   30

And yet, in ways outpassing thought,
Men worship me that know me not.
They work my will. I shall arise
In that last dawn of atom-fire,
To stand upon the planet's pyre   35
And cast my shadow on the skies.

If Winter Remain

Hateful, and most abhorred,
about us the season
of sleet, of snow and of frost
reaches, and seems unending
as plains whereon   5
lashed prisoners go,
chained, and enforced
to labor in glacial mines,
digging the baubles of greybeard kings,
of bleak Polarian lords.   10

Benumbed and failing,
we languish for shores Canopic
that foulder to vaults of fire,
for streams of ensanguined lotus
drinking the candent flame   15
with lips unsered, unsated,
for valleys wherein no shadow,

whether of cassia or cypress,
shall harbor the ghost of ice,
the winter's etiolate phantom.   20
Benumbed and failing,
we languish for shores Canopic
that foulder to vaults of fire.

Fain would we hail the summer,
like slaves endungeoned   25
beneath some floe-built fortress,
greeting their liberator,
the hero in golden mail. . . .

But . . . if summer should come no more,
and winter remain   30
a stark colossus
bestriding the years?
If, silent and pale,
with marmorean armor,
the empire of cold   35
should clasp the world
to its rimed equator
beneath the low,
short arc of the sun,
out-ringed by the far-flung   40
orbit of death?

Almost Anything

Superlatively sonorous
Like a saxophone full of brass tacks and coffin-nails;
Reverberantly rhythmical and rhythmically reverberant
Like a foetus four months old
In the womb of a she-baboon;   5
Romantic and picturesque
Like a merd-brown fog slinking away through slum alleys
And over the city dump;
Fair and pulchritudinous as a female Hottentot with buttocks
    two axe-handles broad
And eyes that shine like rotten mackerel by moonlight;   10
More savorous than Gorgonzola buried for two months
At the bottom of a ship-load of guano;
Soft and voluptuous

Like the bosom of a jellyfish that is more than slightly moribund;
And redolent as a room   15
Where a cat was shut in by mistake . . .

But you say that my meaning is obscure,
And that it is hard to understand what I am referring to:
I ask you,
Hypocrite lecteur, mon semblable, mon frère,   20
What is the use of writing this Modernist poetry
If one is not permitted
To be decently or indecently cryptic on occasion? . . .
And as for the meaning—
Well, I am not any too sure myself,   25
But if you are really determined to know,
I suggest that you refer the matter to some Modernist critic.

"That Motley Drama"

O meaningless and sterile wars!
O senseless virtue! stupid sin!
Our puerile drama will not win
The hoots or plaudits of the stars.

O world, with vulture beaks agape!   5
What god will care to curse or bless
Nature, the crouching leopardess,
Or man, the homicidal ape?

Pour Chercher du nouveau

Call up the lordly daemon that in Cimmeria dwells
Amid the vaults untrodden, long-sealed with lethal spells,
Amid the untouched waters of Lemur-warded wells.

Call up the wiser genius who knows and understands
The lore of night and Limbo, who finds in tomb-dark lands   5
The pearls and shells and wreckage that strew the dawnless strands—

Remnants of elder cargoes, lost, enigmatic spars
From seas without horizon, washing occulted stars,
From shadow-sunken cycles of vaster calendars.

Call up the vagrant daemon, whose vans have haply strayed   10
Through subterranean heavens by dead Anubis bayed,
Who has seen abysmal evil, aloof and undismayed;

Beholding fouler phantoms no necromancer wakes,
Reptilian bulks that cumber the thick putrescent lakes,
And pterodactyls brooding their nests in charnel brakes;   15

Hearing the unspent anger of troglodyte and Goth,
The rote of gods abolished, the moan of Ashtaroth,
The hunger and the fury of famished Behemoth.

Call up the sapient daemon, whose eyes have haply read
The cipher-graven portals in planets of the dead,   20
Who knows the dark apastrons of stars for ever sped;

Who has seen the lost eidola hewn from no earthly stone,
The unrusting magic mirrors, in chambers chill and lone,
That hold supernal faces from heavens overthrown;

Who has heard the vatic voices of witch-wrought teraphim;   25
The wailing fires of Moloch, the flames that swirl and swim
Around the blood-black altars of ravening Baalim;

Who has heard the sands of ocean, far-sifted on the beach,
Repeating crystal echoes of some sidereal speech;
Who has heard the atoms telling their legend each to each.   30

Call up the errant daemon, the pilgrim of strange lands,
And he will come, arising from shadow-tided strands,
With gifts of bale and beauty and wonder in his hands.

Dans l'univers lointain

Dans l'univers voilé d'un vague violet,
De larges fleurs sans nom sur leurs soucoupes frêles
Promènent les rubis, portent les rubicelles
Que leur soleil vermeil verse de son coffret
Dans l'univers voilé d'un vague violet.   5

Ces fleurs sont les seuls rois d'une rouge luisante.
Nulle nuit, nul hiver leur lustre n'a terni;
D'une floraison énorme, en le soir qui reluit,
Une lune rosée allume l'amarante.
Ces fleurs sont les seuls rois d'une rouge luisante.   10

Elle se mirent là par somptueux milliers
Aux mares de grenat, aux fleuves qui refoulent
En écarlate où des palais rouillés s'écroulent
Et des temples tombés entassent leurs piliers.
Elles se mirent là par somptueux milliers.   15

Dans leur oubli sanguin les tribus inconnues,
Qui troublaient leur empire en un Avril d'antan,
Disparaissaient ainsi qu'un papillon volant,
Ainsi qu'un souvenir de soleils et de nues.
Leur néant engouffra les tribus inconnues.   20

Où des fantasques dieux se fendent les autels,
Sous l'ancien ciel sans vent, sans aile et sans nuée,
Monte des fleurs une fumée exténuée
Comme un encens voué aux trônes éternels . . .
Où des fantasques dieux se fendent les autels.   25

Le temps, oiseau glué à l'aile languissante,
S'est englouti dans leur léthé de cramoisi;
Et leur linceul énorme et rouge ensevelit
Un monde qui s'abîme en ses cieux d'amarante
Comme un oiseau glué à l'aile languissante.   30

Dans l'univers voilé d'un vague violet,
De larges fleurs sans nom sur leurs soucoupes frêles
Promènent les rubis, portent les rubicelles
Qui leur soleil vermeil verse de son coffret
Dans l'univers voilé d'un vague violet.   35

In a Distant Universe

In the universe veiled by a violet vastness,
The large and nameless flowers on their frail salvers
Flaunt the rubies, bear the rubicelles
An old vermilion sun pours from its coffer
In the universe veiled by a violet vastness.   5

These flowers are the kings of [. . .]
[. . .] of this enormous flowering.
[. . .] the kings of a red, bright star.
[. . .]
[. . .]

They mirror themselves there in sumptuous thousands
In garnet pools, in scarlet streams that ebb
Where rusty palaces crumble
And fallen temples heap their pillars.
They mirror themselves there in sumptuous thousands.   15

In their red oblivion the unknown tribes
That troubled their empire in an April of yesteryear,
Have vanished even as a flown butterfly,
Even as a memory of suns and clouds:
Their nothingness engulfed the unknown tribes.   20

Where lie the riven altars of fantastic gods,
Under the sky without wind, without wing or cloud,
Mounts from the flowers an attenuated smoke
Like an incense vowed to the eternal thrones . . .
Where lie the riven altars of fantastic gods.   25

Like a lime-caught bird with drooping wing
Time is swallowed up in their crimson Lethe;
And their red, enormous winding-sheet enshrouds
A world that drowns in skies of amaranth
Like a lime-caught bird with drooping wing.   30

In the universe veiled by a violet vastness,
The large and nameless flowers on their frail salvers
Flaunt the rubies, bear the rubicelles
An old vermilion sun pours from its coffer
In the universe veiled by a violet vastness.   35

High Surf: Monterey Bay

Like fins of numberless white sharks, the foam
Cleaves the blue, wrinkled surface of the bay,
And on the cliffs the massive combers build
Fragile ephemeral lattices of spray.

This was the bay the slant-browed fishers sailed   5
In boats of raddled reeds; and this shall be
The shrunken salt-thick water seined by none
When the last sun, a red and rusty hinge
Torn from the sky, lets down eternity.

Isaac Newton

Stems break, wax melts;
A thorn of thought worked earthward through his mind.
Apples and gods and mortals all came down

By natural causes or by accident.
Some not unmixed with glory: 5
That sweet boy, who like a murdered bird,
Fell wingless from the sun.
Rain fell, snow fell.
The magnet at the centre of the earth
Drew stars and stones and red-cheeked apples down.   10
What wonders fell towards that sleepless mole!
What little birds, what great and exiled wings!
Ripeness hung still and heavy from the bough.
He waited for apocalypse to fall,
Feeling the lodestone like another moon   15
Drawing the earth-shaped apple through the leaves.

La Muse moderne

In muddled sleep a soused neurotic bawd,
Chemised with bumwad, burps beneath the sink,
And when she farts, the whoreson bardlets think
Some new divine afflatus blows abroad.

The Mystical Number

Three crows
On the scarecrow,
In the pear-orchard;
Three rabbits,
Peacefully nibbling in a corner of the cornfield;   5
Three cockroaches,
Floating belly-up in a pail-ful of cream
In Mrs. Hoskins' pantry;
Three Peruna bottles,
All empty but one,   10
On the bureau in Mrs. Hoskins' bedroom;
Three jugs of hard cider,
Under the seat of Farmer Hoskins' buggy,
Returning from the corner store. . . .
O! mystical number!   15

Pantheistic Dream

In the heart of the old woodland
The world is a mirage
More wan and dim
Than the pool that reflects,
In another planet,   5
The pale nenuphar.

Scarcely can I remember,
Nor recognize my pain:
[. . .] this green twilight
[. . .] depart, grown strange   10
[. . .] masks,
[. . .]ith love.

[. . .]nd my arbor
The sunbright mere
Lulls asleep my dazzled eyes,   15
Like a crystal whence has come
The flame of an ecstasy
To the swooning mage.

The incredible nothingness
Plucks at me, inenarrable,   20
From the heart of its covert;
I lose myself, I graze
The thing that flies,
Too vast for the spirit.

I know not if the oak   25
Sighs with my breath,
Nor if I sigh in the oak;
Sometimes I am the wild poppy
And sometimes the cat-tail
That scatters its seed on the clear ripple.   30

For me all thought
Is leafed and wood-like
And mingles with the elder-trees:
Sap that escapes not thence,
It ripens the berries   35
And spreads in the boughs.

Rêve panthéistique

Au fond du vieux bocage
Le monde est un mirage
Plus terne et plus blafard
Que l'étang qui réfléte,
Dans une autre planète   5
Le pâle nénufar.

Je me souviens à peine,
Je meconnais ma peine:
De ce vert demi-jour
_____ vois partir, étranges   10
_____ marques qui se changent,
_____ joint à l'amour.

_____llée,
_____ ensoleilée
_____ort l'oeil ébloui,   15
_____e un cristal d'où passé
_____a flame d'une extase
Au mage évanouî.

La néant incroyable
M'accroche, inénarrable,   20
Du fond de son abri;
Je me perds, et je frôle
La chose qui s'envole,
Trop vaste pour l'esprit.

Je ne sais si le chêne   25
Soupire à mon haleine,
Ni si jen pousse l'air;
Parfois je suis l'oeillette,
Et parfois la massette
Qui s'égrene au flot clair.   30

Pour moi toute pensée
Est feuillue et boisée
Et se mêle aux sureaux:
Sève qui s'en n'échappe,
Elle mûrit la grappe   35
Et s'épand aux rameaux.

Poèmes d'amour

She said: "They're beautiful, but bad for you, your poems."
I thought that I had paid her a compliment
In well-timed verse designed to praise and woo,
And was taken quite aback.

                Yet maybe she was right,   5
Or partly right at least. We poets turn
Our slender loves to swollen verse, and thus
The verse builds up the complex of our loves,
Refining and exasperating them
Ad infinitum, past the scope of nature.   10
How much is love, how much is poesy?
But it's a pretty game and hardly matters
Beyond the morgue, when toothless maggots eat
The hand that wrote, the fingers that caressed
Or, peradventure, failed to make the curves.   15
We only hope the poem, by some chance,
May last a little longer than the amour.

Sandalwood and Onions

I kissed you once,
And left in half an hour
Without kissing you again:
You had perfumed yourself with sandalwood,
And also, you had been eating fried onions   5
    For supper.
I like sandalwood,
And I like onions, too,
    In their place;
But I simply couldn't stand the mixture!   10

The Dark Chateau

The mysteries of your former dust,
Your lives declined from solar light—
These would you know, or these surmise?
Beneath a swathed and mummied sun,
Descend where dayless dials rust,   5
Where the void hourglass fills with night;
And seeing with still-living eyes
Dim Acherontic rivers run,

Follow where shrouded barges float
And fall, in regions of the dead,   10
Into the sable-foaming depths.
Then over ghostland mountains go
To find, beyond a bridgeless moat,
What stairs with shadows carpeted
Crumble behind the climber's steps   15
In some foreknown forlorn chateau.

Where exiled ghosts of gales that blew
At eve from vintages antique
Still stir the blurring tapestries,
And empty armor guards the rooms   20
By rotting portraits that were you,
Pass on. From airless cupboards bleak
Startle memorial spiceries
And plagues adrowse in attared glooms.

By oriels charged with stifled stains,   25
With night-blent purples, gules embrowned,
And spring's lost verdure, graver now
Than cypress at the set of day,
Pause, and look forth: no ghost remains
Save you to gaze on that dim ground   30
Where once the budding almond-bough
Waved, and the oleander-spray.

Hoar silence is the seneschal
Of court and keep, of niche and coigne.
With drumless ear no lute annoys,   35
Nor clang from jarring jambarts drawn,
Death, with dulled arrasses for pall,
Waits whitely there; and none will join
Your quest, nor ever any voice
Speak from the chambered epochs gone: 40

Till from the vaults with shadows brimmed
Shall come a cowled lampadephore,
Holding his lamp, by no breath blown,
To mirrors moony-clear and still
Where never living face is limned,   45
But wan reflections fixed of yore—
Long-mouldered shapes that were your own—
Graven in glass, unchanged and chill.

Don Quixote on Market Street

Riding on Rosinante where the cars
With dismal unremitting clangors pass,
And people move like curbless energumens
Rowelled by fiends of fury back and forth,
Behold! Quixote comes, in battered mail,   5
Armgaunt, with eyes of some keen haggard hawk
Far from his eyrie. Gazing right and left,
Over his face a lightning of disdain
Flashes, and limns the hollowness of cheeks
Bronzed by the suns of battle; and his hand   10
Tightens beneath its gauntlet on the lance
As if some foe had challenged him, or sight
Of unredresséd wrong provoked his ire. . . .

Brave spectre, what chimera shares thy saddle,
Pointing thee to this place? Thy tale is told,   15
The high, proud legend of all causes lost—
A quenchless torch emblazoning black ages.
Go hence, deluded paladin: there is
No honor here, nor glory, to be won.
Knight of La Mancha, turn thee to the past,   20
Amid its purple marches ride for aye,
Nor tilt with thunder-driven iron mills
That shall grind on to silence. Chivalry
Has flown to stars unsooted by the fumes
That have befouled these heavens, and romance   25
Departing, will unfurl her oriflammes
On towers unbuilded in an age to be.
Waste not thy knightliness in wars unworthy,
For time and his alastors shall destroy
Full soon, and bring to stuffless, cloudy ruin   30
All things that fret thy spirit, riding down
This pass with pandemonian walls, this Hinnom
Where Moloch and where Mammon herd the doomed.

The Isle of Saturn

In one of these (islands) the barbarian feign that Saturn is
held prisoner by Zeus.

—Plutarch

Say, what seer, what poet has beheld Saturnia?
Clio or Euterpe, tell, if this you know:
Zones of guardian storm unslackening, sempiternal
Doldrums of the flat untraversable foam
Drive the encroaching keels to leeward,   5

So no sailor glimpses it, no chart includes.
Never yet has man profaned it, never printed
Xanthic sands whereover duskier flames the blue
For tall marble cliffs whereon the hippogriffin
Rears his head and gazes seaward,   10

Unalarmed, and all replete with grainy grasses.
Slant with wind, and drenched by spindrift, walls of cypress
Closely ward untended crofts where mellowed apples
Fall not from the bough to break the cyclic silence
Of a mighty myth that slumbers.   15

There, in calamus and the lush hemlock matted,
By the muffled windings of unmurmurous streams,
Black gigantic swans that winter in strange planets,
Age to age returning, make their nests, and rear
Shadowy broods that no one numbers.   20

There the dragon-mother, couched amid the boulders,
High on rugged fells that rim the smoothed main,
Hatches out her blotched and horny young, with folded
Wings that open soon in fluttered, brief essays—
Tumbling on the downs and tors.   25

Darkly in the gaunt and gleamless mountain-sides,
Drowse the metals for the mail of gods rewakened;
And the trees of savage forests hold on high
Still-unshapen hafts of Titan battle-maces
To be wielded in vast wars.   30

Stretched between two peaks, within a lea-wide valley,
Saturn, slumbering, heals his wounds through halcyon cycles:
Rains and dews like balm anoint him; wild grapes clamber

Over him with ripening clusters; and black ivy
Plaits his golden beard uncombed.   35

Others there are sleeping. . . . Will they haply waken—
Monstrous phantoms, striding down from fell and highland,
Crawling like to rivered lava through the dale-beds?—
Gods who rose and reigned and died before the Titans,
Lying in topless tombs undomed.   40

"O Golden-Tongued Romance"

We found, we knew it dimly
Within a dead life grimly
By guarding time inurned—
A glamor far and olden,
A fulgor night-enfolden,   5
A flame that in long-darkling Eden burned.

Though hardly then we claimed it,
We yet adored and named it
With a name forgotten now—
A faery word and dawn-like,   10
A word of gramarie, gone like
An opal bird from off a purple bough. . . .

Ah! vain the lamp reluming
The unhaunted vault inhuming
The cold Canopic jar,   15
And vain the charm recovered
From out the daemon-hovered,
Worm-traveled page of pentacled grimoire.

And yet the thing we yearned for,
The thing that we returned for,   20
From tomb and catacomb,
It may not wholly dwindle
While moon or meteor kindle
A phantom beacon on the ebon foam.

Through ghoul-watched wood unthridden,   25
By goblin mere and midden,
No ivory horn will blow,
No gold lamp lighten gloom-ward,
But we will carry doom-ward
The broken beauty caught from long ago: 30

An echo half evading
The ear, remotely fading
From a far-vibrant lyre,
A long-plucked flower blooming
In the dry urn, a fuming   35
Myrrh-fragrant ember in a darkened pyre.

Averoigne

In Averoigne the enchantress weaves
Weird spells that call a changeling sun,
Or hale the moon of Hecate
Down to the ivy-hooded towers.
At evening, from her nightshade bowers,   5
The bidden vipers creep, to be
The envoys of her malison;
And philtres drained from tomb-fat leaves
Drip through her silver sieves.

In Averoigne swart phantoms flown   10
From pestilent moat and stagnant lake
Glide through the garish festival
In torch-lit cities far from time.
Whether for death or birth, the chime
Of changeless bells equivocal   15
Clangs forth, while carven satyrs make
With mouths of sullen, somber stone
Unending silent moan.

In Averoigne abides the mage.
So deep the silence of his cell,   20
He hears the termless monarchies
That walk with thunder-echoing shoon
In iron castles past the moon—
Fast-moated with eternities;
And hears the shrewish laughters swell   25
Of Norns that plot the impested age
And wars that suns shall wage.

In Averoigne the lamia sings
To lyres restored from tombs antique,
And lets her coiling tresses fall   30
Before a necromantic glass.
She sees her vein-drawn lovers pass,

Faintly they cry to her, and all
The bale they find, the bliss they seek,
Is echoed in the tarnished strings   35
That tell archaic things.

Zothique

He who trod the shadows of Zothique
And looked upon the coal-red sun oblique,
Henceforth returns to no anterior land,
But haunts a latter coast
Where cities crumble in the black sea-sand   5
And dead gods drink the brine.

He who has known the gardens of Zothique
Where bleed the fruits torn by the simorgh's beak,
Savors no fruit of greener hemispheres:
In arbors uttermost,   10
In sunset cycles of the sombering years,
He sips an amaranth wine.

He who has loved the wild girls of Zothique
Shall not come back a gentler love to seek,
Nor know the vampire's from the lover's kiss: 15
For him the scarlet ghost
Of Lilith from time's last necropolis
Rears amorous and malign.

He who has sailed in galleys of Zothique
And seen the looming of strange spire and peak,   20
Must face again the sorcerer-sent typhoon,
And take the steerer's post
On far-poured oceans by the shifted moon
Or the re-shapen Sign.

Le poéte parle avec ses biographes

O goules des minuits funèbres et fétides,
Que découvrîtes vous dans vos tristes labeurs?
—Nous avons déterré l'Empuse de tes peurs
Et la Gorgone affreuse aux prunelles livides
Dans nos mornes labeurs.   5

O terrassiers si diligents, ô goules sages,
Qu'avez-vous trouvé dans vos prodigues travaux?
—Nous avons exhumés à leurs antiques maux
Tes amours, dont les vers effondrent les visages,
Dans nos vastes travaux.   10

Ouvreurs salis de pyramide et d'ossuaire,
Qu'avez-vous révélé hier au rouge soir?
—Nous avons défoncé le sol cendreux et noir
Pour anatomiser la nymphe sans suaire
Que l'on a couché au soir.   15

Goules, que faites-vous, ce soir, pour vos délices,
Dans ces sépulcres bas, lugubres et béants?
—Nous venons pour démailloter des morts vivants—
Des faunes pas châtrés jamais de tes vieux vices—
Dans ces tombeaux béants.   20

Pourquoi dans ces efforts, ô goules Chaldéennes,
Blanchissez-vous la terr' du sel de vos sueurs?
—Nous y trouvons toujours d'ineffables douceurs:
Les senteurs des morts mûrs, les épices anciennes,
Embaument nos sueurs.   25

The Poet Talks with the Biographers

O ghouls of fetid and funereal midnights,
Say, what do you uncover in your sad labors?
—We have disinterred the Empusa of thy fears
And the frightful Gorgon with her livid eyeballs
In our mournful labors.   5

O diggers all so diligent, O sapient ghouls,
What have you found in your prodigious toils?
—We have exhumed with all their antique evils
Thy loves, with features gutted by the worms,
In our enormous toils.   10

Grimed openers of pyramid and ossuary,
What revealed ye yesterday at crimson evening?
—We have dug up the black and ashen soil
To anatomize the shroudless nymph
Who was laid to sleep at evening.   15

Ghouls, what would ye do, tonight, for your pleasure,
Within these low, lugubrious and gaping tombs?
—We come to disenswathe the living dead—
The never-gelded fauns of thine old vices—
Within these gaping tombs.   20

Wherefore in such efforts, O Chaldean ghouls,
Whiten ye the earth with the salt of your sweat?
—Therein we find ineffable pleasures always:
Odors of the ripe dead, and ancient spices,
Embalsam our sweat.   25

Beauty

Whoso follows thee, O mystic Beauty,
will find, before the ultimate abyss,
thy face a pearl that founders and is lost
in the black billows of oblivion.

La Hermosura

Quien te siga, mística Hermosura,
allará, ante la final hondura,
tu faz una perla allí perdida
en las negras olas de la olvida.

Las Poetas del optimismo

Sómos los dueños
de todos los sueños
de la noche y del día.

Reitermos
y siempre bordamos   5
esta melodía:

El mundo es el suyo,
el sol es el tuyo,
la luna es la mía.

The Poets of Optimism

We are the masters
of all the dreams
of daylight and night.

We repeat
and always we embroider   5
this melody:

The world is his,
the sun is yours,
the moon is mine.

El Cantar de los seres libres

Gato montés, hermano de mi alma,
indómito sé tú, y sin cadena;
no sigas senda alguna de los hombres,
y vélate en vistillas y malezas.

Halcón del cielo, compañero alado,   5
sino para cazar, nunca descendas;
y como en torre, anídate en peñasco
que rodean fosos anchos de torrentes.

Gran cárabo, transnochador conmigo,
en claustro cavernoso de cipréses,   10
guárdate los secretos escondidos
a quien no ve la luz en las tinieblas.

Song of the Free Beings

Cat of the wilderness, my soul's own brother,
be thou untamed and tetherless;
follow no path that men have made,
be watchful on the heights and in the thickets.

Hawk of the heavens, winged companion,   5
descend never save to seek thy plunder;
and even as in some tower, make thy nest
in a craggy mountain moated round with torrents.

Great hornéd owl, that has outwatched the night with me,
in thy cavernous cloister of cypresses,   10
guard thou the secrets hidden
from him that sees no light in darkness.

¿Donde duermes, Eldorado?

Vida miá, en tu alteaza
Nunca olvides nuestro amor;

En tu dulce gentileza
No rechazes mi dolor.

Siempre soy un desterrado   5
De las playas mágicas

Bellas y gentílicas.
(¿Donde duermes, Eldorado?)

Nunca olvides este amor
En los besos venideros . . .   10

Y recuerda el gran calor
Sobre los laureados cerros;

Y recuerda nuestro mar
Soñoliento en la lejana

Dicha de una edad pagana. . . .   15
No rechazes mi pesar.

Where Sleepest Thou, O Eldorado?

Mistress mine, in thy loftiness
Forget never our love;

In thy sweetness and grace
Reject not my grief.

I am still an exile   5
From the magic shores

Beautiful and pagan.
(Where sleepest thou, O Eldorado?)

Forget not this love
In future kisses . . .   10

And remember the heart
Upon the laurelled hills;

And remember our sea
Sleeping in the distance

And the bliss of a pagan day. . . .   15
Reject not my repentance.

Los Dueños

¿Dimè, gran Satanás, que estás haciendo
En tu inferno más caliente y negro?
—Ando en borracheras con las diablas;
Estupro cada noche una diosa blanca;
Y bebo muentras mi vino más caliente y negro.   5

¡Oh! ¿soberano Mammón, que estás mirado
Desde tu altar mayor de oro sangriento?
—Miro el pueblo trepando en la mierda
Para recuperar mis monedas ensuciadas;
Y bebo de mi prensa el vino sangriento.   10

¡Oh! ¿despótico Muerte, que estás diciendo
De tu píramide de los cuerpos podridos?
—Digo de mi potencia, mi gloria, mi alteza,
Como un vasto upas asombrando la tierra;
Y bebo los licores de los cuerpos podridos.   15

¡Oh! ¿portentoso Amor, que estás pensando
Sobre los flúidos dudables en tu alembique?
—Pienso de toda tumba, toda cama y toda cuna
Que yo he llenado durante las centurias . . .
Pero no bebo las piciónes de mi alembique.   20

Dominium in Excelsis

Exalt thyself: be more than man,
Be saint or be magician,
And where the burning Sword awaits
Defy the old seraphic ban.

Thy will, that climbs from dark estates,   5
Shall divinize the godless fates,
This fiery ecstasy of dream
Melt down the grim, forbidden gates

That open into spheres extreme
Beyond the starry-bubbled stream—   10
Beyond Capella, past Altair—
Where amaranthine gardens gleam.

Thy feet shall tread the Scorpion's lair,
Thy hands shall catch the comet's hair;
Or over Endor thou shalt ride   15
Unfrighted on the tamed Nightmare,

And thence go down where ghosts have died
And famished ghouls and vampires glide;
Or tarry in years behind the tomb;
Or in the multiple futures bide.   20

Thou shalt respire the flame and fume
Of Beltis' altars drowned in gloom
Under her sharded fanes; or share
The fabled Atlantean doom,

And rise unharmed to light and air   25
Out of old death, once more to dare
With antinomian deed and thought
The planet of thy slain despair—

Till stones and atoms, shadow-wrought,
Dissolving shall return to naught,   30
Or into fairer shapes be brought.

Parnaso

Al pie de Parnaso
trashuman los rebaños
de chivas, de carneros
y de puercos
desarraigando las hierbas   5
y rumiando
en los pantanos y en los marjales
fangosos
que han descubierto sus pastores.

Pero alzando sus cimas   10
llenadas de flores ye de nubes
y de capullos y de joyas,
la montaña de las Musas,
siempre sin escalador,
sobresale, sola y limpia,   15
en el cenit tenido
de los azores de oro.

Parnassus

At the foot of Parnassus
from pasture to pasture roam the herds
of she-kids, of sheep
and of swine
rooting and ruminating   5
in the fens and moorlands
full of mud
that their herders have discovered.

But, elevating its summits
filled with flowers and clouds,   10
with buds and jewels,
the mountain of the Muses,
still unclimbed,
soars immaculate and lone
in a zenith held   15
by the golden hawks.

Las Alquerías perdidas

Amo los compos huertos, los vergeles
que las selvas han invadido
y las hierbas han recogido
a abrir sus florecitas fieles
llenas de oleres y de mieles.   5

Amo los yermos manzanales—
los moribundos ábroles
forrados de los liquenes—
amo la yid en los frutales—
los muérdagos en los perales.   10

Hallo en el fondo del boscaje
las piedras de un fogón caído
donde crece el rosal perdido
que tira de todo el paisaje
los vivos colibris en viaje.   15

Al borde de las espadañas,
conozco un viejo cobertizo
con muro mohoso y rojizo—
casa de hongos ye musarañas
y factoriá de telarañas.   20

Isleta de los cambronales,
he visto un prado sin sendero
donde el anciano membrillero
deja sus frutos invernales
al agua de las cenegales.   25

He visto de crepúsculo,
cerca de un destechado suelo,
blanquean los flores del ciruelo
como un fantasma pálido
que evoca un cano mágico;   30

a cuando los murciélagos
aleatan en la anochecita,
huelo de una pasada vida
los vola doros petalos
en los ramajes místicos.   35

Lost Farmsteads

I love the fields and gardens
invaded by the wilderness,
retaken by weeds and herbs
that open their faithful flowerets
full of perfumes and honies.   5

I love the desolate apple-orchards—
the dying trees
lined with lichens—
I love the vines in the fruit-trees—
the mistletoe in the pear-tops.   10

I find, in some woodland bower,
the stones of a fallen fire-place
where springs a forsaken rose-bush
to which from all the country-side
voyage the vivid humming-birds.   15

At the edge of the cat-tails,
I know an ancient shed
with moss-grown reddish wall—
a house for vermin and fungi,
a factory of cobwebs.   20

Enisled amid the bramble-thickets,
I have seen a pathless meadow
where an aged quince-tree
bequeathes its wintry fruit
to the water of quagmires.   25

I have seen in the twilight,
beside a roofless pavement,
the flowers of the plum-tree whiten
like a pale phantom
called up by some grey magician.   30

And when the flickering bats
veer through the evenfall,
I scent the flying petals
of former life
in the mystic boughs.   35

Cantar

Cuando en el desierto
relucen las aguas salinas,
veo los verdes ojos
de mi zagala atrevida.

Cuando en medio de espinas   5
maduran del cambronal las bayas,
miro los rubios pezones
de mi querida pagana.

Cuando vuela la polilla
fuera del almarjal   10
buscando las flores del anochecer,
siento a su alma fugaz.

Cuando oigo de medianoche
al mochuelo en su pino,
comprendo un aviso prudente   15
que presto olvido.

Song

When in the desert
shine the saline waters,
I see the green eyes
of my saucy lass.

When amid thorns   5
ripen the bramble-berries,
I behold the ruddy nipples
of my pagan love.

When flies the moth
beyond the marish   10
seeking the flowers of nightfall,
I know her volatile soul.

When I hear at midnight
the owl in his pine,
I understand a prudent warning   15
that I soon forget.

Eros in the Desert

I am the Love that wandereth alone
In weary lands beside a weary sea.
Grey reefs whereon the shoaling waters moan,

Marshes where salt and sterile blossoms be,
And all the sleep of mountain-ending sands,   5
Are mine to range, and roam eternally.

But emptier than these mine idle hands,
And hot as my insatiable soul,
Fulfilled with light, the fiery desert stands;

And roofed with flame, the mighty skies unroll.   10

Dice el soñador

Mi sueño preve un páramo
de la futura Atlántida
donde el fénix fogao hará
su nido nigromántico.

Él mira en Marte los canales   5
sin agua donde juguetean
las salamandras que flamean
como los fuegos infernales.

Él suerbe todo el amargor
de las lagunas Mercuriales,   10
y proba de las invernales
brescas en Venus el sabor.

Él sabe cómo los dragones,
frezas de un sol azafranado,
sacuden un llano arbolado   15
de sus enormes conjunciones.

Él oye cómo, sin aliento,
cantan en Júpiter las flores
la parca de los vencedores
que vienen de otro firmamento.   20

Él toma del seráfico
las alas y el feliz retiro;
él siente la sed del vampiro
y el hambre del licántropo. . . .

Pero si mi hado debatido   25
es fábula de mi pavor,
o es sueño de otro Soñador,
nunca mis sueños han sabido.

Says the Dreamer

My dream foresees the wilderness
of a future Atlantis
wherein the fiery phoenix will build
his necromantic nest.

It beholds in Mars the waterless   5
canals where frolic wantonly
the salamanders that flame
like infernal fires.

It knows how the dragons,
spawn of a saffron sun,   10
shake a wooded plain
with their enormous copulations.

It sips the bitterness
of the Mercurial lakes,
and proves the savor   15
of winter honeycombs in Venus.

It hears the unbreathing flowers
that sing in Jupiter
the doom of conquerors
that come from another firmament.   20

It assumes the wings of the seraph
and shares his blissful retreat;
it suffers the thirst of the vampire
And the hunger of the lycanthrope. . . .

But whether my mooted fate   25
is a fable of my fear,
or is the dream of another Dreamer,
my dreams have never known.

Memoria roja

Esta memoria vuelve todavía
de un jardín de amaranto más retinto:
los lagos del ocaso, colorando
mi desvarío como un vino tinto;
y los rubíes, hundidos talismanes,   5
en tus profundos ojos de jacinto.

Un esplendor de bermellón bañaba
las hiedras y las flores fúnebres;
y de tus labios yo bebía la sangre
que un dios sangraba fuera del ciprés;   10
y mi alto corazón llovía la vida,
la esencia de sanguinos árboles. . . .

Pero la noche vino a apagar
los mágicos rubíes y el fuego rojo
con el icor del dios. . . . En vano busco   15
aquella claridad en cielo y en ojo . . .
hallando ya símbolos y palabras
a limitar el río leteo y flojo.

Red Memory

This memory still returns
from a garden of darkest amaranth:
the pools of sunset, coloring
my fevered fantasy like some rich wine;
and the sunken, talismanic rubies   5
at bottom of your hyacinthine eyes.

Vermilion splendor bathed
the ivies and the tall funereal blooms;

and from your lips I drank the blood
a god was bleeding past the cypress;   10
and from my lofty heart rained down
the essence and the life of sanguine trees. . . .

But the night came to quench
the magic rubies and the flames made red
with a god's ichor. . . . Vainly now I seek   15
that light in any heaven, in any eye . . .
finding at last these words, these symbols
to circumscribe the slothful lethean river.

Dos Mitos y una fábula

¿A dónde vais, guerreros orgullosos,
con cotas fúlgidas como la luna?
—Salimos a matar al basilisco
en sima que sus ojos solo alumbran.

¿A dónde vais, valientes marineros,   5
en bajel de los tintes del otoño?
—Cruzamos a buscar verdina playa,
postrer asilio de los unicornios.

¿A dónde vais, innominados brujos,
con mantos más bermejos que el ocaso?   10
—Vamos a hallar de Salomón las jarras,
y a libertar los genios encerrados.

Two Myths and a Fable

Whither go ye, haughty warriors,
with coats of mail effulgent like the moon?
—We sally forth to slay the basilisk
in some deep gulf his eyes alone illumine.

Whither go ye, valiant mariners,   5
in your vessel colored like the leaves of autumn?
—We sail to seek some bright and verdant shore,
the last asylum of the unicorns.

Whither go ye, nameless wizards,
with robes outreddening the sunset gleam?   10
—We fare to find the jars of Solomon
and liberate the imprisoned genii.

La Nereida

Deseándola, declinan ya los astros.
A su lugar llevan los mares lentos
la sombra de los buscadoros vientos
que vagan en espuma y fuego vano.

Con luz de perlas su belleza brilla. 5
¡Qué ocasos, sueños y planetas hacen,
muriendo, los crepúsculos que yacen
alrededor de ella! Disuelto diá

fluye en el submarino firmamento,
para tejer vislumbres y visions 10
de bellas fugitivas ilusiones;
y la noche es un sueño sin ensueños.

No ha conocido mal de noche inquieta,
Ni blanco tósigo de diá claro;
¡que temblor de borrasca, en su amparo, 15
como un flojo placer su pecho besa!

Con berilina palidez, su cara
alumbra en reino de los ahogados.
En ella amor y anhelos ignorados,
rapto sin flor, y soterrada gracia, 20

esperan amador perdido y solo,
descaminado dios, que no viniere,
si, mudo al fin, el gran océano fuere
hundido en piedra estrecha de sus pozos.

¡Ay! pero nunca piensa en él, quizás; 25
su liso sueño, en lontananza ignota,
con su purpurando pelo, flota
en grutas de postrera fábula.

Del fuego antiguo serena inmanencia,
quédala siempre, espíritu que mura 30
la esmeralda del mar, inmensa y pura.
Deseándola, se ponen las estrellas.

La Isla de Circe

Ido su pétalo postrero,
decae de Circe el jardín;
el mudo olvido lastimero
sus filtros ha bebido al fin.

Las trenzas de la encantadora   5
sus amapolas han cambiado
por una mas helada fora
que crece en el sazón nevado.

Los cerdos vagan en el hielo
y no pueden desarraigar   10
ninguna raiz; al vano cielo,
sin proa, brama el vano mar.

Circe no sueña donde está
Ulisses en los negros años,
y nunca sepa adonde va   15
ningún dolor de sus antaños.

The Isle of Circe

Its final petal gone,
the garden of Circe decays;
mute and sorrowful oblivion
has drunken her philtres at last.

The tresses of the enchantress   5
have changed their poppies
for a white flower that remains
and grows in a snowy parterre

The swine wander in the sleet
and cannot dig   10
any root; to the vain sky,
prowless, bellows the vain sea.

Circe dreams not where
Ulysses is in the black years,
and knows not whither goes   15
any sorrow of yesteryear.

Lo Ignoto

Las bóvedas del tiempo y del abismo
no tienen ejemplar de tu beldad;
y ningún escultor cincela el mismo
concepto de tu forma y de tu faz.

Tirados por mentido magnetismo,   5
buscamos y no hallamos tu fugaz
palacio . . . y el farol del ocultismo
no te ha mostrado en tu proximidad.

¿Te escondes en la noche constellada?
¿o moras en el átomo profundo?   10
¿Descubierta, serás pira apagada,
o llama nueva de inaudito mundo? . . .

¿o luz cielo en faros terrenales? . . .
¿o fuego fatuo de los tremedales?

The Unknown

The vaults of time and space
hold no exemplar of thy beauty;
and no sculptor has chiseled the same
conception of thy form and of thy features.

Drawn on by some mendacious magnetism,   5
we seek and never find thy perishable
palace . . . and the lantern of paths occult
has never shown thee in thy nearness.

Hidest thou in the constellated night?
or dwellest in the atom's deep abyss?   10
Discovered, wilt thou be a burnt-out pyre,
or the new flame of an unheard-of world? . . .

or light from heaven in terrestrial beacons? . . .
or ignis fatuus of the quagmires?

Leteo

Sombrías son las aguas y sin ola
a quien demora ay muelle del Leteo,
sintiendo los temores del deseo
a ensayar ya la noche enorme y sola.

*   *   *

Los campos encantados de amapola   5
susurran en el perezoso oreo
de un cielo sin Polar. . . . En paseo
machaca del ignoto ser la cola.

[Lethe]

Somber and waveless on the waters
for him that lingers at the wharf of Lethe,
enduring the tremors of an old desire
to essay the lonely and enormous night.

For him the enchanted fields of poppy   5
sigh and whisper in a wind
from the pole that has no pole-star; in his passing
he tramples the dark tails of nameless things.

Añoranza

Mirando las mudanzas del azur otoñal,
leyendo en los soles un fúnebre señal,
oyendo las aves lamentosas en su vuelo
al fin del último cielo,
he sentido un soplo de amargura   5
de las alas de la hermosura.

¿Han ennegrecido el campo de cuervos los piñones
en su húida de un lugar de maduras corrupciones?
¿Qué sombra más funesta amortaja mi corazón? . . .
¿En esta venenosa poción   10
que ma boca ha bebido
qué verdín es fundido? . . .

¿Bruja sabia, de dónde viene esta añoranza
que ha amargado las vendimias de la mudanza?
¿Es nacido del nocturno   15
polo de Saturno?
¿o del pecho más amado
que los gusanos han besado?

¿Bruja ladina, dime, en qué páramo vernal
crece el antídoto de su veneno letal?   20
¿y qué herba cura los saetazos de los dolores? . . .

¡Oh! los moribundos amores
que sienten un soplo funeral
de las alas del mal!

Melancholia

Beholding the change of the autumnal azure,
reading in the suns a funereal sign,
hearing the plaintive birds in their flight
to the end of the ultimate heaven,
I have felt a breath of bitterness   5
from the wings of beauty.

Have the pinions of ravens darkened the field
in their passage from a place of ripe corruptions?
What baleful shadow enshrouds my heart? . . .
In this poisonous potion   10
that my heart has drunken
what verdigris is melted? . . .

Sagacious witch, whence comes this melancholia
that has embittered the vintages of mutation?
Is it born from the nocturnal   15
pole of Saturn?
[or fro]m a most beloved bosom
[. . .] have kissed?

[. . .]
[. . .]al wilderness   20
[. . .]thal poison?
[. . .]s of sorrows? . . .

El Vendaval

Viento, soplas de la playa
donde flotan los fantasmas
del pasado, y las futuras
horas lloran en las brumas.

(¿De aquel país de mi delicia,   5
a buscar otra rapiñia
como el voladoro halcón,
a dónde has volado, Amor?)

Viento, soplas de los pinos
llenos de suspiras míos,   10
del ciprés abovedado
donde queda mi alma en vano.

¿Vendaval, hablan a solas
ante él las amargas ondas? . . .
¿Per siempre jamás, caerrá   15
la piñuela en soledad?

¿Siempre vagan sobre el cielo
y las olas con las vientos
nuestras alejadas lágrimas
en la luz y en la nubada?   20

¿Dura bajo en mediodia
de la ninfa alguna risa
como un eco que demora
dentro la enroscada concha?

Viento, soplas de la playa   25
donde flotan los fantasmas
del pasao y del futuro
que lamentan en las brumas.

El Vendaval

Wind, thou blowest from the strand
where float the phantoms
of the past, the future hours
weep in the mists.

(From that land of my delight,   5
to seek other prey
like the swiftly flying falcon,
whither hast thou flown, O love?)

Wind, thou blowest from the pines
filled with my sighs,   10
from the vaulted cypress
where my soul vainly lingers.

Wind hesperian, speak alone
before it the bitter waters? . . .
shall the cypress-fruit fall always   15
in solitude? . . .

Wander still through heaven
and over the billows with the winds
our olden tears
in the light and in the rain?   20

Does there abide beneath the noon
any laughter of the nymph
like an echo that still lingers
within the convoluted shell?

Wind, thou blowest from the strand   25
where float the phantoms
of the past and future
lamenting in the mists.

Farmyard Fugue

Cockadoodle dooo!
Baa baa baa baa mooo!
Oink oink quack quack gobble gobble
Christ bime it yer a lot of trouble
Baa baa baa baa mooo   5
Move yer goddam leg back so I can milk yuh.
Cluck cluck baa baa baa baa
cluck cluck quack quack
puppies (From the cornfield) caw caw caw
The better squirt squirt squirt   10
Oink oink hee haw hee haw
Cluck cluck baa baa haw haw
Caw caw quack quack gobble gobble
Spit mraar mraar <ms. burned>
Hee haw hee haw   15
Mriau spit mraw mriaw
Cocka doodledooo
Hey but I heave a block a wood at these goddam cats
gome gome caw caw
Oink oink baa baa   20
    mriaw spit spit mriaw
Here she goes paw
Hee har
Mriar cluckity cluck brup brup mrioow
    Cluck cluck quack quack pegs pegs mooo   25

Spit mriair spir mriow
  moooo
Cockadoodledoooo.

Didus Ineptus

Absurd, magnificent, and huger
than swan or turkey-cock, this flightless antique pigeon
once roamed at his anachronistic leisure
among the broad-leaved travelers' trees and aloes
upon that manless isle,   5
dawnward from Madagascar,
which may have been old Pliny's isle of Cerne.
Laying in peace the large, the one white egg
on the mat of woodland grass
through ages of that slothful paradise,   10
the dodo flourished in his archaic fashion,
learning no need of wings and having but few feathers,
exempt from competition
save of his only fellow-islanders,
the wingless rail, the short-winged heron,   15
some curious doves and parroquets
and the fruit-gorging bat:
of which the well-winged have survived alone.
Then came the eastward-driving Portuguese,
the Dutch, the French, the English,   20
to try in turn the dodo's meat, to find no mode
nor amount of cooking made it palatable,
and yet to leave of him no remnant
other than drawings, paintings, and a legend
of something great and harmless and grotesque . . .   25
And no one knows
what colonist it was who killed the last
of the prodigious brood, nor in
what century he earned this dim distinction . . .
So he passes wonder   30
unnoted and unrumored from the earth.

Amithaine

Who has seen the towers of Amithaine
Swan-throated rising from the main
Whose tides to some remoter moon
Flow in a fadeless afternoon? . . .
Who has seen the towers of Amithaine   5
Shall sleep, and dream of them again.

On falcon banners never furled,
Beyond the marches of the world,
They blazon forth the heraldries
Of dream-established sovereignties   10
Whose princes wage immortal wars
For beauty with the bale-red stars.

Amid the courts of Amithaine
The broken iris rears again
Restored from gardens youth has known;   15
And strains from ruinous viols flown
The legends tell in Amithaine
Of her that is its chatelaine.

Dreamer, beware! in her wild eyes
Full many a sunken sunset lies,   20
And gazing, you shall find perchance
The fallen kingdoms of romance,
And past the bourns of north and south
Follow the roses of her mouth.

The trumpets blare in Amithaine   25
For paladins that once again
Ride forth to ghostly, glamorous wars
Against the doom-preparing stars.
Dreamer, awake! . . . but I remain
To ride with them in Amithaine.   30

Malediction

While the black perennial snows
Piled about the pole of night
Swell the fount whence Lethe flows;

While the worm, apart from light,
Eats the page where magians pored;   5
While the kraken, blind and white,

Guards the greening books abhorred
Where the evil oghams rust—
In accurst Atlantis stored;

While beneath the seal of dust   10
Dead mouths mutter not in sleep
To betray oblivion's trust;

While the dusky planets keep,
Past the outlands of the sun,
Circuits of a sunless deep,   15

Never shall the spell be done
And the curse be lifted never
That shall find and leave you one

With forgotten things for ever.

Shapes in the Sunset

Daylong was my slumber. At the sunset,
Wakening, I beheld the clouds, a hundred
Shapes of antic gods and beasts of wonder
Gathered on the horizon.

Vulcan, with his forge behind him, towered,   5
Greaved with aureate fire, against the boundless
Concave west; and whirling Scylla spouted
Purple spray on Triton.

There, with gaping mouth, the Mantichora
Showed his teeth and uttered silent roarings;   10
Light and silky as thistle-down, the Astomians
Came from lands of marvel.

Wafted on their ether; and the headless
People followed after them, the Blemmyes,
Bearing on humped shoulders through the heavens   15
Their enormous fardels.

There, across dismembered Titans crawling,
Python rolled his volumes; there the Gorgon,
Eyed with blinding gold, through rack amorphous
Trailed her sinuous ringlets.   20

There, with skyward soles, with head inverted,
Hung the Sciapod, torn from his earthy
Plot remote; and swam the cod-tailed Mermaid,
From the surges riven.

While the sunset, deepening and rubious,   25
Limned the bestiary shapes in lurid
Salamandrine hues, and robed with murex
Gods from myths forgotten,

I, the watcher, cried: "O clouds of wonder,
Fables, carry me, where an age-long sunset   30
Arches your lost Thule, by no sullen
Earth-born shadows blotted!"

Sinbad, It Was Not Well to Brag

Sinbad, the Barnacle Bill of Araby
Carried upon his back the Old Man of the Sea,
Over crag, down ravine,
Round and round in a cane-brake green,
Tramp, tramp,   5
Under the coconuts, through the swamp,
Between the camphors, into the swale
Where the upas dropped its blooms of bale—
Tangling with the tough rattans,
Staggering under the hammers of noon   10
Over the sands
Of a steamy lagoon
A-crawl with crabs and *bêche-de-mer*—
Lurching through the gamboge glare
Of sunset into the damaskeened   15
Twilight where the tree-ferns leaned,
Chasing a saffron-bellied moon
That swayed like a drunken temple-girl
On beaches paved with coral and pearl—
Bemoaning his fate   20
Like the sad estate
Of a Baghdad porter, a Caliph's flunky—
Slipping on rotted mangosteens,
Tripping on jades and tourmalines,
Sliding on dung of tapir and monkey,   25
Startling the bug-eyed lemur, sending

The flying-fox to a farther landing,
Nights, days,
Half-blind in a clotted haze,
Hay-foot, straw-foot,   30
All in an Indonesian Tophet:—
Till, seeing the vines that ran
Over rock and tree he contrived a plan
More clever than rash,
And he made a mighty calabash   35
From the island-grapes a vintage new
With bubbles like rubies clustering thick
And all the strength of an ostrich-kick;
And the old man sipped the sailor's brew
And swore by Allah's vicar   40
He had never tasted a better liquor,
Then took the calabash in his talons
And swigged the pints and swilled the gallons
Till even the thickest lees were downed,
And the grip of his arms and legs grew slack   45
On Sinbad's back,
And he slid at last to the jungle-ground,
Happy as a hinny
In the clover of June,
Soused like a sultan, full as any   50
Tick that drops from a fat baboon. . . .

This was the story that Sinbad
Told to astonish Hinbad:
The story was new,
Whether fantastic or true.   55

But, granting that your narration
Was free from extravagation,
Sinbad, it was not well to brag
At the sunset end of your ocean-road:
For others have carried a heavier load   60
On aching shoulders a-sag—
A load that they could not lose.

My incubus is the classic hag
Yclept the Muse.

El Eros de ébano

Escultor de demonios y de diosas,
también cincelo un ídolo de amor
en ébano, adornándole de rosas
negras y con espinas de dolor.

Sus cejas y su boca, caprichosas,   5
mezclan su miel con un gran amargor;
al hombro, de sus garras rigurosas
y de ojos duros, se posa un azor.

Vendiendo todos mis icones viejos,
venero al nuevo dios: ante su altar   10
llevo las frutas míticas de lejos

y mi botín de las tumbas del mar. . . .
El dios es ciego . . . y mis oblaciones
tieñan de sangre vana sus talones.

Eros of Ebony

Sculptor of demons and of goddesses,
I chisel also an eidolon of love
in ebony, adorning him with black roses
that bear the thorns of pain and sorrow.

His mouth and brows, capricious,   5
mingle their honey with a great bitterness;
upon his shoulder, with tightening talons,
there perches a hard-eyed hawk.

Selling all my ancient idols,
I worship the new god; before his altar   10
I bring the mythic fruits of distant lands

and cast the loot of ocean-sepulchres. . . .
The god is blind . . . and my oblations
have vainly hued his ebon heels with blood.

The Dead Will Cuckold You

1950

The Dead Will Cuckold You

A Drama in Six Scenes

PERSONAE
Smaragad, King of Yoros
Queen Somelis
Galeor, a wandering poet and lute-player, guest of Smaragad
Natanasna, a necromancer
Baltea, tiring-woman to Somelis
Kalguth, Natanasna's negro assistant
Sargo, the King's treasurer
Boranga, captain of the King's guards
Waiting-women, court-ladies, courtiers, guards and chamberlains.

THE SCENE: *Faraad, capital of Yoros, in Zothique*

SCENE I

A large chamber in the Queen's suite, in the palace of Smaragad.
Somelis sits on a high throne-like chair. Galeor stands before her, holding
a lute. Baltea and several other women are seated on divans, at a distance.
Two black chamberlains stand in attendance at the open door.

> *Galeor (playing on his lute and singing):*
> Make haste, and tarry not, O ardent youth,
> To find upon the night,
> Outlined in fuming fire,
> The footsteps of the goddess Ililot.
>
> Her mouth and eyes make fair the bourns of sleep, 5
> Between her brows a moon
> Is seen. A magic lute
> Foretells her with wild music everywhere.
>
> Her opened arms, which are the ivory gates
> Of some lost land of lote 10
> Where from charmed attars flow,
> Will close upon you 'neath the crimson star.

> *Somelis:* I like the song. Tell me, why do you sing
> So much of Ililot?

> *Galeor:*   She is the goddess
> Whom all men worship in the myrrh-sweet land 15

Where I was born. Do men in Yoros not
Adore her also? She is soft and kind,
Caring alone for love and lovers' joy.

   Somelis: She is a darker goddess here, where blood
Mingles too often with delight's warm foam. . . .   20
But tell me more of that far land wherein
A gentler worship lingers.

   Galeor: By a sea
Of changing damaskeen it lies, and has
Bowers of cedar hollowed for love's bed
And plighted with a vine vermilion-flowered.   25
There are moss-grown paths where roam white-fleecèd goats;
And sard-thick beaches lead to caves in which
The ebbing surge has left encrimsoned shells
Like lips by passion parted. From small havens
The fishers slant their tall, dulse-brown lateens   30
To island-eyries of the shrill sea-hawk;
And when with beaks low-dipping they return
Out of the sunset, fires are lit from beams
And spars of broken galleys on the sand,
Around whose nacreous flames the women dance   35
A morris old as ocean.

   Somelis: Would I had
Been born in such a land, and not in Yoros.

   Galeor: I wish that I might walk with you at evening
Beside the waters veined with languid foam,
And see Canopus kindle on cypressed crags   40
Like a far pharos.

   Somelis: Be you more tacit: there are ears
That listen, and mouths that babble amid these halls.
Smaragad is a jealous king—(*She breaks off, for at this moment
King Smaragad enters the room.*)

   Smaragad: This is a pretty scene. Galeor, you seem at home
In ladies' chambers. I am told you entertain   45
Somelis more than could a dull sad king
Grown old too soon with onerous royalty.

   Galeor: I would please, with my poor songs and sorry lute,
Both of your Majesties.

Smaragad: Indeed, you sing
Right sweetly, as does the simorgh when it mates. 50
You have a voice to melt a woman's vitals
And make them run to passion's turgid sluice.
How long have you been here?

    Galeor: A month.

    Smaragad: It has been
A summer moon full-digited. How many
Of my hot court-ladies have you already bedded? 55
Or should I ask how many have bedded you?

    Galeor: None, and I swear it by the crescent horns
Of Ililot herself, who fosters love
And swells the pulse of lovers.

    Smaragad: By my troth,
I would confirm you in such continence, 60
It is rare in Yoros. Even I when young
Delved deep in whoring and adultery. (*Turning to the queen*)
Somelis, have you wine? I would we drank
To a chastity so rathe and admirable
In one whose years can hardly have chastened him. 65
(*The queen indicates a silver ewer standing on a taboret together with goblets of the
same metal. Smaragad turns his back to the others and pours wine into three
goblets, opening, as if casually the palm of his free hand over one of them. This he
gives to Galeor. He serves another to the queen, and raises the third to his lips.*)
See, I have served you with my royal hand,
Doing you honor, and we all must drink
To Galeor that he persevere in virtue,
And he must drink with us. (*He drinks deeply. The queen raises her goblet to
her lips but barely tastes it. Galeor lifts the wine, then pauses, looking into it.*)

    Galeor: How strangely it foams.

    Smaragad: Indeed, such bubbles seem 70
To rise as if from lips of a drowning man
In some dark purple sea.

    Somelis: Your humor is strange,
Nor are there bubbles in the cup you gave me.

    Smaragad: Perhaps it was poured more slowly. (*To Galeor*)
Drink the wine, 75
It is old and cordial, made by men long dead.

(*The poet still hesitates, then empties his goblet at one draught.*)
How does it taste to you?

    Galeor: It tastes as I have thought that love might taste,
Sweet on the lips, and bitter in the throat. (*He reels, then sinks to his
knees, still clutching the empty goblet.*)
You have poisoned me, who never wronged you. Why   80
Have you done it?

    Smaragad: That you may never wrong me. You have drunk
A vintage that will quench all mortal thirst.
You will not look on queens nor they on you
When the thick maggots gather in your eyes,   85
And issue in lieu of love-songs from your lips,
And geld you by slow inches.

    Somelis (*descending from her seat and coming forward*):
                    Smaragad,
This deed will reek through Yoros and be blazed
Beyond the murky marches of the damned. (*She sinks to her knees beside
Galeor, now prostrate on the floor and dying slowly. Tears fall from her eyes as she
lays her hand on Galeor's brow.*)

    Smaragad: Was he so much to you? Almost I have a mind   90
That the bowstring should straiten your soft throat,
But no, you are too beautiful. Go quickly,
And keep to your bed-chamber till I come.

    Somelis: I shall abhor you, and my burning heart
Consume with hate till only meatless cinders   95
Remain to guest the mausolean maggots. (*Exit Somelis, followed by Baltea
and the other women. The two chamberlains remain.*)

    Smaragad (*beckoning to one of the chamberlains*):
Go call the sextons. I would have them drag
This carcass out and bury it privily. (*Exit the chamberlain. The king turns to
Galeor, who still lives.*)
Think on your continence eternalized:
You had not fleshed as yet your rash desire,   100
And now you never will.

    Galeor (*in a faint but audible voice*): I would pity you,
But there is no time for pity. In your heart
You bear the hells that I have never known,
To which the few brief pangs I suffer
Are less than the wasp-stings of an afternoon   105

Sweet with the season's final fruit.

(*Curtain*)

SCENE II

The king's audience hall. Smaragad sits on a double-daised throne, a
guard bearing a trident standing at each hand. Guards are posted at each
of the four entrances. A few women and chamberlains pass though the
hall on errands. Sargo, the royal treasurer, stands in one corner. Baltea,
passing by, pauses to chat with him.

Baltea: Why sits the king in audience today?
Is it some matter touching on the state?
Still thunder loads his brow, and pard-like wrath
Waits leashed in his demeanor.

Sargo: 'Tis a wizard,   110
One Natanasna, whom he summons up
For practise of nefandous necromancy.

Baltea: I've heard of him. Do you know him? What's he like?

Sargo: I cannot wholly tell you. It's no theme
For a morning's tattle.

Baltea: You make me curious.

Sargo: Well,   115
I'll tell you this much. Some believe he is
A cambion, devil-sired though woman-whelped.
He is bold in every turpitude, as those
Hell-born are prone to be. His lineage
Leads him to paths forbanned and pits abhorred,   120
And traffic in stark nadir infamies
Not plumbed by common mages.

Baltea: Is that all?

Sargo: Such beings have a smell by which to know them,
As olden tomes attest. This Natanasna
Stinks like a witch's after-birth, and evil   125
Exhales from him, lethal as that contagion
Which mounts from corpses mottled by the plague.

Baltea: Well, that's enough to tell me, for I never
Have liked ill-smelling men.

(Enter Natanasna through the front portals. He strides forward, bearing a staff on which he does not lean, and stands before Smaragad.)

Sargo: I must go now.

Baltea: And I'll not linger, for the wind comes up   130
From an ill quarter. (*Exeunt Sargo and Baltea, in different directions.*)

Natanasna (*without kneeling or even bowing*): You have summoned me?

Smaragad: Yes. I am told you practise arts forbid
And hold an interdicted commerce, calling
Ill demons and the dead to do you service.
Are these things true?

Natanasna: It is true that I can call   135
Both lich and ka, though not the soul, which roams
In regions past my scope, and can constrain
The genii of the several elements
To toil my mandate.

Smaragad: What! you dare avow it
The thing both men and gods abominate?   140
Do you not know the ancient penalties
Decreed in Yoros for these crimes abhorred?—
The cauldron of asphaltum boiling-hot
To bathe men's feet, and the nail-studded rack
On which to stretch their scalded stumps?

Natanasna: Indeed   145
I know your laws, and also know that you
Have a law forbidding murder.

Smaragad: What do you mean?

Natanasna: I mean but this, that you the king have filled
More tombs than I the outlawed necromancer   150
Have ever emptied, and detest not idly
The raising of dead men. Would you have me summon
For witness here against you the grey shade
Of Famostan your father, in his bath
Slain by the toothed envenomed fish from Taur   155
Brought privily and installed by you? Or rather
Would you behold your brother Aladad,
Whose huntsmen left him with a splintered spear
At your instruction, to confront the fen-cat
That he had merely pricked? Yet these would be   160

Only the heralds of that long dark file
Which you have hurried into death.

    Smaragad (half-rising from his seat): By all
The sooted hells, you dare such insolence?
Though you be man or devil, or be both,
I'll flay you, and leave your hide to hang in strips   165
Like a kilt about you, and will have your guts
Drawn out and wound on a windlass.

    Natanasna: These be words
Like froth upon a shallow pool. No finger
Of man may touch me. I can wave this staff
And ring myself with circles of tall fires   170
Spawned by the ambient space arcane. You fear me,
And you have reason. I know all the secrets
Of noisome deed and thought that make your soul
A cavern where close-knotted serpents nest.
Tell me, was there not yestereve a youth   175
Named Galeor, who played the lute and sang,
Making sweet music for an evil court?
Why have you slain him? Was it not through your fear
Of cuckoldom, thinking he pleased too much
The young Somelis? But this thing is known   180
To me, and I know moreover the dim grave
Where Galeor waits the worm.

    Smaragad (standing erect, his features madly contorted): Begone! begone!
Out of my presence! Out of Faraad!
And here's a word to speed you: when you entered
This hall, my sheriffs went to find your house   185
And seize Kalguth, your negro neophyte
For whom 'tis said you have the curious fondness
That I might keep for a comely ebon wench.
Ponder this well: Kalguth must lie by now
Embowelled in our dankest dungeon-crypt.   190
He will rejoin you if tomorrow's sun
Meet you outside the city. If you linger,
I'll give him to my sinewy torturers.

    Natanasna: King Smaragad, if young Kalguth be harmed,
Hell will arise and sweep your palace clean   195
With fiery besoms and with flails of flame. (*Exit Natanasna.*)

(*Curtain*)

SCENE III

The necropolis of Faraad. Dying and half-decayed cypresses droop over creviced headstones and ruinous mausoleums. A gibbous moon shines through wispy clouds. Enter Natanasna, humming:

A toothless vampire tugs and mumbles
Some ancient trot's whitleather hide,
But he'll fly soon to the abattoir
And the pooling blood where the stuck pig died.   200

(*Kalguth emerges from behind the half-unhinged door of a tomb close at hand. He carries a dark bag, which he lays on the ground at Natanasna's feet.*)
Kalguth: Greetings, O Master.

Natanasna: It was well I sent you
To wait me here among the tacit dead—
Lugging you from your slumber at morning dusk
While none but blind-drunk bowsers were abroad.
As I prevised, the king took advantage   205
Of my commanded presence in his halls,
And sent his hounds to sniff for you. He'll not
Venture to harry me, who have climbed too high
In magedom's hierarchy, but would fang
His baffled spleen on one not fully armed   210
And bucklered with arts magical. We must
Depart from Yoros promptly, leaving it
To all its many devils, amid which
This king is not the least. (*He pauses, looking about him at the tombs and graves.*) It is a land
Where murder has made much work for necromancy,   215
And there's a task to do before we go
That we be not forgotten. I perceive,
My good Kalguth, that you have found the spot
Which my strix-eyed familiar did describe:
Those yonder are the yellowing cypresses   220
That death has pollarded, and this the tomb
Of the lord Thamamar, which sheltered you
Daylong from eyes still mortal. . . . See, where it bears
The lichen-canceled legend of his titles
And the name itself, half-blotted out. (*He paces about, peering closely at the ground, and holding his staff extended horizontally. Over a certain spot the staff seems to twist violently in his hand, like a dowser's wand, until it points downward with the tip almost touching the earth.*)   This is

The grave that covers Galeor. The turf
Was lately broken here, and spaded back
With the grass turned upward. (*He faces in the direction of Faraad, whose
towers loom indistinctly beyond the necropolis. Raising both arms, he intertwines
his fingers with the thumbs pointing skyward in the Sign of the Horns.*)
By this potent Sign,
O jealous king who dreaded cuckoldom,
Murder shall not avert from your proud head   230
The horns of that opprobrium: for I know
A spell whereby the dead will cuckold you. (*Turning to Kalguth*)
Now to our ceremonies. While you set
The mantic censers forth, I'll make the circles. (*Taking a short sword, the
magic arthame, from under his cloak, he traces a large circle in the turf, and a smaller
one within it, trenching them both deeply and broadly. Kalguth opens the dark bag and
brings out four small perforated censers whose handles are wrought in the form of the
double triangle, Sign of the Macrocosm. He places them between the circles, each censer
facing one of the four quarters, and lights them. The necromancers then take their
positions within the inner circle. Natanasna gives the arthame to Kalguth, and retains
his magic staff, which he holds aloft. Both face toward the grave of Galeor.*)

    Natanasna (*chanting*):

    Mumbavut, maspratha butu,   235
    *Varvas runu, vha rancutu.**
    Incubus, my cousin, come,
    Drawn from out the night you haunt,
    From the hollow mist and murk
    Where discarnate larvae lurk,   240
    By the word of masterdom.
    Hell will keep its covenant,
    You shall have the long-lost thing
    That you howl and hunger for.
    Borne on sable, sightless wing,   245
    Leave the void that you abhor,
    Enter in this new-made grave,
    You that would a body have:
    Clothed with the dead man's flesh,
    Rising through the riven earth   250
    In a jubilant rebirth,
    Wend your ancient ways afresh,

* Mumbavut, lewd and evil spirit,
  Weresoever thou roamest, hear me.

By the mantra laid on you
Do the deed I bid you do.
Vora votha Thasaidona   255
Sorgha nagrakronithona.†
(*After a pause*)
Vachat pantari vora nagraban‡
Kalguth: Za, mozadrim: vachama vongh razan.§
(*The turf heaves and divides, and the incubus-driven Lich of Galeor rises from the grave. The grime of interment is on its face, hands, and clothing. It shambles forward and presses close to the outer circle, in a menacing attitude. Natanasna raises the staff, and Kalguth the arthame, used to control rebellious sprits. The Lich shrinks back.*)

The Lich (*in a thick, unhuman voice*): You have summoned me,
And I must minister   260
To your desire.

Natanasna: Heed closely these instructions:
By alleys palled and posterns long disused,
Well-hidden from the moon and from men's eyes,
You shall find ingress to the palace. There,
Through stairways only known to mummied kings   265
And halls forgotten save by ghosts, you must
Seek out the chamber of the queen Somelis,
And woo her lover-wise till that be done
Which incubi and lovers burn to do.

The Lich: You have commanded, and I must obey.   270
(*Exit the Lich. When it has gone from sight, Natanasna steps from the circles, and Kalguth extinguishes the censers and repacks them in the bag.*)

Kalguth: Where go we now?

Natanasna: Whither the first road leads
Beyond the boundary of Yoros. We'll
Not wait the sprouting of the crop we've sowed
But leave it to lesson him, who would have crimped
My well-loved minion and my acolyte   275
For the toothed beds of his dark torture-chambers. (*Exeunt Natanasna and Kalguth, singing:*)

---

†By (or through) Thasaidon's power
 Arise from the death-time-dominion.
‡The spell (or mantra) is finished by the necromancer.
§ Yes, master: the *vongh* (corpse animated by a demon) will do the rest. (These words are from Umlengha, an ancient language of Zothique, used by scholars and wizards.)

The fresh fat traveler whom the ghouls
Waylaid in the lonesome woodland gloom,
He got away, and they'll go now
For gamy meat in a mouldy tomb.   280

(*Curtain*)

SCENE IV

The queen's bed-chamber. Somelis half-sits, half-reclines on a
cushioned couch. Enter Baltea, bearing a steaming cup.

Baltea: With wine that stores the warmth of suns departed,
And fable-breathing spices brought from isles
Far as the morn, I have made this hippocras
Slow-mulled and powerful. Please to drink it now
That you may sleep.

Somelis (waving the cup away): Ah, would that I might drink   285
The self-same draft that Galeor drank, and leave
This palace where my feet forever pace
From shades of evil to a baleful sun.
Too slow, too slow the poison that consumes me—
Compounded of a love for him that's dead   290
And loathing for the king.

Baltea: I'll play for you
And sing, though not as gallant Galeor sang. (*She takes up a dulcimer, and sings*):

Lone upon the roseate gloom
Shone the golden star anew,
Calling like a distant bell,   295
Falling, dimming into death.

Came my lover with the night,
Flame and darkness in his eyes—
Drawn by love from out the grave—
Gone through all the loveless day—   300

(*She pauses, for steps are heard approaching along the hall.*)

Somelis: Whose footsteps come? I fear it is the king.
(*The door is flung open violently, and the fiend-animated Lich of Galeor enters.*)

Baltea: What thing is this, begot by hell on death?
Oh! How it leers and slobbers! It doth look
Like Galeor, and yet it cannot be.
(*The Lich sidles forward, grinning, mewing and gibbering.*)

Somelis: If you be Galeor, speak and answer me   305
Who was your friend, wishing you only well
In a bitter world unfriendly to us both.
(*Baltea darts past the apparition, which does not seem to have perceived her presence,
and runs from the room.*)
But if you be some fiend in Galeor's form,
I now adjure you by the holy name
Of the goddess Ililot to go at once.   310
(*The features, limbs, and body of the Lich are convulsed as if by some dreadful
struggle with an unseen antagonist. Then, by degrees, the convulsions slacken, the
lurid flame dies down in the dead man's eyes, and his face assumes a look of gentle
and piteous bewilderment.*)

Galeor: How came I here? Meseems that I was dead
And men had heaped the hard dry earth on me.

Somelis: There is much mystery here, and little time
In which to moot the wherefores. But I see
That you are Galeor and none other now,   315
The dear sweet Galeor that I thought had died
With all the love between us unavowed,
And this contents me.

Galeor: I must still be dead,
Though I behold and hear and answer you,
And love leaps up to course along my veins   320
Where death had set his sullen winter.

Somelis: What
Can you recall?

Galeor: Little but night-black silence
That seemed too vast for Time, wherein I was
Both bounded and diffused; and then a voice
Most arrogant and magisterial, bidding   325
Me, or another in my place, to do
A deed that I cannot remember now.
These things were doubtful; but I feel as one
Who in deep darkness struggled with a fiend
And cast him forth because another voice   330
Had bade the fiend begone.

Somelis: Truly, I think
There is both magic here and necromancy,
Though he that called you up and sent you forth

Did so with ill intent. It matters not,
For I am glad to have you, whether dead   335
Or living as men reckon bootless things.
'Tis a small problem now: Baltea has gone
For Smaragad, and he'll be here full soon,
Mammering for twofold murder. (*She goes to the door, closes it, and draws the*
ponderous metal bars in their massive sockets. Then, with a broidered kerchief and
water from a pitcher, she washes the grave-mould from Galeor's face and hands, and
tidies his garments. They embrace. He kisses her, and caresses her cheeks and hair.)
                              Ah, your touch
Is tenderer than I have known before.   340
And yet, alas, your lips, your hands.
Poor Galeor, the grave has left you cold:
I'll warm you in my bed and in my arms
For those short moments ere the falling sword
Shatter the fragile bolts of mystery   345
And open what's beyond.
(*Heavy footsteps approach in the hall outside and there is a babbling of loud, confused*
voices, followed by a metallic clang like that of a sword-hilt hammering on the door.)

(*Curtain*)

SCENE V

    The king's pavilion in the palace-gardens. Smaragad sits at the head of a
long table littered with goblets, wine-jars and liquor-flasks, some empty or
overturned, others still half-full. Sargo and Boranga are seated on a bench near
the table's foot. A dozen fellow-revelers, laid low by their potations, lie sprawled
about the floor or on benches and couches. Sargo and Boranga are singing:

    A ghoul there was in the days of old,
    And he drank the wine-dark blood
    Without a goblet, with never a flagon,
    Fresh from the deep throat-veins of the dead.   350
    But we instead, but we instead,
    Will drink from goblets of beryl and gold
    A blood-dark wine that was made by the dead
    In the days of old.

(*A silence ensues, while the singers wet their husky throats. Smaragad fills and empties*
his flagon, then fills it again.)

    Boranga (*in a lowered voice*): Something has ired or vexed
The king: he drinks   355
Like one stung by the dipsas, whose dread bite

Induces lethal thirst.

    Sargo: He's laid the most
Of our tun-gutted guzzlers 'neath the board,
And I'm not long above it. . . . This forenoon
He held much parley with the necromancer   360
Whose stygian torts outreek the ripened charnel.
Mayhap it has left him thirsty. 'Twas enough
For me when Natanasna passed to windward.
I'm told the king called for incensories
To fume the audience-hall, and fan-bearers   365
To waft the nard-born vapors round and round
And ventilate with moa-plumes his presence
When the foul mage was gone.

    Boranga: They say that Natanasna
And his asphalt-colored ingle have both vanished,   370
Though none knows whither. Faraad will lose
One bone for gossip's gnawing. I would not give you
A fig-bird's tooth or an aspic's tail-end feather
For all your conjurers. Let's bawl a catch. (*They sing:*)

    —There's a thief in the house, there's a thief in the house,   375
    My master, what shall we do?
    The fuzzled bowser, he called for Towser,
    But Towser was barking the moon.

(*Enter Baltea, breathless and disheveled.*)

    Baltea: Your Majesty, there's madness loose from hell.

    Smaragad: What's wrong? Has someone raped you without leave?   380

    Baltea: No, 'tis about the queen, from whose bed-chamber
I have come post-haste.

    Smaragad: Well, what about her? Why
Have you left her? Is she alone?

    Baltea: She's not alone
But has for company a nameless thing
Vomited forth by death.

    Smaragad (half-starting from his seat): What's all this coil?   385
A nameless thing, you say? There's nothing nameless.
I'd have a word for what has sent you here,
Panting, with undone hair.

Baltea: Well, then 'tis Galeor.

Smaragad: Hell's privy-fumes!
He's cooling underground, if my grave-diggers   390
Shirked not their office.

Baltea: And yet he has returned
To visit Queen Somelis, with dark stains
Of earth upon his brow, and goblin torches
Lighting his torrid gaze.

Smaragad (standing up): Tell me about it,
Though I cannot believe you. Though he be   395
Quick or dead, by Thasaidon's dark horns
What does he in the chamber of the queen?

Baltea: I wot not how he came nor why. But she
Was parleying with him, speaking gentle words
When I ran forth to seek you.   400

Smaragad: Sargo, Boranga, hear you this? Attend me,
And we'll inquire into this nightmare's nest
And find what's at the bottom. (*He starts toward the door, followed by the
others.*) By all the plagues
Afflicting the five senses, there's too much
That stinks amid these walls tonight. . . . Where were   405
The guards? I'll prune their ears with a blunt sickle
And douche their eyes with boiling camel-stale
For such delinquency as lets
Goblin or man or lich go by them.

(*Curtain*)

SCENE VI

The hall before Somelis' bed-chamber. Enter Smaragad, Sargo,
Boranga and Baltea, followed by two chamberlains. Smaragad tries the
queen's door. Finding that it will not open, he beats upon it with the hilt
of his drawn sword, but without response.

Smaragad: Who has barred this door? Was it the queen? I vow   410
That she shall never close another door
When this is broken down. I'll bolt the next one for her,
And it will be the tomb's. Boranga, Sargo,
Give here your shoulders, side by side with mine. (*All three apply their
weight to the door but cannot budge it. Sargo, more intoxicated than the others,
loses his balance and falls. Boranga helps him to his feet.*)

Truly, my stout forefathers built this palace 415
And all its portals to withstand a siege.

    Boranga: There are siege-engines in the arsenal,
Great rams, that have thrown down broad-builded towers
And torn the gates of cities from their hinges.
With your permission, Sire, I'll call for one 420
Together with men to wield it.

    Smaragad: I'll not have
A legion here to witness what lies couched
In the queen's chamber. Nor am I accustomed
To beat on closen doors that open not.
In all my kingdom, or in Thasaidon's 425
Deep tortuous maze of torments multi-circled,
There is no darker gulf than this shut room
Which reason cannot fathom, being shunted
From the blank walls to madness.

    Sargo: Your Majesty,
If this indeed be Galeor, it smells 430
Of Natanasna, who has called up others
From tomb or trench, inspiriting with demons
Malign or lewd their corpses. There'll be need
Of exorcism. I would have the priests
Brought in, and rites performed.

    Smaragad: I hardly doubt 435
That the curst necromancer is the getter
Of this graveyard fetus. But I will not have it
Either your way or Boranga's. (*Turning to the chamberlains*) Bring to me
Fagots of pitch-veined terebinth, and naphtha.

    Boranga: Sire, what is your purpose?

    Smaragad: You will see full soon. 440

    Baltea: Your Majesty, bethink you, there are windows
To which armed men could climb by ladders, finding
Ingress to the queen's room. It may be she's
In peril from this intruder, who had about him
The air of an incubus.

    Smaragad: Truly, I think 445
That he is no intruder to the queen
Who has barred these portals. Nor am I a thief

To enter in by a window.
(*The chamberlains return, bearing armfuls of fagots and jars of oil.*)
Pile the wood
Before the door, and drench it with the naphtha. (*The chamberlains obey.*
Smaragad seizes a cresset from one of the sconces along the hall, and applies it to the
fagots. Flames leap up immediately and lick the cedarn door.)
I'll warm the bed of this black lechery   450
That lairs within my walls.

    Boranga: Have you gone mad?
You'll fire the palace!

    Smaragad: Fire's the one pure thing
To cleanse it. And for fuel we lack only
The necromancer and his swart catamite.
(*The fire spreads quickly to the curtains of the hallway, from which flaming patches begin*
to fall. Baltea and the chamberlains flee. A section of the burning arras descends upon
Sargo. He reels, and falls. Unable to rise, he crawl away, screaming, with his raiment
ignited. A loosened splotch sets fire to the king's mantle. He flings the garment from him
with an agile gesture. The flames eat steadily into the door, and assail its heavy wooden
framework. The heat and smoke compel Boranga and Smaragad to stand back.)

    Boranga: Your Majesty, the palace burns about us.   455
There's little time for our escape.

    Smaragad: You tell me
A thing that's patent. Ah! the goodly flames!
They will lay bare the secret of this chamber
Whose mystery maddens me. . . . And at the last
There will be only ashes   460
For the summoning of any sorcerer.

    Boranga: Sire, we must go.

    Smaragad: Be still. It is too late for any words,
And only deeds remain.
(*After some minutes the charred door collapses inward with its red-hot bars, Boranga*
seizes the king's arm and tries to drag him away. Smaragad wrenches himself loose
and beats at Boranga with the flat of his sword.)
               Leave me, Boranga.
I'll go and carve the lechers while they roast   465
Into small collops for the ghouls to eat.
(*Brandishing his sword, he leaps over the fallen door into the flaming chamber beyond.*)

(*Curtain*)

The Sorcerer Departs

1951–1961

The Stylite

Upon his pillar stands upright
The rigid anchoret: his pose,
Over the desert, toward the sky,
Prolongs the rectitude of stone,
The rising and unbroken line.   5

Emmets and men go by beneath.
The veering vultures fan his brow:
He sees them not: his sanctity
Enfolds him like the fuming cloud
A thousand thuribles might yield.   10

At evening pass in pompous file
The larvae sent by Satanas.
To mock him, on a pagan height
The rampant sagittary stands,
Stallion of maenads half-equine;   15

And pulsing soft horizons fall
And swell with forms the heathen shun—
Dark sisters of the Ashtaroth
That crawl from undescended gulfs
Or slither over sliding scaurs.   20

With kelpy tresses wreathed with foam,
Voluptuous cold Nereides
Upon the surging desert float;
And Cypris, as from out the sea,
Rises reborn with veil nor zone.   25

Behind dissolving peristyles
Lithe sphinxes crouch and rear in rut;
And mincing from Gomorrah's night,
Vague-membered gods androgynous
Invert an ithyphallic sign.   30

The reeking shames of Sheol glow
And writhe before him. . . . Still upright
The saint exalts the columned stone
With folden arms and changeless eyes—
In chastity long ankylosed.   35

Two on a Pillar

Two on the Stylite's lofty pillar—
Which was above and which below?
Or still upright, did the Stylite thrill her
With many a happy thrust and throe?

The saint and his leman on the pillar   5
Jiggled dizzily to and fro,
And lustily he tried to fill her
While the Devil laughed in hell below.

His dick that was hard as the high hard pillar,
It melted away, to his shame and woe,   10
Too soon, and she left him there on the pillar
By the rope that hung to the ground below.

Not Theirs the Cypress-Arch

Dream not the dead will wait,
Slow-crumbling in the allotted ground,
Nor rise except to some sonorous trump
And searing splendors of the doomsday sun:
They rise, they gather about us now,   5
Crowding the quiet day.

To us, entombed in time,
Asleep within a vaster vault,
They use a speech we seem not to have known,
Yet guide us like sleep-walkers to and fro—   10
By those forgotten voices drawn
With secret tacit guile.

Not theirs the cypress-arch,
The sexton's haunt, the hallowed stones,
The charnel morris stilled by chanticleer: 15
Dark demons, through the forum and the street
They move, and we, their fleshly ghosts,
Like driven demoniacs are.

Alpine Climber

Above the zone of scented pines, above
The stance of granite-mortised junipers,
He climbs by cliff-won inches. The bleak sun

Flames like a titan pharos based with snows
Upon the untaken tower he covets. Earth   5
Broadens afar its bowl of vertigo

With peak-fanged chasms deepening underneath. . . .
As one who mounts a throne of vanished gods,
Wind-clean and vacant, gazing on stark visnes
Of white-horizoned Thule, he takes hold   10
Of the ultimate ice-sharp edge, and rears upon
That glacial source from which no trickle flows

To torrents nursed by lesser alps. He stands
Till, tranced amid the hawkless heavens lone,
He feels the world turn under him, he hangs   15
Nadirward-pointing from an inverse peak,
And hears the cataracting eons roar
And crash adown the planet-bouldered deeps.

Hesperian Fall

The season brings but little gold,
And only rusty gules and sanguines dull
To these rude hills with darkling lava cored
And with thick, somber rock embossed
That yield small pasture to the mordant sun;   5
And leaves of toneless brown and fawn
Cluster the glaucous foliage of blue-oaks
Amid the fallow grasses leonine;
And the live-oaks' grave and winter-waiting green
And the dim greys and dusky verdures of the pines   10
Seem to turn darker with October's heat.
In lowland and ravine
By dwindled rill and narrowed river, willow
And poplar and wild grape
Will burn to purer yellows,   15
To ruddier or more empurpled stains;
And in the rows of fruit-plucked orchard trees
Exotic pomp, deciduous splendor royal-hued
Of other climes and orient autumns flame:
But here the desiccate and sun-struck fells   20
No similar gauds assume.

Watching the tardy portents of slow change
Prolonged unnotably through changeless days,

I walk in solitude
Where memories return   25
That die not with a single season's leaves
But still delay the blind nepenthean doom,
And gather stranger hues
Than these that clothe the tree
Or fold the autumnal earth.   30
Love walks with me, a spectre beautiful
With fallen seasons and with suns that were,
And on the ground our linkèd shadows run
Together, and her heavy hair is blown,
The invisible sending of a witch's web,   35
On winds from off the sea
Whose autumn shore we followed long ago;
And ecstasy and teen
Wild as the spray of combers reaching us
On crags that held the perilous paths of love,   40
Return to haunt these uplands calm and sere;
And wafts of cypress-balsam, keen and sweet,
From the sped years blow over me,
And Lobos rises like a granite ghost
To crown the sealess wold.   45

Thus conscious and remembering,
I move across a land
That seems oblivion's self—
A land whose primal languors drowse the will,
Whose sleepy light and dim-horizoned air   50
Proffer the earth's antique forgetfulness.
But for awhile I spurn
The peace that comes to all or rathe or late,
And clasp the cherished pain
As one with face amid thorned blossoms pressed   55
Who finds them fragranter
Than those that bear no thorn.
Now, where the stones lie still
And taciturn and secret and withdrawn
In that dark entity we cannot share,   60
And where the pines their level branches swing
Lightly in gusts that rise and pass,
But stir not ever from their rooted stance,
I hear a voice that sings
Some old-world measure magical and clear,   65

Or catch the glimmer of a girl's white feet
Moving in moonlit saraband.
O voice none other hears, that sings for me!
Now must I muse on passions that unfold
Slow as the lichen grows,   70
Or swiftly as the fungus of the night;
And think on how
The many have withered but the one abides. . . .

The shadow of a cloud
Falls on the gnarled and boulder-buttressed oak   75
Beneath whose boughs I pause,
Noting the mistletoe
Already pearled with wintry berries white
'Mid leaves of mottled bronze and feuillemort.
Haply the days draw nigh   80
When dark-toothed wind and tempest will assail
Such spare, sad splendor as these hills put on,
And wildly strew
Green leaves and sere together to that doom
Which waits for all.   85
Meanwhile the southward-drooping sun shines warm
On grasses pale and foliages that fade
And on the fadeless lichen of the stone;
And still, O season of Circean dreams
Preferred from long ago,   90
I find a music far and sorcerous
Like one who hears the dryad singing from her tree;
And still, beneath this latter sun,
Love is the freshness of your shadows, love
The flame that in your distant azure sleeps.   95

"Not Altogether Sleep"

Blithe love, what dubious ponderings bemuse
Thy lover's mind! . . . In me thy memories are
As attar in some alabaster jar . . .
Wholly must I the rose-drawn essence lose
Upon unbalmed oblivion, and diffuse   5
Its odor on the dust? And shall no star
Of ours illume that ebon calendar
I keep beneath the taproots of the yews?

       *   *   *

Or shall, in some ineffable permanence,
The senses merge into one only sense   10
Holding thine image evermore apart
From suns expired and cycles yet to come?—
Where time shall have none other pendulum
Than the remembered pulsings of thy heart?

Seeker

In valleys where the lotos falls
And rots by lily-stifled streams,
A sleeper, dreaming of the sea,
Shall rise, and leave the halcyon lawns,

And follow fainting trails alone   5
Into the waste that has no well,
Or fare on some fantasmal quest
To climes beyond the boreal snow.

For, sated with the lotos-fruit,
He craves again the vanished brine,   10
The sunken ships, the siren isles,
The maelstroms haunted by the mew.

Amid chimera and mirage
He plucks the acrid outland pome
And mordant herbs that make him whole,   15
And trails the meteor and the star,

To leave his vulture-burnished bones
In lands of knightlier sleep than they
Shall haply share whose bones are laid
Where now the lotos-blossoms blow.   20

Soliloquy in a Ebon Tower

The poet speaks, addressing a framed picture of Baudelaire upon a bookcase:

The lamp burns stilly in the standing air,
As in some ventless cavern. Through wide windows
The midnight brings a silence from the stars,
And perfumes that the planet dreams in sleep.
The hounds have ceased to bay; and the cicadas   5
To ply their goblin harps. The owl that whilom
Hooted his famine to a full-chapped moon,

Has pounced upon his gopher, or has gone
To fresher woods behind a farther hill;
And Hecate has grounded all the witches   10
For some glade-hidden Sabbat.

                In my room
The quick, malign, relentless clock ticks on,
Firm as a demon's undecaying pulse,
Or creak or Charon's oar-locks as he plies
Between the shadow-crowded shores. Evoked   15
Within the vaults of my funereal brain,
Voices awaken, sibilant and restless—
Tongues of the viper's charnel-fostered brood,
Half-grown, amid the shreds of winding-sheets
And crumbling wicker of old bones. They sing,   20
Those little voices, all the poisonous,
Importunate melodies you too have heard,
O Baudelaire, in midnights when the moon
Sank, followed by some cloudy hearse of dreams,
Into the skyless nadir of despond.   25
Black-flickering, cloven tongues! Though we distill
Quintessences of hemlock or nepenthe,
We cannot slay the small, the subtle serpents
Whose mother is the lamia Melancholy
That feeds upon our breath and sucks our veins,   30
Stifling us with her velvet volumes.

                Now
My thoughts pursue the santal and sad myrrh
Sighed by the shrouds of all hesternal sorrows.
Busied with old regrets, they carry on
Such commerce as the burrowing necrophores   35
Conduct from grave to grave; or pause to mumble
Snatches of ancient amorous elegies,
Deploring still some splendid, stately love—
Gone like the pomps of void Ecbatana—
That only lives in epodes, but will rise   40
To ghost the goldless morrows, clothed about
With hues of suns declining and decayed,
And crowned with ruinous autumn.

                Other thoughts
Exhume the withered wing-shards of ideals
Brittle and light as perished moths, or bring   45

To sight the mummied bats of blear mischance,
By dismal eves and moons disastrous flying,
But fallen now, and dead as are the heavens
Their vans have darkened. On beloved deaths
I muse, and through my twice-wept tears re-gather   50
The threads that Clotho and Lachesis have spun
And Atropos has cut; and see the bleak
Sinister gleaming of the steely shears
Behind the riven arrasses of time. . . .

What weapon can we arm us with? what bulwark   55
Build against grief and time? What moat renewed
With waters mortal as those that shroud Gomorrah,
Will the sea-going termite never ferry
To gnaw the ebon tower, the ebon ark
Holding the Muses' covenant? Splendor-brimmed,   60
What grail of God or Satan will suffice
For all the breadless days, the unguerdoned labors?

Yet, for a toll so light, by Song transported
To sail beyond Elysium and Theleme,
And see, from oblivion looming, balmier shores   65
Of fables infinite! To light our dreams
At rose Aldebaran or sky-huge Antares,
Then quench their heat, or temper Damascus thought
In cold aphelions and apastrons far!
To pace the sun's Typhoean ramparts vast!   70
To couch on Saturn's outmost ring, or roll
With Pluto through his orb of eventide
Whose Hesper is the dwindled sun! To flaunt
Before the blind an immarcescible purple
Won from the murex of Uranian seas,   75
And fire-plucked vermeil of Vulcan, worn against
These aguish mists and wintry shadows! Thus
We triumph; thus the laurel overtops
The upas and the yew; and we decline
No toil, no dolor of our votive doom.   80

High-housed within the Alchemic Citadel,
We are served by Azoth and by Alkahest.
Out of the gleamless mire and sand we make
Pactolian metal. Fumed from our alembics,
The world dissolves like vapors opium-wrought,   85
Or drips, condensed, to philtres and to venoms

That Circe nor Simaetha dreamed. We build,
Daedalus-like, a labyrinth of words
Wherein our thoughts are twi-shaped Minotaurs
The ages shall not slay. Our ironies,   90
Like marbled adders creeping on through time,
Shall fang the brains of poets yet to be.
Our nacred moons and corposants of beauty
Shall float on ever-mootful lands retained
By Lar and Lemur; where Chimera flies,   95
And still the Sphinx unanswerably rules;
Where the red phantoms we have loosed from Dis
Still haunt the thickets and the cities; where
Our phosphor lamps may serve as well as any
Along the rutted way to Charon's wharf.   100

The Twilight of the Gods

All the satyrs have been dehorned,
And wappened are Mohammed's houris;
Pluto lies supremely corned
Amid the snakeless Furies.

Every mermaiden I have seen   5
Was sunning her hams in a bathing-suit,
Melpomene is on the screen,
Pan is tootling a night-club flute.

The jinnees all are in the jug
(I mean the kind with a seal and stopper)   10
The famous flying Arabian rug
Has somewhere come a cropper.

Great Hercules by mail doth sell
Lessons for building muscles rightly . . .
But the witch of Endor is doing well   15
With séances given nightly.

The Golden Fleece, a trifle crummy,
Hangs in a shop with three gold spheres;
Apollo is a dry-goods dummy,
Atropos wields a sempstress' shears.   20

Adonis runs a bill at the tailor's,
Diana hunts the genus homo,

The Cyprian goddess is chiseling sailors
In a dive with a Bouguereau chromo.

Old Pegasus, that spavined nag,   25
Is out to grass with the cows and hinnies,
While Bacchus has gone on another jag
At Angelo's or Dinny's.

Qu'Importe?

What matters love, what matters pain
if out of pain and love a little wisdom is drawn?
These things came not to flower in the world
but in the spirit they have flowered,
and the flower stands, and overtops the suns of time.   5

¿Qué sueñas, Musa?

¿Dime qué sueñas, mi Musa indolente:
¿En un profundo páramo encantado
oyes y ves al fénix blasonado
de plata con su cresta más fulgente
que el oro que los grifos han guardado?   5

¿Huyes, quizás, del vasto círculo de horror
en donde rueda el basilisco en su espiral
con ojos de bitún quemando de su mal?
¿O, sin querer, escuchas al encantador
que llama a su satán del hondo cipresal?   10

¿Miras, cerca de un golfo sin corriente,
saliendo de su lago nacarado,
la ninfa con cabello asoleado
como la sosa enreda allí pendiente?
¿Hablas con ella por un sol parado?   15

¿Encaras de tus pesadillas el pavor?—
¿la bruja más leprosa en su deseo letal
tocando tus pezones con su faz infernal?—
¿del gnomo abigarrado el detestable amor? . . .
—Poeta, no sueño ni con la beldad ni con el mal.   20

What Dreamest Thou, Muse?

Tell me thy dream, my indolent Muse:
In some profound, enchanted wilderness
hearest and seest the emblazoned phoenix
of silver with its crest outshining far
the griffin-guarded gold?   5

Fleest thou, perhaps, from the huge circle of horror
where rolls the basilisk in his spiral
with eyes of bitumen flaming forth their evil?
or listenest, against thy will, to the enchanter
who calls to his demon from the deep cypress-grove?   10

Beholdest, by some tideless ocean-bay,
arising from her pool enlaid with nacre,
the nymph with sunburnt hair
like tangled sea-weed trailing from the reef?
Speakest thou with her by a halted sun?   15

Confrontest thou the terror of thy nightmares—
the leprous hag in her deadly desire
touching thy nipples with her hellish face?—
the abominable love of the mottled gnome? . . .
—My poet, I dream neither of beauty nor of evil.   20

Que songes-tu, Muse?

Que songes-tu, ma Muse somnolente?
Dans un désert profond et enchanté
Écoutes-tu, vois-tu cet oiseau blasonné
D'argent avec sa huppe plus brillante
Que l'or fabuleux qui les griffons ont gardé?   5

Fuis-tu, peut-être, un cercle illimité d'horreur
En quoi le basilic roule dans sa spirale
Aux yeux bitumineux s'embrasant de leur mal?
Ou, malgré ton vouloir, entends-tu le sorcier
Appelant son démon du fond de la cyprière?   10

Au bord d'une mer plus antique et indolente,
Sourdant de son étang tout marqueté de nacre,
Vois-tu la nymph à la crinière basanée
Comme le long varech tortillé et traînant?
Parles-tu avec elle à son cap empourpré?   15

Confrontes-tu la peur des cauchemars intimes?
La furie à la barbe blanche en son désir fatal
Touchant tes mamelons de sa face infernal?
De gnome bariolé le détestable amour? . . .
Je ne sais pas . . . songe-tu ni à la bonté ni au mal? 20

Ye Shall Return

Ye who have dwelt in palaces
Opulent and decayed and lone
Upon oblivion's closer shore,
But in some daemon-stirred unrest

Departing thence, sojourn awhile 5
By fevered fens and driven seas,
Or in the moil of towns unclean
And fumes of toiling titan fires;

Or climb the sharpened mountain-horns
To see earth's kingdoms gleam afar, 10
Litten with promise and mirage
Beneath a mistless diamond vault;

Or, pausing in Mylitta's vales
At yonic altars carved to sin,
Purchase the ancient carnal kiss 15
Forewritten on the lips of clay:—

Know surely that ye shall return
Into the shadow-land ye left,
And draw again your languored breath
Where breathe the poppies of the dusk. 20

Lives of the Saints

(with no apologies to Ogden Nash)

Little find we that is fiery
In the monkish old papyri.
History affords no highlight
On the love-life of the Stylite.

Secret Worship

Veiled is the altar, and the liturgy
is undivulged, and undivulged the vows.
The fire no vestal builds or keeps
consumes its smoke in burning,
flames not outward;   5
low-fuming are the censers;
discreet, the sacrifice
contains itself, nor bleeds for eyes profane;
and the soft-beaten psalteries
are stilly toned as is the twilight bat.   10

Goddess, thou goest cowled,
though not as does the chaste and sober nun.
Dark as the Cloven Hill thy hidden shrine,
thy nakedness
revealed alone to inward-shining lamps   15
and to thy worshipper.

The Song of Songs

Purest aroma, and amber exquisite
Savorous honey that the bees have sucked;
The immaculate whiteness of the fleece of sheep;
The sanguine freshness of pomegranate-flowers,

The curling petals of the perfumed iris,   5
eyes filled with _____ and ardor; vermilion n__ntels
Kisses of fire; amorous complaint
Caresses of the lover and the beloved

fruition of delight; fountain of life;
reflection cast by _____ luminaries;   10
intensest passion, born interiorly;
the celestial hymn that opens from human hearts . . .
such images the saddened soul will dream
at any mention of the Song of Songs.

STYES WITH SPIRES

A PIG PREFERS TO ROOT IN MIRE,
A ROSE THRIVES WITH ITS ROOTS IN MUCK:
AND GOD, THE COINER, THRU THE FIRE,
PUTS MAN TO TEST THE COIN HE'S STRUCK.

DROSS WITH THE GOLD! BUT WHY REPINE?   5
HIGH DEEDS MAY BLEND WITH LOW DESIRES.
ROAST PORK IS GOOD, A ROSE DIVINE.
SO LET US BUILD OUR STYES WITH SPIRES.

In Time of Absence

Why come you not, as formerly you came,
Bringing the wine-jug and the loaf of bread?
Have you forgot the kisses without stint,
The hair disheveled, and the tumbled bed?

What is it comes between and keeps you far,   5
While the stars change and chapless moons crow old,
While the green grasses whiten, and their seeds
Fall pale and parching on the rainless wold?

Silence and sunderance, with serpent fangs,
Would put their furtive poison in my blood;   10
I tear distorted masks of doubt, that fold
Your image with a false similitude.

I know the stifling horror of loneliness—
A horror that you too, my dear, have known:
In the dusty path conducting to my door   15
There are no other footprints than my own.

Nada

This wakeful death affords not any rift
where root of weed or blossom cleaves the tomb.
Ungrown as yet, no yewen bowers lift,
bringing serene misericordal gloom
upon this sepulture adust and bare,   5
writ with a legend plain to one alone
whose voice could quicken the unvital air,
recalling Lazarus from his room of stone.

Oblivion's river flows in other lands
than this where memory feeds a mordant spring:
the walking dead beseech with parching hands
the cool, far shadow of the raven's wing;
and, leaning from the mouldered bed of lust,
love's skeleton writes *Nada* in the dust.

Seer of the Cycles

I am that saint uncanonized, who saw
the copulation of the toad-like stones
and spawning of the sere, sun-mumbled bones
to golden efts and flowers without flaw.
The clouds were squared to temples of the Law,
the clouds were sphered to pandemonian thrones.
Out of the beaked and feathered telephones
there came the falcon's cry, the raven's caw.

Riding the inland sunset rose anew
triremes of Carthage and Columbian sails
convoyed by sirens with their fan-like fins.
Over the mountains a mad tortoise flew,
spouted upon by levitating whales
that in the zenith hung like Zeppelins.

I Shall Not Greatly Grieve

Is it your final wish that I forget
Your cool sweet kisses in the fervent eve?
Upon my lips their savor lingers. Yet,
Though the blood chafe, I shall not greatly grieve
If these, the first, remain a scented score—

Chary lest passion, like a Sirian noon,
Bring not your fruit to sweetness at the core,
But haply mar or ripen oversoon.

What ardors wake, what fears restrain your blood,
Where Christus wars with pagan gods? I guess
In you the untamed falcon's fretful mood,
The immature green orchard's earthliness.

Love has no will to harm you. I shall stand
With empty arms, and find a strange delight:

The unplucked apples hanging close at hand;   15
The leashless veering of the wild hawk's flight.

Geometries

Your body and mine, upon the bed opposed,
presented changing forms and lines Euclidean.

Our heads' irregular and hairy spheres
pillowed in close conjunction, or describing
tangents, diagonals, parabolas,   5
in the unresting play of love.

Your tongue's obtuse triangle
parting and rounded curves of our four lips,
advancing vibrantly, and vibrantly retracting.

The spiral of my kisses   10
climbing from base to nipple gradually
about your full maternal breasts unspoiled,
whose hemispheres were flattened later
beneath the planes of low male breasts.

Caresses of our straight-drawn fingers   15
in tender parallels,
caresses
of fingers bent, half-angled and half-arced,
of concave palms enfolding knee or buttock
or breast or shoulder;   20
and intersections multi-angular
of arms and legs embracing.

And lastly
the lingham's rigid rectilinear line
bisecting the yoni's cloven, soft triangle.   25

All these were figures formed in time,
figures that changed and vanished,
and passed, perhaps, into eternity,
rejoining their Platonic absolutes.

And afterward   30
you went away, and I was left to ponder
on love's geometries of straight and curved.

Alchemy

In smoke, in tapered darkness, and in mist,
Above the fateful suspect Flame suspended
My foaming loves distill. I watch, as might
Some other and some darker Alchemist
Observe the starry bubbles dim or splendid   5
With the immense alembic of the night.

You have not come . . . and time stands over me,
A torturer, inquisitorial, and I seem
Supine in some colossal hour-glass, where the sands,
Burning and rasping, fall in my bared heart   10
_____ days.

Sacraments

Four sacraments have we partaken,
four sacraments unite us.

The sacrament of mutual desire
when we were still half-strangers yet not strange
like wanderers meeting in the mist   5
drawn darkly to that common motherland
whose moons are borne upon Astarte's brow.

The sacrament of joy
whereof your body was the tilted chalice,
with breasts adored beneath the autumnal sun,   10
with limbs and loins that opened
within the room darkened against the morning
or under the secret lamps that shone not streetward.

The sacrament of mirth—
full-bellied, earthy, Rabelaisian laughters   15
at quips and tales the bawdy gods might relish
after ambrosial banquets.

The sacrament of pain
when the strange illness bowed you, and your head,
nestling upon my shoulder,   20
slipped downward in that cryptic agony
I could not follow, could not fathom,
yet must share obscurely

through nerves of some profound and love-wrought nexus.

Let not the sacraments be broken.   25

Delay

You have not come . . . and time stands over me,
a torturer pouring
sluggish, slow-burning drops of molten p____ [burned]
which are the minutes numbered into days.

How shall I suffer this delay? Accurst   5
the lover who must wait, and waiting, doubt:
until your promised coming, better it were
to be the satyr hibernating
dim months within the icy-chitoned oak,
the snake that sleeps beneath the winter stone.   10

Verity

Beneath a lover's ardent sophistries,
Perhaps you read the truth,
And find, beyond the blood's impassioned pleas,
Love that is made of tenderness and ruth,

An exile cast upon the world's dark shore,   5
Something in you I seek
Of that long-vanished motherland of yore
Beyond the deepest sea, the bluest peak;

Some hint of fallen banners, loves foregone,
The soft and sad perfume   10
Of jasmines blown, and salt of waters drawn
By moons no latter sun shall re-illume.

La Isla del náufrago

Huérfano de naufragio,
estoy en un terreno sin jardín,
sin campo cultivado,
una isla que el volcán ha desolado
en parte, y los salvajes han invadido,   5
teniendo ahora la mitad mayor,
las frutas y el pescado su botín.
Ellos me sitian, me detenen

lejos de los bananos y del mar:
De este lugar   10
no tengo que la deshojada roca,
en donde crecerán
un día los liquenes con hojas
que todas las mañanas no pueden marchitar. . . .

Ninguna vela   15
blanquea los verdinegros mares. . . .
   ¿En tal isleta
   puedo sobrevivir los otros insulares?

Isle of the Shipwrecked

Orphan of shipwreck,
I am in a gardenless terrain
with no tilled fields, an isle
which the volcano has desolated,
in part, and savages have invaded,   5
holding now the greater half,
the fruits and the caught fish their booty—
they besiege me, and they keep me
afar from the bananas and the sea:
Of this domain,   10
I have only the leafless rock
in which will grow
one day the lichens with their leaves
and with their semblances of flora
that all the mornings cannot wither. . . .   15

No sail
whitens the dark-green seas. . . .
In such an islet,
can I outlive the other islanders?

Thebaid

Here is the solitude
Unknown to Stylites or Anthony;
A place of bleak illumination
Clean-stripped of clouds and dust,
Ultimate as the apogean moon;   5
Where codes and cults, philosophies and gods

Thin out and vanish on the waste and vast
Like smoke of fires gone cold
In nomad camps deserted yesterday.

Here is the infinite unveiled   10
In visions not of evil or of good;
And the night looks down on us
With only suns for eyes;
And knowledge is our delirium,
The bringer of new appearances,   15
The breeder of new apparitions.

What shall we do
For whom the heavens are throneless, and there is
No demon prince to supplicate and serve?
Shall we pray for succor to the rocks   20
Or beg the sea for aid?
The breath of prayer, the windiness of imploration,
Puffs not against the gale
Nor blows with it in power and violence
Beyond the failing of the owlet's cry.   25

Saturnian Cinema

How many a new and strange neurosis
    The film-producer vexes
When love requres a symbiosis
    Of nine or seven sexes.

Seduction too is problem-laden—   5
    (Picture it if you can)
Calling for several kinds of maiden,
    Several kinds of man.

Picture the complicated clinches
    At crises of the plot   10
The sevenfold or ninefold cinches
    That tie the nuptial knot.

Heros and heroines must fill in
    Their roles of plural sex,
The parts of villainess and villain   15
    Are also multiplex.

Dedication: To Carol

From this my heart, a haunted Elsinore,
I send the phantoms packing for thy sake:
Sea-wind and sun walk now the halls; I take
Funereal wreath and fanon from my door;
I banish demons called by mantic lore: 5
The pentagrams are changed, the circles break
For thee in whom, by twofold thirst to slake,
Naiad and saint unite forevermore.

Here the grey seas have drunk an azure day:
The goblin-shaped miasmas of the night   10
And ghostly dragons of the mist take flight
Where the re-risen Cypris leads us on,
Unzoned, along a vervain-flowered way
Behind the fervent footprints of the sun.

The Centaur

I belong to those manifold Existences
Once known, or once suspected,
That exist no more for man.

                    *   *   *

Was it not well to flee
Into the boundless realms of legend   5
Lest man should bridle me?

Sometimes I am glimpsed by poets
Whose eyes have not been blinded
By the hell-bright lamps of cities,
Who have not sent their souls   10
To be devoured by robot minotaurs
In the infamous labyrinths of steel and mortar.

I know the freedom of fantastic things,
Ranging in fantasy.
I leap and bound and run   15
Below another sun.
Was it not well to flee
Long, long ago, lest man should bridle me?

Lawn-Mower

The grass too we truncate
Into flat uniform monotonous lawns.

And man must amputate himself and his fellows
To fit the Procrustean beds,
To pass beneath the low lintels   5
And along the cramped ways
Of conformity.

Tired Gardener

Cherish them not,
the ostentatious roses grown with care
extravagant, the Tyrian fuchsias drooping
with heaviness of over-nurtured bloom,
and orchid-miming irises that speak too loud   5
of opulence and sumptuous circumstance:
cherish them not, O gardener,
knowing how soon
the desert breathes in every Babylon
and withers all things that man has tilled and trained   10
too often not for mere beauty's sake
but only to prove the old Mammonian power;
knowing how soon
the lovely weeds half-disinherited
return, and banished grasses break   15
the squares and circles of the flowery plots
and beard the creviced fountains.

Turn rather
to sand-verbenas yellow as the sun
that flourish on the crumbling dunes,   20
to yarrow, and the blackbird-ridden reeds
and willows following the dark sunken channel
of marsh-lost waters toward the sea.
Turn rather
where springs the pale and migniard mountain-phlox   25
in basins granite-rimmed,
and the dwarf alpine manzanitas
make arabesques upon the sheeted stone;
turn rather

to lichens charting upon trunk and boulder   30
the track of centuries unclocked:
these shall be planted, these be tended
never by swink and sweat of any laborer;
and these
shall flower the unmanned eternity of earth   35
when the last empire dies, a fat mandragora
uprooted by its rebel gardeners.

High Surf

Loud as the trump that made the mortised walls
Of Jericho to tremble and lean and sway,
The voice of ocean sweeps this granite verge.
The cormorants today,
Back-diving through the falling walls of surge,   5
Float not too near the rocks;
And smoky, white-haired phantoms ride the long-spined rollers
Curving across the bay
From gulfs that round Cipango, arc Cathay.

For me,   10
Who stand enchanted and exalt,
Seized up into a short eternity,
No anger and no sorrow that men feign
Informs the risen main:
I hear alone the impassible roar   15
Of years and centuries and cycles rolling
Under the solar and galactic vault,
Over the cliffs and cities, over the mountains
From shore to crumbled shore.

H. P. L.

Outside the time-dimension, and outside
The ever-changing spheres and shifting spaces—
Though the mad planet and its wrangling races
This moment be destroyed—he shall abide
And on immortal quests and errands ride   5
In cryptic service to the Kings of Pnath,
Herald or spy, on the many-spangled path
With gulfs below, with muffled gods for guide.

Some echo of his voice, some vanished word
Follows the light with equal speed, and spans   10
The star-set limits of the universe,
Returning and returning, to be heard
When all the present worlds and spheres disperse,
In other Spicas, other Aldebarans.

Cycles

The sorcerer departs . . . and his high tower is drowned
Slowly by low flat communal seas that level all . . .
While crowding centuries retreat, return and fall
Into the cyclic gulf that girds the cosmos round,
Widening, deepening ever outward without bound   5
Till the oft-rerisen bells from young Atlantis call;
And again the wizard-mortised tower upbuilds its wall
Above a re-beginning cycle, turret-crowned.

New-born, the mage re-summons stronger spells, and spirits
With dazzling darkness clad about, and fierier flame   10
Renewed by aeon-curtained slumber. All the powers
Of genii and Solomon the sage inherits;
And there, to blaze with blinding glory the bored hours,
He calls upon Shem-hamphorash, the nameless Name.

Fragments and Untitled Poems

[1]
Al borde del Leteo

Som brías son las aguas y sin ola
a quien demora al muelle del Leteo,
llamado por un espectral deseo
para ensagar la noche enorme y sola.

Los secos patalos del aura pola   5
susurran en el eregoso oreo
del cielo sin Polar; en su paseo,
el hocla de las vébora la cola

[2]
Ballad of a Lost Soul

Unseen, without a sound, were closed
    The irremeable doors of clay;
Debarred from earth, to space exposed
    The spirit took her outward way.

She rose, at first on cautious wings—   5
    New to the freedom of the sky,
E'en a wind, from wanderings
    In devious forests thick and high

Coming into the day at last
    But soon, upon ascended heights,   10
A sense of barriers overpassed
Came on her, and she met the vast
    Swiftening unto its wider flights.

To her, with backward gaze,
    The earth was shaken from its place,   15
And flung returnless, unredeemed,
    In gulfs that closed without a trace;

Where the precipitated moon
    A glittering pebble followed swift;
And shot the sun, that dwindled soon—   20
    A plummet in an endless rift.

"As to the vortices of dread
    That wast beyond the nether bars
They fell," said she, above her head—
    A night that bristled with its stars.   25

"Methinks that yonder suns, in rows
    Serried, innumerable, shine
As the angels where disclose
    The portals of the place divine."

Tow'rd eyries of the clustered spheres—   30
    Their vantages remotely seen—
She soared apace, nor thought to face
    The gulfs that drave between:

By night resistless pushed apart,
    The systems, on each side   35
Divided swift, and through the rift
    She saw the blackness wide
Field of ulterior suns, that stood
    In far-assembled pride.

[3]

The Brook

Mark the brooklet leap and dash,
Like an unsheathed sabre flash,
Down the hillside steep and bare
Cleaving through the drowsy air,
Scattering wide a million gems,   5
Where some mossy boulder stems
And then rippling quietly
Where the shadows come and flee—
Shifting spots of light and shade—
In some deep and leafy glade.   10
Here the bales and alders lean
O'er some lucid pool to see
Each its own self faithfully
Imaged in the brooklet's mien.
Now the stream forsakes the glen,   15
Swiftly seeks the light again.
Laughs and sings for happiness
'Neath the sunbeams soft caress
Plunges down its rocky bed
And now runs a slower race   20
Where the willows interlace
In a network overhead.
Now the river beckons nigh,

Then it takes a final leap
Down a cliff face steep and high   25
Where the river beckons nigh.
To its bosom broad and deep

[4] [Christmas card verses]

When Christmas-time is overpast,
The mistletoe shall fade at last,
The holly be forgot:
But friendship has a hardier leaf,
A fruit less brittle and less brief—   5
A fruit that withers not.

A message true is sent to you
By friends from far away
To wish you cheer for all the year
As well as Christmas day.

For you may all the Christmas time
Be fortunate and fair;
For you may every Yuletide chime
Ring out the knell of care.

[5]

Demogorgon

And Demogorgon, a tremendous gloom—
                    —*Prometheus Unbound.*

ARCTURUS

Ye fires of Night and pow'rs of the Abyss,
Tremendous, archetypal,—ye prime rays
Of asterism, constellation, sun,
And the flame-semblance of all moons and worlds,
Your ministers innumerable, made strong   5
But with imparted strength—how have I seen,
From this high throne of vast and shifting night,
Your mustering to my summons from all shores
And streams of the wide aeon-drift: My summons,
Whose import, by the efferent deeps diffused,   10
With thundrous trepidation of all ether,
Thrills now the moons of some remotest world

Beyond some austral sun—ye answer
With quick innumerous thunder of your coming.
Ye, Spica, Procyon, Betelgeuse, I note,   15
Rutilicus, Alderamin, Altair,
And ye, great names of Rigel, Bellatrix,
Aludra, Mirzam, Phurud, Fomalhaut,
With Saiph, Achernar, and supreme Canopus—
Cinctured with lesser suns innominate,   20
And followed by what might of suns unknown,
Fires of the further infinite, and pow'rs,
Whose thrones, encroaching on the outer dark,
Envisage emptiness . . . Now that ye stand
Close round in silence and   25
In flaring flame ten-thousandfold enranked,
Declare, O glorious and puissant suns,

[6]

Despondency

_____ moments of despondency
_____ shattered hopes about us lie
_____clear and sober eyes we see
_____ our future causes lie
And discouragement may teach   5
New ways whereby success to reach
And heeding well the lesson taught.

[7]

The Flight of the Seraphim

Through some eternal land of sand and stone,
I wandered with the wandering moon alone—

[8]

For Iris

Nymph of the harvest-coloured hair,
Thine eyes of warm, unclouded grey
Are lit with some autumnal ray
From lands forgot, from lives afar.

Where hast thou been, O sylvan love   5
Since o'er thy face, and limbs, and breast
My kisses wandered without rest,
In the dim woods of Mytelene?

Where hast thou lain, O dryad fair,
Whom a faun loved in forest-wise—?   10
With love beween thy lips and thighs,
Asleep beyond the dream of pain?

Lo, to what old and wintering moon
Thine amber beauty waned and died,
I know not, nor what forest wide,   15
With leaves of red and pallid gold,

Was made thy lonely sepulcher:

[9]
Haunting

All things incomprehensible, unseen,
    These, these shall haunt me, harmèd unaware
    With pain-sharp presence of the Otherwhere;
And with the unmeasured years' besieging mien
Encompassed ever: Time and these between,   5
    I see them shift upon the crumbling air;
    As with wide wings the horizons hover there—
Uncertain, till the long world intervene.

Eternities are stationed on the night,
    And ministrant upon the steps of day,   10
    The <menace of infinities> supreme
Abysmal shadows touch the world in flight, [. . .]

[10]
The Milky Way

O night, what causeway strange is this, which flung
Across the star-strewn skies—their gulf to span
Begins in space no human eye may scan
And endeth unseen stars and planets 'mong?
Of what is built this structure long and wide?   5
Mayhap 'tis wrought of broken shattered stars

That crashed to doom in deadly cosmic wars
When stellar armies met in combat's swaying tide?

Mayhap this luminous road

[11]

Night

Twilight dim and gray,
    The last, red rays of the sun;
And slowly dieth the day,
    Its work is done.
Darkness cometh on apace,   5
    The shadows into darkness merge;
All is black before thy face,
    All things the night doth purge.

Darkness—and the stillness of the tomb:
    Thou canst feel an oppressing weight.   10
Suddenly the yellow moon doth loom,
    Like the impending hand of fate.
The second day hath come,
    The night in silver light
Is bathed. Nature, stricken dumb,   15
    Is silent all the night.

Blacker seem the shadows dark,
    In contrast with the silver gleam;
The trees stand gaunt and stark,
    Like spectres in a dream.   20
And over all the silver pall,
    The bright and silent beam,
Shining on illuminating all,
    The hills, the woods the silent stream.

The yellow ball on the water shines,   25
    The shadows dance in a sudden breeze;

[12]

The Night Wind

Forever its voice is a voice of unrest
Wildly, oh madly it sobs and it raves
    From its mountain caves

Like a voice of humanity's misery—
And its burden of vain desire.   5

    The fugitive moon peers on
And seemeth a lost and phantom thing—
Like a phantom of dead desire.

[13]

No-Man's-Land

Bales of fantasy from No-Man's-Land.
              Edwin Markham.

What phantoms move within the masque of Sleep!
    Muffled of face, one ever comes to me,
    Whispering a tale half-heard, incessantly,
Like far-off music of a mighty deep,
        Faint with infinity.   5

As one that strives to shape his thought in mist
    Some Titan will would fashion with my dream
    Processionals of images that seem
Such as _____ might exist
        In other spheres extreme.   10

It is as if the nadir of swift hours
    That soar beyond our sight, then descend
    And with our colors lowlier zenith blend,
But, ah! the cloudy dreams that drift and fuse
        Ere thought may comprehend!   15

[14]

Ode on Matter

Once from the labyrinth of earthly things
I found escape;
Thought's burdened, incommunicable shape
Assumed unfettered wings
Whose flight, ascendant, met the immediate dark   5
Where led the wisp of Time
Above the silences sublime.
Soon fell the inadequate and doubtful spark;
And guideless in the stark
Firm cosmic night dimensionless   10

My soul continued, and obtained egress
In light's definable domains,
Wherein the suns are suzerains,—
The stars
That stand light's multitudinous avatars.   15
The pulses of the universe,
They throbbed about me as I sped:
With keener sight I saw disperse
The yellow rays and rays of red;
As with innumerable veins   20
They pierced the ether through and through;
Blue rays and green I saw ensue
As blood that ceases not nor wanes.
Like blots of night upon the solar disks
The planets moved, and e'en as obelisks   25
Their shadows thwarted far-exterior noons.
I saw the manifold concentrated rings
That form the universe of outward things—
Suns within worlds, and worlds in maze of moons.

Then was I made aware   30
Of subtler rays that thrilled the deep—
The bonds wherewith the suns are knit:
A strand of silk is not so fine,
No gossamer as rare,
And yet they keep   35
Certain and true o'er space unlit
The cosmic balance unto which combine
Remotest spheres.
No system shall evade
The pull and the repulse of each,   40
Cogent across the years—
Of nebulae that reach
Into the future fatefully;
And lightless orbs that clutch from out the shade
With power to darken or degrade   45
Or to exult throughout infinity:

[15]

The Regained Past

Within what harbour of the gathered years
With all their dusty dead, and phantom freight—

Strange, mystic argosies—for us doth wait
The Past, its relumed hopes and joys and fears,
Ends but half-reached ungained desires—and tears?   5
Blown thither by what occult winds elate,
Across what darkness-billowed seas of Fate
Shall we sail on, till dim that bay appears
Its shore by buried beacons starred, whose glare
Staineth the eager waves as if with blood?   10
And on whose barren beach a multitude
Of sepulchres lie open to the air,
The tombs of kings once augustly enthroned
And now by listless, dusty winds bemoaned?

[16]

The Saturnienne

Emblazoned by vast flames of cycle-grounded snow,
The surging roar and susurration of the past,
                Upon whose tongue
Strange savors drip from fruits of gardens dead.

[17]

Sonnets of the Desert

I

From pitiless torrid deserts of the sky,
Where far his dreadful flaming throne is raised,
Day tyrannously dominates the waste.
Its tortured sallow reaches quivering lie—
Mirage of earthquake—in the oppressive glare,   5
But all is silent save the jackal's cry
And its sardonic echoes; earth and air
Are voiceless, in exhaustion and despair.
Tormented by the cruel spears of heat
The Day-God ceaseless casts, unrestingly   10
Shudders the air in hazy, tenuous waves.
Unreachable, a sea of mirage laves
And breaks about the far-off mountains' feet,
But gleam no waters undebatably.

II

Outstretches prone and far the solitude,
Whose desolate and dismal unity
Unbroken lies, where ne'er a lonely tree
Uprears its crested head. How black and nude
Beneath the unclouded skies' infinitude,   5
Its lifeless reach! With the ascending sun
Shrink the rock-shades, till daylight doth include
And utterly devour them, one by one.
How merciless, how unendurable
Day's reign, now at its zenith! To the sand   10

[18]

The Temptation

Lilith, queen of all delight,
Nude for all desire, and fain,
Came with her luxurious train,
In a low, fantastic light robe—
When the red moon had vanished.   5
Vampires that the saints have banished,
Nymphs that tempted Antony
With their hair
Parted by descending breasts, and blending
With the closer curled fleece that covers portals of mystery   10
Only proved by happy lovers,

[19]

To a Comet

O visitant from out the starry skies
Whose long and awful blade of light
Doth sudden burst upon our startled sight
Provokant [sic] of fear, wonder and surprise,
What secrets past our knowledge or surmise   5
Are thine, what things lost as in thy flight
Thou wingest through the star-mad night,—
Behold? What wonders on thy ken arise,
What distant stars and suns we cannot see
What satellites, what countless planets great   10
Majestic circling in immensity?

And then, in empty space beyond at last
The

[20]

To Iris

Nymph of the harvest-coloured hair,
Thine eyes of warm and glamorous
Are soft with some remembered grey
Of autumn in a world afar.

Where hast thou slept, with purple leaves,
And leaves of amber for thy bed,   5
While ancient sunsets burned to red,
And thy dead mouth my kisses kept?

Where hast thou lain, O dryad fair,
Whom a faun loved in forest-wise—
With love between thy lips and thighs,   10
Asleep beyond the dream of pain?

Where hast thou been, O sylvan love,
Since over thee, from limb to limb
Wandered the mouth and hands of him
Whose form was mine in Mytilene?   15

O mouth alive with amorous dreams
When mine hath found, in slow pursuit,
The savour of the forest fruit,
And honey from a woodland hive.

[. . . ?]

[21]

To Iris

Hidden within thy heart, as in some
      shadowy forest, a lonely
dryad waits, dreaming of
strange kisses and violent loves—

[22]

To the Sun

Thou most august and everlasting one
    Whose light and warmth-bestowing ray

[23]

The Vampire Night

The darkness falls like some great, silent doom,
With clouds that seem its huge, portentous wings.
A desert swart, it eats the azure fields;
Its jaws engulf the few and trembling stars,
And swallow quick the silver-pallid moon.   5

From out the silence leaps a sudden wind,
As if the night had spoken and her words
Were shuddering through the stillness like a fear.
It fills the mute, unstirring forest trees,
Endowing them as if with breathing souls;   10
They cry a wordless horror to the night,
And toss uplifted arms that writhe with pain.
Hark! is it but the wind that shrieks and wails?
Wake not the dead to wander as a sound
Within the gloom? It seems the Night hath spewed   15
Her phantoms forth to tread the pathless air—
Her dreams of terror, and her fancies wrought
Of gloom and silence. As a sea they surge,
Brimming the wind with potency malign,
That beats and presses on the subtler sense,   20
Albeit intangible to sight. The gloom
Grows darker with them—unimagined shapes
Wherewith the air is crowded and alive.
I feel their influence as a mighty wave—
An iron-gripping terror; and their hands   25

[24]
Space rolls to-day her splendour round!
Unbridled, spurless, without bound,
Mount we upon the wings of wine
For skies fantastic and divine.

[25]
No more of love, for love is doubly cursed,
Being wrought but of desire and weariness
And Circe's wine is vain and magicless
For men no more enchanted of than theirs.

[26]
Beauty! in the garden wherein thou dwellest,
I have gathered the hours of love.

[27]
Like a thousand cows in heat, bellows the sea,
with waves that leap up and climb . . .
We walk upon the shore,
And meanwhile passion enchants us
like the rainbow of the foam   5
that crumbles away in a moment.

[28]
Always I am an exile
from the shore of pleasures
and of Hellenic yesterdays
that a halted sun illumines.

[29]
I sought the solemn cloister of the dead,
      When, thrown athwart the riven funereal gloom,
      On many a glimmering monument or tomb
The sunset wrought a ghostly seal of red.

Dreaming above the marbles and the mould,   5
      I saw the mausolean shadows rouse,
      While slowly in the long-sufusing[?] boughs
The fingered light found out a sullen gold.

[30]
Nor when the mountain lake
      Lulled by the pine-dark ranges,
      To sombre crystal changes,
The moon therein doth make

Her dwelling, and doth lie   5
      Untouched of wind and air,

Forever perfect there
As in another sky . . .

[31]
To loose the dragon darkly curled
About the Hesperidean spheres;
To exorcise the demon years,
The monstrous specter, called the world.

[32]
When myrtle spiced the moonless air,
Under red Antares blown,
Only the garden-god has known
What lady made the darkness fair
With starry jasmine for her zone.   5
          —Christophe des Laurières

[33]
With kisses warmer than the red September sun,
We shall restore awhile our lost oblivion,
Some even, when on twice-trodden paths we have wandered far,
And found upon the hills the cold hesperian star,
And lost beyond the peaks the red September sun.   5

[34]
Lo! fleeter than the rays of distant suns,
That in a thought stab through the deeps of gloom,
For distances immeasured, on I flew,
With stars as flashing meteors on the sight.
Mid unfamiliar systems soon I plunged—   5
Colossal worlds that in uncharted skies,
Revolve to Cyclopean suns; and vasts
Of dark, unstarred, intense, that intervene
Impassible to light twixt universe
And universe; rays of stars we know   10
Were drowned to me in seas of changeless night.

[35]
Triste thuriféraire!
Ton noir encensoir fume
De myrrhe et d'amertune.
Ton chant, O Baudelaire,

Assombrit la Cythère,   5
Et ses flammes funèbres
Blasonnent les ténèbres.

[36]
From the beautiful infinite west, from the happy memorial places,
Full of the stately repose and the lordly delight of the dead
When the fortunate islands are lit with the light of ineffable faces,
And the sound of a sea without wind is about them, and sunset is red.

[37]
Par délà les plaisirs qui revennent pour l'on
Qui mange ta racine, ancien satyrion!

Dessous au ciel tu t'endors ou planent des condors.

J'écoute encor, avec d'oreilles assourdus!
D'enorme grondement des roues d'Antarés.   5
Dans leur néant pourpré des peuples inconnues,
Qui courbaient leur empire en l'arr___ de l'antan,
Disparaissaent aussi qu'un papillon volant,
Ainsi qu'un souvenir des soleils et des nues
Leur néant avalaient des peuples inconnues.   10
Avec ses pieds leniés et ses plumes mourantes
Le temps s'en gloutte en leur Léthé de cramoiri;
Et leur linceul enorme en rouge ensevelit
Un monde qui pourrit d'orbites amarantes
Avec ses ans _____, ses legendes mourantes.   15

[38]
In the great wold where glacial winds are revelling,
Where wheels the weathervane through the delaying night,
Better than in soft April dawns, or summer's light,
My soul most amply will unfurl her raven wing.

To a heart replete with funeral memories numberless,   5
Whereon autumnal frosts have fallen from old time,
Naught is more sweet, O queenliest seasons of our clime,

Than the abiding train of your pale darknesses—
Unless it be, some evening when the moon is dead,
To enslumber all our grief on a chance-chosen bed.   10

[39]
The surges rolled the reflex of the skies
Before my portals, mingling mystically
Their music opulent and melancholy
With the nacre and rose ignited in mine eyes.

[40]
The guileless paradise, replete with hidden joys,
Is it already more remote than the _____ main?
Can one recall it with a wistful golden voice,
Or with an argent music make it live again?
The guileless paradise, replete with hidden joys?   5

The sea, the sempiternal sea, consoles our pain!
What kindly demon gave to this enchantress hoarse
Who sings the queenly organ of the hurricane,
Her power to cradle us like some Titanic nurse?
The sea, the sempiternal sea, consoles our pain!   10

[41]
When breaks upon the debauchee the _____ morn
Leagued with the ideal that gnaws and gnaws the mordant worm,
Through workings of some vengeful mystery dire and firm
As _____ from the sopor of the heart is born.
And softly, greatly balancing   5
On whirlwinds of the conscious air
With indolent delirous wing,

I hate you, ocean! all your rampant rage and vain
Tumult resounds within my soul;

[42]
Till all about me rose the waves of Night.
Among the stars I sped nor counted hours;
For, lo! I deemed Time's tyrant reign had ceased,
Or that his might was stayed in truce: I seemed
A nameless wanderer, forever lost   5
Within the icy, bleak infinitudes,
And awful silence of Eternity.

[43]
Why practice, love, this small economy
Of your heart's favour? Can you keep a kiss

To be enjoyed in age? And will the free
Expense of pleasure leave you penniless?
Nay, nay, be wise. Believe me, pleasure is   5
A gambler's token, only gold to-day.
The day of love is short, and every bliss
Untasted now is a bliss thrown away.
'Twere pitiful in truth such treasures should
Lie by like miser's crusts till mouldy grown.   10
Think you the hand of age will be less rude
In touching your sweet bosom than my own?
Alas, what matter, when our heads are grey,
Whether you loved or did not love to-day.
     From "The Love-Sonnets of Proteus"

[44]
Ecstasy in love is something ill-defined.
Color, form and life design a face, however lined
Yet still I cannot grasp the words that in the Book I find
Which deal with neo-platonism and Ovid and with Time.
And worst of all is Spencer's style.   5

[45]
Ah, fill the cup, and in the fire of spring
  Your winter garments of repentance fling;
The bird of time has but a little way
  To flutter—and the bird is on the wing!

[46]
Old Adam the carrion crow,
The old crow of Cairo,
He sat in the shower and let it flow
Under his tail and over his breast
  And through every feather   5
  Leaked the wet weather,
And the bough swung under his nest.

Is that the wind dying? Oh, no,
'Tis only two devils that blow
Through a murderer's bones, to and fro,   10
In the ghosts' moonshine.

Splendid and chill those gardens shone
Where sound is not and tides are winds,

Where, fugitive, the naiad finds
Eternal autumn, hushed and lone.   15

    Hell's white flame
Set upon thee for a crown,
See forgotten kingdoms drown
In the darkness without name.

[47]
"War!" was thy shout through the land,
"War! War!" is the ringing command.
"War!" the cry from a thousand throats,
  The thundrous cry that onward floats.
With martial show and gleam of steel   5
I watch the warriors marching past.
In battle fierce the legions reel
And men are falling thick and fast.
When shall the awful carnage cease
The endless war of man 'gainst man   10
And o'er the fields of battle Peace
Unfurl the standards of her van?

[48]
Past any dream of those who would deplore him,
Some fainting seraph sees expand before him
The portals of the rose and azure suns.

[49]
Time who but jests with s_od and sovereignty,
Confirming these as phantoms in his gloom,
Or bubbles that his arid hours consume,
Shall mould an undeparting light of thee,
S__tar whereby futurity shall see   5
How song's eventual majesties illume,
Beyond Augustan pomp or battle-doom,
His annals of abiding heraldry.

Time, though his mordant ages gnaw the crag,
Shall blot no hue from thy seraphic wings,   10
Nor vex thy crown and choral glories won,
Albeit the solvents of oblivion drag
To dust the sundered sepulchres of kings
In desolations splendid with the sun.

[50]
His toil a moment's flurry of the dust
Amid the unbending heedlessness of laws
Limitless, sempiternal, yet to him
Life, for its evanescence, realized
As past divine renewal, grew more sweet;   5
And Nature's disregard, made known at last,
Prompted him but to more defiant flights,
Above the dust's inevitable plane.
Retraded by the sullying earth, yet crowned
With ever-heightening, more rebellious dreams,   10
He clomb on gradual, culminating paths,
And sank at last wherein the eventual end
Protesting dream and passive dust unite.

[51]
Blue waters endlessly are whirled
Between the quays of malachite,
And quays of sard, that run in light
A thousand leagues athwart the world;

A world of magic mineral,   5
And magic billow; shore and sea,
A dazzling cold immensity
Redoubling and reflecting all!

In silence from a vault profound,
Great rivers negligently turn   10
The treasure of each gleaming urn
Adown the gulfs of diamond.

An architect of Faery,
I make, with softly murmured spell,
A cavern wrought of rubacelle   15
That passes 'neath the conquered sea.

And all things, pale or sable, shine
Like furbished armour; flameful spaces
The flameful, foamless tide enchases,—
With gulfs and glories crystalline!   20

No foreign star, no sun has flown
To climb the insuperable skies,
And dawn above these prodigies
That burn with lambence all their own,

And on this world of gramerie   25
Incumbent falls (O! dread demesne,
Where naught is heard and all is seen!)

[52]
Dead voices cried as back past peak and scaur—
But still no _____, when sunless heavens bend
The fortress-guarded shrine at the world's end,
The raven-circled towers of Utressor.

[53]
Constrained in channels subterrene
     I heard relentless Acheron roar,
     Where hellish wheels forevermore
Serve at an evil toil unseen.

From out the mighty courts resound   5
     Some slow, malign, tremendous loom
Dismally underground.

[54]
White flowers with colored shadows crost;
     Translucent-wingèd butterflies,
     And hueless birds of haunted skies,
In iridescent twilight lost.

[55]
Remembered in the dreaming blood,
The lentor of thy clinging tresses
Across my face in heavy flood
Falls endlessly; thy deep caresses
Linger within my haunted blood.   5

[56]
Once more the scattered memories of you
     (Lost petals on Lethean waters borne)
     Adown my thoughts flow seaward with the morn,
And vainly gleam, and vanish.

[57]
If I have cried aloud,
Or if my sorrow made a sonant horn

In passes hunt with cloud—
It was to hide what none should know,
It was to keep a deeper, stranger owe   5
In silence unbetrayed

[58]
We have blasphemed the might of Jesus,
Of gods the most irrefutable;
And, like a parasite at the table
Of some malign, abhorrent Croesus,
To please the monstrous animal,   5
Digne servant of great Asmodai,
We have denied and flouted all
The things we love, eternally,
And all the things that we despise,
Greeted with slavish flattery;   10
A servile excutioner,
Bemoaned the wrong of our mesprise;
Bowed to immense stupidity,
Stupidity, the minotaur;
Kissed with devotion prodigal   15
The brainless Matter's red and white,
And praised the dim, phosphoric light
That is corruption's final pall.

Likewise, to drown the vertigo,
The dolour and delirium febrile,   20
We, the proud servant of the Lyre,
The Lyre, whose glory is to show
The drunkenness of things funebral,
Again have drunk with no desire
And eaten still with no delight . . .   25
—Be swift! blow out the lamp, that we
May shroud us in the clemency
And dark forgetfulness of Night!

[59]
Time is a bootless alchemy, a ceaseless transmutation
    Of gold to lead, of lead to gold;
Ever and evermore the old dreams are the new dreams,
    The new dreams are the old.

[60]
Fairer are my proud and lonely dreams to me
Than the communal dream men call reality.

[61]
On Carmel shore the breakers moan
Like pines that breast a gale;
O whence, ye winds and billows flown
To cry your wordless tale?

[62]
À la très bonne, à la très belle,
Qui remplit mon coeur de clarté;
À l'ange, à l'idole immortelle,
Salut en immortalité.

Ella se rèpand dans ma vie   5
Comme un air impregné de sal;
Et dans mon ame inassouie,
Vers le gout de l'éternal.

[63]
Oh! in what lost Edenic isles shadest those,
In strange, serene white beauty, like a hidden moon,
When storming seas have sought thy far and still lagoon
With crowns of foam and broken coral for thy brow?

[64]
And one there was—a garden close
Whose blooms are grown of ancient sea
And death _____ says that _____ and _____
The spirits weigh that dwell

And one I knew, where strident chords of pain   5
Are strings upon the soul's lyre
And one, where Beauty's olden chain
Is forged anew with stranger loveliness,
In flame-soft links of never-quenched desire
And ineluctable duress.   10

[65]
Here the dim seas have drunk an azure day.
The goblin-shaped miasma of the night

And ghostly dragons of the mist take flight,
And Cypris and Apollo rise for us
In twin renascence from a halcyon bay.   5

[66]
Black City! Moloch with the many maws
Devouring youth and beauty, dreams and love,
I wait the _____ of your destruction.

[67]
And thou sometimes art like the lovely horizons
Lit by the furbished flame of brief and brumal suns.
O! splendour of the storm-wet vales and hills ashine,
Under a sunset heaven where fires and clouds decline!

[68]
His vagrant soul would haunt a vaster night,
Lit only by the inclement light
Of all the quer_____ galore.

[69]
O blesséd Land of Dreams, whereto in vain
       Entrance is never craved by slave or king!
       Though winter lie about, therein is Spring
Enwreathed with flowers bright with freshening grain,
Whose perfume holds an anodyne for pain.   5
       Alas! that there should be awakening
       From that fair realm, where birds sweet-throated sing
'Neath suns e'er bright and moons that never wane!
And yet therein are halls of black Despair—
       Haggard profounds and dreadful vastitudes   10
       With mocking mirages of peace, where Fear,
The Spirit of the place, in stillness broods—
Pursued by awful Shapes down valleys drear
The traveller seeks refuge that e'er eludes.

[70]
Death, and the hordes of Death, whence called upon
Of what mad necromancer's rune, or chant
Of sorceress, brow-bound with mauccon, [?]
Came they, across what _____ vigilant,
O Time and place, with hands determinant   5

Of silence tyrannous and iron _____ fear—
Unseen, unheard, apparent, puissant? . . .
How far is that vague land of theirs? How near?
Did Death arise that night or Life but disappear?
Like the loosed stress and burden of a swoon—   10
An infinite release. And winds were light
And swift of foot to some ethereal tune
What that strong silence moved before—& soon,
In faery glades where dews and lilies were,
There stole the holier witchcraft of the moon,   15
While sorcery that was peace without demur,
Save for the nightingale, in fretted shades astir.

[71]
Unfathomably then thy tears were shed
Into the wells of night, and silently
As leaves on Lethe falling fell thy dreams.

[72]
                                frenzy-driven
What dreamer is he whose mad, tormented lips
                                with mordeant kisses thus,
By some Cimmerian moon in uttermost eclipse,
Mouth the bosom of the succubus?

[73]
On what sombre and eventual shore-line
Sinks the roaring,
Thins the foam of time
Out beyond the cosmos?

[74]
Sodden and muddled are those dreams
Which are found in the dregs of slumber.

[75]
What shades eloign thee, and what suns bring back—
O pale Persephone that art my April?

[76]
For in your voice are voices from beyond the tomb,
And in your face a shadow risen from vast vaults.

[77]
Banded with gold and ebon, on broad vans,
The dragons rose from mausolean domes
In dead, gulf-girt atamanes [*sic*].

[78]
Black cities, domed with suns that never sank,
Gave forth the eternal tolling of strange bells.

[79]
Overhead a monstrous comet reached
In fire from Xiphias to the Zodiac.

[80]
Where, xanthic-sailed, on whitening waters ran
Some xebec blown from Yoros toward Ayair.

[81]
Measure the boundless arpents of the night.

[82]
He that drinks the wine of mandrakes
Knows not yesterday and dreams of no tomorrow.

[83]
Quaint quills whereon the aegipan has played.

[84]
Drawn by dead moons the waters wane,
Till kings re-risen from the main
Over the strand shall stride to land
And take command of thy domain.

[85]
                    Warring
With errant sphinxes out of ruined spheres.

[86]
Desconocido, en páramo olvidado,
Por siempre canta el pájaro dorado.

[87]
(In his forgotten wilderness, unheard,
Forever sings the golden bird.)

[88]
    From out its winding tube
The serpent sobs a music old and quaint
As antic quills blown by the aegipan.

[89]
Zoned with green zircon and with palest gold.

[90]
Rest on thine ears the clamor and the band,
For which they famish in a voiceless land.

[91]
The marbled viper crawls where crawled the melon-vine.

[92]
    Taught by me, they will
Reject the fading phantoms called the Real,
And choose in place of them those other phantoms
That fade not, being immaterial.

[93]
O bustling emmets of the lamplit streets,
Fear ye the baleful wisdom that I bring
From gulfs where chaos drops and breaks the egg
And crawls from out its fragments.

[94]
    Saturn
Rose, a realmless phantom, on the wind of chaos.

[95]
Seek the fabulous mountain-crag where roosts the roc.

[96]
Pebbles and pearls the turbid water sifts.

[97]
Knowledge is often most concealed when most divulged;
And haply none will harken if I whisper
The secrets wooed from lipless mystery,
Or cry aloud a tomb-extorted lore.

[98]
                    The Earth has other pits
Than quarries, caverns, wells, and unfilled graves,
Or craters, and shafted mines. Beware lest you
Should step between two atoms, and go plunging
Down to the nadir of a molecule.   5

[99]
                    Restore
Their primal mystery to things profaned.

[100]

Broceliande

As a child, I wandered beside a fen
Where the sunset, falling through a cloudless air,
Stained with scarlet the still and sedgy pools.
There I entered a silent evening wood
(Knowing not that the wood was Broceliande.)
Then, in the twilight of / great oaks, a voice that I / heard
and yet heard not / seemed to dictate un-/known words,
and I, / constrained by some weird / power, repeated them aloud.
        . . . .
In the same sunset (or / was it haply in another?) / I came forth
again from / the wood beside the / fenland where the /
tarns and ponds were still crimson / with a flaring
afterglow. / And peering into a / pool, I saw not the / face
of a child neglected, but the hoar and / many-wrinkle visage
of / the ancient warlock Merlin!

[101]
Disburse a thin and phantom opulence.

[102]
    Raven and owl
Afar from oak or cypress bough,
Errant above a poleless plain.

[103]
Ivrae [?] lubber fay
Falls arsiturvy on
Elfheim's tedded hay.

[104]
And he alone shall steer aright
By deviating sign and sun,
Whose compass draws to poles occult
And harbors past the senses five.

[105]
Forlorn, upon some savage promontory,
A blinded Cyclops roaring to the sun.

[106]
Clepsydrae dribbled on the sands
Of sightless, earless Acheron,
And cuckoo clocks in sarabands
Went measuring time through timeless lands,
And Big Ben swam in Phlegethon,   5
Telling the hour with flame-tipped hands.

[107]
    Nor falls upon the lyre
The plectrum of the skeleton's white hand,
Striking a final chord.

[108]

Twilight Pilgrimage

We sought, where unreturning suns descend,
That shrine and fortress at the world's dark end—
The raven-circled towers of Utressor.

[109]
                        Man
In whom illusion doth itself behold.

[110]
Through ultimate cycles, as in cycles old,
Phantoms, and apparitions manifold,
Shall pass before the spectral eyes of man
In whom illusion doth itself behold.

[111]
My dreams are marble and clay:
Some will endure for an age,
Some will the rains wash away
Or the thunder smite in its rage.

[112]
To sleep, assured of Devachanic dreams.

[113]
                        I seem to hear
Some lover's ghost, who cries for old delight;
Or dead king telling of the state he had:
An ancient voice grown shrill and frail and sad
Like the cicada in late summer night.

[114]
Se tu caballo volador, saliendo
Sobre las lontananzas de la luna.

[115]
The dreadful and enormous pomp of dreams,
The silver wind of eventide.
The sound of hidden flutes
And viols heard through doors of ivory.
The summer of the red and purple suns.

[116]
Jade, malachite, vermilion, amber, amethyst.

[117]
The silver wind before the dawn
That warns the sun-awaiting star.

[118]
With gems and filigrane
Engaud the marble beauty of the moon.

[119]
Where the brazen griffins guard
From the satin-footed pard,
And the lion of the sands,
All the wealth of elder lands—
Rich and unremembered things,—   5
Tombs and crowns of crumbled kings,
Ebon lutes with silver strings,
Pearls, and ivory, and nard.

[120]
O dauntless child of beauty and of dross,
My verdant love enzones thy lonely tomb.
Like some eternal sunset brave with gold,
The perils and the glamour shared of old
Outsoars corruption and the restless mould   5
                    —Fetlain's *Elegy for Vixeela.*

O dauntless child of beauty and of dross,
My verdant love surrounds thy lonely tomb
With secret, proud fluorescence and perfume.
Like some delaying sunset, brave with gold,
The glamour and the perils shared of old   5
Outsoar the shrunken empire of the mould.
                    —*Elegy for Vixeela.*

Thy name, an invocation, calls to light
Dead moons, and draws from long outdated night,
The rosy-breasted spectre of delight.

Vixeela, daughter of beauty and of doom!
Thy name, an invocation, calls to light
Dead moons, and draws from overdated night
The rosy-bosomed spectre of delight,
Like some delaying sunset, brave with gold,

The glamors and the perils shared of old
Outsoar the shrunken empire of the mould.

[121]
But the Russians still rule the barranca
And a man there is never alone—
For the Soviet agents will peep down his pockets
And run a periscope far up his ass-hole.

[122]

Limericks

In Egypt there was a young Wac
Who had to get up from her sack.
She pissed in a dusty old tomb,
Then, wiping herself in the gloom,
She crept through the crypt on her crack.

Oh the she-cat sat on the barb-wire fence
And the tom-cat sat on the ground
    Old tom made a pass at the she-cat's ass
And they went round and round.

Ripe Mulberries

Under the spreading mulberry tree
When the purple fruit was falling free,
I got horny and had some nooky
With my hot cooky
And she had some with me*

A Siamese hierophant
Once fucked a white she-elephant.
But when they wiped him dry again
    And told him not to try again
He cussed and said, "The hell I can't."

An Abyssinian maid there was
Who loved a hippopotamus.
But when they found the little fool
Stuck fast upon his mighty tool,
Her parents cried, "O what a muss!"

*God damn! The cleaners' bills!

A lady athletic and handsome
[Was ca]ught one night in a transom.
When she offered much gold
For release, she was told
That the view was worth more than the ransom.

A lady athletic and handsome
Was ravished one night in a hansom.
When she clamored for more,
The young man on the floor
Said, "The name is Simpson, not Samson."

Alas for the newlyweds Kelly,
Fast stuck with belly to belly
Because in their haste
They used library paste
Instead of petroleum jelly.

There was a young woman named Alice
Who pissed in a Catholic chalice:
But 'tis my belief
She pissed for relief
And not out of Protestant malice.

There was an old man of Nantucket
Whose cock got so hard that he bruk it;
So he went over to France
With the stump in his pants
To look for someone to suck it.

There was yogi of Bangalore
Whose astral lay with an Afghan whore,
And his astral prick and balls alas
Got caught in the hair beneath her ass
And wouldn't come back no more.

A white girl met a brave Mohican
With a painted prick that shone like a beacon.
She didn't run, so he got ruder
And he screwed her—
Though she was the daughter of a puritan deacon.

In a chair of the kind called peacock
A Lesbian played with a meacock.
    They jounced all night,

In their strange delight,
But tell me, which had the he-cock?

A pert little girl named Leacock
Decked her rump with the plumes of a peacock.
Her boy friend lifted together
Dress and petticoat and feather
And pushed her with his wee cock.

There was a young buck of the tribe called Digger
Who greatly fancied himself as a frigger.
    He made many passes
    At brown and white asses
But was much too fast on the trigger.

A maiden lady who longed to sin
Found it exceedingly hard to begin:
    No man made a jump
    For her bubbies or rump,
So she rogered herself with a bowling-pin.

A hot young hussy named Hunt
Was possessed of a most capacious cunt.
    She was wont to diddle
    The crevasse in her middle
With a big church-candle round and blunt.

[123]

From "Ode to Antares"

Star of strange hope,
Pharos beyond our desperate mire,
Lord of unscalable gulfs,
Lamp of unknowable life.

[124]

From "The Song of Xeethra"

Thasaidon, lord of seven hells
Wherein the single Serpent dwells,
With volumes drawn from pit to pit
Through fire and darkness infinite—
Thasaidon, sun of nether skies,
Thine ancient evil never dies,

5

For aye thy somber fulgors flame
On sunken worlds that have no name,
Man's heart enthrones thee, still supreme,
Though the false sorcerers blaspheme.   10

[125]

From "Song of the Galley Slaves"

Dead longing, sundered evermore from pain:
How dim and sweet the shadow-hearted love,
The happiness that perished lovers prove
In Naat, far beyond the sable main.

[126]

From "Song of King Hoaraph's Bowmen"

Let the grape yield for us its purple flame,
    And rosy love put off its maidenhood:
By blackening moons, in lands without a name,
    We slew the Incubus and all his brood.

[127]

From "Ludar's Litany to Thasaidon"

Black Lord of bale and fear, master of all confusion!
By thee, thy prophet saith,
New power is given to wizards after death,
And witches in corruption draw forbidden breath
And weave such wild enchantment and illusion   5
As none but lamiae may use;
And through thy grace the charneled corpses lose
Their horror, and nefandous loves are lighted
In noisome vaults long nighted;
And vampires make their sacrifice to thee—   10
Disgorging blood as if great urns had poured
Their bright vermilion hoard
About the washed and weltering sarcophagi.

[128]
From "Ludar's Litany to Thasaidon"

Lord of the sultry, red parterres
And orchards sunned by hell's unsettling flame!
Amid thy garden blooms the Tree which bears
Unnumbered heads of demons for its fruit;
And, like a slithering serpent, runs the root   5
That is called Baaras;
And there the forky, pale mandragoras,
Self-torn from out the soil, go to and fro,
Calling upon thy name:
Till men new-damned will deem that devils pass,   10
Crying in wrathful frenzy and strange woe.

Appendix

Prospective Tables of Contents

The Jasmine Girdle

1. The Chatelaine of Dream [The Nevermore-to-Be?]
2. Fantaisie d'antan
3. Un Madrigal
4. One Evening
5. Song at Evenfall
6. Trope
7. Canticle
8. Answer
9. Madrigal of Evanescence
10. Tristan to Iseult
11. Souvenance
12. Venus
13. To Antares
14. Immortelle
15. Amor Autumnalis
16. Temporality
17. Offering [a prose poem]
18. Song
19. Credo
20. The Autumn Lake
21. November
22. Chanson de Novembre
23. Sonnet lunaire
24. Exorcism

Nine Poems from Charles P. Baudelaire
1. L'Irremediable
2. Les Hiboux
3. Sed non satiata
4. Spleen (LXXX)
5. Le Revenant
6. Brumes et pluies
7. Epigraphe pour un livre condamné
8. Chant d'automne
9. Le Balcon

Incantations
1. The Nightmare Tarn
2. Warning
3. Necromancy
4. The Saturnienne
5. Sonnet
6. A Fable
7. After Armageddon

Mandragoria
1. October
2. December
3. Au bord du Léthé
4. L'Espoir du néant

The Jasmine Girdle and Other Poems

Euphrasees
1. On a Chinese Vase
2. Jungle Twilight
3. Nyctalops
4. The Envoys
5. Le Refuge

Four Poems from P. Verlaine
1. Clair de lune
2. En Sourdine
3. Le Faune
4. IX Ariettes Oubliées

Madrigals and Memories
1. Septembral
2. Ode
3. Poplars
4. Un Couchant
5. L'Ensorcellement

Interregnum
1. Ennui
2. Bâillement
3. A Mi-Chemin

Incantations

Song at Evenfall
Trope
November
Le Miroir des blanches fleurs
The Autumn Lake
Madrigal of Evanescence
Moon-Sight
Calendar
September
Indian Summer
The Dragon-Fly
Sufficiency
Mystery
Dominion

Three Poems from Paul Verlaine
En Sourdine
Le Faune
IX (Ariette Oubliées)

Nine Poems from Charles Pierre Baudelaire
The Balcony
Sed non satiata
The Phantom
Spleen (LXXX)
Song of Autumn
Mists and Rains
The Sick Muse
The Owls
Epigraph for a Condemned Book

Prose Pastels
Chinoiserie
The Lotus and the Moon
The Mirror in the Hall of Ebony
The Passing of Aphrodite

The Abalone Song

Oh! Some folks boast of quail on toast
    Because they think it's tony;
But I'm content to owe my rent
    And live on abalone.

Oh! Mission Point's a friendly joint,
    Where every crab's a crony;
And true and kind you'll ever find
    The clinging abalone.

He wanders free beside the sea,
    Wheree're [*sic*] the coast is stony;
He flaps his wings and madly sings—
    The plaintive abalone.

On Carmel bay, the people say,
    We feed the lazzaroni
On Boston beans and fresh sardines
    And toothsome abalone.

Some live on hope, and some on dope,
    And some on alimony;
But my tom cat, he lives on fat
    And tender abalone.

Oh! Some drink rain and some champagne,
    Or brandy by the pony;
But I will try a little rye
    With a dish of abalone.

Oh! Some like jam, and some like ham,
    And some like macaroni;
But bring me in a pail of gin
    And a tub of abalone.

Some stick to biz, some flirt with Liz,
    Down on the sands at Coney;
But we, by Hell! Stay in Carmel,
    And nail the abalone.

We sit around and gaily pound,
    And hold no acrimony,
Because our object is a gob
    Of toothsome abalone.

Our servant girl is sure a pearl—
 Her name is Mag Mahoney:
You ought to see the way that she
 Serves up the abalone.

He hides in caves beneath the waves—
 His ancient patrimony;
And so 'tis shown that faith alone
 Reveals the abalone.

The more we take the more they make
 In deep sea matrimony;
Race suicide cannot abide
 The fertile abalone.

————

I telegraph my better half
 By Morse or by Marconi;
But if the need arises for speed
 I send an abalone.

Oh! Some think that the Lord is fat,
 And some think he is bony;
But as for me I think that He
 Is like an abalone.

Oh! Some are named for persons famed,
 And some are named Mahoney;
But when I get a kid, you bet
 I'll name it Abalone.

Song

Past the flown horizon's wall,
And the flight of any wind,
Where the sunken sunsets fall,
Lies the land that Love would find—
Past the flown horizon's wall.   5

Past the fens of Oon and Orm,
Far within the mystic west,
Where the golden dragons swarm
And the sable wyverns nest—
Past the fens of Oon and Orm.   10

Past the mountain Ulmalor,
Builded on the world's extreme,
Whence the moon, in magic war,
Smites the world to mist and dream—
Past the mountain Ulmalor.   15

Past the flown horizon's wall,
And the flight of any wind,
Where the sunken sunsets fall,
Lies the land that Love would find.
Past the flown horizon's wall.   20

Voices

                    The madman speaks.

The night is my sister. Do you know it? Hush,
The night is my sister.
Always she comes to seek and visit me
And to make sweet my sadness.
If you deny it, I'll kill you. I have no longer   5
Any family save her . . .
My promised bride? She has left me and has gone
To live in another planet,
Far, very far. What do you wish? Poor child!
They carried her away by violence.   10
She had black eyes
Surrounded by dark violet circles
That were the twins of two abysses
Crowned with ivies:
Abysses deep, unfathomably deep,   15
From which the stars peered forth.
The night . . . I have already told you? Doubt it not,
The night is my sister.
See you not that she, like me, is clad in mourning?
When the night knew my bride   20
Had gone for ever, when she knew that I
Was perishing of grief,
She came and found my dwelling-place: "Come, friend,"
She said to me, "come, poet."
Because I am a poet . . . What! You do not know?   25
You do not know, perhaps, my poem
Made up of laughters and of tears? a song
That bears her name?

No? It is best, is best! Ah! I have told you—
What have I told you? Yes, yes, that the night,   30
So sad and pale,
The night so sad and so benign,
Is my sister.
See you not that she, like me, is clad in mourning?
And see you not the stars that she possesses   35
Like me? If you should look into my soul
You will behold in the thick shadow
A swarm of luminous bees,
A splendor like the blaze of some bright fire.
Our origin is taken from the night   40
Whence I draw light and darkness.
Blackness of mourning and the dayspring's gold,
Whiteness of Annunciation and Chimera.
Today I am happy. If you will not repeat it
To anyone, I'll tell you why my sorrow   45
Is changed into this shining jubilation.
You will not tell? Then listen, then so be it:
Because the night will come in the end to bear me
To the far planet
Where my bride lives; because at last   50
I shall see in her eyes, in her serene
Eyes, oh! the sad
Eyes, oh! the sweet and tranquil
Eyes encircled
By violet—   55
    (And the madman laughs and weeps, while a nun prays,
      running a rosary between her fingers.)
Twelve slow tollings of a bell are given.

Notes

Abbreviations:

BB   *The Black Book of Clark Ashton Smith.* Sauk City, WI: Arkham House, 1979. Ms. at JHLS.

BS   *The Burden of the Suns.* Glendale, CA: Roy A. Squires, 1977. Xiccarph edition, sixth volume.

DC   *The Dark Chateau and Other Poems.* Sauk City, WI: Arkham House, 1951.

DD   *¿Donde Duermes, Eldorado? y Otros Poemas.* As by "Clérigo Herrero." Glendale, CA: La Imprenta de Rojo Escuderos [Roy A. Squires], 1964.

EC   *Ebony and Crystal: Poems in Verse and Prose.* Auburn, CA: Printed by The Auburn Journal Press, 1922.

FD   *The Fanes of Dawn.* Glendale, CA: Roy A. Squires, 1976. Xiccarph edition, fourth volume.

GF   *Grotesques and Fantastiques.* Saddle River, NJ: Gerry de La Ree, 1973.

GL   *Genius Loci.* Sauk City, WI: Arkham House, 1948.

GS   *To George Sterling: Five Poems.* Glendale, CA: Roy A. Squires, 1970. Zothique edition, fourth fascicle.

HD   *The Hill of Dionysus: A Selection.* Pacific Grove, CA: Roy A. Squires and Clyde Beck, 1962. TMS at JHLS. Any citation of *HD* implicitly includes the TMS.

KML *Klarkash-Ton and Monstro Ligriv.* Saddle River, NJ: Gerry de la Ree, 1974.

LO   *The Last Oblivion: Best Fantastic Poems of Clark Ashton Smith.* Ed. S. T. Joshi and David E. Schultz. New York: Hippocampus Press, 2002.

LW   *Lost Worlds.* Sauk City, WI: Arkham House, 1944.

N1   *Nero and Other Poems.* Lakeport, CA: The Futile Press, 1937.

N2   *Nero* [broadside]. Glendale, CA: Roy A. Squires, 1964.

NU   *Nostalgia of the Unknown: The Complete Prose Poetry of Clark Ashton Smith.* Ed. Marc and Susan Michaud, Steve Behrends, and S. T. Joshi. West Warwick, RI: Necronomicon Press, 1988; rev. ed. 1993.

OS   *Odes and Sonnets.* San Francisco: Book Club of California, 1918.

OST *Out of Space and Time.* Sauk City, WI: Arkham House, 1942.

PD   *The Potion of Dreams*. Glendale, CA: Roy A. Squires, 1975. Xiccarph edition, third volume.

PJ   *The Palace of Jewels*. Glendale, CA: Roy A. Squires, 1970. Zothique edition, second fascicle.

S   *Sandalwood*. Auburn, CA: Printed by The Auburn Journal Press, 1925.

Sx   *Sandalwood*. TMS c. 1952 (in private hands).

S&P   *Spells and Philtres*. Sauk City, WI: Arkham House, 1958.

SC   *Seer of the Cycles*. Glendale, CA: Roy A. Squires, 1976. Xiccarph edition, fifth volume.

SH   *A Song from Hell*. Glendale, CA: Roy A. Squires, 1975. Xiccarph edition, second volume.

SP   *Selected Poems*. Sauk City, WI: Arkham House, 1971. [Prepared 1944–49.] TMS at JHLS. Any citation of *SP* implicitly includes the TMS.

SS   *Strange Shadows: The Uncollected Fiction and Essays of Clark Ashton Smith*. Ed. Steve Behrends with Donald Sidney-Fryer and Rah Hoffman. Westport, CT: Greenwood Press, 1989.

SSU   *Shadows Seen and Unseen: Poetry from the Shadows*. Ed. Raymond L. F. Johnson. San Jose, 2006. [All poems in the volume save "The Horizon" and "The Sorcerer Departs" are facsimile reprints of CAS's TMSs.]

ST   *The Star-Treader and Other Poems*. San Francisco: A. M. Robertson, 1912.

SU   *The Shadow of the Unattained: The Letters of George Sterling and Clark Ashton Smith*. Ed. David E. Schultz and S. T. Joshi. New York: Hippocampus Press, 2005.

SZ   *The Sword of Zagan and Other Writings*. Ed. W. C. Farmer. New York: Hippocampus Press, 2004.

TS   *The Tartarus of the Suns*. Glendale, CA: Roy A. Squires, 1970. Zothique edition, first fascicle.

TSS   *Tales of Science and Sorcery*. Sauk City, WI: Arkham House, 1964.

TT   *The Titans in Tartarus*. Glendale, CA: Roy A. Squires, 1974. Xiccarph edition, first volume.

UV   *In the Ultimate Valleys*. Glendale, CA: Roy A. Squires, 1970. Zothique edition, third fascicle.

AJ *Auburn Journal*

DM *Dark of the Moon: Poems of Fantasy and the Macabre.* Ed. August Derleth. Sauk City, WI: Arkham House, 1947; Freeport, NY: Books for Libraries Press, 1969; Miami, FL: Granger, 1976.

EOD Donald Sidney-Fryer. *Emperor of Dreams: A Clark Ashton Smith Bibliography.* West Kington, RI: Donald M. Grant, 1978.

FSC *Fire and Sleet and Candlelight.* Ed. August Derleth. Sauk City, WI: Arkham House, 1961.

IM *In Memoriam: Clark Ashton Smith* (Baltimore: Mirage Press, 1963.

OED *Oxford English Dictionary* (1933 ed.)

WT *Weird Tales*

AH [manuscipt enclosure with letter to August Derleth] Arkham House/Place of Hawks, Sauk City, WI

BL Bancroft Library, University of California, Berkeley

FSC Mss of CAS's poems for *Fire and Sleet and Candlelight,* SHSW

JHLL H. P. Lovecraft Papers, John Hay Library, Brown University, Providence, RI

JHLS Clark Ashton Smith Papers, John Hay Library, Brown University, Providence, RI

MCL Mills College Library, Oakland, CA

NYPL New York Public Library

SFPL San Francisco Public Library

SHSW State Historical Society of Wisconsin, Madison

SU Stanford University, Palo Alto, CA

UCLA University of California–Los Angeles

CAS Clark Ashton Smith

DAW [manuscipt enclosure with letter to] Donald A. Wandrei

DSF Donald Sidney-Fryer

GK [manuscipt enclosure with letter to] George Kirk

GS George Sterling

MH Margery Hill

MStC M. St. Claire

RAH Rah A. Hoffman

SL Samuel Loveman

MS manuscript

TMS typescript

Tr. transcript

À **Mi-Chemin** [English]. MS (JHLS). The title is French for "Halfway." For a poem in French of this title, see p. 284. It is unclear which was written first.

À **Mi-Chemin** [French]. MS (JHLS). For an English version of this poem, see p. 285.

Abandoned Plum-Orchard. MS (AH; DAW). In *SP, S&P. See also "Distillations," "Haiku," and "Vignettes and Indexes."

L'Abîme. MS (JHLS).

Absence. MS (JHLL; *JHLS). The ms. is dated 28 May 1929.

The Absence of the Muse. MS (NYPL). *Lyric West* 1, No. 6 (October 1921): 14. In *EC, *SP. Written before 4 June 1919. First title: "To an Absent Muse." Altair (l. 14) is the brightest star in the constellation Aquila and one of the fifteen brightest stars in the sky.

Abstainer. MS (AH). See "Pagans Old and New." Pentheus (l. 1), in Greek myth, infiltrated the rites of the maenads or Bacchantes but, when discovered, was torn to pieces by them.

The Abyss Triumphant. *Town Talk* No. 1041 (3 August 1912): 8. In *EC. Current Literature* 53, No. 4 (October 1912): 473. *SP, LO.

Adjuration. MS (JHLS). For Tantalus (l. 16), see note on "The Incubus of Time."

Adjuration. See "Classic Epigram."

Adventure. MS (JHLS; NYPL; *Sx). *AJ* 24, No. 18 (14 February 1924; 30 lines only): 6. In *S*. In *Today's Literature,* ed. Dudley Chadwick Gordon, Vernon Rupert King, and William Whittingham Lyman (New York: American Book Co., 1935), pp. 448–49. In *SP, LO*. The ms. is dated 21 January 1924. CAS sent the poem to GS on 21 April 1924. GS commented: "I think 'Adventure' very lovely—and *alive"* (letter to CAS, 28 May 1924; *SU* 241). GS quoted the first ten lines in his article "Poetry of the Pacific Coast—California" (1926), writing: "No idealization, in his woodland music, of the great machine of today, rather a turning away from industrialism and, as Max Nordau would say, the lies of civilization" (cited in *SU* 291–92).

After Armageddon. MS (DAW; JHLL; JHLS). *Recluse* (1927): 15. In *SP, LO*. The ms. is dated 19 December 1926. In the Bible, Armageddon is the location for the final battle between the angels of God and the forces of evil. The name is cited once in Revelation (16:16) and probably refers to the valley of Megiddo in Israel.

Afterglow. MS (JHLS).

Aftermath of Mining Days. In *SP*.

Afterwards. MS (JHLS; NYPL; Sx). *AJ* 23, No. 44 (16 August 1923): 6. In *S*, *SP.

Alchemy. MS (JHLS). The ms. is dated 12 September 1952. In an early version, the second line reads "Suspended on the flame that makes or mars."

Alexandrines. MS (JHLS). In *OS, EC*, *SP. Written May 1917. The title refers to the meter of the poem (12-syllable line). For CAS's translation of the poem into French, see "Alexandrins" (p. 396).

Alexandrins. MS (JHLS). In *SP. The ms. is dated 14 April 1929. A French translation of "Alexandrines" (p. 167). CAS remarked to SL (15 April 1929; ms., BL): "'Alexandrins' is an attempt to gallicize the poem of that name in 'E. & C.' There's a loss of force, concision and plangency, I fear."

Alien Memory. MS (NYPL). Later rewritten as "Exotic Memory." CAS mentions this poem in a letter to SL (26 June 1915; ms., BL) as having been written "a few weeks ago," adding: "It's very crude, and obviously wouldn't 'do' for any respectable periodical. I shan't publish it, anyway. English is too brutal a language for erotic verse."

Alienage. MS (JHLS [2 mss., one titled "Iris"]; NYPL; *Sx). *AJ* 23, No. 38 (5 July 1923): 6. *Wanderer* 1, No. 6 (November 1923): 4–5. In *S, SP, LO*. First title: "Iris." The first draft was written on 18 April 1923; the final draft was completed in June 1923. CAS sent the poem, with "Moments," to GS on 23 June 1923. GS commented: "These poems are both beautiful, and finely passionate, though I prefer 'Alienage'" (letter to CAS, 29 June 1923; *SU* 233). For "Paphos" (l. 7), see note on "The Ghoul and the Seraph." For "Hesperèan" (l. 18), see note on "Autumn Orchards" (on Hesperia).

Alienation. See "The Outer Land."

"All Is Dross That Is Not Helena." MS (JHLS). In *SP. The ms. is dated 9 February 1942. The title is derived from Christopher Marlowe's *Dr. Faustus* (1604), Scene 13, l. 98. For Paphos (l. 9), see note on "The Ghoul and the Seraph."

Almost Anything. MS (JHLS). In *SP, S&P*. The ms. is dated 15 February 1949. L. 20 is a direct quotation of the last line (l. 40) of the preface ("Au lecteur") of Baudelaire's *Les Fleurs du mal* (see Vol. 3, p. 30). It is translated by CAS as "Hypocritical reader, my fellow-man, my brother!"

Alpine Climber. MS (JHLS). The ms. is dated 13 January 1951. For Thule (l. 10), see note on "Desolation."

Las Alquerías perdidas. MS (*JHLS). In *DD*. Written 12 April 195[_] (ms. mutilated). For an English translation, see "Lost Farmsteads," p. 577. It is not clear which poem was written first.

The Altars of Sunset. MS (JHLS).

Alternative. MS (JHLS; SHSW). *Raven* 2, No. 2 (Summer 1944): 13. In *SP, S&P*. The ms. is dated 5 January 1944. Baaltis (l. 6) is is an alternate name for Astarte, by reason of her relation to Baal (see note on "Pour Chercher du nouveau"). For Lilith (l. 7), see note on "The Tears of Lilith."

Amithaine. MS (AH; DAW; JHLS). *Different* 7, No. 3 (Autumn 1951): 9. In *DC, LO*. The ms. is dated 21 October 1950. The name Amithaine is CAS's invention.

Amor. MS (SHSW; UCLA). *Acolyte* 2, No 2 (Spring 1944): 7. In *SP, HD*. The ms. is dated 25 February 1943. The title is Latin for "Love." Hestia (l. 1) is, in Greek myth, the daughter of Kronos and Rhea and the goddess of the hearth. Selene (l. 3) is the Greek word for the moon; "Latmian boy" refers to Endymion, a beautiful young boy who slept eternally on Mount Latmos in the Greek province of Caria. Melkarth (l. 4) is the tutelary god of Tyre (see "The Sorrow of the Winds") and an aspect of Baal. In Cyprus he was worshipped along with Adonis.

Amor Aeternalis. MS (DAW; FSC; JHLS; NYPL [as "To Love"]). In *SP*. In *FSC* 186. The ms. is dated 1 January 1920. First title: "To Love." The title is Latin for "Eternal Love."

Amor Autumnalis. MS (JHLL; *JHLS). In *BS*. The ms. is dated 28 December 1927. The title is Latin for "Autumnal Love."

Amor Hesternalis. MS (JHLS; UCLA). *Wings* 5, No. 7 (Autumn 1942): 17. In *SP, HD*. The ms. is dated 5 January 1942. The title is Latin for "Yesterday's Love" (the adjective *hesternalis* does not appear in extant classical Latin literature; the only adjective with this meaning is *hesternus*). For Theocritus (l. 13), see note on "Classic Reminiscence." In l. 14, Heliodorus (third or fourth century C.E.) is the author of a romantic novel, the *Aethiopica* (or *Theagenes and Chariclea*). For Sappho (l. 17), see note on "Song of Sappho's Arabian Daughter." For Catullus (l. 18), see note on "Classic Epigram." Ashtoreth (l. 24) is an alternate spelling of Astarte, the Semitic goddess of fecundity and love.

Amour bizarre. MS (JHLS). The title is French for "Bizarre Love."

L'Amour suprême [English]. MS (JHLL; *JHLS; SHSW). In *GF*. For a French translation, see below.

L'Amour suprême [French]. MS (SHSW). The ms. is dated 25 March 1929. The title is French for "Supreme Love." For an English translation, see above. It is not clear which poem was written first.

The Ancient Quest. In *SH, LO*.

Anodyne. See "Mors."

Anodyne of Autumn. MS (JHLS). In *SP. The ms. is dated 18 October 1942.

Añoranza. MS (JHLS). A Spanish version of "Melancholia."

Answer. MS (JHLL; *JHLS).

Antepast. In *EC* (as "Anticipation"), *SP, LO.

Anteros. In *SP*, *S&P, SSU. The title refers to a god, cited only rarely in extant Greek literature, who either avenged slighted love (*eros*) or struggled against Eros, the god of love. CAS appears to use the name here in the latter sense.

Anticipation. See "Antepast."

Antony to Cleopatra. MS (JHLS). Cf. "Cleopatra" (p. 230). A fragmentary 8-line draft also exists at JHLS. Ur (l. 21) was an ancient Mesopotamian city and the center of Sumerian civilization. It was founded sometime in the fourth millennium B.C.E. and survived up to the end of the fourth century B.C.E.

Any Shadow, Any Dream. See "Postlude."

Apologia (O gentlest love, I have not played). MS (JHLS, *Sx). *AJ* 25, No. 1 (16 October 1924): 6. *Step Ladder* 10, No. 3 (February 1925): 49. *United Amateur* 24, No. 1 (July 1925): [1]. In *S, SP*.

Apostrophe. MS (JHLS [as by Timeus Gaylord]). In *SP. The original ms. (JHLS; NYPL; titled "Bâillement" [French for "yawn"]) is dated 20 January 1926. First title: "Sempiternal." CAS sent the poem to GS on 8 May 1926. GS commented that it was "up to sample, which is going some" (letter to CAS, 15 May 1926; *SU* 273).

Arabesque. MS (JHLS). In *EC*, *SP. Written before 15 June 1916. When capitalized, the word *Arabesque* (an adjective) means simply "Arabian, Arabic" (l. 10), or "Arabian or Moorish in ornamental design" (*OED*). Lower-cased, the word (as a noun) means "A species of mural or surface decoration in colour or low relief, composed in flowing lines of branches, leaves, and scroll-work fancifully intertwined" (*OED*). CAS sent the poem (with others) to GS on 15 June 1916, remarking that "Some of the poems enclosed may interest you, since they are more personal than most of my work" (*SU* 135). GS commented of the poems: "They're delicate and lovely. 'Arabesque' is quite as good, but somewhat less salable, probably" (letter to CAS, 17 June 1916; *SU* 136). CAS said the magazine *Art World* purchased the poem, but it did not appear there.

Arctica Deserta. See "Thebaid."

Artemis. MS (JHLL; JHLS; NYPL). In *EC*, *SP. The ms. is dated 16 May 1922. CAS sent the poem, along with "Chance," to GS on 11 June 1922. GS commented: "I like your two poems very much, especially the 'Artemis,' which is work of *very high quality*—a noble poem" (letter to CAS, 14 June

1922; *SU* 207). For the Greek goddess Artemis, see note on "The Masque of Forsaken Gods." In this poem, CAS seems to be emphasizing Artemis's original function as a goddess of wildlife.

Ashes of Sunset. In *EC*, **SP*.

Aspect of Iron. MS (JHLS). For "Memnons" (l. 4), see note on "Echo of Memnon."

At Midnight. MS (JHLS).

At Nadir. MS (JHLS). The poem contains a final stanza that CAS has deleted: "Then, like a wavering taper's flare, / Extinguished by some vagrant wind, / The star forsakes the midnight air / And leaves nor ray nor glow behind."

At Sunrise. In *EC*, **SP*. First title: "Before Sunrise." "Favonian" (l. 9) refers to Favonius, a Latin term for the west wind (equivalent to the Greek Zephyros).

At the Last. See "We Shall Meet."

Atlantis. MS (JHLS). In *ST*. *California News* 1 (January 1913): 1. *Tesseract* 2, No. 5 (May 1937): 9. *Tesseract Annual* 1, No. 1 (1949): 11. In **SP, LO*. The myth of the sunken island or continent of Atlantis goes back at least to Plato's *Timaeus* (c. 350 B.C.E.). CAS also set a prose-poem, "From a Letter" (*NU* 16), in Atlantis, as well as five of his tales of fantasy and science fiction.

Attar of the Past. See "Essence."

Au bord du Léthé. MS (DAW; JHLS). In **SP*. The ms. is dated 7 January 1927. The title translates to "At the Edge of Lethe."

August. See "Septembral."

Autumn Dew. MS (JHLS).

The Autumn Lake. MS (JHLL; JHLS; MCL). In **SP*. The ms. is dated 29 October 1928. For CAS's French translation of this poem, see "Le Lac d'automne."

Autumn Orchards (Templed beneath unmoving skies,). MS (JHLS).

Autumn Orchards (Walled with far azures of the wintering years,). MS (JHLS; **Sx*). *AJ* 24, No. 5 (15 November 1923): 6. *Buccaneer* 1, No. 2 (October 1924): 3. In *S*. In *A Day in the Hills*, ed. by Henry Meade Bland (San Francisco: Taylor & Taylor, 1926), p. 69. In *Songs and Stories*, ed. Edwin Markham (Los Angeles: Powell Publishing Company, 1931; Freeport, NY: Books for Libraries Press, 1974), pp 424–25. In *California Poets: An Anthology of 224 Contemporaries* (New York: Henry Harrison, 1932), pp. 665–66. In *SP*. The ms. is dated 5 November 1923. "Sabean" (l. 3) refers to the people of the ancient pre-Islamic kingdom of Sheba (Saba) in Yemen. For "Tyrian" (l. 5), see note on "The Sorrow of the Winds." "Hesperian" (l. 9) refers to Hesperia, Latin for "the western land" (from the Greek *hespera*, west).

Autumn Twilight. See "November Twilight."

Autumnal. MS (JHLS). In *EC.* Written before 23 July 1917. CAS said that *Art World* had purchased the poem, but it did not appear there.

Autumn's Pall. MS (JHLS). First title: "The Wizardry of Winter."

Ave atque Vale. MS (JHLS; NYPL). In *OS, EC. Step Ladder* 13, No. 5 (May 1927): 136. In *SP.* Written before 29 April 1917. The title, Latin for "hail and farewell," is frequently addressed to the recently dead, as in Catullus' celebrated elegy to his brother: "Atque in perpetuum, frater, ave atque vale" (101.10). CAS sent the poem to GS c. August 1917; GS commented that it was a "big sonnet" (letter to CAS, 19 September 1917; *SU* 152). "Maremma" (l. 11) (usually lower-cased) is a "low marshy insalubrious country by the sea shore" (*OED*). Capitalized, it refers to a region on the coast of Tuscany in Italy.

Averoigne. MS (AH; JHLS). *Challenge* 1, No. 4 (Spring 1951): 6. In *DC, LO, SSU.* An early draft appears in *SZ.* The title is the name of a fictitious region in medieval France invented by CAS and used as the setting of many stories, beginning with "The End of the Story" (1929). For Hecate (l. 3), see note on "The Witch in the Graveyard." Norns (l. 26) are the Fates in Norse mythology. They are usually represented as three virgin goddesses dwelling at the foot of the world-tree Yggdrasil.

Averted Malefice. In *ST, *SP, LO.*

Aviol's Song. See *The Fugitives.*

Avowal. MS (DAW). *Arkham Sampler* 2, No. 1 (Winter 1949): 31. In *SP.* Written 15 October 1948. For "Paphian" (l. 7), see note on "The Ghoul and the Seraph." For "Bacchantic" (l. 11), see note on "Bacchante." For "Canopic" (l. 12), see note on "Cleopatra."

Bacchante. MS (MCL; SHSW). *WT* 34, No. 6 (December 1939): 84. In *SP, HD, LO.* Written before 29 April 1939. A Bacchante is a woman inspired by the god Bacchus (an alternate name of Dionysus), as described by Euripides in *The Bacchae.* Traditionally, such women are depicted wearing the skins of animals and holding a thyrsus (a wand wreathed in ivy and vine leaves; cf. "thyrse" [l. 6]). Maenad (l. 22) is an alternate name for a Bacchante; a Bassarid is a Bacchante from the Greek province of Thrace. Cithaeron (l. 24) is a mountain that separates the provinces of Attica and Boeotia; it contained a celebrated cave of the nymphs.

Bacchants and Bacchante. Tr. (DSF). See "Pagans Old and New."

Bacchic Orgy. MS (AH). "Bacchic" refers to Bacchus (see note on "Bacchante"). See "Pagans Old and New" and "Strange Miniatures."

Bâillement. See "Apostrophe."

The Balance. In *ST*, **SP*. "On" (l. 2) is the Egyptian name for the city of Heliopolis in lower Egypt. It was a seat of learning and of the worship of the sun-god Ra. Carthage (l. 2) was the Phoenician city in what is now Tunisia, in north Africa, traditionally founded in 814 B.C.E. and destroyed by the Romans in the Punic Wars in 146 B.C.E.

The Barrier. MS (JHLS; NYPL; **Sx*). *AJ* 23, No. 48 (13 September 1923): 6. In *S. Step Ladder* 13, No. 5 (May 1927): 130. In *SP, IM*. First title: "Fear." The ms. is dated 22 August 1923. CAS sent the poem to GS on 4 November 1923. GS commented: "'The Barrier' is damned good! Too good for our more erotic periodicals, but why not try it on one of them" (letter to CAS, 28 November 1923; *SU* 236). GS apparently was unaware the poem had already appeared in *AJ*, although perhaps he did not regard that as preventing publication in a magazine.

Basin in Boulder. In *SP*.

Beauty. MS (JHLS). For CAS's Spanish translation, see "La Hermosura."

Beauty Implacable. MS (JHLS; MCL). *AJ* 1, No. 141 (23 December 1914): 1. In *EC. Step Ladder* 13, No. 5 (May 1927): 136. In **SP, BS*. First title: "The Unmerciful Mistress."

Bed of Mint. In *SP*. See "Pulse-Beats of Eros."

Before Dawn. MS (JHLS; SHSW [as "Now, Ere the Morning Break"]). In **SP. Carmel Pine Cone* 42, No. 9 (1 March 1956): 6. In *HD*. The ms. is dated 7 November 1942. First title: "Now, Ere the Morning Break."

Before Sunrise (I rose in that hushed house before the dawn). MS (NYPL). Written 1910.

Before Sunrise. See "At Sunrise."

Behind Each Thing a Shadow Lies. See "The Price."

Behind the Abatoir. See "Field Behind the Abatoir." See also "Neighboring Slaughter-House."

Belated Love. MS (JHLS). In *OS, EC. Step Ladder* 13, No. 5 (May 1927): 132. In **SP*. CAS first sent the sonnet to GS on 15 June 1916. GS later commented: ". . . let me say that I think that 'Belated Love' is a *very* lovely sonnet. Its last three lines are beyond praise" (letter to CAS, 3 November 1922; *SU* 214). "Circean" (l. 2) refers to Circe, the enchantress whom Odysseus encounters on the island of Aeaea (*Odyssey* 10.133f.). She changed his men into swine until he demanded that their human forms be restored.

Berries of the Deadly Nightshade. In *SP*.

The Besieging Billows. MS (JHLS).

The Best Beloved. See "Dedication: To Carol."

Beyond the Door. In *PD*.

Beyond the Great Wall. MS (JHLS; NYPL). In *EC. Asia* 24, No. 5 (May 1924): 359. In *SP*, *LO*. The ms. is dated 21 December 1919. GS remarked of the poem that it is "undiluted poetry" (letter to CAS, 20 January 1920; *SU* 179). The poem refers to the Great Wall of China, a 1500-mile wall constructed in 214–204 B.C.E. as a defense against northern invaders. "Cathayan" (l. 1) refers to Cathay, a name for China derived from the Chinese *Ch'i-tan*, the name of a tribe in Manchuria.

Bird of Long Ago. MS (JHLS). In *SP*.

Black Enchantment. MS (JHLS).

The Blindness of Orion. MS (NYPL). *Arkham Sampler* 1, No. 1 (Spring 1948): 20. In *SP*, *S&P*. Written before 22 April 1915; rev. 1947? First title: "Orion." CAS sent the poem to GS in August 1915; GS noted that it was "good stuff—a few more unbroken lines than I fancy. That 'heard the ascending eagles hail the sun' [l. 12] is *great*" (letter to CAS, 21 August 1915; *SU* 127). CAS later asked GS: "Do you think the 'Orion' good enough to include [in *EC*]? The poem is too 'tame' for my taste" (letter to GS, 9 September 1915; *SU* 128). Although GS replied that "'Orion' is all right" (*SU* 130), CAS did not include the poem in *EC*. Elsewhere CAS notes that it was rejected by the *Atlantic Monthly* (CAS to SL, 7 October 1916; ms., BL). Orion, in Greek myth, was a giant who was blinded by Oenopion, son of Dionysus, because he had raped Oenopion's bride, Merope. He regained his sight by traveling to the island of the Cyclops and appealing to Helios. "Pentelic marble" (l. 8) refers to the mountain of Pentelicus, near Athens, where a superior grade of marble was quarried. Phosphorus (l. 13), in Greek myth, is the morning star, the son of Astraeus and Eos.

Bond. MS (MCL; MStC; SHSW). In *SP*, *HD*. The ms. is dated 17 March 1941. For Poseidonis (l. 3), see note on "Tolometh." For Pompeii (l. 5), see note on "Enchanted Mirrors." For Ys (l. 10), see note on "The Prophet Speaks." Naishapur (l. 11) is a variant spelling of Nishapur, a city in Persia that for a short time in the 11th century was the capital of Persia. It was sacked in the 13th century by the Mongols under Genghis Khan.

Borderland. MS (DAW). In *SP*. See "Strange Miniatures (Haiku)."

Boys Rob a Yellow-Hammer's Nest. MS (AH). In *SP. See "Childhood: Seven Haiku."

Boys Telling Bawdy Tales. MS (AH). In *SP. See "Childhood: Seven Haiku" as "Bawdy School-Boy Tales." For Rabelais (l. 3), see note on "Humors of Love."

Braggart. See "Epitaphs."

Brumal. MS (*JHLS; NYPL). *AJ* 24, No. 3 (1 November 1923): 6. Variant title: "Winter Song."

Buckeyes. See "Harvest Evening."

Builder of Deserted Hearth. In *SP*.

The Burden of the Suns. In *BS*. Mizar (l. 6) is the name of a second-magnitude star in the constellation Ursa Major. For Algebar (l. 7), see note on "The Envoys." For Procyon (l. 8), see note on "Demogorgon."

But Grant, O Venus. MS (DAW [as "Sonnet"]; JHLS [2 mss., one as "Sonnet"]). In *SP. First title: "Sonnet." The ms. is dated 20 February 1941.

The Butterfly. MS (JHLS [fragment: 20 lines only]; NYPL). In *ST*, *SP. The poem was one of the first that CAS sent to GS, c. January 1911. GS commented (letter to CAS, 31 January 1911): "The poems are rich in promise, and the 'Butterfly' one qualifies as performance" (*SU* 19). "Signs" (l. 12) refers to the constellations.

By the River. MS (JHLS). *AJ* 23, No. 49 (20 September 1923): 6. In *SP (as a translation of "Christophe des Laurières"). The ms. is dated 9 March 1923. For Pan, see note on "The Masque of Forsaken Gods."

Bygone Interlude. Tr. (DSF). See "Pagans Old and New."

Calendar. MS (JHLL; JHLS). *Troubadour* 2, No. 6 (February 1930): 11. In *SP. The ms. is dated 2 February 1929.

Calenture. MS (SHSW; DAW). *Arkham Sampler* 2, No. 4 (Autumn 1949): 17–18. In *SP, DC*. Written 1947.

Californian Winter. MS (AH). First version of "January Willow." See "Strange Miniatures."

The Call of the Wind. In *UV*. Written c. 1910.

Cambion. MS (JHLS; SHSW [both as "The Unnamed"]). In *SP*, *DC, LO*. First title: "The Unnamed." The ms. is dated 5 December 1943. The title signifies the half-human offspring of a human male and a succubus or of a human female and an incubus. Alecto (l. 6) is, in Greek myth, one of the three furies, spirits of punishment who avenge wrongs.

Cantar. MS (*JHLS). In *SSU.* A Spanish version of the English poem "Song." Probably the Spanish version was written first, then translated into English.

El Cantar de los seres libres. MS (JHLS). In *DD. A Spanish version of the poem "Song of the Free Beings." Probably the Spanish version was written first, then translated into English.

Canticle. MS (DAW; JHLL; JHLS; MCL). *Troubadour* 3, No. 8 (July 1931): 26. In *SP, LO. The ms. is dated 22 May 1927.

The Canyon. *Rosary Magazine* 40, No. 2 (February 1912): 204.

Canyon-Side. See "River-Canyon."

The Castle of Dreams. In *PD, LO.

Catch. See *The Dead Will Cuckold You.*

A Catch. MS (NYPL; *Sx). *AJ* 24, No. 51 (2 October 1924): 6 (as "Song"). In *S, SP.* First title: "Song." The ms. is dated 12 September 1924.

Cats in Winter Sunlight. MS (DAW). In *SP, S&P. See "Distillations," "Haiku," and "Vignettes and Indexes."

Cattle Salute the Psychopomp. In *SP.* See "Neighboring Slaughter-House." In Greek myth, a psychopomp is one who ferries the souls of the dead to the underworld; usually an attribute of Hermes.

Le Cauchemar. MS (JHLS). The title is French for "The Nightmare."

Censored. See "Lives of the Saints."

The Centaur. In *S&P, BB.

Chainless Captive. In *SP.*

Chance. MS (JHLS; MCL; NYPL). *AJ* 23, No. 35 (14 June 1923): 6. *Bloodstone* 1, No. 2 (November 1937): [4]. In *SP, LO. The ms. is dated 19 May 1922. CAS sent the poem to GS on 11 June 1922. GS wished to send the poem to H. L. Mencken for the *Smart Set,* saying it was a "damn good" poem (letter to CAS, 21 June 1922; *SU* 208); but if he did so, it was rejected.

Change. MS (JHLS; NYPL). *AJ* 23, No. 39 (12 July 1923): 6. In *SP. The ms. is dated 7 March 1923. CAS sent this poem, along with "A Valediction," to GS on 16 July 1923. GS made note of "the *very beautiful* lyrics," adding: "Indeed, they are lovely, lovelier than you think, I imagine, especially 'Change.' I'm glad to see you leaving behind the demoniac, which you have done more justice to than any other poet, and turning to more important things, which include love. These lyrics are heart-piercing" (letter to CAS, 20 August 1923; *SU* 235).

Chanson de Novembre [English]. MS (JHLS). An English translation of "Chanson de Novembre." The original title was "Chant de Novembre."

Chanson de Novembre [French]. MS (JHLL; *JHLS). The ms. is dated 16 November 1928. The title is French for "Song of November." For an English translation, see above.

Chanson de rêve. MS (JHLL; *JHLS). The title is French for "Song of Dream."

Chansonette (Mon amour, la chair des roses). MS (JHLS). CAS habitually misspelled the French word *chansonnette*.

Chansonette (Mon coeur n'a trouvé point de valeur, par delà). For an English version, see "Chansonette" [3] (p. 384). Written 1928?

Chansonette [English]. MS (JHLS). In *SP (as a translation of "Christophe des Laurières"). CAS's English version of "Chansonette" (p. 384). Avalon (l. 6), in Arthurian legend, is the Isle of Souls, an earthly paradise where the great heroes are transported after death.

Chant of Autumn. MS (JHLS). *Lyric West* 2, No. 6 (October 1922): 3. In *EC*, *SP. CAS may not have been aware at this time that one of the poems in Baudelaire's *Les Fleurs du mal* was titled "Chant d'automne" (translated by CAS as "Song of Autumn" [see Vol. 3, p. 113]).

Chant to Sirius. MS (SU). In *ST, N1,* *SP. The ms. is dated 12 July 1911. Sirius, the so-called Dog Star, is the brightest of the fixed stars.

Chatelaine. See "The Nevermore-to-Be."

The Cherry-Snows. In *ST.* In *California State Series: Sixth Year Literature Reader,* ed. LeRoy E. Armstrong (Sacramento: Robert L. Telfer, Superintendent State Publishing, 1916; 11th ed. 1928), p. 86. In *SP.

Le Cheveu. MS (JHLL). The title is French for "The Hair."

Childhood: Seven Haiku. MS (AH). In *SP* under "Experiments in Haiku." Comprises "School-Room Pastime"; Bawdy School-Boy Tales"; "Fight on the Play-Ground"; "Water-Fight"; "Boys Rob a Yellow-Hammer's Nest"; "Grammar-School Vixen"; and "Girl of Six." *SP* omits "Fight on the Play-Ground."

The Chimera. MS (NYPL [as "The Chimaera"]). In *EC* (as "The Chimaera"), *SP. CAS sent the poem to GS on 13 October 1918, noting that "One sonnet (which I enclose) makes up the sum total of my work during August, September, and the present month" (*SU* 165). GS commented: "You may not have written a great deal of late, but to have written the very powerful sonnet you send me ('The Chimaera' [*sic*]) is a good deal to have done—

more than to have composed several tons of the usual verse we find in the magazines of to-day" (letter to CAS, 26 October 1918; *SU* 165). In Greek myth, the Chim(a)era was a fire-breathing monster with the head of a lion, the body of a she-goat, and the tail of a snake. It was killed by Bellerophon riding the winged horse Pegasus.

The City in the Desert. MS (JHLS; NYPL). In *EC, *SP, LO*. CAS noted that "The lines entitled 'The City in the Desert' were remembered out of a dream. They're a bit disordered, but seem to present a sort of picture" (letter to SL, 22 April 1915; ms., BL). The Phoenix (l. 7) is the Greek name for an Egyptian mythological bird that, after living about 500 years, builds a funeral pyre for itself and, after being burned, rises from the ashes new and young.

City Nocturne. See "Nocturne: Grant Avenue."

The City of Destruction. MS (JHLS; SHSW). *Arkham Sampler* 1, No. 1 (Winter 1948): 22. In *SP*. The poem was begun on 13 May 1914. "Babelian" (l. 4) refers to Babel, a city in the valley of Shinar where, according to the Bible, the descendants of Noah built a tower that sought to reach the heavens. God, angered by this temerity, created a confusion of languages so that the builders could not understand one another (see Gen. 9:1–9). "Briarean" (l. 19) refers to Briareus, one of three hundred-armed giants who fought with Zeus against the Titans and were rewarded by being set to guard the Titans in Tartarus.

The City of the Titans. MS (JHLS). In *SP*. *Challenge* 1, No. 2 (Fall 1950): [12]. In *LO*. Written 12 May 1913. CAS sent this poem to GS on 16 May 1913, remarking that it was one of "two or three moderately rotten sonnets" (*SU* 88) he had recently written. GS commented that "I like the sonnet you sent very much, especially the strong ending and the great adjective 'thunder-named' [l. 8]" (*SU* 89). The title of the poem appears to derive from a line in GS's poem "Duandon": "As tho' a city of the Titans burned" (l. 99). For the Titans, see note on "The Return of Hyperion." Erebus (l. 3), in Greek myth, is one of the primeval deities sprung from Chaos; he is usually regarded as the personification of darkness.

Classic Epigram. Ms. (JHLS). In *SP* (as a translation of "Christophe des Laurières"), *SC*. The ms. is dated 29 September 1942. The poem was originally titled "Adjuration" (and was published under that title in *SC*); another ms. has the title "To Lesbia." The person addressed in the poem is probably the Lesbia who was the subject of many of the poems of the Latin author Catullus (C. Valerius Catullus, 84?–54? B.C.E.). She is thought to have been Clodia, sister of P. Clodius Pulcher and the wife of Q. Metellus Celer.

Classic Reminiscence. In *SP*. First title: "Reminiscence." Theocritus (l. 3) was a Greek poet (first half of the third century B.C.E.) who originated pastoral or bucolic poetry.

Cleopatra. MS (JHLS; MCL; NYPL). In *EC*, **SP*, *LO*. The ms. is dated 18 May 1921. Cf. "Antony to Cleopatra" (p. 57). The poem is a paean to Cleopatra, the Egyptian queen (69–30 B.C.E.) who was conquered by Octavian at Actium in 31 B.C.E., later committing suicide. Canopus (l. 6) was an Egyptian seaport 15 miles northeast of Alexandria. It gave its name to Canopic jars, used to hold the internal organs of the mummified dead. Cythera (l. 18) is an island off the coast of Greece in the Aegean Sea, where Aphrodite (the goddess of love) is said to have landed after being born from the sea-foam (for that reason Aphrodite is sometimes referred to as Cytherea).

The Cloud-Islands. MS (JHLS [as "The Sunset Islands"]). In **ST*. *San Francisco Call* (1 December 1912): 6. *Current Opinion* 54, No. 2 (February 1913): 150 (as "Cloud Islands"). In *LO*. First title: "The Sunset Islands." For Hesperides (l. 4), see note on *The Fugitives* ("Song"). In this case, the term refers to putative islands on which the Hesperides dwelt.

Cloudland. MS (JHLS). In **UV*. Written c. 1910. In both texts, l. 13 appears to be deficient.

The Clouds. MS (NYPL). CAS sent the poem to GS on 21 March 1913; GS made no specific comment on it.

Cocaigne. *AJ* 23, No. 40 (19 July 1923): 6. For Cocaigne, see note on "One Evening."

The Cohorts of the Storm. MS (JHLS as "The Storm"). **Rosary Magazine* 42, No. 2 (February 1913): 182. First title: "The Storm and After."

Coldness. MS (JHLS). In *EC*, **SP*. CAS sent the poem, along with others, to GS on 20 June 1916. GS noted: "I like these last poems you send. . . . But I like best the lyric 'Coldness,' especially 'A dreaming crystal, clear and cold' [l. 10], and 'Thou knowest life and life's desire / As a bright mirror knows the moon' [ll. 19–20]. There may be a better adjective than 'bright,' by the way" (letter to CAS, 8 July 1916; *SA* 138). In l. 10, CAS changed "clear" to "pure," but did not alter "bright" in l. 20.

Companionship. MS (NYPL). Written 1910.

Concluding Lines for "Saturnian Epic." See "Saturn."

Concupiscence. MS (DAW; JHLS). In **SP* (as a translation of "Christophe des Laurières"). CAS sent the poem to GS on 6 March 1925. GS commented: "This 'Concupiscence' is especially fine. Baudelaire would have given a back tooth to have been its author" (letter to CAS, 8 March 1925; *SU* 248). Lais (l. 13) was the name of two different courtesans in Corinth.

Connaissance. MS (JHLL; JHLS; SHSW [as "Knowledge"]; another in copy no. 2 of *HD* [JHL]). In **SP, LO*. First title: "Knowledge." Written 26 January 1929. The title is French for "Acquaintance" (or "Knowledge").

Consolation. MS (NYPL; *Sx). In *S. Step Ladder* 13, No. 5 (May 1927): 130. In *California Poets: An Anthology of 224 Contemporaries* (New York: Henry Harrison, 1932), p. 666. In *Today's Literature*, ed. Dudley Chadwick Gordon, Vernon Rupert King, and William Whittingham Lyman (New York: American Book Co., 1935), p. 449. In *SP*. First title: "Éloignement." For "Xanadu" (l. 6), see note on "The Mirrors of Beauty."

Consummation. MS (*JHLS; SHSW). The ms. is dated 15 October 1941. It is evidently part of the *Hill of Dionysus* cycle, as it appears to deal with CAS's relations with Eric Barker and Madelynne Greene.

Contra Mortem. MS (JHLS). The title is Latin for "Against Death." *BB* contains early versions of several passages. In l. 2, "invariably" originally read "inevitably" (*BB* 36). L. 3 originally read "What lacks the scurvy, lack-brained Demiurge" (*BB* 36). L. 8 originally read "Mark not with immortality one man" (*BB* 36). Ll. 10–11 originally read: "Will no man / Cry out against this abatoir of time" (*BB* 33).

Contradiction. MS (NYPL; Sx). *AJ* 23, No. 31 (17 May 1923): 6. In *S, *SP*. CAS sent the poem, with others, to GS on 15 March 1923. GS commented: "'Contradiction' is mature, too. I don't see why you should feel depressed when you can do such work" (letter to CAS, 6 April 1923; *SU* 230).

Copan. MS (JHLS). In **ST*. Copán was an ancient Mayan city that flourished in the 8th and 9th centuries C.E. and then was abandoned. It was a seat of learning, especially astronomy.

Copyist. In *SP*.

Un Couchant [English]. See "A Sunset."

Un Couchant [French]. MS (DAW; *JHLS; MCL). In a typescript of a poem sent to Albert Bender, CAS has written: "My first attempt in French!" CAS apparently wrote an English version, "A Sunset" (below), at about the same time. CAS appears to have sent the poem to GS on 25 December 1925. GS forwarded the poem to James Hopper, an author who had lived in France for many years. In reference to l. 3, CAS remarked: "I thought one of his criticisms a trifle meticulous. 'Fané' means 'faded' or 'discoloured' as well as 'withered' or 'wilted': my phrase 'sang fané' meant simply 'faded blood.' His other comments were just enough—though he didn't spot *all* my slips" (letter to GS, 19 February 1926; *SU* 269).

Credo. MS (JHLL; *JHLS). The ms. is dated 28 October 1928.

Crepuscule. MS (NYPL and MCL [as "Crepuscule"]). In *EC* (as "Crepuscle"), **SP*. The poem was accepted by the *Thrill Book*, but the magazine folded before the poem could be published.

Crows in Spring. MS (AH [as "Crows in March"]). In **SP*. See "Strange Miniatures."

The Crucifixion of Eros. MS (JHLS). In *OS, EC. Step Ladder* 13, No. 5 (May 1927): 132. *Golden Atom* No. 10 (Winter 1943): 23. In **SP*. CAS sent the poem, along with others, to GS on 15 June 1916. GS commented (letter to CAS, 17 June 1916): "'Belated Love' and 'The Crucifixion of Eros' are beautiful and moving things" (*SU* 136). CAS noted to SL that the poem "is a good enough conception, but the phraseology seems flat, and the versification intolerably monotonous" (letter to SL, 26 April 1916; ms., BL). For the same general theme of love and death, see the story "The Disinterment of Venus" (1932).

Cumuli. MS (JHLL; DAW; JHLS). *Interludes* 8, No. 1 (Spring 1931): 11. In **SP*. The ms. is dated 12 December 1929.

The Cycle. MS (JHLS).

Cycles. MS (*AH; RAH; UCLA). In *IM, BB, LO*. CAS's last poem, dated 4 June 1961. The first three words duplicate the title of a poem written c. 1943 (see p. 516).

Cyclopean Fear. Either non-extant or a variant title of an unidentified poem. It was sent by CAS to GS c. July–August 1913 (see *SU* 93). GS commented only that "'Cyclopean Fear' I cared less for" (letter to CAS, 19 August 1913; *SU* 94). The ms. of the poem does not survive among the poem mss. sent by CAS to GS at NYPL.

Dancer. In *SP*.

Dans l'univers lointain. MS (*JHLS). Written before 7 December 1949. For an English translation, see "In a Distant Universe."

The Dark Chateau. MS (JHLS). In *DC, LO*. Written c. 1950. For "Acherontic" (l. 8), see note on "Solution."

Dawn. See "The Sunrise."

Day-Dream. MS (JHLL, in letter to R. H. Barlow [c. November 1935]). An English translation of "Rêvasserie" (p. 401).

De Consolation [English]. An English translation of the French poem of the same title (p. 378).

De Consolation [French]. MS (JHLS). Written August 1927. The title is French for "Of Consolation."

De Profundis. MS (SHSW). In *SP. The ms. is dated 4 September 1943. The title (Latin for "From the Depths") is perhaps meant to evoke Oscar Wilde's celebrated essay *De Profundis* (1905), his account of his two years in prison. The phrase is taken from the Vulgate (*De profundis clamavi* ["I have cried from the depths"]: Psalms 129:1 [= 130.1 in the King James Bible]). Cf. Baudelaire's poem of that title, translated by CAS (Vol. 3, pp. 72–73).

A Dead City. In *ST*, *SP, *LO*. In l. 14, the use of "weird" as a noun (= doom) anticipates CAS's later story, "The Weird of Avoosl Wuthoqquan" (1931).

Dead Love. In *GF*.

The Dead Will Cuckold You. In *IM*, *SS. Verse drama. The play, written c. 1950/51, is set in CAS's imaginary realm of Zothique (see note on "Farewell to Eros"). None of the characters appear in his short stories in the Zothique cycle. Mss. of four "songs" from the play are extant: "Catch" (MS [AH; JHLS] = ll. 197–200 and 277–80; "Drinking-Song" (MS [JHLS]) = ll. 347–54; "Incantation" (MS [JHLS]) = ll. 234–58; and "The Song of Galeor" (MS [AH; JHLS]) = ll. 1–12.

Death. MS (*JHLS). In *TS*.

Decadence. In *SP*.

December. MS (DAW; JHLS). *AJ* 24, No. 8 (6 December 1923): 6. *Poetry* 33, No. 3 (December 1928): 123. In *SP. CAS sent the poem to GS on 7 October 1925, wishing it to appear in the *Overland Monthly*, as he was not including it in *S*. GS replied, "I'm very glad to have 'December' for the Overland, but we don't want to use it till the Dec. number" (letter to CAS, 9 October 1925; *SU* 259); but the poem did not appear in the *Overland* at all.

Declining Moon. MS (AH; DAW). In *SP. See "Haiku" and "Vignettes and Indexes."

Dedication: To Carol. Ms (JHLS [2 mss., one as "The Best Beloved," the other as "To Carol"]). In *S&P. The ms. is dated 19 February 1955. The dedicatory poem to *S&P*. Elsinore (l. 1) (the English name for the Danish town of Helsingør) is the setting for Shakespeare's *Hamlet*. Cypris (l. 12) is an alternate name for Aphrodite (see note on "The Ghoul and the Seraph").

Delay. MS (JHLS). The ms. is dated 12 September 1952. On the ms., Carol Smith has written: "Obviously a poem to Ede Hoppmoor."

Departure. MS (JHLS, in one ms. under general title "Tankas"). *AJ* 24, No. 7 (29 November 1923): 6. In *S. The ms. is dated 16 November 1923.

Desert Dweller. MS. (JHLS; MCL; SHSW). *WT* 36, No. 12 (July 1943): 71. In **SP, DC, LO, SSU.* The ms. is dated 13 August 1937. The Hanging Gardens (l. 16), built within the walls of the royal palace at Babylon, were regarded as one of the seven wonders of the world. They were probably built between 810 and 561 B.C.E.

The Desert Garden. See "Song of Sappho's Arabian Daughter."

Desire of Vastness. MS (JHLS). In *EC, *SP, LO.* CAS sent the poem to GS on 8 June 1913. GS commented: "'Desire of Vastness' is big too, with a *very* good ending. Its octave is pretty obscure; I get it, but fear that few others will" (letter to CAS, 22 June 1913; *SU* 91). "Cyclopean" (l. 14) is the adjectival form of Cyclops, the one-eyed giant encountered by Odysseus in the *Odyssey* (9.105f.).

Desolation. MS (JHLS). In *EC, *SP, LO.* GS said of the poem: "'Desolation' is a powerful and touching sonnet" (letter to CAS, 17 June 1916; *SU* 136). "Thulean" (l. 6) refers to Thule, an unspecified northern locale (possibly to be identified with Greenland) cited by Greek explorers and astronomers of the 4th and 3rd centuries B.C.E., including Pytheas, Eratosthenes, and Ptolemy. Cf. Poe's "Dream-Land": "From an ultimate dim Thule" (l. 6).

Dialogue. MS (JHLL; JHLS; SHSW). *WT* 36, No. 11 (May 1943): 67 (as by Timeus Gaylord). In **SP, S&P.* The ms. (as by Timeus Gaylord) is dated 28 July 1941. For "Gorgon" (l. 8), see note on "Medusa."

The Dials. MS (JHLS).

Dice el soñador. MS (UCLA; JHLS). In **SSU.* Written c. 1950. For an English version, see "Says the Dreamer."

Didus Ineptus. MS (AH; DAW; JHLS). In **S&P.* The ms. is dated 10 October 1950. The title is Latin for "The Clumsy Dodo." *Didus* is CAS's neo-Latin coinage. "Pliny's isle of Cerne" (l. 7) refers to an island off the western coast of Africa cited by Pliny the Elder (*Natural History* 6.198–99), purportedly settled by the Carthaginian Hanno. It may be identical to the small island of Arguin.

¿Dime tu sueñas, Musa? See "¿Qué sueñas, Musa?"

Dirge. See "Requiescat."

Disenchantment. See "Disillusionment."

Disillusionment. MS (JHLS; NYPL [as by Arzè Dnüöp]). In **SP, S&P.* First title: "Disenchantment." One ms. is titled "Disenchantment"; it has slightly different line divisions.

Dissidence. See "Diversity."

Dissonance. MS (JHLS; NYPL). *Thrill Book* 2, No. 6 (15 September 1919): 149. In *EC, *SP, LO.* Written before 24 April 1918. GS commented that the eighth line of the poem is "terrific" (letter to CAS, 12 May 1918; *SU* 160). Later, GS called it "a big sonnet" (letter to CAS, 3 November 1922; *SU* 214).

Distillations. MS (JHLS). Comprises "Fence and Wall"; "Growth of Lichen"; "Cats in Winter Sunlight"; "Abandoned Plum-Orchard"; "Harvest Evening"; "Willow Cutting in Autumn"; "Late Pear-Pruner"; "Nocturnal Pines"; "Geese in the Spring Night"; "The Sparrow's Nest"; and "The Last Apricot." In *SP*, the subsection "Distillations" includes these and numerous other haiku.

Diversity. MS (JHLS, under "Tankas"; *Sx). *AJ* 24, No. 7 (29 November 1923): 6. In *SP* (as "Dissidence"). The ms. is dated 16 November 1923. CAS restored the original title in Sx.

Do You Forget, Enchantress? MS (SHSW). *WT* 42, No. 3 (March 1950): 29. In *SP*, *S&P*. The ms. is dated 9 July 1946. A hamadryad (l. 3) is a nymph of the trees; a naiad is a water-nymph. A hippocentaur (l. 4) is a variant term for the centaur, a creature that is half man and half horse (from the Greek *hippos*, horse).

Dolor of Dreams. MS (JHLS). *AJ* 23, No. 46 (30 August 1923): 6. In *SP*, LO.

Dominion. MS (DAW; JHLS; MCL). *WT* 25, No. 6 (June 1935): 724. In *SP*, *S&P*, SSU. The ms. is dated 26 January 1935. For Cimmeria (l. 5), see note on "Ode on Imagination." For Erebus (l. 15), see note on "The City of the Titans." For "Sabean" (l. 16), see note on "Autumn Orchards." An Afrit (l. 17) is a devil in the Islamic religion.

Dominium in Excelsis. MS (AH; JHLS). In *DC, BB, IM.* The ms. is dated 13 February 1950. The title is Latin for "The Lord in the Highest"; the phrase as such is not actually found in the Vulgate, although the words are frequently found separately. "Burning Sword" (l. 3) refers to the Sword of Orion, the common name for a series of stars lying beneath Orion's Belt. Capella (l. 11) is the fifth brightest star in the sky, situated in the constellation Auriga. For Altair (l. 11), see note on "The Absence of the Muse." "Scorpion's hair" (l. 13) refers to the constellation Scorpio. Endor (l. 15) is a village in Palestine, 13 miles southwest of the Sea of Galilee. It was where Saul consulted a witch on the eve of his final battle against the Philistines. Beltis (l. 15) is a variant spelling of Baaltis (see note on "Alternative").

Don Juan Sings. MS (JHLS; NYPL; *Sx). *AJ* 23, No. 30 (10 May 1923): 6. *Wanderer* 2, No. 3 (March 1924): 30. In *S, SP*. The ms. is dated 7 March 1923. CAS sent the poem, with "Song (from *The Fugitives*)," to GS on 7 March 1923. GS commented: "I like both these poems—the Don Juan one the more, as being maturer. If you'll send me a better copy I'll sell it to Mencken [for the *Smart Set*] for you—if it's not sold already" (letter to CAS, 9 March 1923; *SU* 229). CAS later reported (letter to GS, 15 March 1923; *SU* 229) that he had submitted it to *Ainslee's*, but it must have been rejected. The ms. contains a discarded stanza (placement uncertain): "Ere the garlands that you bear / Turn to stricter chains and bind you / Lay them gently by and find you / Other flowers to weave and wear."

Don Quixote on Market Street. MS (JHLS). In *DC, BB. WT* 45, No. 1 (March 1953): 11. Written 1950. The Market Street of the title is a busy thoroughfare in San Francisco. Rosinante (1. 1) is Don Quixote's undernourished horse. For Hinnom (1. 32), see note on "The Outer Land." For Moloch (1. 33), see note on "Some Blind Eidolon." For Mammon (1. 33), see note on "The Envoys."

¿Donde duermes, Eldorado? MS (JHLS [2 mss., one titled "Súplica"]). In *DD, *SSU.* Eldorado (*El dorado,* "The golden man") is a legendary city of fabulous wealth believed during the 16th and 17th centuries to exist somewhere in the northern part of South America. For an English translation of the poem, see "Where Sleepest Thou, O Eldorado?"

The Doom of America. MS (JHLL). CAS sent the poem to GS on 11 May 1913, remarking that it is "a sort of Bible prophecy, in about fifty verses. I don't suppose it's poetry. It's a sort of round-up of all my grudges and kicks against the present age. I even took a swat at the suffragettes. I'm glad it's out of my system" (*SU* 87). (CAS appears at a later date to have removed his "swat" against the suffragettes.) GS commented: "The 'Doom of America' is also a magnificent thing, even though, like my 'Job' stuff, it's an echo of the Bible" (letter to CAS, 22 June 1913; *SU* 91). GS refers to his own poem, "The Forty-third Chapter of Job," in *The House of Orchids and Other Poems* (1911). The phrase "after strange gods" (1. 1) is derived from several passages in the Bible, e.g., Deut. 31:16: "And this people will rise up, and go a whoring after the gods of the strangers of the land." For Baal (1. 1), see note to "Pour Chercher du nouveau." For Mammon (1. 1), see note to "The Envoys." For Moloch (1. 1), see note to "Some Blind Eidolon." Alcyone (1. 11) is, in Greek myth, a woman who was changed into a bird, the halcyon (kingfisher). The relevance of this name in the poem is not apparent. For Altair (1. 11), see note on "The Absence of the Muse." For Babel (1. 21), see note on "The City of Destruction." For Abaddon (1. 42), see note on "A Dream of the Abyss." For Tyre (1. 48), see note on "The Sorrow of the Winds."

Dos Mitos y una fábula. MS (JHLS). In *DD, SSU.* For an English translation, see "Two Myths and a Fable." An early version of the poem exists (MS [JHLS]) as "Mito."

The Dragon-Fly. MS (JHLL; JHLS; MCL). In *SP. The ms. is dated 11 September 1929.

Dream. See "The Nymph."

The Dream. MS (JHLS).

The Dream-Bridge. MS (NYPL). In **ST, LO*. Written c. 1911.

The Dream-God's Realm. MS (JHLS [as "Sonnets on Dreams"]). In **PD, LO*. For "Cimmerian" (l. 2), see note on "Ode on Imagination."

Dream-Mystery. See "Lunar Mystery."

A Dream of Beauty. MS (JHLS). *Academy* 81 (12 August 1911): 196. In *ST, N1*. In *A Collection of Verse by California Poets: From 1849 to 1915*, ed. Augustin S. Macdonald (San Francisco: A. M. Robertson, 1914), p. 54. *Golden Atom* 1, No. 8 (May 1940): 3. In *SP. In *Unseen Wings: The Living Poetry of Man's Immortality*, ed. Stanton A. Coblentz (New York: Beechhurst Press, 1949), pp. 261–62. In *LO*.

A Dream of Darkness. MS (JHLS). Line 5 lacks two syllables. The blank space in l. 6 was left by CAS; the line lacks three syllables.

A Dream of Oblivion. In **PD, LO*. For Nirvana (l. 9), see note on "Nirvana."

A Dream of the Abyss. MS (JHLL; JHLS). *Fantasy Fan* 1, No. 3 (November 1933): 41. In **SP, LO*. For Azrael (l. 35), see note on "The Flight of Azrael." Abaddon (l. 35), "the place of destruction," is the depth of Hell mentioned in the Talmud and in Milton's *Paradise Regain'd* (1671), 4.624. Sometimes (as in CAS's poem) it refers to the angel of the bottomless pit, cited in the Bible as Apollyon (Rev. 9:11).

The Dream-Weaver. MS (JHLS). The ms. is dated 3 April 1911.

Drinking-Song. See *The Dead Will Cuckold You.*

Duality. MS (NYPL [as "Sonnet"]; JHLS [as "Sonnet"]; Sx). *WT* 2, No. 1 (July–August 1923): 69 (as "The Garden of Evil"). *AJ* 24, No. 20 (28 February 1924): 6. In *S*, *SP. First title: "Sonnet." The poem was one of the first by CAS to be published in *WT*. CAS was presumably referring to this poem when he spoke of the phrase "water-weeds of Lethe" (cf. l. 5): "By 'water-weeds of Lethe' I mean the water-hemlock, from which the Greeks got their poison. It's a pale-green, pernicious-looking sort of plant, and grows in this neighborhood, along with two or three kinds of night-shade, one of which has violet-coloured, rose-scented flowers, and livid berries—a weird and sinister object" (CAS to SL, 1 June 1915; ms., BL).

Los Dueños. MS (JHLS). The ms. is dated 30 January 1950. The title is Spanish for "The Masters." The poem is addressed to four "masters," Satan, Mammon (see note on "The Envoys"), Death (Muerte), and Love (Amor).

Dying Prospector. MS (JHLS, under "Quintrains").

The Earth. See "Epitaphs."

Echo of Memnon. MS (NYPL). In *EC*, **SP*, *LO*. Written before 27 May 1912. CAS sent the poem to GS on 30 December 1912. GS commented: "Your 'Echo of Memnon' is a fine and impressive lyric" (letter to CAS, 11 January 1913; *SU* 78). The poem, like "Memnon at Midnight" (p. 151), makes use of the legend of a colossal statue of Memnon (a king of the Egyptians who purportedly fought with the Trojans against the Greeks in the Trojan War) at Thebes that sang at dawn when the sun struck it.

The Eclipse. MS (JHLS).

Ecstasy. MS (JHLS; NYPL). *Pearson's Magazine* 48, No. 10 (October 1922): 32. In *EC*, **SP*. The ms. is dated 19 May 1921. CAS sent the poem, along with others, to GS on 27 May 1921, noting that "They're the first writing I've done for a year" (*SU* 195). GS commented: "Your poems are all peaches.... 'Ecstasy' and 'Nightfall' seem the finest to me, especially the former" (letter to CAS, 6 June 1921; *SU* 196).

Eidolon. MS (NYPL). In *EC*, **SP*. Written before 24 April 1918.

Eight Haiku. MS (JHLS). In *SP* as part of "Experiments in Haiku" (but without title) in the subsection "Distillations." Comprises "The Sparrow's Nest"; "The Last Apricot"; "Mushroom Gatherers"; "Spring Nunnery"; "Nuns Walking in the Orchard"; "Improbable Dream"; "Night of Miletus"; and "Tryst at Lobos."

The Eldritch Dark. In *ST*, *N1*, **SP*. In *DM* 319–20. In *LO*.

Ellos Resurgem. See "Not Theirs the Cypress-Arch."

Éloignement. MS (DAW; *JHLL). The title is French for "Remoteness."

Éloignement. See "Consolation."

Éloignement. See "Postlude."

Empusa Waylays a Traveler. MS (AH). See "Strange Miniatures." The name Empusa (Empousa) appears in Aristophanes' *Frogs* (l. 293) and *Ecclesiazusae* (l. 1056) as a shape-changing hobgoblin sent by Hecate.

Enchanted Mirrors. MS (DAW; JHLS; *Sx). In *S. AJ* 26, No. 4 (5 November 1925): 4. *Overland Monthly* 83, No. 11 (November 1925): 407. In *SP*, *LO*. The ms. is dated 16 March 1925. "Pompeiian" (l. 5) refers to Pompeii, the city in central Italy that, along with Herculaneum, was destroyed by the eruption of Mt. Vesuvius in 79 C.E. Saturnia (l. 7) apparently refers to the time and place in which the primitive Italian god Saturnus (later identified with the Greek god Kronos, overthrown by Zeus) reigned. Devachan (l. 14) corresponds to heaven in theosophical literature. Cf. CAS to GS, 11 June 1922: "'Devachan', as I understand it, is merely a temporary Paradise of beatific illusions—in which the discarnate soul is permitted to abide for a time before its return to mortal existence" (*SU* 207).

The End of Autumn. MS (JHLS; Sx). *AJ* 24, No. 7 (29 November 1923): 6. *Wanderer* 2, No. 11 (November 1924): 153. In *S*, *SP. CAS appears to have sent this poem, with others, to GS on 21 September 1924. GS commented: "Thanks very much for the poems! I hardly know which one I prefer, for all are very charming—first-class work. And the short one ['The End of Autumn'?] levels up with the others by reason of a deep poignancy" (letter to CAS, 28 September 1924; *SU* 245).

Enigma. MS (DAW; JHLL; NYPL; Sx). *AJ* 25, No. 18 (12 February 1925): 4. In *S*, *SP. Written before 20 January 1925.

Ennui (My days are as a garden, where the dust). MS (DAW; JHLL; *JHLS [some mss. have the title "The Ennuyé"]; NYPL). *AJ* 25, No. 14 (15 January 1925): 5. In *KML* as "The Ennuye." The ms. is dated 22 December 1919. CAS later revised the poem in alexandrines (see p. 466). Cf. CAS's prose-poem "Ennui" (1918; *NU* 12–13).

Ennui (Thou art immured in some sad garden sown with dust). MS (JHLS; SHSW). *WT* 27, No. 5 (May 1936): 547. In **SP, LO*. A recasting of the sonnet "Ennui" (p. 193) in alexandrines. Written before 11 December 1935. Sodom (l. 2) was, with Gomorrah and other cities of the plain, destroyed because of its wickedness in the time of Abraham (Gen. 17–19).

L'Ensorcellement. MS (DAW; *JHLS). The title is French for "Witchcraft." CAS has misspelled the title as "L'Ensorcelement."

The Envoys. MS (DAW; JHLS; NYPL). *AJ* 26, No. 13 (7 January 1926): 4. *Overland Monthly* 84, No. 5 (June 1926): frontispiece. *Overland Monthly* 84, No. 7 (July 1926): 230 (corrected version). In *DM* 342–43. In **SP, LO*. The ms. is dated 1 December 1925. CAS sent the poem to GS on that date. GS commented: "'The Envoys' is pure poetry: Poe would have hugged you for it—if he didn't stab you! I'm not sure I get the symbolism, and some of the words sent me to the dictionary. But that's no fault of *yours*" (letter to CAS, 10 December 1925; *SU* 264). GS arranged to have the poem published in the *Overland Monthly* (June 1926), but it was so misprinted that it was reprinted correctly in the July 1926 issue. "Cimmerii" (l. 7) refers to the inhabitants of Cimmeria (see note on "Ode on Imagination"). Algebar (l. 23) is the Arabic name for the constellation Orion; Capricorn is the constellation Capricornus (the goat). Taurus (l. 25) is the constellation (the bull). Mammon (l. 34) is, in the Old Testament, an Aramaic word used as a personification of wealth.

Ephemera. MS (JHLS).

Epitaph for an Astronomer. In *SP*.

Epitaph for the Earth. In *SZ*. Cf. GS's letter to CAS, 11 February 1912: "That's a great title, the 'Epitaph to [*sic*] the Earth!' See that you use it!" (*SU* 37). The letter by CAS—January or February 1912—in which CAS apparently mentioned this title is non-extant (see *SU* 35).

Epitaphs. Comprises "Braggart"; "Slaughtered Cattle"; and "The Earth." Apparently non-extant. Cited in *EOD* 50.

Erato. MS (JHLS; SHSW). In *SP*. The ms. is dated 2 October 1942. Erato was the muse of the lyre, hence of lyric poetry (often referring specifically to the poetry of love or eroticism). Helicon (l. 15) is a large mountain Boeotia believed to be frequented by the Muses.

El Eros de ébano. MS (*JHLS; UCLA). In *SSU*. Written c. 1950. For an English translation, see "Eros of Ebony."

Eros in the Desert. MS (JHLS).

Eros of Ebony. MS (JHLS; UCLA). In *DC, SSU*. An English translation of the Spanish poem "El Eros de ébano."

Essence. MS (DAW; JHLS, under "Quintrains"). In *SP* (as "Attar of the Past"), *S&P*.

Esperance. See "The Hope of the Infinite."

L'Espoir du néant. MS (DAW; JHLS; MCL). In *SP*. The title translates to "The Hope of Nothing [or Nonexistence]."

Estrangement. MS (JHLL; JHLS; Sx). *AJ* 24, No. 50 (25 September 1924): 6. *Step Ladder* 10, No. 4 (March 1925): 80. In *S*, *SP*. The ms. is dated 9 September 1924.

The Eternal Gleam. MS (JHLS).

The Eternal Snows. MS (*JHLS; NYPL). Publication in 1911–12 not found. In *UV*. This was one of the earliest poems that CAS sent to GS, on 2 February 1911 (*SU* 19). In his letter of 28 February 1911, GS made a number of comments on the draft (*SU* 21), including the suggestion to remove "Doth drench" and substitute "Drenches."

Evanescence. Tr. (DSF) from ms. dated 15 September 1929; MS (JHLS [untitled fragment]).

Even in Slumber. MS (JHLS). In *SP*. The ms. is dated 11 November 1943.

Evening. MS (JHLS).

Exchange. MS (NYPL). *AJ* 23, No. 34 (7 June 1923): 6. *Buccaneer* 1, No. 5 (January 1925): 17.

The Exile. *Bohemia* 2, No. 2 (March 1917): 20. In *EC. Stars* (June–July 1940): [2]. In **SP.*

Exorcism. MS (JHLS). *Troubadour* 3, No. 5 and 6 (February–March 1931): 6. In **SP, LO.* The ms. is dated 14 January 1929.

Exotic. See "Exotique [English]."

Exotic Memory. MS (JHLS). In **SP* (as a translation of "Christophe des Laurières"). First version: "Alien Memory" (p. 156). CAS sent the poem (then still titled "Alien Memory") to GS on 26 September 1921 (see *SU* 200); GS made no specific comment on it.

Exotique [English]. MS (JHLS; NYPL [as "Exotic"]). In *OS, EC, *SP, LO.* Variant title: "Exotic." The ms. is dated 14 June 1915. For a French translation of this poem, see p. 287.

Exotique [French]. MS (JHLS). A French translation of "Exotique" (p. 155).

The Expanding Ideal. MS (JHLS). First draft: "The Unattainable."

A Fable. MS (DAW; JHLL; JHLS; MCL). *WT* 10, No. 1 (July 1927): 76. In **SP.* Solomon (l. 3), in the Bible, was the king of Israel (c. 973–933 B.C.E.), the son of David and Bathsheba. He became renowned for his wisdom.

Le Fabliau d'un dieu. MS (JHLS). The title translates to "The Fabliau of a God." A *fabliau* is a type of French poem in octosyllabic meter, popular in the 13th and 14th centuries.

Fairy Lanterns. In *ST.*

Fallen Grape-Leaf. MS (AH). In **SP.* See "Strange Miniatures." The first version reads: "Newly fallen, the red leaf in my heart / Meets a sadder scarlet / Cadent too."

The Falling Leaves. MS (JHLS). The ms. contains the following variant lines: The Leaves are falling, brown & sere / Like whirling showers of autumn rain / Enveloping the dying year / As in his final counterpane.

Fame. See "That Last Infirmity."

The Fanes of Dawn. MS (*NYPL). In *FD.*

Fantasie. MS (JHLS).

Fantasie d'antan. MS (DAW; JHLS; MCL). *WT* 14, No. 6 (December 1929): 724. In *DM* 343–44. In **SP, LO.* The ms. is dated 1 April 1927. The title is French for "Fantasy of Yesteryear." For "Aquilonian" (l. 17), see note on 'Farewell to Eros." For "Hyperboreans" (l. 22), see note on "October."

Farewell to Eros. MS (JHLS; MCL; SHSW). *WT* 31, No. 6 (June 1938): 759. In *SP*, *S&P*, *LO*. Written c. March 1937. In Greek myth, Eros (sometimes declared the son of Aphrodite) is the god of love, especially physical love. "Stygia" (l. 10) is a Latin adjectival form of Styx (see note on "In Slumber"); CAS envisions it as a land or planet. Zothique (l. 13) is a continent in the far future where CAS set many of his tales. For "Thule" (l. 13), see note on "Desolation." "Aquilonian" (l. 21) refers to Aquilonia, a realm cited by Robert E. Howard in his stories of Conan the Cimmerian. In l. 26, Dis is the Latin name for Pluto, the Greek god of the underworld.

Farmyard Fugue. MS (JHLS). Written c. 1 October 1950. A parody of Modernist poetry, with its emphasis on treating mundane subjects in a poem.

Fashion. MS (JHLS). The ms. is dated 9 March 1923.

Fawn-Lilies. MS (*JHLS). In *GF*. The ms. is dated 19 April 1922.

Fear. See "The Barrier."

Feast of St. Anthony. MS (AH; DAW). In *SP*, *S&P*. See "Strange Miniatures" and "Strange Miniatures (Haiku)." The poem refers to St. Anthony (251?–350?), an Egyptian hermit who withdrew from society and lived on a mountain near the Nile River, tormented by temptations from the Devil in numerous forms. His feast day is 17 January. See Flaubert's novel *La Tentation de Saint Antoine* (1872; translated as *The Temptation of St. Anthony*).

February. MS (*JHLS). In *KML*. The ms. is dated 2 February 1929.

Fellowship. MS (JHLL; JHLS [fragment]). *WT 16, No. 4 (October 1930): 550. The ms. is dated 15 September 1929.

Felo-de-se of the Parasite. MS (AH; JHLS). In *SP*. See "Strange Miniatures" and "Mortal Essences." "Felo-de-se" is Latin for "felon of himself," an archaic term for suicide.

Fence and Wall. MS (AH; DAW; JHLS). In *SP*, *S&P*. See "Distillations," "Haiku," and "Vignettes and Indexes."

Field Behind the Abatoir. In *SP*. First title: "Behind the Abatoir." The final word of the title is normally spelled abattoir.

Fight on the Play-Ground. MS (AH). In *SP*. See "Childhood: Seven Haiku."

Finis. MS (SFPL). In *ST*. In *Literary California*, ed. Ella Sterling Mighels (San Francisco: Harr Wagner Publishing Co., 1918), p. 381. *Tesseract* 2, No. 3 (March 1937): 9. In *SP*. Written 1912. The title is Latin for "end," and the work not only is the concluding poem in *ST* but deals with the end of the universe.

Fire of Snow. MS (JHLS). *Poetry* 6, No. 4 (July 1915): 178. In *SP*.

Flamingoes. *Asia* 19, No. 11 (November 1919): 1134. In *EC*, *SP.

The Flight of Azrael. *Fantastic Worlds* 1, No. 1 (Summer 1952): 15. In *SP, *LO*. Written before 10 May 1915. The third of CAS's poetic dialogues, following "The Masque of Forsaken Gods" (p. 102) and "The Witch in the Graveyard" (p. 140). It was followed by "The Ghoul and the Seraph" (p. 195). CAS noted that the poem was a "hasty scribble which is probably not worth preserving, and is rather 'too much of a sameness', with many other things that I've written, anyway. A good theme for a painting, tho, don't you think?" (letter to SL, 10 May 1915; ms., BL). CAS sent the poem to GS on 20 June 1916, noting that it had been written in 1915 (*SU* 137). GS commented that the poem "has more than a touch of the sublime" (letter to CAS, 8 July 1916; *SU* 138). Azrael is, in Judaic and Islamic writings, the angel who separates soul from body at the moment of death. Algol (l. 24) is a second-magnitude variable star in the constellation Perseus. "Antarean" (l. 26) refers to Antares (see note on "The Star-Treader").

Flight of the Yellow-Hammer. In *SP*.

Flora. In *SP*. Flora was the Italian goddess of flowers and spring; the name later came to be used as a generic term for any kind of plant life.

The Flower of the Night. MS (JHLS).

Foggy Night. MS (AH; DAW). In *SP. See "Haiku" and "Strange Miniatures."

For a Wine Jar. MS (BL), in letter to Samuel Loveman, of 14 February 1920. Written c. 1919. "Omar" (l. 2) refers to Omar Khayyam (see note on "To Omar Khayyam").

For an Antique Lyre. MS (MCL; SHSW). *Agenbite of Inwit* 3, No. 1 (January 1946). In *SP, *HD*, *SSU*. Vesper (l. 12) is Latin for "evening."

For the Dance of Death. MS (JHLS). In *SP. See "Mortal Essences."

Foreknowledge. See "Future Pastoral."

Forgetfulness. MS (JHLS). *Sonnet* 4, No. 2 (May–June 1919): 2. In *EC*, *SP. CAS sent the poem to GS on 2 February 1919. GS commented: ". . . this exquisite sonnet that you send me is worth more than several books of poorer verse" (letter to CAS, 11 February 1919; *SU* 168).

Forgotten Sorrow. MS (Sx). *AJ* 23, No. 42 (2 August 1923): 6. In *S*, *SP, *LO*. Palmyra (l. 9) was a city in Syria reputedly founded by Solomon. Siam (l. 11) is the name formerly applied to the nation of Thailand.

La Forteresse. MS (*JHLS; MCL; SHSW). Written 25–26 November 1935. Revised version of "Le Refuge."

The Fortress. MS (JHLS). English translation of "La Forteresse" (p. 465).

The Fountain of Youth. MS (MH).

Fragment. MS (JHLS; SHSW). *Wings* 5, No. 5 (Spring 1942): 6. In *SP*. Rpt. *Unseen Wings: The Living Poetry of Man's Immortality*, ed. Stanton A. Coblentz (New York: Beechhurst Press, 1949), pp. 210–11. In **HD*. The ms. is dated 11 September 1941.

A Fragment. MS (JHLL; NYPL). In *EC*. *Argonaut* (16 December 1922): 388. *Step Ladder* 13, No. 5 (May 1927): 134. In **SP*.

The Freedom of the Hills. MS (JHLS). In l. 18, CAS has left a blank space for a word never filled in.

From Arcady. MS (SHSW). In **SP*. Arcady is an anglicized spelling of Arcadia, a mountainous province in central Greece that became associated with Pan and hence with pastoral tranquility.

The Fugitives. In *ST*.

The Fugitives. A verse drama begun on 17 September 1922 but never completed. CAS does not discuss the scope or direction of the play in any extant correspondence. A mutilated fragment of the opening scene description survives (MS [JHLS]). CAS published four "songs" separately, as follows:

The Song of Aviol. MS (MCL; JHLS [2 mss., one a fragment and the other titled "Aviol's Song"]; NYPL). *AJ* 23, No. 25 (5 April 1923): 6. *Lyric West* 3, No. 11 (March 1924): 28. In *S*, **SP*, *SS* (as "Song"; see Appendix). The ms. is dated 17 September 1922. CAS sent the poem to GS on 29 September 1922. GS commented: "I like the lyric very much . . . and am greatly interested in the projected drama" (letter to CAS, 1 October 1922; *SU* 211).

Song. MS (JHLS). The ms. is dated 7 March 1923. The Hesperides (l. 14) were the daughters of Nyx (night) and Erebus (darkness) who lived in the extreme West (their name derives from the Greek *hespera*, west).

The Love-Potion. MS (NYPL; Sx). *AJ* 23, No. 29 (3 May 1923): 6. In *S*. *Step Ladder* 13, No. 5 (May 1927): 135. In **SP*. Written before 10 May 1923.

The Song of Cartha. MS (JHLL; JHLS). *AJ* 23, No. 29 (3 May 1923): 6. *Wanderer* 2, No. 8 (August 1924): 103. In *S*, **SP*. Written before 10 May 1923. The ms. contains the following discarded second stanza: Goal of love's immortal quest, / Land for love to search and plunder! . . . / Slowly now the throbbing wonder / Lessens, and our veins would rest.

The Funeral Urn. MS (DAW). *AJ* 23, No. 45 (23 August 1923): 6. In **SP* (as a translation of "Christophe des Laurières"), *LO*. In the ms. and *AJ*, the second stanza originally read: "Where wan immortal flowers twine / As in a wreath funereal; / Where autumn leaves forever fall / To crown the dim and rich design. . . ."

The Future. MS (JHLS).

Future Meeting. MS (AH). In *SP. See "Strange Miniatures."

Future Pastoral. MS (JHLS [2 mss., one titled "Foreknowledge"]; SHSW). *Wings* 6, No. 1 (Spring 1943): 20. In **SP, HD*. The ms. is dated 28 February 1942. First title: "Prescience"; variant title: "Foreknowledge." For "Favonian" (l. 3), see note on "At Sunrise."

The Garden of Dreams. In *GF*. Written 1911.

The Garden of Evil. See "Duality."

Garden of Priapus. In *SP*. See "Pagans Old and New." In Greek myth, Priapus was the god of fertility and was usually depicted with an enormous erect phallus. In Italy he became the god of gardens, and statues of him were frequently placed in gardens.

Geese in the Spring Night. MS (AH; DAW; JHLS). In **SP, S&P*. See "Distillations," "Haiku," and "Strange Miniatures."

Geometries. MS (JHLS). The ms. is dated 9 August 1952. "Euclidean" (l. 2) refers to Euclid (c. 300 B.C.E.), the Greek mathematician whose *Elements* is the foundation of all geometry. "Platonic absolutes" (l. 29) refers to the notion of "forms" (or "ideas") conceived by the Greek philosopher Plato (427–347 B.C.E.), the perfect forms of terrestrial objects of which all actual objects are flawed reproductions.

The Ghost of Theseus. MS (AH; DAW). In *SP. See "Strange Miniatures" and "Strange Miniatures (Haiku)." The poem alludes to the Athenian hero Theseus' defeat of the Minotaur, the mythological beast part man, part bull, imprisoned in a stone labyrinth by King Minos of Crete.

The Ghoul. MS (JHLS). The ms. is dated 16 February 1913. For "Hecatean" (l. 8), see note on "The Witch in the Graveyard."

The Ghoul and the Seraph. MS (GK; JHLS; NYPL). In *EC*, **SP, The Ghoul and the Seraph* (Gargoyle Press, 1950), *LO*. The fourth of CAS's poetic dialogues, following "The Masque of Forsaken Gods" (p. 102), "The Witch in the Graveyard" (p. 195), and "The Flight of Azrael" (p. 154). In early 1913 CAS was considering writing a work entitled "The Ghoul, the Cypress, and the Grave." He describes it in a letter to GS (19 February 1913) as "a three-cornered dialogue among the entities of the title. The ghoul comes to claim the grave, and finds his rights disputed by the Cypress, which is already 'on the spot'. They have an argument, at the end of which the Grave also speaks. The idea is ghastly enough for Bierce, don't you think?" (*SU* 81). Elsewhere CAS describes the work as "an unusual mixture of horror and sublimity" (CAS to SL, 31 December 1919). CAS did not actually complete the poem until the very end of 1919; he referred to it (letter to GS, 29 January 1920) as "a philosophical fantasy . . . The philosophical thesis is a plain statement of scientific fact—the immortality of matter, and the evanescence and commutation of its forms" (*SU* 179). GS commented: "I like some of this new poem, 'The Ghoul and the Seraph,' very much. You strike a mighty deep note in that last soliloquy of the ghoul. Have you tried the poem on The Ladies Home Journal yet?" (letter to CAS, 23 March 1920; *SU* 180). Malebolge (l. 18) ("evil trench") is, in Dante's *Inferno*, the eighth circle of Hell. A Kobold (l. 20) (usually not capitalized) is, in Germanic myth, a familiar spirit of a tricky disposition. For Acheron (l. 26), see note on "Solution." For the Latin phrase "In Pace" (l. 40), see note on "Requiescat." Apollyon (l. 45) is, in the Bible, the angel of destruction, residing in the bottomless pit (Rev. 9:11). Belial (l. 48) is a name mentioned once in the New Testament (2 Corinthians 6:15) as a synonym for Satan. Ulysses (l. 51) is the Latin name for the Greek hero Odysseus. "Paphian" (l. 78) refers to Paphos, a city on the coast of Cyprus where Aphrodite was reputed to have been born from the sea-foam; it is also the site of a noted temple to Aphrodite. Python (l. 90) was an immense snake whose killing by Apollo helped to usher in the reign of the Olympian gods. Phlegethon (l. 95) is a river of fire in the Greek underworld. Ophiuchus (l. 105), from the Greek *ophis*, snake, is the constellation Ophiuchus et Serpens.

Girl of Six. MS (AH). In *SP*. See "Childhood: Seven Haiku."

Give Me Your Lips. MS (*JHLS). *Live Stories* 10, No. 1 (February 1917): 48. The ms. is dated 3 October 1916.

Goats and Manzanita-Boughs. In *SP*.

Gopher-Hole in Orchard. In *SP*.

Götterdämmerung. See "The Twilight of the Gods."

Grammar-School Vixen. MS (AH). In *SP*. See "Childhood: Seven Haiku."

Grecian Yesterday. MS (JHLS). In *SP*. The ms. is dated 17 February 1941. Leda (l. 2) was the wife of Tyndareus, king of Sparta, and the mother of Clytemnestra and Helen of Troy. She was seduced by Zeus (in the form of a swan [cf. l. 3]) and gave birth either to Helen or to the twins Castor and Polydeuces. Syrinx (l. 10) is the name of a nymph pursued by Pan, in whose honor he named the instrument made of seven reeds.

Greek Epigram. Tr. (DSF). The poem is a satire on T. S. Eliot (1888–1965), the American-born Modernist poet who emigrated to England and became an English citizen. CAS frequently criticized the obscurity of much of his poetry, notably *The Waste Land* (1922). See also "On Trying to Read *Four Quartets*" (p.

514). In l. 2, CAS alludes to the fact that lower-class British "Cockneys" were accustomed to add an aspirate before a word beginning in a vowel.

Growth of Lichen. MS (AH; DAW; JHLS). In *SP, S&P.* See "Distillations," "Haiku," and "Vignettes and Indexes."

H. P. L. MS (JHLL). In H. P. Lovecraft and others, *The Shuttered Room and Other Pieces,* ed. August Derleth (Sauk City, WI: Arkham House, 1959), p. 204. In *LO.* The ms. is dated 17 June 1959. CAS's second poem about H. P. Lovecraft (see "To Howard Phillips Lovecraft"). Pnath (l. 6) is an imaginary realm cited in some of Lovecraft's "dreamland" tales, notably *The Dream-Quest of Unknown Kadath* (1926–27). For Spica (l. 14), see note on "Demogorgon"; Aldebaran is the brightest star in the constellation Taurus.

Haiku. MS (DAW). In *SP* as part of "Experiments in Haiku," in the subsection "Distillations." Comprises "Fence and Wall"; "Growth of Lichen"; "Cats in Winter Sunlight"; "Abandoned Plum-Orchard"; "Harvest Evening"; "Willow-Cutting in Autumn"; "Declining Moon"; "Late Pear-Pruner"; "Nocturnal Pines"; "Phallus Impudica"; "Stormy Afterglow"; "Geese in the Spring Night"; "Foggy Night"; "Love in Dreams"; "The Sparrow's Nest"; "Improbable Dream"; and "Night of Miletus."

The Harbour of the Past. In *BS.*

The Harlot of the World. MS (JHLS). *Town Talk* No. 1115 (27 March 1915): 5. In *OS. Town Talk* No. 1361 (21 September 1918): [15] ("Golden Gate Literary Number"). In *EC, *SP.* Variant title: "To Life." GS wrote to CAS (4 February 1915): "[Harry] Lafler says of your 'Harlot of the World,' 'What a tremendous sonnet! It says the last word. How does that lonely boy ever *get* such stuff?'" (*SU* 118). CAS later told GS (23 April 1915) that he gave the poem to *Town Talk,* adding: "It was 'impossible', I suppose, for any of the respectable eastern publications" (*SU* 122).

Harmony. MS (*JHLS). In *SC.* The ms. is dated 29 January 1929. First title: "Harmony," changed to "Similitude" but ultimately back to "Harmony."

Harvest Evening. MS (AH; DAW; JHLS). In *SP, S&P.* First title: "Buckeyes." See "Distillations," "Haiku," and "Vignettes and Indexes."

The Hashish Eater; or, The Apocalypse of Evil. MS (JHLL [microfilm]; JHLS [fragment]; NYPL [without subtitle]; SU [without subtitle]). In *EC.* In *DM* 321–38. In *SP, LO.* CAS began the poem in January 1920 and completed it on 20 February 1920. He wrote to SL on 14 January 1920: "I've blocked out fifty lines of a new poem in blank verse, entitled 'The Hashish-Eater.' It's to be a tour-de-force of monstrous imagery—'Continents of serpent-shapen trees, With slimy trunks that lengthen league on league' [ll. 14–15] is a fair sample. I'm putting all the delirium into it that I can; but it's damned hard writing. Some of the images will remind you of the 'Wine of Wizardry'—'forgotten glyphs By sinful gods in torrid rubies writ For ending of a brazen book—' [ll. 30–32]; but it's darker in colour, and more cosmic in scope, than George's poem." He wrote to GS on 29 January 1920: "I've been at work on a much longer poem, 'The Hashish-Eater,' but am 'stuck' at the end of three hundred lines. It will take another hundred to finish the thing. I'm afraid it's too long and incoherent. It has some monstrous images . . . I've left the poor devil of a Hashish-eater in mid-air, fleeing on the back of some providential hippogriff, from a python as big as a river" (*SU* 179). CAS sent the unfinished poem to SL on 26 January 1920, noting: "I feel horribly discouraged about the thing—it seems altogether too long and incoherent—and find it impossible to go on at present" (ms., BL). SL commented on this fragment on 2 February 1920: "'H. E.' is the greatest poem you have ever written—far greater than the 'Wine of Wiz.'" (ms., JHLS). On 20 February 1920, the day he finished the poem, CAS wrote to Loveman: "It contains a wonderful menagerie, toward the end—partly 'lifted' from Flaubert, 'The Faery [*sic*] Queene,' and Sir John Maundeville, and partly of my own invention" (ms., BL). Only on 29 March 1920 did CAS send the poem to GS, writing: "The poem is imaginative, but, to me, the technique is so intolerable that I can take no pride or pleasure in it" (*SU* 181). GS commented: "'The Hashish-Eater' is indeed an amazing production. My friends will have none of it, claiming it reads like an extension of 'A Wine of Wizardry.' But I think there are many differences, and at any rate, it has more imagination in it than any other poem I know of. Like the 'Wine,' it fails on the aesthetic side, a thing that seems of small consequence in a poem of that nature" (letter to CAS, 10 June 1920; *SU* 183). CAS replied: "I'm sorry that people think 'The H. Eater' a mere extension of 'A Wine of Wizardry'. That's no mean compliment, however—The 'Wine of Wizardry' has always seemed the ideal poem to me, as it did to Bierce. But the ground-plan of 'The H. E.' is really quite different. It owes nearly as much to [Flaubert's] 'The Temptation of Saint Anthony' as to your poem" (letter to GS, 10 July 1920; *SU* 184). Many years later CAS wrote to S. J. Sackett: ". . . 'The Hashish-Eater', a much-misunderstood poem, . . . was intended as a study in the possibilities of cosmic consciousness, drawing heavily on myth and fable for its imagery. It is my own theory that if the infinite worlds of the cosmos were opened to human vision, the visionary would be overwhelmed by horror in the end, like the hero of this poem" ("Letters from Auburn," *Klarkash-Ton* No. 1 [June 1988]: 22). For an exhaustively annotated edition of the poem, see *The Hashish-Eater*, ed. Donald Sidney-Fryer (New York: Hippocampus Press, 2008).

CAS wrote an "Argument of 'The Hashish-Eater'" (first published in *SS* 245–26): "By some exaltation and expansion of cosmic consciousness, rather than a mere drug, used here as a symbol, the dreamer is carried to a height from which he beholds the strange and multiform scenes of existence in alien worlds; he maintains control of his visions, evokes and dismisses them at will. Then, in a state similar to the Buddhic plane, he is able to mingle with them and identify himself with their actors and objects. Still later, there is a transition in which the visions, and the monstrous and demonic forces he has evoked, begin to overpower him, to hurry him on helplessly, under circumstances of fright and panic. Armies of fiends and monsters, many drawn from the worlds of myth and fable, muster against him, pursue him through a terrible cosmos, and he is driven at last to the verge of a gulf into which falls in cataracts the ruin and rubble of the universe; a gulf from which the face of infinity itself, in all its awful blankness, beyond stars and worlds, beyond created things, even fiends and monsters, rises up to confront him."

For Armageddon (l. 40), see note on "After Armageddon." For Asmodai (l. 48), see note on "Interrogation"; Set is, in Egyptian myth, an animal-headed god, the god of darkness, night, and evil, and the brother, opponent, and slayer of Osiris. For Ombos (l. 57), see note on "Ombos." For "Antarean" (l. 66), see note on "The Star-Treader." Hecatompylos (l. 176) means "hundred-gated" in Greek; it is usually an attribute of the city of Thebes. For Achernar (l. 202), see note on "Demogorgon." Narcissus (l. 287), in Greek myth, is a lovely boy who, as punishment for the rejection of the love of Echo, fell in love with his own image as seen in a pool of water and wasted away. For Typhon and Enceladus (l. 314), see note on "Saturn." For "Aidennic" (l. 343), see note on "October." Antenora (l. 355) refers to a section of Cocytus (l. 365), the ninth and lowest circle of Hell in Dante's *Inferno*, where traitors to there are found (it is named after Antenor, an elder in Homer's *Iliad* who recommended that Helen be returned to the Greeks; later tradition made him a traitor to the Trojans). Cocytus was, in Greek myth, one of the rivers of the Greek underworld. For Babel (l. 369), see note on "The City of Destruction." For Afrit (l. 423), see note on "Dominion." For Rutilicus (l. 429), see note on "Demogorgon." Alioth (l. 438) is a star in the constellation Ursa Major. For Saiph (l. 446), see note on "Demogorgon." For Kobold (l. 505), see note on "The Ghoul and the Seraph."

Haunting (There is no peace amid the moonlight and the pines:). MS (JHLS; NYPL). *Lyric West* 1, No. 10 (February 1922): 6. In *EC*, *SP. Written before 24 April 1918.

Hearth on Old Cabin-Site. In *SP*.

Heliogabalus. MS (NYPL). In *SP (as a translation of "Christophe des Laurières"). CAS sent the poem (comprising two sonnets) to GS on 28 August 1919. GS commented: "As I intimated, your sonnets seemed very poetical to me, nor can I come on anything I'd care to see changed. I note you're wavering between 'glad, intolerable' and 'unimaginable.' ¶ What on earth put you up to glorifying that idiotic pervert Heliogabalus?" (letter to CAS, 27 September 1919; *SU* 175). As for their source, see CAS's letter to SL (6 August

1919; ms., BL): "Glad you liked the sonnets on Heliogabalus. I shall dedicate them to you, if they are ever published—and providing you are not afraid of the dedication! Without your suggestion, I should scarcely have thought of writing them. I know little enough about the gentleman, apart from the reference in [Edgar Saltus's] 'Imperial Purple,' and a long, minutely excoriating review of the Stuart Hay book you mention. The review, I believe, was in the London 'Academy,' but I am unable to lay hands upon it at present. The reviewer, after the manner of his kind, gloated with a fearful rapture over the details that he decried." The book referred to is *The Amazing Emperor Heliogabalus* (1911) by John Stuart Hay, which SL said he was attempting to procure for CAS (SL to CAS, 4 February 1918; ms., JHL). It does not appear that SL actually sent the book to CAS. Heliogabalus (more properly Elagabalus), Emperor of Rome (218–22 C.E.), became so notorious for the obscene rites he practiced in worship of the Syro-Phoenician sun-god from whom he took his name that he was killed by the Praetorian Guard. It is not clear what GS's comment on "glad, intolerable" vs. "unimaginable" refers to. For "Pentelic" (l. 7), see note on "The Blindness of Orion." Hermaphroditus (l. 20) was, in Greek myth, the son of Hermes and Aphrodite and reputedly had both male and female sexual organs. See SL's long poem *The Hermaphrodite* (1926).

Hellenic Sequel. MS (JHLS). *Arkham Sampler* 1, No. 1 (Spring 1948): 22. In *SP, DC.

La Hermosura. MS (JHLS). The poem is a translation of "Beauty."

The Heron. MS (JHLS). In *SP.

Hesperian Fall. MS (AH; JHLS [2 mss., one as "Hesperian Autumn"). In *DC, HD, SSU. Written before 22 February 1951.

The Hidden Paradise. MS (JHLS; NYPL). In *EC*, *SP. The ms. is dated 24 May 1921.

High Mountain Juniper. MS (AH). In *SP. See "Strange Miniatures."

High Surf. *Lyric* 37, No. 2 (Spring 1957): 42. In *S&P. "Walls / Of Jericho" (ll. 1–2) refer to Jericho, a city in Palestine that was captured by Joshua after he destroyed its walls. Cipango (l. 9) is the name given by Marco Polo for an island east of Asia—a possible reference to Japan. For Cathay (l. 9), see note on "Beyond the Great Wall."

High Surf: Monterey Bay. In *SC*.

The Hill of Dionysus. MS (DAW; JHLS [as "Hill of Dionysus"]; SHSW [as "Hill of Dionysus"]). In *SP, HD, LO. The ms. is dated 5 November 1942. In Greek myth, Dionysus is the son of Zeus and Semele, and his worship was associated with intoxication, ecstasy, and even madness. For Anteros (l. 40), see note on "Anteros."

The Hill-Top. MS (DAW; JHLL; JHLS). In *The Laureate's Wreath: An Anthology in Honor of Dr. Henry Meade Bland, Poet Laureate of California,* ed. The Edwin Markham Poetry Society (San Jose: The Edwin Markham Poetry Society, 1934), p. 108. In *The Golden Year: A Calendar of the Poets,* ed. Rufus Rockwell Wilson (NY: Wilson-Erickson, 1936): 15. In *SP. In *The Music Makers,* ed. Stanton A. Coblentz (New York: Bernard Ackerman, 1945), pp. 225–26. The ms. is dated 21 March 1929.

The Hope of the Infinite. MS (JHLS; NYPL). In *EC, *SP, LO.* First title: "Esperance." The ms. is dated 17 September 1919.

The Horizon. MS (JHLS). *Overland Monthly* 58, No. 2 (August 1911): 119 (as by C. Ashton Smith). In *SSU.* One ms. is titled "The Horizon Line."

The Horologe. MS (JHLS; FSC). In *SP.* In *FSC* 186.

The Hosts of Heaven. MS (JHLS).

Humors of Love. MS (DAW; JHLS; SHSW). *Saturday Review of Literature* 29, No. 33 (17 August 1946): 11. In *SP, HD.* Written before 29 October 1941. In l. 12, CAS refers to Jonathan Swift (1667–1745) and François Rabelais (1494?–1553?), authors known for their humorous and satirical writings. In l. 14, he refers to Giovanni Boccaccio (1313–1375), author of the *Decameron.*

A Hunter Meets the Martichoras. MS (AH; DAW). In *SP, S&P.* See "Strange Miniatures" and "Strange Miniatures (Haiku)." A martichora (variant spelling of "manticore") is a fabulous creature with the head of a man, the body of a lion, the quills of a porcupine, and the tail of a scorpion.

Hymn. MS (JHLS; another in copy no. 7 of *HD* [JHL]). In the dedication, "Puliakamon" is unidentified.

I Shall Not Greatly Grieve. MS (JHLS; one ms. as "Haply I Shall Not Greatly Grieve"). The ms. is dated 5 August 1952. "Sirian" (l. 15) refers to Sirius (see note on "Chant to Sirius").

Idylle païenne [English]. MS (JHLL). An English translation of "Idylle païenne" (p. 281).

Idylle païenne [French]. MS (JHLL; JHLS [as "Païennerie"]). First title: "Païennerie." An early version of "Paysage païen" (p. 400).

If Winter Remain. MS (AH; JHLS; RAH). In *SP.* The ms. is dated 26 January 1949. "Polarian" (l. 10) refers to Polaris (see note on "Outlanders"). "Canopic" (l. 12) is an adjectival form of Canopus (see note on "Cleopatra").

Lo Ignoto. MS (*JHLS). In *DD*. The ms. is dated 22 May 1950. For CAS's English translation, see "The Unknown." The Spanish version probably was written first.

Illumination. MS (JHLS; SHSW). In *SP, HD*. The ms. is dated 9 September 1943.

Illuminatus. Tr. (DSF).

Illusion. MS (DAW; *JHLS; NYPL). Written c. 1910.

Image. MS (JHLS; NYPL). In *EC*, *SP*. Written before 24 April 1918.

Imagination. MS (JHLS [first page only]; *NYPL). In *LO*. For "Nereid" (l. 31), see note on "The Nereid." For "Cyclopean" (l. 60), see note on "Desire of Vastness." The ms has several notes written by GS. Cf. "Ode on Imagination" (p. 109).

Immortelle. MS (*JHLS). *AJ* 25, No. 10 (18 December 1924): 4. In *SC*. The ms. is dated 2 September 1924.

Impression. MS (JHLS; NYPL). In *EC*. In *Great Poems of the English Language*, comp. Wallace Alvin Briggs (New York: Robert M. McBride, 1927; London: George C. Harrap & Co., 1928), p. 1338; rev. ed. New York: Tudor Publishing Co., 1936, p. 1338. In *SP*. The ms. is dated 20 November 1916. CAS sent GS this poem c. August 1917. GS commented: "'Impression' is absolute—very Gallic" (letter to CAS, 19 September 1917; *SU* 152).

Improbable Dream. MS (AH; DAW; JHLS). In *SP*. See "Eight Haiku," "Haiku," and "Strange Miniatures." In 1940, the Sisters of Mercy moved their motherhouse to and established a novitiate at the Teagarden Ranch in Auburn. CAS alludes to the convent in this haiku and also "Spring Nunnery" and "Nuns Walking in the Orchard."

In a Distant Universe. MS (JHLS). An English translation of "Dans l'univers lointain." Written before 7 December 1949. The only extant ms. is burnt, so that the second stanza is partly illegible.

In Alexandria. In *SP* (as a translation of "Christophe des Laurières").

In Another August. MS (SHSW). The ms. is dated 11 September 1942. The poem apparently belongs to the *Hill of Dionysus* cycle.

In Autumn. MS (JHLS). The ms. is dated 9 September 1924.

In Extremis. MS (JHLS). The title is Latin for "In the final throes [i.e., of death]." CAS has written a stanza between the first and second stanzas, but later crossed it out: "Strange tho it seem I feel no fear, / And yet I know the light / With nearing dark grows narrower / And soon will end in night."

In Lemuria. MS (JHLS; NYPL). *Lyric West* 1, No. 4 (July–August 1921): 6. In *EC*, *SP. *Outré* No. 3 (c. 1956): 24. In *LO*. The ms. is dated 24 December 1919. For Lemuria, see note on "Mirrors." CAS sent the poem to GS on 27 December 1919; GS commented: "'In Lemuria' is a gorgeous thing. I greatly like 'Pallid and pure as jaspers from the moon' [l. 14]" (letter to CAS, 20 January 1920; *SU* 179).

In November. MS (JHLS; NYPL). *Ainslee's* 44, No. 5 (December 1919): 121. In *EC. Written before 24 April 1918.

In Saturn. MS (JHLS; NYPL [as "Upon the Seas of Saturn"]). *Sonnet* 2, No. 2 (January–February 1919): 2. In *EC*, *SP, *LO*. Written before 24 April 1918. First title: "Upon the Seas of Saturn."

In Slumber. MS (MCL; SHSW). *WT* 24, No. 2 (August 1934): 253. In *SP, *DC*. Written before 21 January 1934. Styx (l. 7) is one of the rivers in the Greek underworld. For Maremma (l. 11), see note on "Ave atque Vale."

In the Desert. In *SP, *LO*. For "Cimmerian" (l. 8), see note on "Ode on Imagination."

In the Grip of Dreams. See "Said the Dreamer."

[In the Ultimate Valleys.] MS (*JHLS [untitled]). In *UV*. Written 17 December 1912. In *UV* the first stanza is repeated at the end.

In the Wind. MS (JHLS). *Poetry* 6, No. 4 (July 1915): 178. In *SP.

In Thessaly. MS (JHLL; JHLS; MCL; SHSW). *WT* 26, No. 5 (November 1935): 551. In *DM* 344–45. In *SP, *LO*. The ms. is dated 24 May 1935. In ancient Greece, the province of Thessaly was reputed to be the haven of witches. For Hecate (l. 3), see note on "The Witch in the Graveyard." "Golden Ass" (l. 9) refers to the *Metamorphoses*, a novel by Lucius Apuleius (2nd century C.E.), usually translated as *The Golden Ass*. It tells of a man who goes to Thessaly and is turned into an ass, finally returning to human form by eating roses.

In Time of Absence. MS (JHLS). The ms. is dated 20 June 1952.

Incantation. See *The Dead Will Cuckold You*.

Incognita. MS (DAW; JHLL; JHLS; NYPL; Sx). *AJ* 25 No. 25 (2 April 1925): 12. In *S. Step Ladder* 13, No. 5 (May 1927): 137. In *SP. Written 15 January 1925. The ms. is dated 15 January 1925. Variant title: "Unique." The title is the feminine singular form of the Latin adjective *incognitus* ("unknown"). CAS sent the poem to GS on 6 March 1925. GS commented: "'Incognita' is *subtle*. I wish you'd try it on the 'Dial.' But change the 'thou'—no magazine will take anything, any more, with 'thou' or 'thy' in it—the more shame to the time-serving swine!" (letter to CAS, 8 March 1925; *SU* 248). CAS used "thou" in lines 2 and 13 in *S*, but changed them to "you" for *SP*.

The Incubus of Time. MS (DAW; JHLS; NYPL; FSC). In *SP. In FSC [184]–85. In LO. Tantalus (l. 5) was a son of Zeus who offended the gods and was therefore punished by being sent to Tartarus, where, in hunger and thirst, he was set in a pool of water that always receded when he attempted to drink from it and where fruit hung down from branches just out of his reach.

Indian Acorn-Mortar. In SP.

Indian Summer. MS (JHLS). In SP.

Ineffability. MS (JHLL; JHLS; MCL). In *SP. First title: "Ineffabilité." The ms. is dated 18 September 1929.

Inferno. MS (JHLL; NYPL). In EC, *SP. The ms. is dated 24 April 1918. CAS sent this poem and "Mirrors" to GS on 17 May 1918, noting that they are "in the metre you dislike" (SU 161), i.e., the alexandrine. GS, in reply, noted that he preferred "Mirrors" to "Inferno" (letter to CAS, 10 June 1918; SU 162). In his pseudonymous review of EC in the San Fransico Bulletin (19 December 1922; as by George Douglas), GS wrote: "Baudelaire himself might have written such things as would make the Alexandrine sonnets 'Inferno' and 'Mirrors' read like perfect translations" (cited in SU 291).

The Infinite Quest. MS (JHLS). Lyric West 1, No. 4 (July–August 1921): 6. In EC, *SP, BS. One ms. has the title "The Unfinished Quest."

Inheritance. MS (MCL; NYPL). In EC, *SP. CAS sent this poem and "Memnon at Midnight" to GS on 11 March 1915. GS commented: "The poems you sent are all good—that 'slow to leave the tavern of thy brain' [l. 16] is terrific" (letter to CAS, 14 April 1915; SU 121). CAS noted (letter to SL, 7 October 1916; ms., BL) that the poem was rejected by the Atlantic Monthly.

Initiate of Dionysus. MS (AH; as "Initiate"). See "Pagans Old and New" and "Strange Miniatures." For Dionysus, see note on "The Hill of Dionysus." The "Mysteries" (l. 3) refer to the Eleusinian Mysteries, a secret religious rite devoted to Demeter and Persephone but also invoking Dionysus.

The Inscription (Science hath found the secret key). MS (JHLS). For Ur (l. 4), see note on "Antony to Cleopatra." Nineveh (l. 3) was the longtime capital of the Assyrian Empire, founded no later than 1950 B.C.E. and overrun in 608 B.C.E. by the Medes and Babylonians.

Interim. MS (DAW; MStC; SHSW). Scienti-Snaps 3, No. 1 (February 1940): 14. AJ 69, No 100 (13 November 1941): 5 (last 10 lines omitted). Wings 5, No. 3 (Autumn 1941): 12. In SP, *HD. Written before 22 February 1940.

Interrogation. MS (JHLL [fragment]; NYPL; *Sx). In S. WT 10, No. 3 (September 1927): 414. In Principal Poets of the World, vol. 1: 1930–1931 (London: Mitre Press, 1932), p. 182. In SP, LO. The ms. is dated 14 September 1925.

Alastor (l. 9) (Greek for "avenger") is a supernatural entity who exacts vengeance for a crime (cf. Shelley's *Alastor; or, The Spirit of Solitude*, 1816); Asmodai is a variant spelling of Asmodeus (Hebrew Ashmodai), a destructive demon in Jewish demonology. For "Erebus" (l. 12), see note on "The City of the Titans." The line "like the souls on Dante's wind of woe" (l. 15) appears to refer to a passage in Dante's *Inferno:* "And like the winds of some unresting wood, / The gathered murmur from those depths of woe / Soughed upward into thunder" (4.9–11; tr. S. Fowler Wright).

Interval. MS (JHLS). The ms. is dated 20 April 1943.

The Invisible Host. *Farm Journal* 35, No. 5 (November 1911): 546.

Iris. See "Alienage."

Isaac Newton. MS (JHLS). The poem is addressed to Sir Isaac Newton (1642–1727), British natural philosopher whose three laws of motion revolutionized the science of his day.

La Isla de Circe. MS (JHLS). In *SSU*. Written 24 September 1950. For an English translation, see "The Isle of Circe." For Circe, see note on "Belated Love."

La Isla del náufrago. MS (*JHLS). In *DD*. The ms. is dated 18 December 1953. For an English translation, see "Isle of the Shipwrecked."

The Island of a Dream. MS (JHLS).

The Isle of Circe. MS (JHLS). In *SSU*. Written 1950. An English translation of the Spanish poem "La Isla de Circe."

The Isle of Saturn. MS (JHLS). In *DC, BB, SZ*. Written 1950. The epigraph is from Plutarch's essay "On the Face Appearing in the Orb of the Moon" (sec. 26), in *Moralia*. Clio and Euterpe (l. 2) are the Muses of history and lyric poetry, respectively. "Xanthic" (l. 8) refers to the Greek word *xanthos* (yellow). "Pontus" (l. 45) refers to the Sea of Pontus (the Black Sea). For Tartarus (l. 50), see note on "The Return of Hyperion." The ms. contains a second section:

> II
> Round Saturnia wax the surges,
> Wonder-teeming, fraught with fable.
> Horned monoceros, crowned sea-serpent,
> Milky, fathom-foiling kraken,
> Spawn of Pontus, dynasts of oceans,
>
> Gilled and finned and deep-sea-colored, fulvous,
> Rising, loll on kelp-lined reefs,
> Sprawl on beeches broad and sun-struck;
> Swimmers of dim under-streams,

That have talked with dungeoned god in Tartarus.

Isle of the Shipwrecked. MS (JHLS). An English translation of "La Isla del náufrago."

January Willow. MS (JHLS). In *SP*.

Jungle Twilight. MS (JHLL [15 lines only]; JHLS [2 AMS versions: 10 lines and 15 lines (as "Night in the Jungle"); TMS 15 lines with five AMS lines added]). *Oriental Stories* 2, No. 3 (Summer 1932): 420 (15 lines only). In *SP*, *S&P, LO*. Written early September 1930.

Kin. MS (JHLS).

The Kingdom of Shadows. In *EC, *SP, LO*. CAS may be referring to this poem when he writes: "'The Kingdom of Madness' is symbolical of a spiritual (or emotional) state" (CAS to SL, 7 October 1916; ms., BL).

The Knoll. *Kansas City Poetry Magazine* 4, No. 4 (January 1944): 4. In *SP*, *HD*. Dodona (l. 7) was a city in the Greek province of Epirus and the site of one of the most famous oracular shrines in the ancient world. The oracle was devoted to Zeus, not to Apollo, as CAS suggests in l. 8 (the oracle at Delphi was devoted to Apollo).

Knowledge. See "Connaissance."

Le Lac d'automne. Tr. (DSF). A French translation of "The Autumn Lake." Written c. 1928.

Lament of the Stars. In *ST*.

Lamia. MS (JHLS; SHSW). *Arkham Sampler* 1, No. 1 (Winter 1948): [20]. In *SP*, *DC, LO, SSU*. The ms. is dated 24 January 1940. *Lamia* is a Latin word referring to a witch, sorceress, or enchantress. Cf. Keats's poem *Lamia* (1820).

The Land of Evil Stars. MS (JHLS). In *EC, *SP, LO*. CAS sent the poem to GS on 19 February 1913. GS commented: ". . . there is much beauty in 'The Land of Evil Stars,' though it has a pretty strong flavor of Poe" (letter to CAS, 17 March 1913; *SU* 83). In his pseudonymous review of *EC* in the *San Francisco Bulletin* (see note on "Inferno"), GS writes that the poem "is so like Poe it might have been foisted on an innocent world as a long lost manuscript of our surest immortal" (cited in *SU* 291).

The Last Apricot. MS (AH; JHLS). In *SP, S&P*. See "Distillations," "Eight Haiku," and "Strange Miniatures."

The Last Goddess. MS (JHLS). In *SP, LO*. CAS appears to have sent the poem to GS on 26 September 1912, under the title "A Fragment." GS (letter to CAS, 4 October 1912) noted the use of the obscure word "nenuphar"

(l. 13), saying that it "is a bit puzzling—I had to look it up in the dictionary" (*SU* 66). For "Circean" (l. 3), see note on "Belated Love."

The Last Night. MS (NYPL). *Town Talk* No. 972 (15 April 1911): 8 (in Edward F. O'Day, "Varied Types: XVII—George Sterling"). In *ST. Science Fiction Fandom* (Winter 1940). In *SP, LO*. CAS sent this poem (with others) to GS on 2 February 1911. GS commented: ". . . you will not set any great value on any of these enclosed poems (good as some of them are), except in the case of 'The Last Night.' There is actual performance" (letter to CAS, 28 February 1911; *SU* 20). GS quoted the entire poem in his interview with Edward F. O'Day, remarking: "This boy has a wonderful gift, if I know anything about such things."

The Last Oblivion. MS (JHLS; Sx). *AJ* 24, No. 17 (7 February 1924): 6. In *S*, *SP, LO*. First title: "Oblivion."

Late November Evening. In *SP*.

Late Pear-Pruner. MS (AH; DAW; JHLS). In *SP, S&P*. See "Distillations," "Haiku," and "Vignettes and Indexes."

Laus Mortis. MS (NYPL). *Pearson's Magazine* 47, No. 3 (September 1921): 100. In *EC*, *SP, LO*. CAS sent the poem to GS on 2 March 1919, noting that he wrote the poem in February. The title is Latin for "The Praise of Death."

Lawn-Mower. *SS* A:3. In *SC*. "Procrustean beds" (l. 4) refers to the Greek myth of Procrustes, a brigand who seized strangers under the guise of hospitality and tied them to a bed, cutting off their limbs if they were too tall for it. Written c. 1954–55.

Lemurienne. MS (NYPL and JHLS under "Tankas"; *Sx). *AJ* 24, No. 10 (20 December 1923): 6 (as "The Lemurienne"). In *SP. Arkham Collector* No. 3 (Summer 1968): 57 (as "The Lemurienne"). For Lemuria, see note on "Mirrors."

The Lemurienne. MS (JHLS under "Tankas"). Perhaps a very early version of "Lemurienne." The ms. is dated 16 November 1923.

Leteo. MS (JHLS). For an English translation, see "Lethe."

Lethe (I flow beneath the columns that upbear). MS (JHLS). In *ST*, *SP, LO*. In Hesiod, Lethe is the personification of forgetfulness. In later Greek tradition, Lethe is a place of oblivion in the underworld. In the Roman poets, Lethe becomes one of the five rivers of the underworld.

Lethe (Seekst thou that Lethe of whose depths profound). MS (JHLS). *Rosary Magazine* 39, No. 5 (November 1911): 555.

[Lethe] (Somber and waveless on the waters). MS (JHLS, on verso of "Leteo"). An English translation of "Leteo."

Lethe (From the nameless dark distilled,). MS (AH; *JHLS). See "Strange Miniatures" (there titled "Oblivion").

Lichens. MS (DAW; JHLL; JHLS; SHSW). *Wings* 1, No. 2 (Summer 1933): 7. *Berkeley Daily Gazette* (1933?). *Stars* (December 1940–January 1941): 2. In *SP, SSU*. The ms. is dated 8 February 1929. For Cathay (l. 7), see note on "Beyond the Great Wall." Tang (l. 8) refers to the dynasty that ruled China from 618 to 906. During its reign, literature and the arts flourished as never before. For Ming (l. 8), see note on "On a Chinese Vase."

Limestone Cavern. Tr. (DSF).

The Limniad. MS (AH; DAW). In *SP. See "Strange Miniatures" and "Strange Miniatures (Haiku)." A limniad is a lake nymph.

Lines on a Picture. MS (SHSW; JHLS [as "To Lilith"]). *Raven* 2, No. 1 (Spring 1944): 22. In *SP. The ms. is dated 3 January 1944. First title: "To Lilith." The "picture" that inspired the poem was a photograph of the poet Lilith Lorraine, sent by her to CAS. Sybil (l. 2) (CAS's error for Sibyl, made also in the story "The White Sybil" [1932]) was the general name given by the Greeks and Romans to a prophetess.

A Live-Oak Leaf. In *ST*. CAS copied this poem in his letter to GS, 6 October 1911 (*SU* 32).

Lives of the Saints. MS (JHLS). Early draft titled "Censored." The subtitle refers to Ogden Nash (1902–1971), American comic poet who attained celebrity by his whimsical light verse, usually in quatrains.

Loss. MS (DAW; JHLS; NYPL; *Sx). In *S. United Amateur* 25, No. 2 (May 1926): 8. In *SP*. The ms. is dated 30 January 1925. CAS sent the poem to GS, with others, on 6 March 1925. GS commented: "And 'Loss' is very beautiful. Of course 'eloigned' [l. 10] would give any magazine editor the Melanesian pip!" (letter to CAS, 8 March 1925; *SU* 248).

Lost Beauty. MS (JHLS).

Lost Farmsteads. MS (JHLS). For a Spanish version of the poem, see "Las Alquerías perdidas" (p. 576).

Love and Death. MS (DAW, on ms. titled "Quintrains"; JHLS [fragment]). In *SP.

Love in Dreams. MS (AH; DAW; JHLS). In *SP. See "Haiku," "Pulse-Beats of Eros," and "Strange Miniatures."

Love Is Not Yours, Love Is Not Mine. In *EC. Step Ladder* 13, No. 5 (May 1927): 134–5. In *SP. First title: "Song." The ms. is dated 25 June 1922.

Love Malevolent. MS (NYPL). *Live Stories* (1916) [not seen]. In *EC. Step Ladder* 13, No. 5 (May 1927): 134. In *LO. It may have been about this poem that

CAS wrote: "I wonder if such poetic deviltry really offends people, in spite of their loud and disgusting pretence of being shocked. It seems to me that many must find it more entertaining than the ordinary banalities. . . . Apropos of some of the things in the sonnet, did you know that mandragora [l. 9] was at one time in great repute as an aphrodisiac? I don't remember to have seen any poetic reference to the fact. Few will get the full force of the lines in which I've made use of this" (CAS to SL, 13 June 1915; ms., BL).

The Love-Potion. See *The Fugitives.*

Luna Aeternalis. MS (DAW; JHLS; UCLA). In *SP. WT* 42, No. 4 (May 1950): 43. In **DC, LO.* Written 12 December 1912; rev. 1948. CAS writes to GS (13 December 1912): "I enclose a rather fantastic experiment, in which I've tried the regular repetition of lines and phrases, and a desultory rhyming of words with themselves. I don't remember seeing it done this way before— only in an arbitrary stanza, as in Poe. I don't know that I've succeeded in making anything of it" (*SU* 74). In a later letter (16 December 1912), CAS made some revisions, but they do not correspond with the text as currently extant. CAS gives the beginning of the second stanza as follows: "Self-shadowed half, upstood the moon, / Yea, tarnished half; but soon / Had her soft light stilled the stars to croon, / Had her low light . . ." (*SU* 75). GS commented (letter to CAS, 18 December 1912): "The poem itself should (or might) have been discovered in one of Poe's old trunks—if the poor fellow had any. In fact, it's so absolutely an echo of Poe that it's more of a curiosity than a credit to you. But soon you will be beyond the 'derivative' stage" (*SU* 75). It appears that CAS at some later time reduced the "repetition of lines and phrases." The title (in Latin) translates to "The Eternal Moon." "Uriel" (l. 32) is one of the seven archangels in Christian legendry. See the apocryphal 1 Enoch 20:1–8. In some apocryphal literature he is referred to as an angel of light. Cf. CAS's comment in a letter to GS (8 June 1913): "I'm beginning a short narrative poem, 'Uriel', the story of the compassionate angel who intercedes with God for the wretchedness of Man, and rebels because of God's equivocal answer. It's a rather new idea, I think" (*SU* 90). The poem apparently was never written.

Lunar Mystery. MS (Sx). In *S, *SP, GF* (as "Dream-Mystery"), *LO.* First title: "Dream-Mystery." The poem is dated 5 July 1915 in *GF.*

The Mad Wind. *San Francisco Call* (2 August 1912): 2. In *ST, *SP.*

Madrigal (Low-lidded eyes thou hast,). MS (DAW; NYPL). In **SP* (as a translation of "Christophe des Laurières"). Written c. 14 September 1925.

Madrigal (You are the golden guerdon). MS (MStC). See "Paean."

A Madrigal. MS (*JHLS [as "Un Madrigal"]). In *SC.* For a French translation, see "Un Madrigal" (p. 279). It is unclear which version was written first.

Un Madrigal. MS (DAW [as "Madrigal"]; *JHLL; JHLS). For an English version, see "A Madrigal" (p. 279).

Madrigal of Evanescence. MS (JHLS). *Kaleidoscope* 2, No. 11 (March 1931): 3. In *SP.

Madrigal of Memory. MS (DAW; SHSW). *Kaleidograph* 13, No. 9 (January 1942): 7. In *SP. Written 15 July 1941.

Malediction. MS (AH; JHLS). In *DC, SSU.

La Mare. MS (JHLL). In *SP. The ms. is dated 3 August 1929. For CAS's English translation, see "The Pool" (p. 453).

Les Marées. MS (JHLS). In *SP. The ms. is dated 24 July 1929. The title is French for "The Tides."

The Masque of Forsaken Gods. In *ST, *SP. The gods in question are Jove (Roman god, also named Jupiter, and later equated with Zeus, chief of the Olympian gods); Pan (Greek god of shepherds and flocks); Artemis (Greek goddess with a variety of functions and attributes; see also the poem "Artemis" [p. 235]); Apollo (Greek god of healing and music, the twin brother of Artemis); Aphrodite (Greek goddess of love); Atè (not a goddess as such, but the Greek personification of blindness or delusion); and nymphs (Greek personifications of natural objects, such as trees, rivers, or mountains). "Huntress" (l. 14) refers to Artemis, frequently depicted as a virgin huntress. Diana (l. 23) is a Roman goddess later equated with Artemis. "Echo" (l. 58) refers to a nymph unsuccessfully wooed by Pan. In l. 86 ("born of sound and foam"), CAS follows a tradition first found in Hesiod (*Theogony* 195–200) stating that Aphrodite was born of the foam in the sea that gathered around the severed parts of the god Uranus. (Other traditions declare Aphrodite to be the daughter of Zeus and Dione.) The citation of Syria (l. 89) alludes to the identification of Aphrodite with the Asian goddess Astarte. L. 105 refers to Pygmalion, the legendary king of Crete who fell in love with a statue and begged Aphrodite to bring it to life, which she did. It is only in Ovid (*Metamorphoses* 10.243f.) that Pygmalion is cited as the actual fashioner of the statue.

Maternal Prostitute. Tr. (DSF).

Maya. MS (DAW; JHLL; JHLS; NYPL; *Sx). *AJ* 25, No. 23 (19 March 1925): 4. In *S. Step-Ladder* 13, No. 5 (May 1927): 135. *Helios* 1, No. 3 (October–November–December 1937): 11. In *SP, LO*. CAS sent the poem to GS on 6 March 1925. GS commented: "'Maya' is excellent too. It reminds me of [Francis] Saltus' 'The chuckle of Satan in Chaos'" (letter to CAS, 8 March 1925; *SU* 248). The word of the title is a term in the Vedantic religion of India meaning "illusion" or "appearance," referring to the illusion of multiplicity in the empirical world.

The Maze of Sleep. In *ST*, **SP*.

The Meaning. MS (NYPL [as "The Mystic Meaning"]). In *ST* (as "The Mystic Meaning"), **SP*. *Los Angeles Science Fantasy Society Newsletter* (23 February 1964) (as "The Mystic Meaning"). Written c. 1911. First title: "The Mystic Meaning."

Medusa. MS (MCL). In *ST*. *Fantasy Fan* 2, No. 3 (November 1934): 46–7. In *N1*, **SP*, *LO*. The ms. is dated 17 May 1911. In Greek myth, Medusa was one of the three Gorgons, whose gaze would turn people into stone. See also "The Medusa of the Skies" (p. 107) and "The Medusa of Despair" (p. 139). "Tellurian" (l. 12) is a synonym for "earthly" or "terrestrial" (from the Latin *tellus*, earth).

The Medusa of Despair. MS (MCL; JHLS). *Town Talk* No. 1113 (20 December 1913): 8. In *OS*, *EC*, **SP*, *LO*. CAS referred to the poem as "easily my most terrific [i.e., terrifying] sonnet" (letter to SL, 1 August 1913; ms., BL). He sent the poem, along with others, to GS on 8 June 1913. GS commented: "But biggest of all is this great 'Medusa of Despair,' a truly terrible sonnet. It's clearer than most of your sonnets, too, and ends wonderfully" (letter to CAS, 22 June 1913; *SU* 91). Evidently GS submitted the poem to *Town Talk* (see *SU* 99). For "Cimmerian" (l. 11), see note on "Ode on Imagination."

The Medusa of the Skies. In *ST*, **SP*, *LO*. The poem is about the moon, suggesting that its light turns all objects white, as if the Medusa had gazed upon them and turned them to stone. CAS later translated the poem into French as "La Méduse des cieux" (p. 288).

La Méduse des cieux (The Medusa of the Skies). MS (JHLL; **JHLS* [one ms. has the French title, another the English]). A French translation of "The Medusa of the Skies" (p. 107).

A Meeting. MS (JHLS). *AJ* 24, No. 12 (3 January 1924): 6. In **S*. First title: "To Columbine."

Melancholia. MS (JHLS). The only extant ms. is burned, rendering the concluding part of the poem illegible. For a Spanish translation, see "Añoranza."

The Melancholy Pool. In *EC*. *WT* 3, No. 3 (March 1924): 21. In **SP*, *LO*.

Memnon at Midnight. MS (JHLS; MCL; NYPL). In *OS*, *EC*. In *Songs and Stories*, ed. Edwin Markham (Los Angeles: Powell Publishing Company, 1931; Freeport, NY: Books for Libraries Press, 1974), p. 425. In **SP*, *LO*. Dedicated to Albert M[aurice] Bender (1866–1941), benefactor and friend of CAS. Written before 11 March 1915. For Memnon, see note on "Echo of Memnon." CAS sent the poem, with others, to GS on 11 March 1915. GS commented: "The poems you sent are all good . . . But I like best the sonnet 'Memnon at Midnight.' The sestet of that is sublime" (letter to CAS, 14 April 1915; *SU*

121). Toward the end of 1915 CAS wrote the prose-poem "The Memnons of the Night" (*NO* 14), which echoes some of the imagery of the sonnet.

Memoria roja. MS (*JHLS). In *DD*. Written 20 May 1950. For an English translation, see "Red Memory."

Memorial. MS (JHLS; NYPL; FSC). In **SP*. In *FSC* 185–86. Written before 24 April 1918.

Memorial to George Sterling. See "To George Sterling: A Valediction."

A Memory. MS (JHLS). Another stanza is found on the verso of the ms., but it does not appear to go with the poem: "As there in rapt commune we stood / The bulbul's song rose clear / From out the dark and scented wood, / And still I seem to hear / Its echo in mine ears / [Down?] faint and sweet adown the years."

The Messengers. MS (NYPL). CAS copied the poem in his letter to GS, 21 May 1911 (*SU* 26). GS commented: "'The Messengers' is a charming lyric. I especially love your exceedingly felicitous use of the verb 'dissolve' [l. 2]" (letter to CAS, 13 July 1911; *SU* 27).

Metaphor. MS (FSC). *AJ* 23, No. 34 (7 June 1923): 6. In **SP*. In *FSC* 185.

Metaphor. See "Simile" (Ah! chide me not for silence, or that I,).

Midnight Beach. MS (JHLS; SHSW). *Wings* 6, No. 7 (Autumn 1944): 14 (25 lines only). In *SP*, **HD, LO*. The ms. is dated 5 September 1943.

The Mime of Sleep. MS (JHLS; SHSW). *Acolyte* 1, No. 3 (Spring 1943): 6. In **SP*. The ms. is dated 28 July 1941. Salome (l. 11), in the Bible, was the daughter of Herodias and caused the death of John the Baptist by her seductive dancing (see Mark 6:14–29; Matt. 14:1–12).

Minatory. MS (*Sx). *AJ* 25, No. 29 (30 April 1925): 6 (16 lines only). In *S* (16 lines only). *Raven* 2, No. 3 (Autumn 1944): 17. In *SP, LO*. Lines 5–8 are not in *AJ* or *S*. Summanus (l. 17) is, in Roman myth, a god of thunderstorms. Demogorgon (l. 19) is a name devised in the early Renaissance period to denote the primeval god of ancient mythology; it is apparently a corruption of the name Demiurge (the creator god of the visible world in Plato's philosophical works).

The Ministers of Law. MS (JHLS). In *OS, EC,* **SP*. Title derives from l. 258 of GS's *The Testimony of the Suns*. Written 7 August 1913.

Mirage. MS (JHLS; MCL; NYPL). In *EC,* **SP*. For the Phoenix (l. 4), see note on "The City in the Desert." Ilion (l. 11) is the proper Greek name of the city rendered as Ilium in Latin, an alternate name for Troy (hence the source of the title of Homer's *Iliad*).

Le Miroir des blanches fleurs [English]. MS (*JHLL). In *LO*. The ms. is dated 9 August 1929. The title is French for "The Mirror of White Flowers." An English translation of a French poem of the same title.

Le Miroir des blanches fleurs [French]. MS (JHLS). Cf. CAS's English translation.

Mirrors. MS (NYPL). In *EC*, *SP*. See note on "Inferno." Lemuria (1. 7) was a putative sunken continent in the Pacific first conjectured by the zoologist P. L. Sclater to account for the existence of the fossils of lemurs and other animals and plants in both the Malay archipelago and the south coast of Asia and Madagascar. It was later taken up by numerous occultists, such as W. Scott-Elliot in *The Lost Lemuria* (1904). In 1. 8, "Alhambran" refers to a Muslim fortress and palace at Granada, Spain, begun in 1248 by Mohammed Ibn Al Ahmar and damaged after the expulsion of the Muslims from Spain in 1492.

The Mirrors of Beauty. MS (JHLS; NYPL). In *EC*, *SP*. The ms. is dated 23 April 1915. CAS sent this poem and "Moon-Dawn" to GS on 9 September 1915. GS commented that "There are some *fine* things in this last batch of yours," singling out 1. 14 (letter to CAS, 1 October 1915; *SU* 129). The Amazons (1. 3) were a legendary nation of female warriors, usually situated in northeast Asia, who fought the Greek heroes. The name derives from *a-* (without) and *mazon* (breast), referring to their purported custom of cutting off the right breast to facilitate the use of weapons (especially the bow and arrow) in battle. In 1. 6, "blades from Damascus" refers to the fact that steel from Damascus was highly sought during the Middle Ages for weaponry, especially swords and knives; Xanadu is the imaginary realm cited in Coleridge's "Kubla Khan" (1798), which, like CAS's "The City in the Desert" (p. 152), was transcribed from a dream.

Mithridates. MS (DAW; JHLS (one ms. under "Quintrains [2]"). In *SP, S&P*. Mithridates IV Eupator was a king of Pontus (r. 120–63 B.C.E.) who, facing death at the hands of the Romans, attempted to poison himself; but he had taken so many antidotes that the poison was ineffective, so he had a slave stab him. Cf. CAS's prose-poem "The Mithridate" (1929; *NU* 23).

Mito. See "Dos Mitos y una fábula."

Moly. MS (JHLS). In *SP. New Atheneum* (Fall 1950): n.p. In *DC*. The ms. is dated 2 December 1943. Moly is a fabulous herb said to have been given by Hermes to Odysseus as a charm against Circe.

Moments. MS (JHLS; NYPL). In *SP* (as a translation of "Christophe des Laurières"). CAS sent the poem, along with "Alienage," to GS on 23 June 1923 (see note on "Alienage"). GS commented: "One thing: I fear you'll have to make a change in the second stanza of 'Moments'. It's almost *comic* at the end—too literal; all one sees is the underwear. The poem is too lovely to have even one flaw in it" (letter to CAS, 29 June 1923; *SU* 233). It does not appear that CAS revised the poem.

The Monacle. MS (AH; DAW). In *SP, S&P*. See "Strange Miniatures" and "Strange Miniatures (Haiku)."

Moods of the Sea. MS (JHLS). In l. 10, CAS has left a blank space for a word never filled in.

The Moon. See "Moonlight."

Moon-Dawn. MS (JHLS [2 mss., one titled "The Red Moon"]; MCL; NYPL [as "The Red Moon"]; Sx). *WT* 2, No. 1 (July–August 1923): 48 (as "The Red Moon"). *AJ* 24, No. 15 (24 January 1924): 6 (as "The Red Moon"). In *S. Golden Atom* (December 1940). *SP, LO.* CAS sent the poem, with others, to GS on 9 September 1915. GS commented: "All the short poems that you enclose in this last letter seem good to me, especially 'Moon-Dawn' and 'The Mirrors of Beauty'" (letter to CAS, 1 October 1915; *SU* 129). GS went on to suggest "demons' ark" for "demon's ark" in l. 7, and CAS made the change. It is not clear why CAS waited until *S* to collect the poem. It was one of his first to be published in *WT*.

Moonlight. MS (JHLS). *Overland Monthly* 56, No. 2 (August 1910): 229. First title: "The Moon." CAS's first published poem. The ms. ends with the following lines: Her light all things enshrouds in mystery / And subtle glamour [   ] realms unknown / It seems a radiance from worlds that lie / Beyond our ken and glimpsed in dreams alone.

The Moonlight Desert. MS (*NYPL). In *LO.* Written before 2 February 1911. The poem was one of the first that CAS sent to GS (see *SU* 19). GS made two comments on the poem in a letter of 28 February 1911 (*SU* 20). The first—"I fear that use of that compound is impossible. It sounds most awkward to *me*"—refers to the compound "darkness-mystified" in l. 1, revised by CAS to read "dark-obscured." GS also notes that "'Burnt-out' [l. 6] is rather too commonplace."

Moon-Sight. MS (*JHLL; JHLS). Written 30 January 1929.

Morning on an Eastern Sea. MS (DAW; *JHLS). In *PJ.* CAS notes that the poem was written in 1915 (letter to GS, 20 June 1916; *SU* 137).

The Morning Pool. MS (NYPL). *San Francisco Call* (2 August 1912). In *ST.* Written c. 1912.

Morning Star of the Mountains. Tr. (DSF). See "Pagans Old and New."

Mors. MS (DAW; JHLS [one ms. as "Anodyne"]; MCL [as "Anodyne"]; NYPL [as "Anodyne"]). First title: "Anodyne." In *SP* (as a translation of

"Christophe des Laurières"). The ms. is dated 12 April 1918. The title is Latin for "Death."

La Mort des amants. MS (JHLS). In **SP.* See "Mortal Essences." The title is French for "The Death of Lovers." It is the title of one of the poems in Baudelaire's *Les Fleurs du mal,* translated by CAS (see Vol. 3, pp. 260–61).

Mortal Essences. MS (JHLS). In *SP* under "Experiments in Haiku." Comprises "Snake, Owl, Cat or Hawk"; "Plague from the Abatoir"; "La Mort des Amants"; "Vultures Come to the Ambarvalia"; "For the Dance of Death"; "Water-Hemlock"; and "Felo-de-se of the Parasite." *SP* lacks "Cattle Salute the Psychopomp"; "Field Behind the Abatoir"; and "Berries of the Deadly Nightshade."

The Motes. MS (NYPL). In *EC, *SP, LO.* CAS sent the poem to GS on 16 March 1922, saying that it "was written years ago" (*SA* 204). GS replied only that it was "very salable" (letter to CAS, 8 April 1922; *SU* 205). The poem, however, did not appear in a magazine.

Mountain Trail. MS (JHLS). In **SP.* See "Pulse-Beats of Eros."

The Mummy. MS (JHLS). *Sonnet* 4, No. 2 (May–June 1919): 3. In **EC, LO.* CAS notes that the poem was written in 1915 (letter to GS, 20 June 1916; *SU* 137). GS commented that it was "a pretty good sonnet" (letter to CAS, 8 July 1916; *SU* 138).

Mummy of the Flower. MS (JHLS, under "Quintrains"; "Quintrains [2]"). In **SP.*

La Muse moderne. MS (JHLS). Another poem satirizing modern poetry, especially its penchant for slangy or obscene diction. The title is French for "The Modern Muse."

Mushroom-Gatherers. MS (AH; JHLS). In **SP.* See "Eight Haiku" and "Strange Miniatures."

The Music of the Gods. MS (JHLS).

Mystery. MS (JHLL; JHLS). In **SP.*

The Mystic Meaning. See "The Meaning."

The Mystical Number. MS (JHLS). Another satire on modern poetry.

Nada. MS (JHLS). *Lyric* 37, No. 2 (Spring 1957): 42. In **S&P.* The ms. is dated 23 June 1952. The title is Spanish for "Nothing." The line "Recalling Lazarus from his room of stone" (l. 8) refers to the story in the Bible of Jesus' raising of Lazarus from the dead. The account is found only in the Gospel of John, where it is stated that Lazarus' tomb was "a cave, and a stone lay upon it" (11:38).

The Nameless Wraith. MS (JHLS [as "The Wraith of Beauty"]). In *SP. Arkham Sampler* 1, No. 1 (Winter 1948): 21. In *S&P, LO. First title: "The Wraith of Beauty." "Hesper" (l. 6) refers to Hesperus, the evening star.

Namelessness. Either non-extant or a variant title of an unidentified poem. Cf. CAS to GS, 18 October 1912: "I enclose one [poem] ('Namelessness') out of a bunch of brief lyrics that I've written lately" (*SU* 68). GS commented: "Your lyric is a delicate and beautiful one. I've no suggestions to make about it, except a half-wish that you'd add another verse and make it a little less tenuous" (letter to CAS, 26 October 1912; *SU* 69).

Nature's Orchestra. MS (JHLS).

Necromancy. MS (DAW; MCL; NYPL; SHSW). *Fantasy Fan* 1, No. 12 (August 1934): 188. *WT* 36, No. 10 (March 1943): 105. In *SP*, *S&P, LO. Written before 21 January 1934.

Neighboring Slaughter-House. MS (JHLS). In *IM*. Comprises "Cattle Salute the Psychopomp"; "Slaughter-House in Spring"; "Slaughter-House Pasture"; and "Behind the Abatoir." The poems were inspired by an old slaughter-house and stockyards located about a mile south of the Smith ranch.

The Nemesis of Suns. MS (SFPL). In *ST. The ms. is dated 10 January 1912.

Neptune. Either non-extant or a variant title of an unidentified poem. CAS sent the poem to GS c. July–August 1913 (see *SU* 93). GS commented: "The sonnet 'Neptune' you sent me is a fine thing, especially (as should be) the sestet" (letter to CAS, 19 August 1913; *SU* 94).

The Nereid. MS (JHLS; SU). *Yale Review* 2, No. 4 (July 1913): 685–86. In *EC*. In *California Poets: An Anthology of 224 Contemporaries* (New York: Henry Harrison, 1932), p. 665. In *SP, LO. CAS sent the poem to GS on 30 December 1912; GS commented that it was an "exquisite poem," going on to say: "I wish I could do as well before I die" (letter to CAS, 11 January 1913; *SU* 78). A nereid, in Greek myth, is a sea-maiden, one of the daughters of Nereus, a sea god. For CAS's much later Spanish translation of the poem, see "La Nereida" (p. 583).

La Nereida. MS (JHLS). The ms. is dated 27 June 1950. A Spanish translation of "The Nereid" (p. 129).

Nero. In *ST. In *Golden Songs of the Golden State*, ed. Marguerite Wilkinson (Chicago: A. C. McClurg & Co., 1917; rpt. Greak Neck, NY: Granger Book Co., 1979), pp. 116–20. In *The Book of Poetry*, ed. Edwin Markham (New York: William H. Wise & Co., 1926 [3 vols.], 1927 [2 vols.], 1928 [10 vols.]), pp. 749–50 (extracts; as "From Nero"); as *Anthology of the World's Best Poems* (New York: William H. Wise & Co., 1948 [6 vols.]), pp. 749–50. In *OS, N1, *SP, N2, LO. The poem is a monologue putatively spoken by Nero (Nero

Claudius Caesar, 37–68 C.E.), Emperor of Rome (54–68), who developed a reputation even in antiquity for his decadence and propensity to violence (he had his mother, Agrippina, killed in 59). Facing a revolt from the Praetorian Guards, he committed suicide on 9 June 68. CAS said of the poem that "It is the emperor's soliloquy after he has watched the burning of Rome" (letter to GS, 28 April 1912; *SU* 45), which occurred in 64. Suetonius (*Nero* 38) reports that Nero himself started the fire and sang an epic poem as Rome burned, but other historians dispute the assertion. When finishing the poem, CAS noted that "About four-fifths of it is prose, and not particularly good prose at that" (letter to GS, 26 May 1912; *SU* 47), but GS said of it, "I rank it higher even than your great odes. It has a maturity, a vertebration, a pertinancy and grasp beyond those other poems, and I'd give a reasonably-sized slice off one of my ears to have done anything so great for this many a year" (letter to CAS, 6 June 1912; *SU* 48).

Nest of the Screech-Owl. Tr. (DSF).

Nevermore. MS (DAW [as "Song"]). In **SP.*

The Nevermore-to-Be. MS (JHLL; JHLS [both as "Chatelaine"]). In **SP.* The ms. is dated 25 March 1927.

Night (The fires of sunset die reluctantly). MS (*JHLS; MH [2nd stanza only]; RAH). In *UV.* Written c. 1910.

The Night Forest. MS (BL). In *ST, *SP.*

Night in the Jungle. See "Jungle Twilight."

The Night of Despair. MS (JHLS).

Night of Miletus. MS (AH; DAW; JHLS). In **SP.* See "Eight Haiku," "Haiku," "Pulse-Beats of Eros," and "Strange Miniatures." Miletus was a city in Asia Minor. Beginning in the 2nd century B.C.E., "Milesian tales"— flamboyant tales of romance and adventure—began to be written; they were the forerunners of the modern novel.

Nightfall. MS (*JHLS; MCL; NYPL). *AJ* 24, No. 13 (10 January 1924): 13. The ms. is dated 18 May 1921. CAS sent the poem, along with "Ecstasy" and other poems, to GS on 27 May 1921. GS commented: "'Ecstasy' and 'Nigh[t]fall' seem the finest to me, especially the former. But they're all fine work" (letter to CAS, 6 June 1921; *SU* 196).

Nightmare. MS (JHLS). In *EC.* In *DM* 338. In **SP, LO.* CAS referred to the poem in a letter to GS (11 May 1913) as "Gothic Nightmare" (*SU* 87). He sent the poem to GS on 8 June 1913. GS commented: "'Nightmare' is good too, especially its tremendous ending" (letter to CAS, 22 June 1913; *SU* 91).

Nightmare of the Lilliputian. MS (DAW). In *SP, S&P*. "Lilliputian" refers to the miniature race that Gulliver comes upon in Part I of Jonathan Swift's *Gulliver's Travels* (1726). Ygdrasil (l. 5) (more properly Yggdrasil) is, in Norse myth, the world-tree that binds Heaven, Earth, and Hell together.

The Nightmare Tarn. MS (JHLL; JHLS). *WT* 14, No. 5 (November 1929): 624. In *SP, LO*.

Nirvana. In *ST, *SP, LO*. In Buddhist myth, Nirvana is the final state to which the soul aspires, a state of release from birth, suffering, death, and rebirth.

No Stranger Dream. MS (AH). *Arkham Sampler* 1, No. 3 (Summer 1948): 20. In *SP, S&P*. For "Lemures" (l. 6), see note on "Mirrors." For Baaltis (l. 10), see note on "Alternative."

Nocturnal Pines. MS (AH; DAW; JHLS). In *SP*. See "Distillations," "Haiku," and "Vignettes and Indexes." For Polaris (l. 2), see note on "Outlanders."

Nocturne (Intensified and re-enforced with clouds,). MS (NYPL). *International* 6, No. 4 (September 1912): 76 (as "Nocturn"). The poem was one of the earliest that CAS sent to GS, on 2 February 1911 (see *SU* 19). In his letter of 28 February 1911, GS made several comments on the poem (see *SU* 21).

Nocturne (A silver sleep is on the vale;). MS (JHLL; JHLS; ms laid in copy #1 of *HD*). In *SP, GF*. The ms. is dated 13 March 1916. CAS sent the poem to GS on 15 June 1916. GS commented: "There is always a demand for very short lyrics such as 'Nocturne' and 'Autumn Twilight,' and I'd send them out too. They're delicate and lovely" (letter to CAS, 17 June 1916; *SU* 136). It is not clear whether CAS ever submitted the poem to magazines.

Nocturne: Grant Avenue. MS (JHLS; SHSW). *Wings* 6, No. 5 (Spring 1944): 15. In *SP, *HD*. First title: "City Nocturne." The ms. is dated 29 September 1942.

The Noon of the Seasons. See "Sonnets of the Seasons."

"Not Altogether Sleep." MS (DAW). In *DC. WT* 44, No. 2 (January 1952): 73. In *HD*. The title derives from GS's sonnet "Afterward" (in *Poems for Vera*, 1938): "And making death not altogether sleep" (l. 12).

Not Theirs the Cypress-Arch. MS (JHLS). In *DC. Wings* 10, No. 4 (Winter 1952): 13. In *LO*. First title: "Resurgam" (Latin for "I shall rise up"); alternate title: "Ellos Resurgen." The ms. is dated 12 January 1951.

November. MS (JHLL; JHLS). In *SP*.

November Twilight. MS (JHLS [as "Autumn Twilight"]). In *EC, *SP*. First title: "Autumn Twilight." Written before 15 June 1916.

Now, Ere the Morning Break. See "Before Dawn."

Nuns Walking in the Orchard. MS (AH; JHLS). In *SP. See "Eight Haiku" and "Strange Miniatures." See also note on "Improbable Dream."

Nyctalops. MS (JHLL; JHLS; MCL). *WT* 14, No. 4 (October 1929): 516. In *The Laureate's Wreath: An Anthology in Honor of Dr. Henry Meade Bland, Poet Laureate of California,* ed. The Edwin Markham Poetry Society (San Jose: The Edwin Markham Poetry Society, 1934), p. 109. In *Today's Literature,* ed. Dudley Chadwick Gordon, Vernon Rupert King, and William Whittingham Lyman (New York: American Book Co., 1935), p. 449. In *DM* 339–40. In *SP, LO, SSU.* The ms. is dated 21 March 1929. One ms. at JHL omits stanzas 4–6; another adds them by hand. The word *nyctalops* is a variant of *nyctalopia,* originally meaning "Night-blindness" but later coming to mean "Inability to see clearly except by night" (*OED*); it is in the latter sense that CAS uses the word.

The Nymph. MS (JHLS; NYPL [both as "Dream"]). In *SP (as a translation of "Christophe des Laurières"). First title: "Dream." The ms. is dated 8–9 March 1923. For nymphs, see note on "The Masque of Forsaken Gods."

"O Golden-Tongued Romance." MS (JHLS). In *DC. WT* 44, No. 3 (March 1952): [33] (as "O Golden-Tongued Romance"). Written 1950. The title derives from John Keats's "On Sitting Down to Read *King Lear* Once Again" (1818), l. 1.

Oblivion. See "The Last Oblivion."

Oblivion. See "Lethe" (From the nameless dark distilled,). See also "Strange Miniatures."

Ocean Twilight. MS (JHLS).

October. MS (DAW; JHLS; NYPL). *Westward* 4, No. 5 (May 1935): 5. In *Poets of the Western Scene,* ed. Hans A. Hoffmann (San Leandro, CA: Greater West Publishing Company, 1937), p. 89. In *SP, S&P.* The ms. is dated 11 October 1925. Aidenn (l. 9) is the Arabic equivalent of Eden. One of its most celebrated usages in poetry is in Poe's "The Raven" (1845): "Tell this soul with sorrow laden if, within the distant Aidenn, / It shall clasp a sainted maiden whom the angels name Lenore" (ll. 93–94). In l. 18, "hyperborean" means "beyond the north wind," used by the Greeks to denote a fabulous people believed to live in bliss in the distant north. CAS would write an entire series of tales set in a realm he called Hyperborea, a prehistoric land in the far north.

Ode (O young and dear and tender sorceress!). MS (JHLS). In *SP, HD. For "maenads" (l. 7), see note on "Bacchante." For "Favonian" (l. 13), see note on "At Sunrise." For "Arcadian" (l. 25), see note on "From Arcady."

Ode (Your name is like the opening of a flow'r,). *AJ 26, No. 8 (3 December 1925): 14.

Ode on Imagination. In *ST, *SP, LO.* "Cimmerian" (l. 35) refers either to an imaginary people cited in Homer (*Odyssey* 11.14) as dwelling beyond the Ocean in perpetual darkness, or to an actual tribe dwelling on the north shore of the Black Sea in the 8th and 7th centuries B.C.E.

Ode on the Future of Song. MS (JHLS).

Ode to Aphrodite. MS (*JHLS). A variant ms. (JHLS; titled "To Aphrodite") includes two lines of a second section: "Goddess of all delight and all desire / How shall our hearts elude thee? Though we take [. . .]" For Aphrodite, see note on "The Ghoul and the Seraph." CAS wrote to GS on 31 January 1921: "I've written almost nothing. I began an 'Ode to Aphrodite', but gave it up as being too conventional" (*SU* 196).

Ode to Beauty. See "To Beauty."

Ode to Light. MS (*JHLS). In *TT, LO.* Written 1912. Unfinished. For Aldebaran (l. 24), see note on "H. P. L."; for Algebar, see note on "The Envoys." Orion (l. 25) is the most brilliant constellation in the sky, situated between Taurus and Canis Major. The following lines of discarded text appear after line 29:

> Or note its fall from paths of light uplifted,
> To where, within the irremeable pit,
> All suns detroned have drifted
> To sunken paths unlit?
> Have all its brethren found that place,
> Where iron-relentless shadow hem,
> Seeing the ruinous maw
> As when the falling Titans saw
> The gulf of Tartarus opening under them
> Like visible oblivion, for the space
> Ere they were one with it?

Ode to Matter. MS (*JHLS). In *TS, LO.* Written 1911. CAS may have been referring to this poem when he wrote to GS (21 May 1911): "I've been trying my hand at some cosmic verse lately . . . . This is about what I've done in four poems, varying in length from 112 to 56 lines" (*SU* 25). This poem is 56 lines. See also CAS's "Ode on Matter" (p. 651), probably written earlier.

Ode to Music. MS (JHLS). *Placer County Republican* 42, No. 23 (26 September 1912): 1. In *ST.* CAS sent the poem to GS in March 1911 (see *SU* 21). GS commented: "I've been meaning for weeks to write and tell you how much I like your beautiful music-ode" (letter to CAS, 13 April 1911; *SU* 22). Later he wrote: "I've prayerfully considered your beautiful 'Ode to Music,' and want to express my utter amazement that a youth of your years is capable of such a production. It is pure poetry of a high order, and I wish *I'd* written it" (letter to CAS, 19 May 1911; *SU* 23). CAS later noted: "I read my 'Ode to Music' before a local woman's club yesterday, where I was the only male person present" (letter to GS, 15 September 1912; *SU* 63). GS had in fact written a poem, "Music," in *The Testimony of the Suns and Other Poems* (1903).

Ode to Peace. MS (NYPL [as by Arzè Dnüŏp]). Written c. November 1918. CAS sent the poem to GS on 16 April 1919. GS commented: "I enjoyed your 'Ode to Peace.' Why not send it to 'The Liberator'?" (letter to CAS, 17 May 1919; *SU* 172). The *Liberator* was a left-wing magazine founded by Max Eastman, absorbing the *Masses*.

Ode to Poetry. MS (JHLS). Written 1911. First draft: "To Poetry." The last seven lines are found only on the handwritten draft.

Ode to the Abyss. MS (MCL). In *ST, OS. Tesseract* 2, No. 3 (March 1937): 9–10. In **SP, LO*. Written 3 May 1911. CAS remarked of the poem that he wrote "practically all of it at a sitting" (letter to GS, 26 May 1912; *SU* 47). GS was enthusiastic about the work, writing (letter to CAS, 13 July 1911): "It is a noble, majestic and delightful thing" (*SU* 27). CAS responded: "Your praise of my 'Ode to the Abyss' is far higher than I had expected or dared hope for. Nor can I concede, after more consideration, that the poem deserves it. It does not seem possible to me that I can have written anything having the merit that you assign to this Ode" (letter to GS, 5 September 1911; *SU* 28). GS submitted it to the *North American Review*, but it was rejected. Through GS's influence, the poem was quoted in a number of California newspapers. GS also sent it to Ambrose Bierce, who remarked of it: "Kindly convey to young Smith of Auburn my felicitations on his admirable 'Ode to the Abyss'—a large theme, treated with dignity and power. It has many striking passages—such, for example, as 'The Romes of ruined spheres' [l. 57]. I'm conscious of my sin against the rhetoricians in liking that, for it jolts the reader out of the Abyss and back to earth. Moreover it is a metaphor which belittles, instead of dignifying. But I like it" (letter to GS, 11 August 1911; quoted in *SU* 289n). Elsewhere (letter to *Town Talk*, 6 August 1912; published in the issue for 10 August 1912), in responding to exaggerated claims of CAS's merits placed in Bierce's mouth, Bierce wrote: "Several weeks ago I had from a correspondent a manuscript copy of Mr. Smith's 'Ode to the Abyss.' It seemed to me uncommonly good work and a promise of better work to come. So I commended it—in just what words I do not recollect, but if I said any of the things recently attributed to me I beg my correspondent to cover me with shame and confusion by quoting them from my letter—and filing the letter in proof" (quoted in *SU* 288–89).

Odysseus in Eternity. MS (DAW). In *SP. See "Strange Miniatures (Haiku)."

Old Hydraulic Diggings. MS (JHLS). In *SP.

Old Limestone Kiln. In *SP*.

An Old Theme. In *SP* (as a translation of "Christophe des Laurières").

The Old Water-Wheel. MS (SHSW). *Poetry* 61, No. 3 (December 1942): 492. In *SP*, *DC*, *SSU*. The ms. is dated 2 August 1941. For "Antares" (l. 11), see note on "The Star-Treader."

Ombos. MS (JHLS). The title is Greek for "thunderstorm."

Omniety. MS (JHLS; SHSW). *Raven* 1, No. 4 (Winter 1944): 21. In *SP*, *HD*, *LO*, *SSU*. The ms. is dated 14 September 1943. The word of the title is a variant spelling of *omneity* ("The condition of being all; 'allness'" [*OED*]). For Dis (l. 4), see note on "Farewell to Eros"; "Hyblaean" refers to Mt. Hybla, a mountain in Sicily where bees abounded (hence used as a synonym for honey).

On a Chinese Vase. MS (DAW; JHLL; JHLS). *Oriental Stories* 2, No. 2 (Spring 1932): 174. In *SP*, *SSU*. The ms. is dated 2 November 1928. Ming (ll. 2 and 5) refers to a dynasty that ruled China from 1368 (when it overthrew the Mongols) to 1644.

On Re-reading Baudelaire. MS (JHLS [as "On Reading Baudelaire"]; NYPL; Sx). *AJ* 24, No. 9 (13 December 1923): 6 (as "On Reading Baudelaire"). In *S* (as "On Reading Baudelaire"), *SP*, *LO*. The poem apparently was written more than a year before CAS began his own translations of *Les Fleurs du mal* in the spring of 1925 (see Vol. 3, pp. 20f.), so his "re-reading" was probably done in English, perhaps in the translation of F. P. Sturm (1906). For "Paphian" (l. 12), see note on "The Ghoul and the Seraph." Proserpine (l. 12) is an Italian goddess whom the Romans identified with the Greek goddess Persephone, queen of the underworld.

On the Canyon-Side. MS (JHLS; NYPL; Sx). *AJ* 23, No. 50 (27 September 1923): 6. In *Continent's End: An Anthology of Contemporary California Poets*, ed. George Sterling, Genevieve Taggard, and James Rorty (San Francisco: Book Club of California, 1925), p. 54. In *SP*. The ms. is dated 4–12 March 1923. CAS sent the poem to GS, with others, on 15 March 1923. GS commented: "I like all these poems you send, and most of all the beautiful 'On the Canyon-Side.' You bid fair to be as successful at the human as at the demoniac. There seems to me to be no flaw in this poem" (letter to CAS, 6 April 1923; *SU* 230). CAS later submitted it, along with "The Witch with Eyes of Amber," to William Rose Benét for the *Saturday Review of Literature*, but "apparently they were too strong for him" (letter to GS, 21 July 1924; *SU* 242).

On the Mount of Stone. MS (AH). *Arkham Sampler* 1, No. 3 (Summer 1948): 31. In *SP*. Alilat (l. 3), or Al-ilat, is a supreme female deity in Arabic myth, analogous to Aphrodite. "Hermes-footed" (l. 8) refers to the fact that the Greek god Hermes was said to have had winged feet.

On Trying to Read *Four Quartets.* MS (JHLS). The poem addresses the long poem *Four Quartets* (1943) by T. S. Eliot (see note on "Greek Epigram"), which CAS apparently found obscure. The ms. (written on an envelope) is mutilated by fire, rendering some portions illegible. "Ella" (l. 8) refers to Ella Wheeler Wilcox (1850–1919), American poet whose work was widely syndicated in newspapers but who was criticized for triteness and sentimentality.

One Evening. MS (DAW; JHLL; JHLS). In *SP.* Cocaigne (l. 3) is, in medieval legendry, an imaginary realm devoted to idleness and wealth. Cf. CAS's prose-poem "In Cocaigne" (1922; *NU* 14–15).

Only to One Returned. MS (AH). *Arkham Sampler* 1, No. 4 (Autumn 1948): 13. In *SP, *S&P.* For Endor (l. 10), see note on "Dominium in Excelsis." For Lilith (l. 12), see "The Tears of Lilith."

The Oracle. MS (JHLS). CAS has written a line of verse or prose at the top of the ms.: "Life and Beauty cannot be more than shapes of carven [?] mist." Also, he has written a second stanza but later crossed it out: "Sombre, mute, sardonical, / From my throne that fools have built / With the flimsy bronze and gilt / Of their dreams terrestial."

The Orchid of Beauty. MS (MCL; NYPL). In *EC* (as "The Orchid"), *SP.* The ms. is dated 21 May 1914. GS commented on the poem in a letter to CAS (4 June 1914): "'The Orchid of Beauty' is very much to my taste. *I* don't find it obscure, nor have I any alterations to suggest" (*SU* 107). (The letter in which CAS sent this poem appears to be lost.) The poem was rejected by the *Atlantic Monthly* (CAS to SL, 7 October 1916; ms., BL).

Orgueil. MS (JHLS). For Benjamin De Casseres, see note on "Le Refuge." The title translates to "Pride."

Ougabalys. MS (DAW; JHLL; *JHLS). *WT* 15, No. 1 (January 1930): 135. In *LO.* The ms. is dated 15 September 1929. The poem was later revised as "Tolometh" (p. 553). For Poseidonis (l. 1), see note on that poem.

The Outer Land. MS (MCL; SHSW [both as "Alienation"]). *Supramundane Stories Quarterly* 1, No. 2 (Spring 1937): 3–4 (as "Alienation"). In *SP.* *Spearhead* 2, No. 2 (Spring 1951): 3–5. In *DC, LO.* The ms. is dated 26 May 1935. Hinnom (l. 24) is the Hebrew equivalent to the Greek Gehenna, a valley south of Jerusalem where children were sacrificed to Moloch. It later became the mouth of Hell.

Outlanders. MS (JHLS [one ms. has octet only]; SHSW; UCLA). In *N1. WT* 31, No. 6 (June 1938): 746. In *DM* 339. In *SP, LO.* The ms. is dated 26 June 1934. Some mss. and the appearance in *WT* are dedicated to David Warren Ryder (1892–1975), author of "The Price of Poetry," *Controversy*

(December 1934); rpt. by the Futile Press (June 1937) and laid in CAS's *N1*. Polaris (l. 8) is a double or triple star in the constellation Ursa Major situated near the north pole of the heavens. It is currently the star around which all the other stars in the heavens appear to revolve.

Paean. MS (SHSW). *Wings* 7, No. 6 (Summer 1946): 14. In **SP, HD.*

The Pagan. MS (DAW; JHLS, as "Pagan"; NYPL). In **SP* (as a translation of "Christophe des Laurières"), *S&P.* The DAW ms. is dated 1923. CAS sent the poem, along with another sonnet, to GS on 2 April 1924. GS commented: "I . . . thought them translations from Baudelaire, so perfectly have you caught his spirit and used his material. I like them better than anything of his, however, especially 'The Pagan'" (letter to CAS, 9 April 1924; *SU* 239–40). GS said he was going to submit the poem to *Measure*, but if so, it was rejected. A Triton (l. 4), in Greek myth, is a merman with human head and shoulders and the tail of a fish from the waist down, the son of Poseidon and Amphitrite. He is usually depicted blowing on a conch-shell.

Pagans Old and New. (No ms. extant; list derived from *EOD.*) Comprises "Initiate of Dionysus"; "Bacchic Orgy"; "Abstainer"; "Picture by Piero di Cosimo"; "Bacchants and Bacchante"; "Garden of Priapus"; "Morning Star of the Mountains"; "Bygone Interlude"; and "Prisoner in Vain."

The Pageant of Music. MS (*JHLS; NYPL). In *TS.* Written c. 1910–11.

Païennerie. First title of "Idylle païenne."

The Palace of Jewels (Fronting the sea's blue chambers fluctuant—). In *PJ.* CAS sent the poem to GS on 8 June 1913, remarking: "'The Palace of Jewels' is an old poem of mine, written about the time of 'The Star-Treader.' I've just exhumed it, and think you might like to have it. It's peculiarly in your line" (*SU* 90). GS commented: "'The Palace of Jewels' *is* 'a gorgeous thing[']! I like it all except that 'intermittently' applied to rubies [l. 20]. It seems to me that the ruby's light is peculiarly steady and *un*intermittent" (letter to CAS, 22 June 1913; *SU* 91).

The Palace of Jewels (It rears beside the cliff-confronted sea,). MS (JHLS). Presumably the first version of a poem later expanded into 16 stanzas (p. 69).

Palms. MS (JHLS; NYPL). *Asia* 20, No. 3 (April 1920): 330. In *EC.* In *Songs and Stories,* ed. Edwin Markham (Los Angeles: Powell Publishing Co., 1931; Freeport, NY: Books for Libraries Press, 1974), p. 424. In **SP.* The ms. is dated 10 April 1918. CAS referred to the poem as "a bit of Oriental colour that I have always fancied" (CAS to SL, 14 April 1920; ms., BL).

Pantheistic Dream. MS (JHLS). An English version of "Rêve panthéistique" (p. 562). It is not clear which version was written first. The ms. is burned, rending some passages illegible.

Paphnutius. MS (DAW). In *SP, S&P*. See "Strange Miniatures (Haiku)." Paphnutius was the Bishop of Thebes in Egypt (fl. 300 C.E.) who was venerated because the Roman emperor Maximianus had his right eye torn out. He later was declared a saint. "Stylitean throne" (l. 1) refers to the Stylites, a sect of Christian ascetics who lived on the tops of pillars.

Parnaso. MS (JHLS). For an English version, see "Parnassus." For Parnassus, see note on "The Thralls of Circle Climb Parnassus."

Parnassus. MS (JHLS). *Asmodeus* 1, No. 1 (Summer 1950): 21. The ms. is dated 24 March 1950. An English translation of the Spanish poem "Parnaso."

Parnassus à la Mode. In *SP, S&P*. For Parnassus, see note on "The Thralls of Circe Climb Parnassus." Erato and Melpomene (l. 1) were the muses of lyric poetry and tragedy, respectively.

Passing of an Elder God. MS (DAW). In *SP, S&P*. For Enceladus (l. 4), see note on "Saturn."

The Past (Naught of the Past is left but memories—). MS (JHLS). CAS has failed to write the final line.

The Past (Drawn hither by the tides of change and chance). MS (JHLS).

Paysage païen. MS (JHLS). In *SP*. The ms. is dated 28 July 1929. The title translates to "Pagan Landscape." A revised version of "Idylle païenne" (p. 281).

Perseus and Medusa. In *SP, S&P*. See "Strange Miniatures" and "Strange Miniatures (Haiku)." In Greek myth, Perseus, the son of Zeus and Danae, cut off the head of Medusa (see note on "Medusa") after Pluto lent him a helmet that made him invisible.

Phallus Impudica. MS (AH; DAW). In *SP*. See "Haiku" and "Strange Miniatures." The title is Latin for "shameless phallus."

The Phantasy of Twilight. MS (*NYPL). In *PD*. Written before 23 June 1914.

Philtre. MS (DAW). In *SP, S&P*. See "Strange Miniatures (Haiku)."

The Phoenix. MS (JHLL; JHLS; MCL). *WT* 35, No. 3 (May 1940): 94. In *SP, S&P*. The ms. is dated 24 May 1935. For the myth of the Phoenix, see note on "The City in the Desert." For "Sabean" (l. 18), see note on "Autumn Orchards."

Picture by Piero di Cosimo. MS (AH). In *SP*. See "Pagans Old and New" and "Strange Miniatures." The painting in question, by the Florentine painter Piero di Cosimo (1462–1521), is "The Discovery of Honey" (c. 1505–10), now in the Worcester (MA) Art Museum.

Pine Needles. In *ST, *SP.*

Plague from the Abatoir. MS (JHLS). In *SP. See "Mortal Essences."

Plum-Flowers. MS (JHLS; NYPL). *L'Alouette* 1, No. 2 (March 1924): 44. In *S. The ms. is dated 17 May 1922. CAS sent the poem to GS on 25 June 1922. GS suggested that he send this poem and "Song" (p. 236) to Ellan McIlvaine of *Snappy Stories.* CAS later reported that McIlvaine had accepted "Plum-Flowers" (letter to GS, 29 September 1922; *SU* 210), but the poem apparently was not published in *Snappy Stories.*

Poemes d'amour. MS (JHLS). The title is French for "Poems of Love."

Poet in a Barroom. MS (AH [as "Poet Drinking in a Barroom"]). In *SP. See "Strange Miniatures."

The Poet Talks with the Biographers. MS (JHLS). In *DC. A burned ms. at JHLS has the title "The Poet Speaks with the Ghouls." For a French version, see "Le Poète parle avec ses biographes." For Empusa (l. 3), see note on "Empusa Waylays a Traveller." Chaldean (l. 21) refers to Chaldaea, a realm in southern Babylonia in existence from at least the 9th century B.C.E. until it was overrun by the Persians in 539 B.C.E.

Los Poetas del optimismo. MS (JHLS [2 mss., one titled "Los Poetas"]). In *DD* as "Los Poetas." A Spanish version of "The Poets of Optimism."

Le Poète parle avec ses biographes. MS (JHLS [2 mss., one titled "Le Poète parle avec les goules"]). A French version of "The Poet Talks with the Biographers."

Poetry. MS (JHLS).

Poets in Hades. MS (DAW; JHLS, under "Quintrains"). In *SP. For "Acherontic" (l. 2), see note on "Solution."

The Poets of Optimism. MS (JHLS). For a Spanish version, see "Los Poetas del optimismo."

The Pool. MS (JHLS). For a French version, see "La Mare" (p. 402).

Pool at Lobos. MS (AH). In *SP. See "Eight Haiku" and "Strange Miniatures." CAS refers to Point Lobos, a rocky promontory in central California just south of Carmel-by-the-Sea. GS, who lived in Carmel, wrote several poems about the site.

Poplars. *Snappy Stories* 70, No. 2 (5 November 1922): 46. In *GF. Written c. July 1922. The appearance in *Snappy Stories* has only 12 lines.

Postlude. MS (JHLS [2 mss., one as "Any Shadow, Any Dream"]; SHSW [as "Éloignement"]). In *SP. *Carmel Pine Cone* 42, No. 1 (5 January 1956): 6. In

HD. First title: "Éloignement"; second title: "Any Shadow, Any Dream." The ms. is dated 22 April 1943. For "Parnassian" (l. 2), see note on "The Thralls of Circe Climb Parnassus."

The Potion of Dreams. In *PD*.

Pour Chercher du nouveau. MS (JHLS; SHSW). *Arkham Sampler* 2, No. 4 (Autumn 1949): 28–29. In **SP, DC, LO*. The title translates to "In Search of the New." For Cimmeria (l. 1), see note on "Ode on Imagination." For "Lemur" (l. 3), see note on "Mirrors." Anubis (l. 11) is a jackal-headed god in Egyptian myth, the ruler of graves and supervisor of the burial of the dead. Ashtaroth (l. 17) is a variant spelling of Ashtoreth, the Hebrew name for the goddess Astarte (see note on "The Masque of Forsaken Gods"). Behemoth (l. 18) is mentioned once in the Bible (Job 40:15) as a large beast (perhaps a hippopotamus). For Moloch (l. 26), see note on "Some Blind Eidolon." "Baalim" (l. 27) is a term applied to a variety of gods related to Baal (the supreme god of the Phoenicians and Canaanites), including Astarte and others.

The Power of Eld. MS (*JHLS). In *TS, LO*.

Prayer. See "Supplication."

A Prayer. MS (*JHLS). In *GF*.

A Precept. MS (JHLS; NYPL). In *EC. Lyric West* 3, No. 9 (January 1924): 4. In **SP*. Written before 24 April 1918.

Prescience. See "Future Pastoral."

The Present. MS (JHLS).

The Price. In *ST*. In *Literary California*, ed. Ella Sterling Mighels (San Francisco: Harr Wagner Publishing Co., 1918), p. 326 (as "Behind Each Thing a Shadow Lies"). In *N1, *SP*.

Prisoner in Vain. MS (JHLS). In **SP*. See "Pagans Old and New" and "Pulse-Beats of Eros."

Proem for Sandalwood. See "Sandalwood."

The Prophet Speaks. MS (JHLS). *WT* 32, No. 3 (September 1938): 348–49. In *SP, *S&P, LO, SSU*. Written August 1937. For "Tyre" (l. 2), see note on "The Sorrow of the Winds." Ys (l. 2) is an ancient city cited in Breton folklore and utilized by A. Merritt in several works, notably *Creep, Shadow!* (1934). Tuloom (l. 26) was a Mayan city in the Yucatan peninsula; Tarshish a city of unspecified locale cited in the Bible (e.g., Ezekiel 27:12) as a source of precious metal.

Psalm (I have sealed my desire upon thee). MS (JHLS). In *SP* (as a translation of "Christophe des Laurières").

Psalm (My belovèd is a well of clean waters,). MS (JHLS). In *EC. The ms. is dated 28 April 1921. The phrase "Abomination of Desolation" (l. 3) occurs frequently in the Old Testament in reference to the desecration of the temple by the Roman Emperor Antiochus Epiphanes in 167 B.C.E. In the New Testament it is cited more generally as a disaster in Judea preceding the Second Coming. CAS wrote a prose-poem of that title (*NU* 21). For Astarte (l. 19), see note on "The Masque of Forsaken Gods." For "Sabean" (l. 24), see note on "Autumn Orchards."

A Psalm to the Best Beloved. MS (NYPL as "Psalm"). In *EC*, *SP. Written 29 April 1921. CAS sent the poem to GS on 18 May 1921, remarking: "I . . . have been writing; but my compositions are all 'personal'—some of them too much so, perhaps, for the official censors (the Anti-Vice Society!)" (*SU* 193). (CAS refers to the New York Society for the Suppression of Vice, founded in 1873 by Anthony Comstock and headed at that time by his successor, John S. Sumner, which was vigilant in seeking the suppression of material considered obscene.) GS commented: "I like the 'Psalm' very much, and shall be glad to receive anything else of the kind . . . Don't fear me as a 'censor!'" (letter to CAS, 19 May 1921; *SU* 194). When the poem was published in *EC*, CAS remarked: "The poor old 'Psalm' on p. 126 [actually p. 121] played havoc with the village proprieties [i.e., in Auburn]. I don't know so many brick-bats were coming my way, till lately . . . I suppose that particular poem was the only one that the villagers could even partially understand" (letter to GS, 15 March 1923; *SU* 229).

Psalm to the Desert. MS (*NYPL). In *KML*. CAS wrote to SL (28 February 1915; ms., BL) that the poem is "pretty rough and scabrous, and I think some of the verses are too metrical, toward the end." In a letter to GS (16 February 1915; *SU* 119) CAS said it was "dismal even for a Bible parody." GS commented (letter to CAS, 6 March 1915; *SU* 119): "Your 'Psalm to the Desert' has much imagination and sublimity in it, as has so much of your work. Even at that, I'm hoping you'll turn to other themes before long." CAS responded (letter to GS, 11 March 1915): "Your comments on 'The Psalm to the Desert' are quite just. Still, why shouldn't the thing be written? It's quite true, and even original, since no one ever wrote anything really like it on the subject before, to my knowledge" (*SU* 120). Herpeton (l. 8) is a Greek word meaning "a creeping animal" or "reptile," usually applied to snakes.

Pulse-Beats of Eros. MS (JHLS). In *SP* as part of "Experiments in Haiku" (but without title) in the subsection "Distillations." Comprises "Night of Miletus"; "Love in Dreams"; "Prisoner in Vain"; "Mountain Trail"; and "Bed of Mint."

The Pursuer (Ascendant from what dead profundity,). MS (JHLS). The ms. is dated 15 May 1912.

The Pursuer (Climbing from out what nadir-fountained sea,). In *SP. Portals* (November 1957). In *LO*. A radical revision of the early poem of the same title (p. 88).

Qu'Importe? MS (JHLS). The title is French for "What Does It Matter?"

Quatrains. See "Omar's Philosophy" under "Juvenilia."

Que songes-tu, Muse? MS (JHLS). A French version of "What Dreamest Thou, Muse?" (p. 629).

¿Qué sueñas, Musa? MS (*JHLS). In *SSU*. A Spanish version of the English poem "What Dreamest Thou, Muse?" (p. 629). There is also a French version, "Que songes-tu, Muse?" (p. 629).

Query. MS (JHLS; NYPL; Sx). *AJ* 25, No. 26 (9 April 1925): 4. In *S. United Amateur* 25, No. 2 (May 1926): 7. *Step Ladder* 13, No. 5 (May 1927): 131. In *SP. First title: "To a Friend." The ms. is dated 20 January 1925.

Quest. MS (JHLS; NYPL). *AJ* 22, No. 10 (22 December 1921): 4. In *EC. Step Ladder* 13, No. 5 (May 1927): 133. *Stars* (June–July 1940): [2]. In *SP. CAS sent the poem, with others, to GS on 10 June 1919. GS commented: "The enclosures are good, as usual—full of that beauty which is its own excuse. My one objection is to the (to me) weakness of 'undelaying mien' [l. 29] as a *last line*" (letter to CAS, 7 July 1919; *SU* 173). Evidently the poem originally ended at l. 29, and GS's criticism led CAS to add the final four lines (an adaptation of ll. 1–2 and 9–10).

Quiddity. MS (JHLS, under "Quintrains" [No. 2]). In *SP, S&P. The word of the title means "The real nature or essence of a thing" (*OED*).

Quintrains. MS (DAW). In *SP*. Comprises "Attar of the Past"; "Passing of an Elder God"; "Nightmare of the Lilliputian"; "Poet in Hades"; "Love and Death"; "Mithridates"; and "Someone." MS (JHLS). One ms. comprises "Attar of the Past"; "Mummy of the Flower"; "Poets in Hades"; and "Dying Prospector." Another ms. comprises "Attar of the Past"; "Mummy of the Flower"; "Bird of Long Ago"; "Late November Evening"; "Mithridates"; and "Quiddity." *SP* also includes "The Heron" and "Epitaph for the Astronomer" and omits "Love and Death" and "Dying Prospector."

Radio. Tr. (DSF).

Reclamation. MS (*NYPL). In *GF*. Written c. 1915.

Recompense. In *EC*. In *Great Poems of the English Language*, ed. Wallace Alvin Briggs (New York: Robert M. McBride, 1927; London: George C. Harrap & Co., 1928), p. 1338; rev. ed. New York: Tudor Publishing Co., 1936, p. 1338. In *SP.

Red Memory. MS (JHLS). For a Spanish version of the poem, see "Memoria roja."

The Red Moon. See "Moon-Dawn."

Refuge. MS (JHLS; SHSW). In *SP*.

Le Refuge [French]. MS (*JHLS; MCL). An early version of "La Forteresse." For CAS's English translation see p. 464. The dedicatee of the poem is Benjamin De Casseres (1873–1945), author of *The Shadow-Eater* (1915) and other volumes of poetry, as well as the critical volume *Forty Immortals* (1926). He wrote the foreword to *SP*.

Le Refuge [English]. MS (BL; *JHLS). A translation of the French poem "Le Refuge." Written before 25 November 1935.

The Refuge of Beauty. MS (JHLS). In *OS, EC. L'Alouette* 1, No. 3 (May 1924): 66. In *SP, LO*. CAS sent the poem to GS on 8 June 1913. GS commented: "'The Refuge of Beauty' is strong, though the clash between 'escape' and 'Hate' [l. 8] jars me" (letter to CAS, 22 June 1913; *SU* 91). Evidently, "Evade" in l. 8 formerly read "Escape." This poem was one of the first read by H. P. Lovecraft when he came into contact with CAS in August 1922; he said of it: "If that ain't supreme poesy, I'm a damned liar!" (Lovecraft to Maurice W. Moe, [September 1922]; *Selected Letters 1911–1924* [Sauk City, WI: Arkham House, 1965], p. 163).

Reigning Empress. MS (AH). In *SP*. See "Strange Miniatures."

Reincarnation. MS (JHLS).

Remembered Light. *Poetry* 1, No. 3 (December 1912): 78. In *EC, *SP, LO*.

Remembrance. MS (JHLS [2 mss., one titled "Song"]; *Sx). *AJ* 24, No. 14 (17 January 1924): 6. In *S, SP*. The ms. is dated 5 November 1923. First title: "Song."

Reminiscence. See "Classic Reminiscence."

Remoteness. Either non-extant or a variant title of an unidentified poem. CAS sent the poem to GS c. August 1917 (see *SU* 151). GS commented: "'Remoteness' is good, but of course not comparable to this big sonnet ('Ave atque Vale')" (letter to CAS, 19 September 1917; *SU* 152).

Requiescat (What was Love's worth,). MS (JHLL; JHLS; NYPL). *Smart Set* 68, No. 4 (August 1922): 102. In *EC, *SP*. First title: "Dirge." The ms. is dated 4 February 1920. CAS sent the poem to GS on 5 September 1920. GS commented: "I showed your lyric 'Requiescat' to [Harry] Lafler yesterday, and we wondered if you realized how sheerly, purely beautiful a thing it is. I cannot conceive of a magazine refusing it" (letter to CAS, 10 September

1920; *SU* 187). CAS responded: "I tried the 'Requiescat' on several magazines, including 'Harper's,' but to no avail" (letter to GS, 29 September 1920; *SU* 187). GS then wrote: "In returning 'Requiescat,' the mag. editors reach a nadir of imbecility heretofore uninfested by them. Better try 'Smart Set'" (letter to CAS, 6 October 1920; *SU* 188). On 11 April 1922 CAS noted that the poem "has been out six or seven times," and that the *Smart Set* and *Snappy Stories* had rejected it (*SU* 205). GS then apparently submitted the poem directly to H. L. Mencken of the *Smart Set*, who accepted it in June 1922 (*SU* 207). The title is Latin for "may he (or she) repose," most often found in the phrase "requiescat in pace" (may he [or she] rest in peace); cf. CAS's poem of that title (p. 175).

Requiescat (Whither, on soft and soundless feet,). MS (JHLS). The ms. is dated 9 November 1938.

Requiescat in Pace. MS (NYPL). *Midland* 5, No. 5 (May 1920): 46–47. In *EC*, *SP. Written before 24 April 1918. For the title, see note on "Requiescat." The poem is dedicated to Mamie Lowe Miller, who died in November 1917. Just before her death CAS wrote: "My best friend here [in Auburn] is very ill. She seems to have developed an attack of brain fever in addition to the consumption from which she has suffered for years. I don't know whether she will live or not. If she dies, I think I will go mad with grief and a guilty conscience" (letter to GS, 11 October 1917; *SU* 141). CAS sent the poem to GS on 24 April 1918. GS noted: "This 'Requiescat' is very beautiful, I think" (letter to CAS, 12 May 1918; *SU* 161). CAS said of Miller: "Yes, her poetic tastes were congenial to mine. We agreed on all things but religion (she was a devout Christian) and I fear that she was made unhappy because I could not share her faith. To-day, strangely enough, is her birthday; and when I go out into the fields, after finishing this letter and certain others, all the flowers that she loved will torture and reproach me. The snow-drops and larkspurs I carried to her a year ago, will ask for her; and I shall have no answer" (letter to SL, 27 April 1918; ms., BL). For Tyre (l. 24), see note on "The Sorrow of the Winds."

Resurgam. See "Not Theirs the Cypress-Arch."

Resurrection. MS (MCL). *WT* 39, No. 11 (July 1947): 85. In *DM* 345–46. In *SP*, *HD, *LO*. Written before 29 April 1939. For "Thessalian moons" (l. 8), see note on "In Thessaly." For "Hecatean goddess" (l. 14), see note on "The Witch in the Graveyard."

The Retribution. MS (JHLS). In *ST*, *OS*, *N1*, *SP. In l. 1, CAS refers to several gods from Egyptian myth: Osiris, the god and judge of the dead; Ammon (more properly Amen), a ram-headed god later associated with the sun-god Ra and worshipped as Amen-Ra; Thoth, the ibis-headed god who was the inventor of speech and hieroglyphics.

Retrospect and Forecast [English]. MS (JHLS; SFPL). *San Francisco Call* (1 December 1912): 6. In *ST*. *Current Opinion* 54, No. 2 (February 1913): 150. In *N1*, **SP, LO*. The poem is dated 11 January 1912. In a letter to GS (13 December 1912), CAS notes a review of *ST* in the *San Jose Mercury* (8 December 1912) in which the reviewer, John Jury, "speaks of the 'sinister' and 'ghoulish' qualities of much of my work, and particularly of the 'vicious spirit' animating the sonnet 'Retrospect and Forecast'" (*SU* 74).

Retrospect and Forecast [French]. MS (JHLS). A French translation of the English poem of the same title (p. 75).

The Return of Hyperion. MS (NYPL). In *ST, *SP, LO*. Written c. 1912. In Greek myth, Hyperion is one of the Titans, a group of older gods overthrown by the Olympian gods and imprisoned in Tartarus, the Greek underworld. Hyperion was also the father (by his sister Thea) of Helios (sun), Selene (moon), and Eos (dawn). In one tradition (as in CAS's poem), Hyperion is identified with Helios. This tradition is also followed by Keats in "Hyperion: A Fragment" (1820). Cf. "To the Sun" (p. 117).

Rêvasserie. MS (*JHLL; MCL). The ms. is dated 30 July 1929. For an English translation, see "Day-Dream" (p. 461).

Rêve panthéistique. MS (JHLS). A French version of "Pantheistic Dream" (p. 561). It is unclear which version was written first. The ms. (as by Christophe de Lauriers) is burned, rendering some passages illegible.

The Revelation. MS (JHLS).

Revenant. MS (DAW; SHSW). *Fantasy Fan* 1, No. 7 (March 1934): 106–7. In **SP, DC, LO*. Written before 22 July 1933. The title is French for "ghost" (specifically, one who returns [*revenir*] from the dead).

Reverie in August. MS (JHLS). In *SP, *HD*.

Rêves printaniers [English]. MS (JHLS). An English translation of the French poem of the same title (p. 468).

Rêves printaniers [French]. MS (JHLS). The title translates to "Spring Dreams." For an English translation, see p. 468.

River-Canyon. MS (AH; JHLS [2 mss., one titled "Canyon-Side"]). In **SP*. Written 7 February 1947. First title: "Canyon-Side."

The Road of Pain. MS (JHLS).

Romance. MS (JHLS).

Rosa Mystica. MS (JHLS; NYPL). *Lyric West* 1, No. 8 (December 1921): 7. In *EC, *SP, LO*. The ms. is dated 5 November 1919. The title (in Latin) translates to "The Mystic Rose." For Atlantis (l. 2), see note on "Atlantis." Persepolis (l. 6) was one of the capitals of the Persian Empire, founded by Darius I around 500 B.C.E. and sacked by Alexander the Great in 330 B.C.E.

Sacraments. MS (JHLS). The ms. is dated 5 August 1952. For Astarte (l. 7), see note on "The Masque of Forsaken Gods." For "Rabelaisian" (l. 15), see note on "Humors of Love."

Said the Dreamer. MS (JHLS). *Vortex* No. 2 (1947): 25–26. In *SP, S&P, LO.* The ms. is dated 5 March 1912; rev. 1944. First title: "In the Grip of Dreams." For "Cimmerian" (l. 21), see note on "Ode on Imagination." "Saracenic" (l. 24) refers to the Saracens, a term devised by Europeans in the Middle Ages in reference to Muslims. The term apparently derives from the Greek *Sarakēnos*, itself derived from the Arabic *sharqiyyin* ("easterners").

Sanctuary. MS (JHLS).

Sandalwood. MS (JHLS [as "Proem for Sandalwood"]). *Leaves* No. 1 (Summer 1937): 49. In *LO.* Written before October 1925. CAS's original proem to *S*, but not included in *S*. A fragmentary ms. (JHLS) contains the final four lines of the poem, followed by a line space and then the following three lines: "O, dutiful sad Helen! Evermore / My song shall build that Ilion of our dreams / To which we could not flee [. . .]"

Sandalwood and Onions. MS (JHLS).

Satan Unrepentant. In *OS, EC, *SP, LO.* CAS reports to GS (20 September 1912) that "I think I'll write another dramatic lyric, somewhat like 'Nero', with 'Satan Unrepentant' for the title and subject. I've only the vaguest idea as to what it'll be like; but the subject seems rather promising" (*SU* 64). In sending the poem to GS on 5 October 1912, CAS noted that it "owes a certain deductible debt to John Milton, but is a somewhat more direct justification of the devil than 'Paradise Lost.' It might have created a row fifty years ago; but I hardly think it would to-day. Still, such a poem seems to me worth writing, for I'm not aware that anything exactly of the same kind has been done" (*SU* 66). GS commented: "Your 'Satan Unrepentant' seems to me a great and noble poem, and one which I would certainly force the magazines to refuse or accept" (letter to CAS, 15 October 1912; *SU* 68). SL spoke of the work enthusiastically: "If that poem doesn't cause comment and an instant valuation of its high qualities, then 'Prometheus Unbound' is minor poetry and 'Hyperion' a failure. I measure it with these" (letter to CAS, 17 March 1918). CAS states that he sent it to the *English Review* and the *Atlantic Monthly* (*SU* 76), where it must have been rejected. In 1915 he noted that he was contemplating using the poem as the title poem of his next collection (letter to SL, 19 March 1915; ms., BL). See Phillip A. Ellis, "Satan Speaks: A Reading Of 'Satan Unrepentant,'" in Scott Connors, ed., *The Freedom of Fantastic Things* (New York: Hippocampus Press, 2007), pp. 132–37.

Satiety (A weary Juan, smothered in boudoirs,). MS (DAW; JHLS). In *SP* (as a translation of "Christophe des Laurières").

Satiety (Dear you were as is the tree of being). MS (JHLS; NYPL). In *EC, *SP*. The ms. is dated 5 March 1922.

Los Sátiros son decornados. See "The Twilight of the Gods."

Saturn. In *ST, *SP, LO*. Lines 254f. are found in a separate ms (MS [JHLS] under the title (or instruction) "Concluding Lines for 'Saturnian Epic.'" For Tartarus (l. 10), see note on "The Return of Hyperion." In a letter to GS (28 April 1912), CAS notes that he has finished the poem, adding: "It's rather an experiment, and I don't feel very sanguine about it" (*SU* 44). CAS appears to have sent the poem to GS in late May (see *SU* 48), but GS made no specific comment about it at the time; he did, however, send the poem to Ambrose Bierce, who made some comments on individual words and passages (see *SU* 58). The poem was rejected by the *Atlantic Monthly* (*SA* 62). It deals with Saturn, an ancient Italian god who was identified with the Greek god Kronos, the father of Zeus. Saturn/Kronos became the leader of the Titans, who were overthrown by Zeus and the other Olympian gods. Even in antiquity, the battle between the Olympian gods and the Titans was confused with the battle between the former and the Giants (one of whom was Enceladus [l. 65]). "Typhonian" (l. 163) refers to Typhon, a monster with a hundred serpent heads; he was defeated by Zeus and cast into Tartarus.

Saturnian Cinema. MS (*JHLS). In *SC.* Written 13 September 1954.

The Saturnienne. MS (DAW; JHLL; JHLS; NYPL). *WT* 10, No. 6 (December 1927): 728. In *SP, LO*. CAS wrote to GS on Christmas 1925: "I enclose one part of a fantastic entitled 'The Saturnienne,' with which I hope to go on presently. It may run to a hundred lines" (*SU* 265). GS commented (5 January 1926): "This 'Saturnienne' is in your best vein. As often, I had to consult the dictionary, and am by so much the wiser. I recall Bierce writing somewhere in praise of archaic words, commenting on their poetic value" (*SU* 266). It is not clear when CAS completed the poem; or perhaps the section that he wrote at this time proved to be the complete poem. "Saturnienne" is a coinage by CAS to denote a female denizen of the planet Saturn. Cf. "Lemurienne" (p. 260). "Aidennic" (l. 11) is an adjectival form of Aidenn (see note on "October").

Says the Dreamer. MS (*JHLS; UCLA). In *SSU.* Written c. 1950. For a Spanish version of the poem, see "Dice el soñador." The Spanish version was probably written first.

School-Room Pastime. MS (AH). In *SP*. See "Childhood: Seven Haiku."

The Sciapod. MS (AH; DAW). In *SP, S&P*. See "Strange Miniatures" and "Strange Miniatures (Haiku)." A sciapod is a fabulous denizen of Libya who used his feet for a sunshade (cf. Aristophanes, *Birds* 1553). The word is attested only in the plural (*Skiapodes*) in Greek literature.

Sea Cycle. *Wings* 8, No. 1 (Spring 1947): 11. In **SP, HD.* "Sirens' isle" (l. 12) refers to an island where the Sirens (mythological creatures, half women and half birds) dwell. In Homer's *Odyssey* (12.55–200), the island of the Sirens is located near Scylla and Charybdis, in the Straits of Messina.

The Sea-Gods. MS (JHLS; MCL). **AJ* 23, No. 36 (21 June 1923): 6. In *BS.* CAS sent the poem to GS in July or August 1913 (see *SU* 93). GS commented: "'The Sea-Gods' is a beautiful thing. My only suggestion is that you don't repeat the first stanza, but write a new one that will be even better than the rest" (letter to CAS, 19 August 1913; *SU* 94). CAS appears to have taken the advice.

Sea-Memory. In *SP.*

The Secret. MS (JHLS; NYPL; Sx). *AJ* 23, No. 27 (19 April 1923): 6. In *S.* In *Today's Literature*, ed. Dudley Chadwick Gordon, Vernon Rupert King, and William Whittingham Lyman (New York: American Book Company, 1935), p. 448. In **SP.* The ms. is dated 13 March 1923.

Secret Love. MS (JHLS; GK). In **SP* (as a translation of "Christophe des Laurières"), *S&P.* The ms. is dated 22 May 1921. CAS sent the poem to GS on 10 August 1921. GS commented: "This sonnet, 'Secret Love,' is very beautiful—a splendid lyric. I'd not use 'Carthage,' though, as that city wasn't destroyed by Time, but by its own inhabitants, at the command of the victorious Roman. I think some Asiatic city would be better, though I can't suggest one" (letter to CAS, 25 August 1921; *SU* 198). Presumably CAS substituted "Syria" (l. 6) for Carthage. For the connection of Venus (Aphrodite) and Syria (ll. 3–6), see note on "The Masque of Forsaken Gods." Adon (l. 12) is presumably short for Adonis, the beautiful youth with whom Aphrodite fell in love.

Secret Worship. MS (JHLS).

Seeker. MS (AH; DAW; JHLS). In **DC, SSU.* Written before 22 February 1951.

Seer of the Cycles. MS (*JHLS). *Epos* 8, No. 1 (Fall 1956): 9. In *SC.* Written 23 June 1952. An early version is titled "Seer" (MS [JHLS]).

Seins. MS (JHLS). The ms. is dated 20 July 1929. The title is French for "Breasts."

Selenique. MS (JHLS [as "Simile"]; *Sx). *AJ* 23, No. 41 (26 July 1923): 6 (as "Simile"). In *S, SP, LO.* The ms. is dated 3 March 1923. The title is French for "Of or pertaining to the moon" (from the Greek *selene*, moon). Selene was a Greek moon-goddess.

Semblance. MS (JHLS; NYPL; *Sx). *AJ* 23, No. 26 (12 April 1923): 6. *AJ* 23, No. 27 (19 April 1923): 6 (with corrections). *Wanderer* 1, No. 2 (July 1923): 7.

In *S. Outré* 1, No. 4 (November 1939): 8. (This entire issue was included in and attached to *Golden Atom* 1, No. 7 (April 1940): [25].) In *SP*. The ms. is dated 4 March 1923. CAS sent the poem to GS on 15 March 1923. GS commented: "'Semblance' is another 'grown-up' poem, and in your best mood" (letter to CAS, 6 April 1923; *SU* 230). For Circe (l. 12), see note on "Belated Love."

Sempiternal. See "Apostrophe."

September. MS (JHLL; JHLS; MCL). In **SP*, LO. The ms. is dated 11 September 1929.

Septembral. MS (JHLS; UCLA [as "August"]; NYPL [as "August"]). **AJ* 23, No. 47 (6 September 1923): 6. Written c. 1923. First title: "August."

Sepulture. MS (GK). *Smart Set* 57, No. 2 (October 1922): 122. In *EC*. In *California Poets: An Anthology of 224 Contemporaries* (New York: Henry Harrison, 1932), p. 664. In **SP*. CAS sent the poem to GS on 8 April 1918. GS commented: "'Sepulture' is very, very beautiful. I'm sorry it has come too late to go in the book [i.e., *OS*]" (letter to CAS, 19 April 1918; *SU* 159).

Sestet. In *SP*.

The Shadow. See "Some Blind Eidolon."

Shadow of Nightmare. In *ST*, **SP*. *Challenge* 1, No. 3 (Winter 1950): 3. *Los Angeles Science Fiction Society Newsletter* No. 22 (23 February 1964): n.p. In *LO*.

The Shadow of the Unattained. MS (*NYPL; JHLS [untitled rough draft]). CAS cited the poem in a letter to GS dated 28 April 1912, writing: "I am trying another poem, 'The Shadow of the Unattained', but it doesn't seem to take shape at all easily. Sometimes I get clear lines like these—'Fainter than winds that breathe / The folds of twilight's drapery' [cf. ll. 11–12] and again—'Beauty, whose lyric laughters hold / A sadder music learned of old, / An echo from the halls of Death—' [ll. 26–28] but, on the whole, what I have done so far is rather unsatisfactory" (*SU* 45).

Shadows. MS (DAW; JHLL; JHLS; MCL). *WT* 15, No. 2 (February 1930): 154. In *DM* 341. In **SP*, LO. The ms. is dated 12 September 1929. For "Xanadu" (l. 12), see note on "The Mirrors of Beauty." For Fomalhaut (l. 21), see note on "Demogorgon."

Shapes in the Sunset. MS (JHLS). In **DC*, BB, SZ. Vulcan (l. 5) (Volcanus) was a Roman god of fire equated with the Greek god Hephaestus. Scylla (l. 7) was a monster living in a cave in the Straits of Messina, between Italy and Sicily, opposite the whirlpool Charybdis. Triton (l. 8) was a merman, with a human head and shoulders and a fish-tail below the waist. For Mantichora (l. 9), see note on "A Hunter Meets the Martichoras." The Astomians

(l. 11) were, according to Pliny the Elder (*Natural History* 7.2.2), an Indian people who had no mouths. The Blemmyes (l. 14) (Blemmyae) were reputed to be without head or eyes and with the mouth in the breast. For Python (l. 18), see note on "The Ghoul and the Seraph." For Sciapod (l. 22), see note on "The Sciapod." For Thule (l. 31), see note on "Desolation."

A Sierran Sunrise. MS (*NYPL). In *UV*. Written c. 1910.

The Sierras. *Munsey's* 43, No. 6 (September 1910): 781 (as by C. Ashton Smith).

The Silence of Eternity. MS (JHLS, now lost). Evidently a fragment.

Silent Hour. MS (JHLS; SHSW). *Wings* 5, No. 2 (Summer 1941): 15. In *SP, HD*. The ms. is dated 30 January 1941.

Silhouette. MS (JHLS).

Simile (Ah! chide me not for silence, or that I,). MS (JHLS). The ms. is dated 12 August 1927. Originally titled "Metaphor."

Simile (Truth is a soundless gong). MS (JHLS).

Similes. See "Similitudes."

Similitude. See "Harmony."

Similitudes. MS (JHLS). Variant title: "Similes." The ms. is dated 1 February 1929.

Sinbad, It Was Not Well to Brag. MS (DAW; JHLS). In *DC*. The poem is about Sinbad (or Sindbad), a sailor who undertook seven remarkable voyages as recounted in the *Arabian Nights*. "Barnacle Bill" (l. 1) refers to "Barnacle Bill the Sailor," an American drinking song.

Slaughtered Cattle. See "Epitaphs."

Slaughter-House in Spring. MS (AH; JHLS). In *SP*. See "Neighboring Slaughter-House" and "Strange Miniatures."

Slaughter-House Pasture. MS (JHLS). In *SP*. See "Neighboring Slaughter-House."

Snake, Owl, Cat or Hawk. MS (JHLS). In *SP*. See "Mortal Essences."

The Snow-Blossoms. In *ST*.

A Snowdrop. See "To a Snowdrop."

Snowfall on Acacia. MS (JHLS). In *SP*.

Solicitation. MS (*JHLS). *Golden Atom* (August 1959, twentieth anniversary issue): 5. The ms. is dated 14 September 1932. For "Cytherean" (l. 10), see note on "Cleopatra." For Cypris (l. 11), see note on "Dedication: To Carol."

Soliloquy in an Ebon Tower. MS (AH). In *DC, BB, LO.* Written before 15 April 1951. For Hecate (l. 10), see note on "The Witch in the Graveyard." Charon (l. 14) was, in Greek myth, the ferryman who conveyed the souls of the dead across the river Styx. Ecbatana (l. 39) is the Greek name for a city in Persia captured by Cyrus the Great in 549 B.C.E. Clotho, Lachesis, and Atropos (ll. 51–52) are the three Fates, represented as three old spinning women: Clotho held the distaff, Lachesis drew the thread, and Atropos cut it short, symbolizing death. For Gomorrah (l. 57), see note on "Ennui." Elysium (l. 64) was the abode of the blest in Greek myth, corresponding to the Christian heaven; Theleme (Thélème) is the name of an abbey in Rabelais' *Gargantua and Pantagruel,* governed by the rule "Do what you wish." For "Typhoean" (l. 70), see note on "Saturn." For Hesper (l. 73), see note on "The Nameless Wraith." For "Uranian" (l. 75), see note on "The Masque of Forsaken Gods." For Vulcan (l. 76), see note on "Shapes in the Sunset." Azoth (l. 81) is an adaptation of an Arabic word meaning "the mercury," and conceived by mediaeval alchemists as the primary seed of all metals; Alkahest is a pseudo-Arabic term purportedly invented by Paracelsus to denote a liquid having the power to dissolve gold and any other substance. For Circe (l. 87), see note on "The Thralls of Circe Climb Parnassus." Simaetha is a witch or enchantress in Theocritus' *Idyls* 2.101–16. Daedalus (l. 88) was the skilled artisan who built the Labyrinth on Crete to house the Minotaur. For Lar (l. 95), see note on "Song of the Necromancer"; for Lemur (l. 95), see note on "Mirrors"; for the Chimera (l. 95), see note on "The Chimera." For Dis (l. 97), see note on "Farewell to Eros."

Solution. MS (JHLS; NYPL). In EC. *WT* 3, No. 1 (January 1924): 32. In *SP.* In *LO.* The ms. is dated 25 December 1919. CAS sent the poem to GS on 27 December 1919. GS commented: "'Solution' is certainly a terror" (letter to CAS, 20 January 1920; *SU* 179). Acheron (l. 10) is one of the rivers in the Greek underworld.

Some Blind Eidolon. MS (AH; DAW; JHLS). *Kaleidograph* 19, No. 2 (June 1947): 2–3. In *SP, DC, LO.* First title: "The Shadow." The ms. is dated 23 March 1947. For "gardened Babylon" (l. 22), see note on "Hanging Gardens" in "Desert Dweller." Moloch (l. 34) is a form of Baal (see note on "Pour Chercher du nouveau") in the Canaanite religion, to whom human sacrifices were made. On the verso of the AH ms., two lines appear: "What Atlantean daemons haunt the day / In the black age of matter and machine." It is not clear whether they are intended to go with the poem or comprise a separate fragment.

Someone. MS (DAW; JHLS). In *SP.*

Somnus (The bottom-lands of Lethe and of Night:). MS (JHLS). In *SP.* "Somnus" is the Latin word for "sleep." It is occasionally personified as a god, the son of Erebus (darkness) and Nox (night), parallel to the Greek Hypnos, son of Nyx (night) and Thanatos (death).

Somnus (The flowing silence of Lethe). MS (JHLS).

Song (I am grown tired of suffering,). MS (*JHLS; MCL). Written 19 December 1927. For "Tyrian" (l. 3), see note on "The Sorrow of the Winds."

Song (I bring my weariness to thee,). In *EC, *SP.* Written before 25 June 1922. CAS sent the poem, along with "Plum-Flowers," to GS on 25 June 1922. GS liked both poems and wished to submit them to *Snappy Stories* (see *SU* 210), but CAS had already submitted "Plum-Flowers" (it was accepted), and "Song" was to be included in *EC* and would not have been able to appear in the magazine prior to book publication.

Song (O mouth by many kissed,). MS (JHLS). Written 12 September 1924. See "A Catch."

Song (Vagrant from the realms of rose,). From *The Fugitives*. MS (JHLS [fragment]; NYPL). *AJ* 23, No. 33 (31 May 1923): 6. *Wanderer* 2, No. 1 (January 1924): 1 (as "The Fugitive"). In *S, *SP.* Written before 7 March 1923.

Song (When in the desert). MS (*JHLS). In *SSU.* An English translation of the Spanish poem "Cantar."

Song. See "Love Is Not Yours, Love Is Not Mine."

Song. See "Nevermore."

Song. See "Remembrance."

Song. See "The Seekers."

Song at Evenfall. MS (DAW; *JHLS). *Overland Monthly* 88, No. 5 (May 1930): 149.

A Song from Hell. In *SH, LO.* CAS sent the poem to GS on 6 October 1911, remarking: "The 'Song From Hell' is a subject that it would take Browning to do rightly. I do not remember to have seen anything of the kind before" (*SU* 31). GS commented: "The 'Song from Hell' is powerful and well-handled, but (to me personally) distasteful, by reason of its subject-matter being inherently and fundamentally untrue: 'hell is the only thing that can't be,' as I once said to a priest-friend" (letter to CAS, 21 December 1911; *SU* 34). GS's disapproval probably led CAS to keep the poem unpublished.

Song (from The Fugitives). See *The Fugitives.*

The Song of a Comet. MS (GK; JHLS). In *ST, N1, *SP, LO*. CAS sent the poem to GS in a non-extant letter of Jan. or Feb. 1912; GS commented (letter to CAS, 11 February 1912): "The 'Comet' ode is a big thing, and of the same rank as your great odes 'To the Abyss' and 'The Star-Treader'" (*SU* 36). At the bottom of the ms. GS has written: "A very great poem. I have no suggestions I dare offer." "Lion's track" (l. 33) refers to the constellation Leo. "The Lyre" (l. 34) refers to the constellation Lyra. Arcturus (l. 59) is the brightest star in the constellation Bootes and the sixth brightest star in the sky.

The Song of Aviol. See *The Fugitives.*

The Song of Cartha. See *The Fugitives.*

A Song of Dreams. In *ST, N1, *SP, LO*.

The Song of Galeor. See *The Dead Will Cuckold You.*

Song of Sappho's Arabian Daughter. *Ainslee's* 43, No. 1 (February 1919): 80 (as "The Desert Garden"). In *EC, *SP*. Sappho, the Greek poet (born c. 612 B.C.E.), is said to have married one Cercylas and had a child, Cleis, but neither Cercylas nor Cleis are believed to have been Arabian.

The Song of Songs. MS (JHLS).

Song of the Bacchic Bards. MS (JHLS). For Bacchus and the Bacchantes (l. 7), see note on "Bacchante." "Plutonian" (l. 3) refers to Pluto (see note on "Farewell to Eros"). For Parnassus (l. 15), see note on "The Thralls of Circe Climb Parnassus." For Rabelais (l. 17), see note on "Humors of Love."

Song of the Free Beings. MS (JHLS). First title: "Song of the Free Creatures." An English translation of the Spanish poem "El Cantar de los seres libres."

Song of the Necromancer. MS (DAW; JHLL; JHLS; MCL). *WT* 29, No. 2 (February 1937): 220. In *SP, BB, LO*. For "Gorgon" (l. 23), see note on "Medusa." Lar is the tutelar deity of a household in ancient Rome (almost always in the plural, *Lares*).

The Song of the Stars. In *ST*.

The Song of the Worlds. In *SH*.

Song to Oblivion. In *ST*. See note on "Sonnet on Oblivion."

Sonnet (Empress with eyes more sad and aureate). MS (DAW; JHLS). *WT* 13, No. 4 (April 1929): 542. In *SP*. For Saturnus (l. 7), see note on "Enchanted Mirrors."

Sonnet (How shall our hearts, those fragile shrines of thee,). MS (MCL). In *SP, HD*. Written before 22 February 1940.

Sonnet (Slowly, sweetly, from the fear that folds or breaks,). MS (JHLS).

Sonnet. See "But Grant, O Venus."

Sonnet. See "Duality."

Sonnet. See "To the Beloved."

Sonnet for the Psychoanalysts. MS (DAW; JHLS [as "Surréaliste Sonnet 2"]). In *SP, *DC. WT* 44, No. 2 (January 1952): 73. Written October 1948. First title: "Surréaliste Sonnet 2." "Falernian" (l. 7) refers to Falernian wine, a celebrated wine among the Romans named after a region in Campania called *Falernus ager* ("the Falernian field").

Sonnet lunaire [English]. MS (*JHLS). An English translation of the French poem of the same title (p. 283). The French poem was written first. CAS has written a note at the bottom of the ms.: "Literal English of French poem by C. A. S."

Sonnet lunaire [French]. MS (DAW; *JHLS; MCL). The title is French for "Lunar Sonnet." For CAS's English translation, see p. 284.

Sonnet on Music. MS (JHLS).

Sonnet on Oblivion. MS (JHLS). GS wrote "Three Sonnets on Oblivion" (*Century Magazine,* September 1908; in *A Wine of Wizardry and Other Poems* [1909]), which were among his most celebrated and frequently reprinted works. For Nirvana (l. 14), see note on "Nirvana."

Sonnet to the Sphinx. MS (JHLS).

Sonnets of the Seasons. MS (*JHLS [2 mss., one containing only the second sonnet, as "The Noon of the Seasons"]). In *UV* ("Summer" only; as "The Noon of the Seasons").

Sonnets on Dreams. See "The Dream-God's Realm."

The Sorcerer Departs. *Acolyte* 2, No. 2 (Spring 1944): 15. In *IM, *BB, SSU.* See also "Cycles."

The Sorcerer to His Love. MS (JHLS). *WT* 39, No. 1 (September 1945): 63. In *SP, HD, LO.* The ms. is dated 16 November 1941. Zimimar (l. 2) is CAS's invention.

The Sorrow of the Winds. *Poetry* 1, No. 3 (December 1912): 80 (as "Sorrowing of Winds"). In *EC, *SP.* "Tyrian" (l. 5) refers to Tyre, the most important city in Phoenicia, located in modern-day Lebanon. It was settled as early as the 13th century B.C.E. and was sacked by Alexander the Great in 332 B.C.E.

The Soul of the Sea. In *ST.*

Souvenance. MS (DAW; JHLS [2 mss., one titled "Verses"]). In *SC. The ms. is dated 25 August 1927. First title: "Verses." The title is French for "Recollection."

Le Souvenir. MS (JHLS). The ms. is dated 28 July 1929. The title is French for "The Memory."

The Sparrow's Nest. MS (AH; DAW; JHLS). In *SP, S&P. See "Distillations," "Eight Haiku," "Haiku," and "Strange Miniatures."

Spectral Life. MS (*JHLL, DAW). In KML. An English version of the French poem "Une Vie spectrale" (p. 397).

Speculation. MS (GK).

Sphinx and Medusa. In PD. For Medusa, see note on "Medusa."

The Sphinx of the Infinite. In GF.

Spring. See "Sonnets of the Seasons."

Spring Nunnery. MS (AH; JHLS). In *SP. See "Eight Haiku" and "Strange Miniatures." See also note on "Improbable Dream."

The Star-Treader. MS (JHLS [fragment]; as "The Sun-Treader": MS [BL (first half); MCL (second half)].). In ST, *SP, LO. Written before 6 October 1911. First title: "The Sun-Treader." CAS said of the poem: "It was written in a mood of midsummer fantasy, and altogether to suit myself. It is frightfully irregular, both in thought and form, and probably a little obscure" (letter to GS, 6 October 1911; SU 31). GS said of it: "It's a magnificent thing wonderfully put, and (to me at least) not at all obscure, though it will be far over the heads of the many. I hardly know how to express myself about it, as I like one part about as well as another. But I *can* say that it's *great poetry*" (letter to CAS, 21 December 1911; SU 34). "Pleiades" (l. 87) refers to a cluster of seven stars in the constellation Taurus. Alcyone (l. 88) is the brightest of the Pleiades. Antares (l. 99) is a red star of the first magnitude in the constellation Scorpio.

The Storm. See "The Cohorts of the Storm."

Storm's End. MS (AH). In *SP. See "Strange Miniatures."

Stormy Afterglow. In SP. First title: "Stormy Sunset." See "Haiku."

Strange Girl. MS (SHSW). Wings 6, No. 3 (Autumn 1943): 12–13. In The Music Makers, ed. Stanton A. Coblentz (New York: Bernard Ackerman, 1945), pp. 224–25. In *SP, SSU. In a letter to August Derleth dated 18 May 1943 (MS, SHSW), CAS wrote regarding the poem: "The girl claimed to be a cousin of Jack London and a niece of the late Henry Van Dyke—a combination of blood-strains that would drive anyone to the devil!" Tanagra (l. 18) was a town in Boeotia, Greece, where the Spartans defeated the Athenians in 457 B.C.E. The terra-cotta figurines discovered there in 1874 made the town famous.

Strange Miniatures. MS (AH). Comprises "Unicorn"; "Untold Arabian Fable"; "A Hunter Meets the Martichoras"; "The Limniad"; "The Sciapod"; "The Monacle"; "Feast of St. Anthony"; "Empusa Waylays a Traveler"; "Perseus and Medusa"; "The Ghost of Theseus"; "Phallus Impudica"; "Story Sunset"; "Foggy Night"; "Geese in the Spring Night"; "Love in Dreams"; "The Sparrow's Nest"; "The Last Apricot"; "Mushroom Gatherers"; "Spring Nunnery"; "Nuns Walking in the Orchard"; "Improbable Dream"; "Night of Miletus"; "Tryst at Lobos"; "High Mountain Juniper"; "Storm's End"; "Slaughter-House in Spring"; "Pool at Lobos"; "Fallen Grape-Leaf"; "Californian Winter"; "Crows in March"; "Felo-de-se of the Parasite"; "Poet Drinking in a Barroom"; "Reigning Empress"; "Oblivion" (= "Lethe"); "Initiate" (= "Initiate of Dionysus"); "Bacchic Orgy"; "Picture by Piero di Cosimo"; and "Future Meeting." This ms. contains only nine of the fourteen haiku that appeared in *SP* in the subsection "Strange Miniatures" under "Experiments in Haiku," lacking "Paphnutius"; "Philtre"; "Borderland"; "Lethe"; and "Odysseus in Eternity"; and including "Empusa Waylays a Traveller." The titles follow "The Ghost of Theseus" in the subsection "Distillations."

Strange Miniatures (Haiku). MS (AH). In **SP, S&P.* Comprises "Unicorn"; "Untold Arabian Fable"; "A Hunter Meets the Martichoras"; "Philtre"; "The Limniad"; "The Sciapod"; "The Monacle"; "Feast of St. Anthony"; "Paphnutius"; "Perseus and Medusa"; "Odysseus in Eternity"; "The Ghost of Theseus"; and "Borderland." *SP* includes "Lethe"; *S&P* lacks "The Limniad"; "Odysseus in Eternity"; "The Ghost of Theseus"; and "Borderland."

Strangeness. MS (JHLS; MCL; NYPL). *Bohemia* 2, No. 4 ([May] 1917): 3. In *EC, *SP* (20 lines; TMS of *SP* has 24 lines, four of which had been added in pen), *LO.* The ms. is dated 3 October 1916. CAS sent the poem to GS on 11 October 1916, and GS commented (letter to CAS, 29 October 1916): "I like the lyric you send, decidedly. It's a jewelled thing" (*SU* 141). Of its appearance in *Bohemia*, CAS noted tartly: "They gave it the place of honour—the entire front page, opposite a photograph of the latest 'movie' actress!" (CAS to SL, 6 June 1917; ms., BL).

STYES WITH SPIRES. MS (JHLS). A parody of modern poetry. The poem is typed in all-capitals in the only extant ms.

The Stylite. MS (JHLS). In **DC.* The ms. is dated 10 January 1951. Satanas (l. 12) is the Greek name for Satan. For Ashtaroth (l. 18), see note on "Pour Chercher du nouveau." For Nereides (l. 22), see note on "The Nereid." For Cypris (l. 24), see note on "Dedication: To Carol." For Gomorrah (l. 28), see note on "Soliloquy in an Ebon Tower." Sheol (l. 31), in the Jewish religion, is the dark underworld abode of the dead.

Sufficiency. MS (JHLS). In *SP. The ms. is dated 5 February 1929. For Ispahan (l. 3), see note on "Surréalist Sonnet."

Suggestion. MS (*JHLS). In GF.

Summer. See "Sonnets of the Seasons."

The Summer Hills. MS (JHLS).

The Summer Moon. In ST, *SP.

The Sunrise. MS (JHLS). *Rosary Magazine 42, No. 1 (January 1913): 96 (last stanza only; as "Dawn").

The Suns and the Void. MS (JHLS). In *TT. For Polaris (l. 29), see note on "Outlanders." For Fomalhaut (l. 31), see note on "Demogorgon."

Sunset. MS (JHLS).

A Sunset (As blood from some enormous hurt). In ST, *SP.

A Sunset (Far-falling from a wounded heaven,). MS (JHLS) [as "Un Couchant"]). Written before 15 November 1925. In SC. For a French version, see "Un Couchant" (above).

The Sunset Islands. See "The Cloud Islands."

Sunset over Farm-Land. In SP.

The Sun-Treader. See "The Star-Treader."

Súplica. See "¿Donde duermes, Eldorado?"

Supplication. MS (JHLS; SHSW). In *SP, HD. First title: "Prayer." The ms. is dated 30 September 1942. For "Stygian" (l. 17), see note on "Farewell to Eros."

Surréalist Sonnet. MS (DAW; SHSW). In SP, *DC. Written 29 December 1945. In a letter to August Derleth dated 9 July 1946 (ms., SHSW), CAS described the poem as "a take-off on [Salvador] Dali." Ispahan (l. 4) is a city in Persia (now Isfahan or Esfahan in Iran) that was founded by the Elamites and was later occupied by the Sassanids, Arsacids, and Parthians. It became a leading city under the Arabs; in the 16th century it became the capital of the Safavid dynasty. In 1722 it was raided by the Afghans and largely destroyed. Regulus (l. 12) is the brightest star in the constellation Leo.

Surréaliste Sonnet 2. See "Sonnet for the Psychoanalysts."

Swine and Azaleas. See "The Thralls of Circe Climb Parnassus."

Symbols. MS (JHLS; NYPL). *London Mercury* No. 33 (July 1922): 245 (as by A. Clark Ashton Smith). In *EC*. In *California Poets: An Anthology of 224 Contemporaries* (New York: Henry Harrison, 1932), p. 664. In **SP, LO*. The ms. is dated 13 August 1919.

Tanka. See "**Transmutation**" and "**You Are Not Beautiful.**"

Tankas. See "**Departure,**" "**Diversity,**" "**The Lemurienne,**" and "**You Are Not Beautiful.**"

The Tartarus of the Suns. In *TS*.

The Tears of Lilith. MS (JHLS; NYPL). In *EC, *SP, LO*. The ms. is dated 26 April 1917. CAS sent the poem to GS on 17 June 1917, noting that he wrote it in May. GS commented: "I like 'The Tears of Lilith'—a lovely lyric" (letter to CAS, 8 July 1917; *SU* 150). Lilith is mentioned once in the Bible (Isaiah 34:14) as a screech owl. In the rabbinical tradition she was believed to be Adam's first wife, created simultaneously with him. In the medieval period she was thought to be a witch or night-demon.

The Temple of Night. MS (JHLS).

Temporality. MS (*JHLS). In *KML, FD, SZ*. The ms. is dated 13 April 1928.

The Temptation (In the close and clinging night,) MS (*JHLS [titled "To Lilith"] and NYPL: drafts only). In "On Fantasy" by Fritz Leiber, *Fantasy Newsletter* No. 33 (February 1981): 4. Begun 23 September 1924; completed 27 October 1924. CAS wrote to GS (3 October 1924): "I have written about 75 lines of a poem called 'The Temptation', which will be unprintable outside of some such collection as 'Poetica Erotica.' Fatigue and depression have kept me from finishing it, so far" (*SU* 245). CAS refers to *Poetica Erotica*, ed. T. R. Smith (1921–22; 2 vols.), a collection of erotic poetry that included 6 poems by GS but none by CAS, even though GS had recommended CAS to the editor. CAS sent the poem to GS on 27 October 1924. GS commented: "All our crowd—the 'Telegraph Hill bunch'—liked 'The Temptation' immensely. It seems, so far, to be written just about as Keats would have done it, had he tried to do something similar. Why don't you go on with it? We'd all like to see more in the same vein. It would be 'indecent' only to 'the booboisie'" (letter to CAS, 24 December 1924; *SU* 247). Erycine (l. 18), or Erycina, is a surname of Aphrodite, derived from Mt. Eryx in Sicily, where her cult was established. Antony (l. 27) refers to St. Anthony (see note on "Feast of St. Anthony").

Tempus. In *SP* (as a translation of "Christophe des Laurières"). The title is Latin for "time." For Acheron (l. 1), see note on "Solution."

"That Last Infirmity." *Wings* 5, No. 1 (Spring 1941): 18 (as "Fame"). In **SP*. The title is from John Milton's "Lycidas" (1638): "Fame is the spur that the clear spirit doth raise / (That last infirmity of noble mind)" (ll. 70–71).

"That Motley Drama." In *SP*, **S&P* (as a translation of "Clérigo Herrero"). Written 21 October 1949. The title derives from Poe's "The Conqueror Worm" (included in "Ligeia," 1838): "That motley drama—oh, be sure / It shall not be forgot!" (ll. 17–18).

Thebaid. MS (JHLS). In **S&P, BB*. Variant titles: "Arctica Deserta" and "Ultima Thule." The ms. is dated 14 February 1954. The title (referring to a poem about the Greek city of Thebes) was used as the title of an epic poem by the Latin poet Statius (P. Papinius Statius, 45?–96? C.E.), dealing with the attempt by Polyneices (son of Oedipus) to regain the throne of Thebes. (The story is also the subject of Sophocles' play *The Seven Against Thebes*.) For Stylites (l. 2), see note on "Paphnutius." Anthony (l. 2) refers to St. Anthony (see note on "Feast of St. Anthony").

The Thralls of Circe Climb Parnassus. MS (JHLS [2 mss., one as "Swine and Azaleas"]; DAW [as "Swine and Azaleas"]; orig. ms. in copy #6 of *HD*). In **SP, SSU*. First title: "Swine and Azaleas." The ms. is dated 16 July 1941. For the myth of Circe, see note on "Belated Love." Parnassus is a mountain in Greece, a few miles north of Delphi, sacred to Apollo and associated with the Muses.

Three Similes. See "Variations."

The Throne of Winter. MS (*JHLS). In *FD*.

Time. MS (JHLS).

Time the Wonder. MS (JHLS).

Tin Can on the Mountain-Top. MS (JHLS). In **SP*. First title: "Tomato-Can on the Mountain-Top." "Donner's peak" (l. 6) presumably refers to the encampment of the Donner party in 1846–47 at Truckee Lake in the Sierra Nevada mountains. Trapped by snow over the winter, the party suffered extreme hardship and survived by resorting to cannibalism. The Coit Memorial Tower (l. 17) on Telegraph Hill, San Francisco, was built in 1933 through the bequest of local benefactor Lillie Hitchcock Coit (1842–1929). "Huysmanesque" (l. 38) refers to Joris-Karl Huysmans (1848–1907), author of such Decadent works as *A Rebours* (1884; *Against Nature*) and *Là-bas* (1891; *Down There*).

Tired Gardener. MS (JHLS). In **S&P*. *Epos* 9, No. 1 (Fall 1957): 16–17. The ms. is dated 5 August 1955. For "Tyrian" (l. 3), see note on "The Sorrow of the Winds." For "Mammonian" (l. 12), see note on "The Envoys."

The Titans in Tartarus. MS (*NYPL). In *TT, LO*. Written before 29 October 1912. CAS wrote of the poem to GS on 30 August 1912: "I've written some more blank-verse lately—a thing called 'The Titans in Tartarus', but I won't be sending it to you for a long time yet. I'm not sure that it's much good, but I am sure that it needs some whole-hearted and hard-handed revision" (*SU*

59). CAS sent the poem to GS on 29 October 1912. GS commented: "Your own 'Titans in Tartarus' I like, for there are some big lines in it, and the whole visualization is sublime. But it is not nearly as good as your poem on the marching Titans—I forget its exact title ['Saturn']" (letter to CAS, 11 November 1912; *SU* 270). For the Titans and Tartarus, see note on "The Return of Hyperion." CAS had begun another poem called "The Titans Triumphant" (see *SU* 50), but it apparently does not survive.

The Titans Triumphant. Either non-extant or a variant title of an unidentified poem. CAS writes to GS (9 June 1912): "I have begun a narrative poem entitled 'The Titans Triumphant', but I may not do much more with it at present. It will inevitably be rather Miltonic" (*SU* 50). When sending "The Titans in Tartarus" to GS on 29 October 1912, CAS noted: "I've begun another thing, 'The Titans Triumphant', which may run to 200 lines or so. It should be better than the poem I enclose" (*SU* 70). CAS then wrote to GS (30 December 1912): "I shall go on with 'The Titans Triumphant' presently. It's a thing I began several months ago. It should be better than 'The Titans in Tartarus,' anyway, for the action that I shall put into it" (*SU* 76).

To a Cloud. MS (JHLS). Tubal Cain (l. 34) (more properly Tubal-Cain) is cited in the Bible (Gen. 4:22) as the first smith, a worker in brass and iron.

To a Fairy-Lantern. See "To a Snowdrop."

To a Friend. See "Query."

To a Mariposa Lily. In *SC.*

To a Northern Venus. MS (*JHLS; NYPL). Friga (l. 21) is, in Norse myth, the principal wife of Odin and the queen of the gods.

To a Snowdrop. MS (JHLS). First titles: "To a Fairy-Lantern" and "A Snowdrop."

To a Yellow Pine. MS (JHLS). Written c. 1910. In *EOD* ll. 23–30 are listed as an untitled poem.

To Ambition. MS (JHLS).

To an Absent Muse. See "The Absence of the Muse."

To Antares. MS (JHLS). In *SP, LO.* The ms. is dated 25 August 1927. For Antares, see note on "The Star-Treader."

To Aphrodite. See "Ode to Aphrodite."

To Bacchante. MS (JHLS [without title]). In *SP (without title), HD.* The dedicatory poem to *HD.* The epigraph is from the *Greek Anthology,* Book 5, no. 98 (attributed to Archias). CAS has used the translation by J. W. Mackail in *Select Epigrams from the Greek Anthology* (London: Longmans, Green, 1928), p. 20.

To Beauty. In *SP, GF* (as "Ode to Beauty"; called "unfinished"). CAS sent the poem to SL in May 1915, noting that it had been written "a year or so ago. I've no present prospect of ever finishing it" (letter to SL, 10 May 1915; ms., BL). MS (JHLS). In *GF* there is a note by CAS: "For George [Sterling]."

To Carol. See "Dedication: To Carol."

To Columbine. See "A Meeting."

To George Sterling (Deep are the chasmal years and lustrums long). MS (JHLS; SHSW). In *SP, GS, SU, SSU*. The first version (dated 20 November 1941) has the first line "The years are many, and the years are long"; another variant version has the first line "What deeply chasmal years, and lustrums long." One ms. has a note by CAS: "Commissioned sonnet written for Rudolph E. Blaettler to publish by Stanford Univ. Press, and criticised by him. See letter to CAS from Rudolph Blaettler, collection of G.S. Later, CAS re-wrote in 1941 when poem becomes a paean of joy rather than a tribute to his dead friend. He [i.e., CAS] had, no doubt, met the dancer Madylynne Greene—when re-written." The epigraph is from GS's "Venus Letalis" (*Smart Set*, March 1923), l. 24. The line "the fleeting plaudits of the throng" (l. 5) is a quotation from GS's poem "To Xavier Martinez, Painter" (l. 7), in *The Caged Eagle and Other Poems* (San Francisco: A. M. Robertson, 1916), p. 110.

To George Sterling (High priest of this our latter Song,). In *GS*. Written 1910.

To George Sterling (His song shall waken the dull-sleeping throng). In *GS*.

To George Sterling (O Beauty, goddess known and sung of old). MS (JHLS).

To George Sterling (What questioners have met the gaze of Time,). In *GS*. CAS sent this poem to GS with his letter of 12 December 1911 (see *SU* 33). GS commented: "I don't know how to thank you for the fine sonnet—Heaven knows I wish I were worthy of it! It is good all through, tho' improving as it goes on, as a sonnet should" (letter to CAS, 21 December 1911; *SU* 34).

To George Sterling: A Valediction. MS (JHLL; MCL; SFPL [as "Memorial to George Sterling"]; UCLA [as "A Valediction to George Sterling"]). *Overland Monthly* 85, No. 11 (November 1927): 338. In *SP, GS, LO* (all as "A Valediction to George Sterling"). Written December 1926, following Sterling's death on 17 November 1926. First title: "Memorial to George Sterling." For "Proserpine" (l. 51), see note on "On Re-reading Baudelaire." For "Cytherean" (l. 59), see note on "Cleopatra."

To Howard Phillips Lovecraft. MS (DAW; JHLL; SHSW). *WT* 30, No. 1 (July 1937): 48. Rpt. H. P. Lovecraft, *Marginalia*, ed. August Derleth and Donald Wandrei (Sauk City, WI: Arkham House, 1944), pp. 370–71. In *SP, LO*. The ms. is dated 31 March 1937. A poem written to Lovecraft (1890–

1937) sixteen days after his death. Providence, R.I. (l. 4), was Lovecraft's home for most of his life. Arkham (l. 8) was a fictional town in New England first mentioned in "The Picture in the House" (1920) and featured in many other tales. "Silver Key" (l. 14) refers to the story "The Silver Key" (1926), where Randolph Carter finds such a key and uses it to return to his childhood. Ulthar (l. 17) is a city invented in "The Cats of Ulthar" (1920); Pnath is a realm invented in the story "The Doom That Came to Sarnath" (1919) and used in several later stories. Kadath (l. 18) is a realm first cited in "The Other Gods" (1921) and used in several later tales, notably *The Dream-Quest of Unknown Kadath* (1926–27) [although CAS had not yet read the short novel at the time he wrote this poem]. Cthulhu (l. 20) is an extraterrestrial entity first cited in "The Call of Cthulhu" (1926). "Old Ones" (l. 23) refers to several groups of extraterrestrial entities, perhaps most notably in *At the Mountains of Madness* (1931). Averoigne (l. 33) is a fictitious region in medieval France invented by CAS and featured in several tales.

To Lesbia. See "Classic Epigram."

To Life. See "The Harlot of the World."

To Lilith. See "The Temptation."

To Lilith. See "Lines on a Picture."

To Love. See "Amor Aeternalis."

To Nora May French. MS (JHLL; JHLS). In *EC, *SP, LO*. Begun c. June 1916, completed before 10 July 1920. Nora May French (1881–1907) was a California poet and friend of GS who committed suicide on 13 November 1907 in GS's home in Carmel. GS and others issued her *Poems* in 1910. GS sent CAS the book in 1912, and CAS commented: "Many, many thanks to you for the lovely volume of Nora May French's poems. They're all wonderful, and some of them have stirred me more than anything I have seen, in many a day. I love them all" (letter to GS, 9 June 1912; *SU* 49). Elsewhere CAS wrote: "No other woman-poet since Sappho (and certainly not the grotesquely overrated Mrs. Browning) is worthy to stand beside her. Nearly every line that she wrote was pure poetry. And of how many poets (irrespective of sex) can you say that?" (CAS to SL, 25 September 1915; ms., BL). GS had been urging CAS to write an elegy to French since 1915, for a book of tributes to French that Harry Lafler was assembling (see *SU* 124), but CAS long demurred, saying: "You ask if I've ever written anything on Nora May French. I'd like to, but I fear I've no talent for personal or memorial verse" (letter to GS, 16 August 1915; *SU* 125). On 27 December 1915 CAS wrote to GS: "Tell Lafler that I'm planning an ode on Nora May French" (*SU* 131), and on 20 June 1916 he wrote: "I began a poem on Nora May French some time ago, but haven't finished it yet" (*SU* 137). CAS finally sent the poem to GS on 10 July 1920, noting: "my blank verses on Nora May French appear tedious, rambling, and uninspired" (*SU* 184). But GS commented: "You don't seem to care for your poem on Nora May French, but to me it seems a very lovely thing, and I'm sure Lafler will think the same of it as soon as I've shown it to him" (*SU* 185). Lafler's volume never appeared. For Lemuria (l. 49), see note on "Mirrors." For Atlantis (l. 49), see note on "Atlantis." "Leucadian" (l. 55) refers to Leucas, a promontory on the island of Leucadia (now Capo Ducato), off the west coast of Greece. CAS used the adjective because it was from here that the Greek poet Sappho reputedly leaped to her death. Mytelene (l. 63) (more properly Mytilene) is one of the chief cities of the island of Lesbos (Sappho was born in the city of Eresus in Lesbos). Erinna (l. 68) was a Greek poet (4th century B.C.E.) from the island of Telos; she died at the age of nineteen, and her work survives only in small fragments. "Hecatean" (l. 75) refers to Hecate, Greek goddess frequently associated with the ghost world.

To Omar. See "To Omar Khayyam."

To Omar Khayyam. MS (GK; NYPL [as "To Omar"]). In *EC. Lyric West* 5, No. 8 (May–June 1926): 216–17. In *SP*, *LO*. First title: "To Omar." The ms. is dated 13 December 1919. The poem is addressed to Omar Khayyam (1050?–1123?), Persian poet and astronomer whose *Rubaiyat* ("quatrains") emphasizes the spirit of hedonism with its focus on the pleasures afforded by wine and women. Many of CAS's juvenile poems were written in the spirit of Omar Khayyam. CAS said of it (letter to GS, 27 December 1919): "I wish the Omar ode were better—it seems a string of pessimistic platitudes" (*SU* 178). GS commented (letter to CAS, 20 January 1920): "I should, I know, have written to you weeks ago and said how beautiful a thing I think the 'Omar' ode is. You are extremely successful with your odes, and I hope you'll give more time to them" (*SU* 178). CAS submitted the poem to *Asia*, but it was rejected; as CAS explains: "'Asia' has just returned my 'Omar' ode. They seemed to like the poem, but, I dare say, thought its publication in their pages not 'advisable.' It might 'get them in bad' with many of their readers. The hedonism (not to mention the pessimism) of the poem would be anathema to a lot of people in this Puritan paradise" (CAS to SL, 25 February 1920; ms., BL).

To One Absent. MS (DAW; JHLS; SHSW). In *SP*, *HD*. The ms. bears the notation: "January 29, 1941; revised 1943." "Cyprian" (l. 15) refers to Cyprus, an island associated with Aphrodite (see note on "The Ghoul and the Seraph").

To Poetry. See "Ode to Poetry."

To the Beloved. MS (JHLS). In *EC*, *SP*, *BS*. First title: "Sonnet." CAS sent this poem to GS on 2 March 1919, noting that it had been written in February (*SU* 169).

To the Chimera. MS (NYPL; *Sx). *AJ* 24, No. 25 (3 April 1924): 6. *United Amateur* 23, No. 1 (May 1924): 7. In *S. Helios* 1, No. 3 (August–September 1937): 10. *WT* 40, No. 6 (September 1948): 79. In *SP, LO.* For the Chim[a]era, see note on "The Chimera."

To the Crescent Moon. MS (JHLS).

To the Daemon Sublimity. MS (JHLS; FSC). In *SP. In *FSC* 184. In *LO.* First title: "To the Spirit of Sublimity." Written 1912.

To the Darkness. In *ST, OS, N1, *SP, LO.*

To the Morning Star (Triumphant rise, O star, on pinions fleet,). MS (*JHLS). In *FD.*

To the Morning Star (Thou art the star of hope that 'fore the dawn). MS (JHLS).

To the Nightshade. In *PJ.* Written c. 1910.

To the Spirit of Sublimity. See "To the Daemon Sublimity."

To the Sun (Thy light is as an eminence unto thee,). In *ST, *SP.* For "Arcturus" (l. 22), see note on "The Song of a Comet." "Hercules" (l. 28) refers to the constellation of that name.

To the West Wind. See "The West Wind."

To Thomas Paine (O priest of Truth and herald of the light,). MS (MH). Apparently a radical revision of CAS's earlier poem on Paine (p. 51).

To Thomas Paine (O thou who dared the sacred truth proclaim). MS (JHLS). The poem concerns Thomas Paine (1737–1809), British author and journalist who came to the American colonies in 1774 and published the pamphlet *Common Sense* (1776), espousing the cause of American independence. The poem addresses Paine's later treatise, *The Age of Reason* (1794–96), condemning religious fanaticism and asserting that the "miracles" recorded in the Bible should be rejected as offensive to reason. Although Paine was a deist, the pamphlet was so controversial that he was accused of being an atheist.

To Whom It May Concern. MS (GK). In *SP.* For Pegasus (l. 7), see note on "The Chimera."

Tolometh. In *SP, S&P.* A revised version of "Ougabalys" (p. 407). The title is a proper name of CAS's invention. Poseidonis (l. 1) is believed by occultists to have been the last portion of the continent of Atlantis to sink into the ocean.

Tomato-Can on the Mountain-Top. See "Tin-Can on the Mountain-Top."

Touch. MS (JHLS). In *SP.*

Town Lights. MS (JHLS; SHSW). *Wings* 5, No. 8 (Winter 1943): 15. In *The Music Makers*, ed. Stanton A. Coblentz (New York: Bernard Ackerman, 1945), pp. 223–24. In *IM*, **SP*. The ms. is dated 15 November 1941.

Transcendence. MS (JHLS; NYPL). In *EC*. *Argonaut* (16 December 1922): 387. In *Continent's End: An Anthology of Contemporary California Poets*, ed. George Sterling, Genevieve Taggard, and James Rorty (San Francisco: Book Club of California, 1925), p. 195. In *Great Poems of the English Language*, ed. Wallace Alvin Briggs (New York: Robert M. McBride, 1927; London: George C. Harrap & Co., 1928), pp. 1338–39; rev. ed. New York: Tudor Publishing Co., 1936, pp. 1338–39. In **SP, LO*. CAS notes that he wrote the poem in February 1919 (letter to GS, 2 March 1919; *SU* 169).

Transmutation. MS (NYPL [under "Tankas"] and JHLS [under "Tanka"). **AJ* 24, No. 16 (31 January 1924): 6.

The Traveller. MS (JHLS). The ms. is dated 21 April 1919.

Triple Aspect. MS (GK; JHLS). In *EC*, **SP, LO*.

Tristan to Iseult. MS (JHLS). *Westward* 4, No. 4 (April 1935): 7. In **SP* (as a translation of "Christophe des Laurières"). The ms. is dated 13–15 August 1927. The poem recounts the story of the celebrated lovers Tristan and Iseult, found in numerous versions in medieval Celtic and Breton literature. For "Acheron" (l. 24), see note on "Solution." For Persephone (l. 28), see note on "On Re-reading Baudelaire."

Trope. MS (DAW; JHLL; JHLS). In **SP*. The ms. is dated 12 August 1927.

Tryst at Lobos. MS (AH; JHLS). In **SP*. See "Eight Haiku" and "Strange Miniatures." For Lobos, see note on "Pool at Lobos."

Tule-Mists. Tr. (DSF).

Twilight. MS (JHLS).

The Twilight of the Gods. MS (JHLS). *Short Stories* 211, No. 5 (May 1951): 65. In **DC, SSU* (as "Los Sátiros son decornados" ["The Satyrs Are De-horned"]). First title: "Los Sátiros son mochos" ["The Satyrs Are Hornless"]. The title is an English version of the German term "Götterdämmerung"; one ms. has this title. For Mohammed (l. 2), see note on "Mohammed." For Pluto (l. 3), see note on "Farewell to Eros." For the Furies (l. 4), see note on "Cambion." For Melpomene (l. 7), see note on "Parnassus à la Mode." For Pan (l. 8), see note on "The Masque of Forsaken Gods." Hercules (l. 13) is the Latin form of the name Herakles, referring to the Greek hero who per-formed remarkable "labors" or feats of strength and bravery. For the witch of Endor (l. 15), see note on "Dominium in Excelsis." The Golden Fleece (l. 17), in Greek myth, was the fleece of a ram sought by the Argonauts. For

Apollo (l. 19), see note on "The Masque of Forsaken Gods." For Atropos (l. 20), see note on "Soliloquy in an Ebon Tower." For Adonis (l. 21), see note on "Secret Love." For Diana (l. 22), see note on "The Masque of Forsaken Gods." For the "Cyprian goddess" (l. 23), see note on "To One Absent." Bouguereau (l. 24) refers to William-Adolphe Bouguereau (1825–1905), French painter who specialized in mythological and historical paintings. For Pegasus (l. 25), see note on "The Chimera."

Twilight on the Snow. In *EC*, **SP, LO*.

Twilight Song. MS (JHLS; SHSW). *Wings* 7, No. 1 (Spring 1945): 18. In **SP, HD*. The ms. is dated 29 September 1942. An oread (l. 8) is, in Greek myth, a nymph of the mountains, a faun a somewhat gentler version of the Greek satyr.

The Twilight Woods. In **FD, LO*.

Two Myths and a Fable. MS (JHLS). In **DC, SSU*. The ms. is dated 20 June 1950. An English translation of the Spanish poem "Dos Mitos y una fabula." The Spanish version was written first.

Two on a Pillar. MS (JHLS). For "Stylite" (l. 1), see note on "Thebaid."

Ultima Thule. See "Thebaid."

The Unattainable. MS (JHLS). First draft of "The Expanding Ideal." Written early 1911?

The Unfinished Quest. See "The Infinite Quest."

Unicorn. MS (AH; DAW). In **SP, S&P*. See "Strange Miniatures" and "Strange Miniatures (Haiku)."

Union. MS (JHLS; NYPL). In **EC*. GS sent the poem back to CAS on 21 June 1922 (see *SU* 208); it is not clear when CAS sent the poem to GS. Lakme (l. 2) is a Westernized rendering of the Indian goddess Lakshmi, the wife of Vishnu and the symbol of creative force.

Unique. See "Incognita."

The Unknown. MS (JHLS). An English translation of the Spanish poem "Lo Ignoto." The Spanish version was probably written first.

The Unmerciful Mistress. See "Beauty Implacable."

The Unnamed. See "Cambion."

The Unremembered. In *ST* (as "The Unrevealed"), **SP*. "Avernian" (l. 8) is the adjectival form of Avernus, a lake in central Italy near which, according to Virgil (*Aeneid* 6.126f.), was a cave leading to the underworld.

The Unrevealed. See "The Unremembered."

Untold Arabian Fable. MS (AH; DAW). In *SP, S&P. See "Strange Miniatures" and "Strange Miniatures (Haiku)." Balkis (l. 1) is the Arabic name for the Queen of Sheba, found in the Koran.

Upon the Seas of Saturn. See "In Saturn."

A Valediction. MS (NYPL; Sx). *AJ* 23, No. 43 (9 August 1923): 6. *Buccaneer* 1, No. 1 (September 1924): 12. In *S*, *SP. The ms. is dated 16 July 1923. For GS's response to this poem, see note on "Change." GS added: "How Bierce would have exclaimed over 'A Valediction!'" (*SU* 235).

A Valediction. See "To George Sterling: A Valediction."

A Valediction to George Sterling. See "To George Sterling: A Valediction."

The Vampire Night (Sunset as of the world's concluding day:). MS (JHLS).

Variations. MS (JHLL). The ms. is dated 4 February 1929. First title: "Three Similes."

Vaticinations. MS (JHLL). In *SP. The ms. is dated 9 February 1929.

El Vendaval [English]. MS (JHLS). An English translation of a Spanish poem of the same title. The Spanish version was probably written first. The title translates to "The Hurricane."

El Vendaval [Spanish]. MS (JHLS). For an English translation of the same title, see p. 587.

Venus. MS (DAW; JHLS). In *SP. The ms. is dated 13 August 1927. The poem refers to the planet Venus, not the goddess (Roman counterpart of Aphrodite, goddess of love).

Verity. MS (JHLS). The ms. is dated 14 September 1952.

Verses. See "Souvenance."

Une Vie spectrale. MS (DAW; JHLL; JHLS; MCL; SHSW). In *SP. The ms. is dated 29 May 1929. The title translates to "A Spectral Life." See CAS's translation, "Spectral Life" (p. 398).

Vignettes and Indexes. MS (AH). In *SP* as part "Experiments in Haiku" (but without title) in the subsection "Distillations." Comprises "Fence and Wall"; "Growth of Lichen"; "Cats in Winter Sunlight"; "Abandoned Plum-Orchard"; "Harvest Evening"; "Willow-Cutting in Autumn"; "Declining Moon"; "Late Pear-Pruner"; and "Nocturnal Pines."

Les Violons. MS (JHLS). The ms. is dated 4 January 1927. The title is French for "The Violins."

A Vision of Lucifer. In *EC*, **SP*, *LO*. Lucifer ("the light-bearer") is cited in Isaiah 14:12 as a "son of the morning" who has "fallen from heaven" (here a figurative reference to the overthrow of the king of Babylon). The phrase was later interpreted as referring to Satan as the leader of the fallen angels. In a letter to GS (16 May 1913) CAS noted that one of the subjects in his notebook was "A Vision of Satan" (*SU* 89). SL commented that the poem was "one of the greatest sonnets ever written and in its proportion as tremendous a work as 'Paradise Lost'" (letter to CAS, 4 February 1918; ms., JHL).

The Voice in the Pines. MS (*JHLS; NYPL). In *IM*. Written c. 1911. GS has commented at the bottom of the ms.: "Beautiful—especially the first line."

The Voice of Silence. MS (*NYPL). In *PJ*. Written c. 1910. The poem was one of the first that CAS sent to GS, on 2 February 1911 (see *SU* 19). GS made several suggestions for revision: "I'd certainly cut out all those capitals, especially since those below seem worth retaining. . . . This last line seems rather unpoetically expressed. Bierce warns me to avoid lines made up entirely of monosyllables. I begin to agree with him more and more" (letter to GS, 28 February 1911; *SU* 21). CAS does not appear to have revised the poem in light of these remarks.

Vultures Come to the Ambarvalia. MS (JHLS). In **SP*. See "Mortal Essences." The Ambarvalia ("the procession around the fields") was a Roman festival to purify the fields, during which animals (usually pigs, sheep, and oxen) were led around the original boundary of Rome and then sacrificed.

The Waning Moon. MS (JHLS). In **FD*.

War. MS (JHLS).

Warning. MS (DAW; JHLL; JHLS). *WT* 12, No. 4 (October 1928): 525. In *DM* 320–21. In **SP*, *LO*. Written 3 March 1928.

Water-Fight. MS (AH). In **SP*. See "Childhood: Seven Haiku."

Water-Hemlock. MS (JHLS). In **SP*. See "Mortal Essences."

We Shall Meet. MS (JHLS [2 mss., one as "At the Last"]; NYPL; *Sx). *AJ* 23, No. 28 (26 April 1923): 6. *Wanderer* 2, No. 5 (May 1924): 60–61. In *S*, *SP*. First title: "At the Last." The ms. is dated 10 March 1923. CAS sent the poem to GS on 15 March 1923. GS commented: "Baudelaire (as translated) has nothing better than 'We Shall Meet.' I don't like that 'flaffing' [l. 33], though—it seems an absurd word *in itself*. I'd keep off the ultra-obsolete" (letter to CAS, 6 April 1923; *SU* 230).

Weavings. MS (*JHLS). In *PJ*. Written c. 1910.

The West Wind. MS (JHLS [as "To the West Wind"]). *Overland Monthly* 56, No. 6 (December 1910): 575. As by C. Ashton Smith. First title: "To the West Wind."

What Dreamest Thou, Muse? MS (*JHLS). *Asmodeus: Combined with Gargoyle* No. 2 (Fall 1951): 32. In *SSU*. For a French version, see "Que songes-tu, Muse?" (p. 629). For a Spanish version, see "¿Qué sueñas, Musa?" (p. 628).

Where Sleepest Thou, O Eldorado? MS (JHLS). An English translation of the Spanish poem "¿Donde duermes, Eldorado?"

The Whisper of the Worm. MS (DAW; JHLS; NYPL). In *SP* (as a translation of "Christophe des Laurières"), *LO*. Written 9 September 1918. "Sisyphean" (l. 3) refers to Sisyphus, the reputed founder of the city of Corinth. When Sisyphus saw the seduction of the nymph Aegina by Zeus and reported it to Aegina's father (the river-god Asopus), Zeus punished him by banishing him to the underworld, to spend eternity attempting to push a rock up to the top of a hill, which would roll back just as he was reaching the summit.

White Death. In *ST*. *Tesseract* 2, No. 5 (May 1937). *Tesseract Annual* 1, No. 1 (1939): 12. In *SP*, *LO*.

A White Rose. MS (JHLS).

Willow-Cutting in Autumn. MS (AH; DAW; JHLS). In *SP*, *S&P*. See "Distillations," "Haiku," and "Vignettes and Indexes."

The Wind and the Moon. In *ST*. CAS wrote to GS (15 September 1912): "It's interesting that you should have picked out 'The Wind and the Moon' as the poorest poem in the book. It's an earlier poem than any of the others, and was written rather more than two years ago. To me it seems that there are several others in the collection just as inferior, if not more so" (*SU* 63). GS's letter commenting on the poem does not appear to be extant.

Wind-Ripples. MS (NYPL). CAS copied the poem in a letter to GS (6 October 1911; *SU* 32). GS, commenting on this one and "A Live-Oak Leaf," copied in the same letter, wrote: "The 'lyrics in little' that you send are exquisite: I advise you to do more of such work, even though it's just about what the magazines want" (letter to CAS, 21 December 1911; *SU* 35).

The Wind-Threnody. In *BS*.

Windows at Lamplighting Time. In *SP*.

The Winds. In *ST*, *N1*, *SP*.

Wine of Summer. *Wings* 5, No. 6 (Summer 1942): 9. In *SP*.

The Wingless Archangels. MS (JHLS; *Sx). *AJ* 23, No. 37 (28 June 1923): 6. In *S*, *SP*, *LO*.

The Wings of Perfume. In *FD*.

Winter Midnight. See "Winter Moonlight" (After our fond, reiterate farewells).

Winter Moonlight (After our fond, reiterate farewells). MS (JHLS [as "Winter Midnight"]). In *SP, FD*. The ms. is dated 23 January 1929. Variant title: "Winter Midnight."

Winter Moonlight (The silence of the silver night). MS (MCL; NYPL). In *EC*, *SP*. Written before 24 April 1918. CAS commented on the poem: "Of its kind, the thing is nearer perfection than most of my verse" (letter to SL, 27 April 1918).

Winter Song. See "Brumal."

The Witch. See "The Witch with Eyes of Amber."

Witch-Dance. MS (MCL; SHSW). *WT* 36, No. 1 (September 1941): 104–5. In *SP, HD, LO*. Written before 29 April 1939.

The Witch in the Graveyard. MS (JHLS; MCL [as "The Witch in the Churchyard"]). Poetic drama. In *EC*, *SP, LO*. The ms. is dated 26–27 June 1913. The second of CAS's poetic dialogues, after "The Masque of Forsaken Gods" (p. 102). It was followed by "The Flight of Azrael" (p. 154) and "The Ghoul and the Seraph" (p. 195). CAS noted (letter to SL, 1 August 1913) that the poem was "my longest and perhaps most successful attempt at the weird and the ghastly" (ms., BL). CAS sent the poem to GS c. July–August 1913 (see *SU* 93). GS noted: "'The Witch in the Graveyard' is grimly impressive. I'd have been wild about it twelve years ago. Now I rather deplore seeing so much imagination on such a theme. But there's great work in it" (letter to CAS, 19 August 1913; *SU* 94). Hecate (l. 1) was a Greek goddess (the daughter of the Titan Perses and Asterie) who eventually became associated with the ghost world, sorcery, and black magic, being an attendant on Persephone in the underworld.

The Witch with Eyes of Amber. MS (JHLS [2 mss., one as "The Witch"]; NYPL). *AJ* 23, No. 32 (24 May 1923): 6. In *SP. Epos* 1, No. 4 (Summer 1950): 14. In *DC, LO*. Alternate titles: "The Witch" and "The Witch with the Heart of Amber." The ms. is dated 11 March 1923. CAS sent the poem to GS on 15 March 1923. GS commented: ". . . let me say I like 'The Witch with Eyes of Amber' immensely! A most luring and imaginative thing! I should think Mencken would fall on it with a whoop. Anyway, Poe would, were he now the editor of 'Smart Set'" (letter to CAS, 6 April 1923; *SU* 230). If the poem was submitted to Mencken for the *Smart Set*, it was rejected. See also note on "On the Canyon-Side."

Wizard's Love. MS (SHSW). In *SP. *Alchemist* (1941; i.e., *Deventioneer Alchemist*); not seen. *Golden Atom* No. 11 (1954–55): 90–91. In *HD*. Written before 20 December 1938. The various versions have 38, 41, and 42 lines.

The Wizardry of Winter. MS (JHLS). First title: "Winter."

The Wizardry of Winter. See "Autumn's Pall."

The Wraith of Beauty. See "The Nameless Wraith."

Ye Shall Return. MS (JHLS). In *DC, BB. The ms. is dated 30 September 1951. Mylitta (l. 13) is a Sumerian goddess of the moon and fertility.

The Years Restored. In *PD*. CAS sent the poem to GS on 8 June 1913. GS commented: "'The Years Restored' is a fine thing. I like particularly the line 'The gold long dim in Herculaneum' [l. 8]" (letter to CAS, 22 June 1913; *SU* 91). For Herculaneum, see note on "Enchanted Mirrors."

Yerba Buena. MS (JHLS; SHSW). *Wings* 7, No. 4 (Winter 1946): 14. In *SP, HD*. The ms. is dated 11 September 1941. The name is Spanish for "good herb." It was initially applied by the early Spanish settlers of California to an island off the coast of San Francisco, then to the early settlement of San Francisco itself.

You Are Not Beautiful. MS (NYPL [under "Tankas"] and JHLS [under "Tanka" and "Tankas"]; Sx). *AJ* 24, No. 10 (20 December 1923): 6. In *S, *SP*.

Zothique. MS (AH; JHLS). In *DC, LO, SSU*. The poem relates to CAS's invented realm of Zothique (see note on "Farewell to Eros"). For Lilith (l. 17), see note on "The Tears of Lilith."

Juvenilia

CAS's juvenilia falls into several discrete categories: (1) poems about the Arab world, largely inspired by Omar Khayyam's *Rubaiyat;* (2) poems about India; (3) poems on general topics, usually with a moralistic bent. It is not possible to determine any exact chronological sequence for these categories or for the poems within these categories. Following CAS's first poem, the juvenilia is printed as follows: (1) the extant poems from an apparent book of verse that CAS had prepared; (2) poems about the Arab world; (3) poems about India; (4) poems on general topics; (5) fragments and untitled poems. Poems in sections 2, 3, and 4 are presented alphabetically.

Alchemy. MS (JHLS).

Allah. MS (JHLS). An earlier version of the poem exists at JHLS.

Arab Song. MS (JHLS). Bendemeer (l. 10) is a river cited in Thomas Moore's Oriental poem *Lalla Rookh* (1817).

Arabian Love-Song. MS (JHLS). The ms. is numbered pp. 1 and 3; p. 2 appears to be missing.

Asia. MS (JHLS).

Aurungzeb's Mosque. MS (JHLS). Aurungzeb (1618–1707) was Emperor of Hindustan (1658–1707) and one of the greatest Muslim rulers of India. John Dryden wrote a verse tragedy about him, *Aureng-Zebe* (1675). Gunga (l. 1) is a variant spelling of the river Ganges. A Nizam (l. 12) is a viceroy in the state of Hyderabad, in south-central India.

Bedouin Song. In *SZ.*

Benares. MS (JHLS). Numbered pp. 20–23 on the ms. Verses VI–XI are found on the ms. of "Odes of Alnaschar." In *SZ* (stanzas I–IV only). Benares is a city in the province of Uttar Pradesh, India, on the north side of the Ganges. It is the holiest of India's cities and a popular resort for pilgrims. A Sudra (l. 21) is a member of the lowest of the four castes in Hindu society; a Brahmin is a member of the highest, or priestly, caste. For Siva (l. 34), see note on "A Dream of India." In regard to "Monkey temple" (l. 36): there are several monkey temples in the India-Nepal area, but CAS is presumably referring to the Durga Temple in Benares, built sometime in the 18th century and known for the many monkeys that inhabit it. For Aurungzebe (l. 39), see note on "Aurungzeb's Mosque."

The Book of Years. MS (JHLS).

The Burning Ghauts. MS (JHLS). Burning-ghauts (or -ghats) are funeral pyres placed at a level spot near the shore of a river in India.

The Burning-Ghauts at Benares. In *SH*. Evidently a revised version of "The Burning Ghauts."

The City of the Djinn. MS (JHLS). Apparently later revised as "The Palace of the Jinn" (p. 334). In the Islamic religion, a djinn (or jinn) is the inhabitant of a subtle and immaterial world who occasionally appears to human beings and performs prodigies. For Solomon (ll. 41 and 48), see note on "A Fable." Chilminar (l. 42), in the Islamic religion, and Balbec were two cities built by Jan ben Jan (l. 43), before the time of Adam. In Persian myth, Soliman Jan ben Jan was the last of forty kings who ruled over a race of gigantic spirits in remote antiquity. He is said to have built the Egyptian pyramids. (See also "Suleyman Jan ben Jan.") Chilminar is believed to be identical to Persepolis (see note on "Rosa Mystica"). "The mighty signet ring of Solomon" (l. 48) refers to medieval legends regarding a magic ring possessed by Solomon that allowed him to control demons or djinns.

Courage. MS (JHLS). Written c. 24 December 1906.

Dawn. MS (JHLS). The title is preceded by a series title, "Oriental Verse," but apparently no others were written.

Dawn. See "The Sunrise."

The Days of Time. MS (JHLS).

Delhi. MS (JHLS). Jumna (l. 1) is a river in northern India, the chief tributary of the Ganges. Alamquire (l. 8) is unidentified. The Moghuls (l. 9), or Mughals, were a Muslim dynasty that ruled northern India from 1526 to 1748. One of its chief leaders was Jellaladin Mahommed Akbar (1542-1605) (l. 8) (r. 1556–1605), who defeated the Hindu usurper Hemu and reestablished the dynasty in Hindustan. Alamgir was a title bestowed upon Aurungzeb, meaning "World Grasper." The Peacock Throne (l. 10) is a throne set up in the Imperial Palace (1638–48) in Delhi by Shah Jahan (r. 1628–58). In l. 10, "the glorious gem of Kohinoor" was a 186-carat diamond probably unearthed in the 14th century and later obtained by Queen Victoria. It has since been recut. For Aurungzebe (l. 25), see note on "Aurungzeb's Mosque."

The Departed City. MS (*JHLS). In *SZ*.

The Desert. MS (JHLS).

A Dream. MS (JHLS).

A Dream of India. MS (JHLS). Morpheus (l. 7) is, in Greek myth, the god of dreams and the son of Hypnos (sleep). "Thakurs" (l. 28) refers to the Thakuri or first Rajput dynasty (c. 633 C.E.) in what is now Nepal. Rajput (l. 43) refers to two separate dynasties in Nepal (the second dynasty ruled c. 1139 C.E.). In l. 47, Mussulmani is an archaic term for a Muslim. Vishnu (l. 65) is one of the three principal gods of Hinduism, the preserver god (Brahma is the creator god and S(h)iva is the destroyer). The poem may be incomplete, or CAS may have decided to end it abruptly with the suggestion that the narrator's dream continues in some other direction.

A Dream of Vathek. MS (JHLS). The title refers to Vathek, the protagonist of the Arabian fantasy *Vathek* (1786) by British writer William Beckford (1759–1844), which depicts the blasphemous Caliph Vathek suffer a series of punishments in the halls of Eblis (the Islamic devil). Many years later CAS wrote "The Third Episode of Vathek" (1932), a completion of a fragmentary tale that was to have been inserted into the latter portion of *Vathek* (it had been published in *The Episodes of Vathek* [1912]). Mahomet is a now archaic spelling of Mohammad (see note on "Mohammed"). Israfel (p. 316) is, in the Koran, one of the four archangels, specifically the archangel of music. He will play the resurrection trumpet on the last day.

A Dream of Zanoni. MS (JHLS). The title evidently refers to Zanoni, the central character of Edward Bulwer-Lytton's novel *Zanoni* (1842), dealing with an ancient Chaldean wizard who has lived for centuries seeking the secret of eternal life.

Eblis Repentant. MS (JHLS). Eblis is the Islamic devil. Suleyman I (l. 38) (1490?–1566), Sultan of Turkey (1520–66), raised the Turkish empire to its greatest extent. For Jan ben Jan (l. 39), see note on "The City of the Djinn." In the ms., CAS has crossed out ll. 65–68.

Fear. MS (JHLS).

The Fear of Death. MS (JHLS).

The Feast. MS (JHLS).

Fortune. MS (JHLS). Numbered p. 65 on the ms.

From the Persian (I read upon a gate in letters bold:). MS (NYPL).

From the Persian (Out of the Great Bazaar there came a cry). MS (JHLS).

From the Persian (I stood amid the ruins of a city great). MS (JHLS). The last two stanzas are largely similar to stanzas 17 and 18 of "The Rubaiyat of Seyyid" (p. 301). Jumsheed (l. 2) is apparently a variant spelling of Jamsheed Quli Qutb Shah (d. 1550), who ruled the Sultanate of Golconda (see note on "Ode from the Persian") from 1543 to 1550. Kaikhosru (l. 6) (or Kaikhausrau), in the Persian epic *Shah Namah*, is the 13th and greatest of the Iranian kings. Kaikobad [or Kaiqubad] the Great (l. 9), in the *Shah Namah*, is the 11th Iranian king. Sultan Mahmud (l. 10) is Mahmud (971?–1030), Sultan of Ghazni (997–1030), best known for his repeated attempts to spread Islam by force in India.

The Ganges. MS (JHLS). The poem is addressed to the longest and holiest river in India. Gaya (l. 2) is a district in the province of Bihar in India; also the chief city in that district. Gungas (l. 4) is a variant spelling of Ganges.

Haroun Al-Raschid. MS (JHLS). The poem is about Haroun Al-Raschid (more properly Harun al-Rashid) (763?–809), Caliph of Baghdad (786–809) who raised the caliphate to its greatest extent. He is frequently cited in the *Arabian Nights.*

Hate and Love. MS (JHLS).

Hope. MS (JHLS).

The Inscription. MS (JHLS).

Jewel of the Orient (Amid palm groves and almond trees,). MS (JHLS). The conclusion of the poem is apparently non-extant. Mahound (l. 14) is a variant spelling of Mohammed, found in medieval and later European literature. For Haroun al-Raschid (l. 62), see note on "Haroun Al-Raschid." The poem may be a fragment.

Jewel of the Orient (In Bagdad, capital of the caliphate,). MS (JHLS). A fragment.

Kismet. MS (JHLS). Kismet is an Arabic and Hindi term referring to fate.

The Land o' Dreams. MS (JHLS).

The Leveler. MS (JHLS).

Love. MS (JHLS).

The Lure of Gold. MS (JHLS). See also note on "Sunrise."

Mercy. MS (JHLS).

Mohammed. MS (JHLS). The poem is about Mohammed (570?–632), the founder of Islam.

The Moon. MS (JHLS).

The Muezzin. MS (JHLS). The poem is headed with a series title, "Oriental Poems," but no others were apparently written. (But see note on "Dawn.")

The Ocean. MS (JHLS). Numbered p. 77 on the ms.

Ode from the Persian. MS (JHLS). A fragment. Bokhara (l. 1) is a city now in Uzbekistan and once an important Muslim intellectual and theological center. Samarkand is a city now in Uzbekistan, originally the capital of Sogdiana. It was conquered by Alexander the Great in 329. Later revived by the Turks and Arabs, it was destroyed by Genghis Khan in 1220. It revived once more and became the home of Tamerlane, who made it the most important city in central Asia. Golconda (l. 3) was a city in the province of Hyderabad, India, known for its diamonds and for the mausoleums of ancient kings. Bokreen is unidentified.

Odes of Alnaschar. MS (JHLS). Alnaschar is a character in the *Arabian Nights*. A seller of glassware, he is so taken with the thought of the wealth he will soon accrue that he breaks all his products. For Ispahan (l. 14), see note on "Surréalist Sonnet."

Omar's Philosophy. MS (JHLS). Variant title: "Quatrains." For Omar Khayyam, the subject of the poem, see note on "To Omar Khayyam."

The Orient. MS (JHLS). Numbered pp. 59–60 on the ms. Tamerlane (l. 29) (variant form of Timur-Leng) (1336?–1405) was a Mongol conqueror who annexed many regions in central Asia and also invaded India (1398f.) and Turkey (1402f.).

The Palace of the Jinn. MS (JHLS). Evidently a fragment. See "The City of the Djinn." For jinns (or djinns), see note on "The City of the Djinn." For "Afrit" (l. 19), see note on "Dominion."

Perseverance. MS (JHLS).

Poem. MS (JHLS). The title, as well as the first two lines, are difficult to read, as the ms. is mutilated.

The Prayer Rug (How calm, O Rug of Persian loom). MS (JHLS). For Ispahan (l. 8), see note on "Surréalist Sonnet." "Mohammedan" (l. 10) is a now archaic term for a Muslim. For Mahmud (l. 24), see note on "From the Persian." Between ll. 15 and 16 CAS has crossed out the following lines: "Oh, sweep aside the veil of years / That mystic bar I may not pierce / And let me still though dimly see / Some shadow of thy thronged past." After l. 36 he has crossed out the following lines: "What magic strange, what spell is it / By which I am and they are not!"

The Prayer Rug (Out of the past thou comest, rug of Persian loom,). MS (JHLS). Numbered pp. 27–28 on the ms.

The Prince and the Peri. MS (JHLS). A peri, in Persian myth, is a member of a race of supernatural beings, originally depicted as evil or malevolent but later deemed to be benevolent and endowed with grace and beauty. Peristan (l. 27) was a pre-Islamic region in what is now northern Afghanistan and northern Pakistan. Ormuz (l. 53) (or Hormuz) was a city on the south coast of Persia at the entrance to the Persian Gulf. It was renowned for its immense wealth. CAS may, however, be referring to the Strait of Ormuz (Hormuz), leading into the gulf.

Quatrain. MS (JHLS). Written on the same page as "Resignation." Kaaba (l. 4) is a cube-shaped building in the center of the Great Mosque at Mecca and the most sacred Islamic shrine. In one corner is a black stone said to have been given to Ishmael by the angel Gabriel, which penitents touch to be forgiven of their sins.

Quatrains (Think not of the past,). MS (JHLS). See also [Fragment 5].

Quatrains (In his path the hunters set). MS (JHLS). For Eblis (l. 5), see note on "Eblis Repentant." Juggurnath (l. 8) (or Juggernaut), in Hinduism, is a form of the god Krishna or Rama, and lord of the world.

Quatrains on Jewels. MS (*JHLS; MH). The quatrain "The Opal" was never written.

Resignation. MS (JHLS). Written on the same page as "Quatrain."

The River. MS (JHLS). A fragment.

The River of Life. In *SZ*.

Rubaiyat (I sought in wingèd flight from star to star). MS (JHLS). The title is derived from the *Rubaiyat of Omar Khayyam* (see note on "To Omar Khayyam"). For Cathay (l. 3), see note on "Beyond the Great Wall."

Rubaiyat (Some talk of paradise and some of Hell,). MS (JHLS). For Ispahann (or Ispahan) (l. 14), see note on "Surréalist Sonnet."

Rubaiyat of Saiyed. MS (JHLS). Evidently a fragment.

The Rubaiyat of Seyyid. MS (JHLS). In *SZ* (fragmentary). The ms. appears to be fragmentary: the first four stanzas are on a page labeled 33; stanzas 17–24 are found on a page labeled 37. Stanzas 21–24 are also found on the verso of "The Book of Years" (labeled p. 38). Stanzas 17 and 18 are largely similar to the final two stanzas of "From the Persian" (p. 328). For Kaikobad the Great (l. 17) and "Sultan Mahmud" (l. 18), see note on "From the Persian." "Shiraz garden" (l. 30) refers to Shiraz, a city in Persia reputedly founded in 693 C.E. and renowned for its gardens.

Sea-Lure. MS (JHLS).

The Sea-Shell. MS (JHLS).

The Seekers. MS (JHLS). First title: "Song." The poem appears on the same page as "Suleyman Jan ben Jan" (p. 345). At the end of the ms., four lines have been crossed out: "They may seek and pant for it, / Still it is forbidden. / In heaven the words are writ: 'These things may never be known to man.'"

Silence. MS (JHLS).

The Skull. MS (JHLS). Numbered p. 58 on the ms.

Solitude. MS (JHLS). A surviving typescript (found on the back of the poem "A Memory") has only one stanza. The complete version is on the verso of the poem "Despondency."

Some Maxims from the Persian. MS (JHLS). Earlier titles for the poem include "Some Maxims" and "Verses of Kamal."

Stamboul. MS (JHLS). Revision of "Haroun Al-Raschid." The title is a Western equivalent for the Turkish city of Istanbul (Constantinople).

Suleyman Jan ben Jan. MS (JHLS). The poem appears on the same page as "The Seekers" (p. 343). For the subject of the poem, see note on "The City of the Djinn."

Summer Idleness. MS (JHLS).

Sunrise. MS (JHLS). Numbered p. 52 on the ms. The poem appears on a list (MS [JHLS]) headed "Poems," as follows: "1. An Egyptian Love-Song. 2. The Lure of Gold. 3. The Song of the Leper. 4. The Outcast. 5. To an Eastern City. 6. The Brazen Idol. 7. To the Nile. 8. To the Orient. 9. Sunrise. 10. Winter. 11. The Crusader's Return. 12. The Marching Song." Aside from nos. 2, 5, and 9, these poems appear to be non-extant.

The Temple. MS (JHLS). The conclusion of the poem appears to be missing.

Time. MS (JHLS). Numbered p. 61 on the ms.

To an Eastern City. MS (JHLS). Numbered p. 62 on the ms. See also note on "Sunrise."

To the Best Beloved. MS (JHLS).

The World (Life is but a fleeting shadow,). MS (*JHLS). In *SZ*. For El Dorado (l. 3), see note on "¿Donde duermes, Eldorado?"

The World (The world is full of ups and downs,). MS (JHLS).

Youth and Age. MS (JHLS).

Zuleika: An Oriental Song. MS (*JHLS). In *SZ*. Zuleika is a popular name for women in Persian poetry.

[Untitled]. *AJ* 2, No. 62 (27 March 1915): 1. CAS's first poem, written when "he was a very little lad" (i.e., c. 1900?).

[Fragment 1]. MS (JHLS). Numbered pp. 8–10 on the ms. Chittore (l. 4) (or Chittur or Chittoor) is a city in the Andhra Pradesh province of India. For Rajput (l. 7), see note on "A Dream of India." Rana (l. 8) refers to a dynasty that ruled Nepal from 1846 to 1953. For Akbar (l. 12), see note on "Delhi." Chitrung Mori (l. 13) was a king of Puar in India and the founder of Chittore; Khoumbhou was a palace built by one of the Rana kings. The Kherut

(l. 14) (or Kheerut) Khoomb is a "Tower of the Victory of Khoumbhou" in Puar. Pudmani (l. 21) was the daughter of one of the Rana kings who married a Muslim sultan.

[Fragment 2]. MS (JHLS). Numbered pp. 13, 15, 16, and 18 on the ms. Ramadan (l. 3) is the ninth month of the Muslim calendar, during which fasting and other actions are observed. The Azân (l. 44), or Athan, is a call to prayer in Islam.

[Fragment 3]. MS (JHLS). Numbered p. 3 on the ms., but it is unclear whether it belongs with the "book" printed above. The ms. also contains a stanza VII, but this is identical to stanza VI in [Fragment 2]. The opening lines are similar to those of "From the Persian" (I stood amid the ruins of a city great). For Jumsheed (l. 2), see note on that poem.

[Fragment 4]. MS (JHLS). For Kamal, see "Some Maxims from the Persian." It is not entirely clear that the final couplet actually belongs with this poem.

[Fragment 5]. MS (JHLS). Apparently an early version of "Quatrains" (Think not of the past,).

[Fragment 6]. MS (JHLS). The item appears on the same page as "Rubaiyat" (I sought in wingèd flight from star to star). "The Afghan Knife" may be a juvenile short story (non-extant).

[Fragment 7]. MS (JHLS). The item appears on the same page as "To the Best Beloved."

Fragments and Untitled Poems

[1] Al borde de Leteo. MS (JHLS). Apparently a fragment. The title is Spanish for "At the Edge of Lethe." It is not a translation of the French poem "Au bord du Léthé" (p. 375).

[2] Ballad of a Lost Soul. MS (JHLS). Between stanzas 7 and 8 the following stanza appears crossed out: "For I who thought to burn a flare / Lighting the infernal roads, / Pass on its scenes, to prove the dreams / Of sky-concealed abodes." The ms. is labeled "unfinished" at the bottom.

[3] The Brook. MS (JHLS). Apparently a fragment.

[4] [Christmas card verses.] Tr. (DSF). Written in 1931, and entered by Ethel Heiple (with three verses of her own), in a Christmas card verse contest. Mrs. Heiple won $25 for one of her verses and gave half to CAS.

[5] Demogorgon. MS (JHLS). CAS has written at the bottom of the ms.: "Fragmentary drama." CAS discusses the work in a letter to GS (3 October 1913; SU 97): "I'm incubating a number of ideas—one of them quite the biggest that I'm ever likely to get hold of. If I manage to handle it with any measure of success, it will dwarf all my past work, and (I fear) will make anything subsequent in the line of the sidereal seem rather tame and anticlimactic. The title will be 'Demogorgon,' and the poem a sort of one-act drama in which the suns gather and take council against God, whom they regard as their common enemy—an invisible, tremendous God who alters and destroys them at will, or sends forth plagues of comets, etc. I shall give 'speaking parts' to the principal suns, such as Antares, Rigel, Betelguese [*sic*], and Vega, and have choruses of constellations and galaxies. I shall fill the speeches of three stars with the most Titanic blasphemies of which my imagination is capable—and I think you'll admit that there are opportunities for what is usually termed blasphemy, in the idea." The epigraph is from Shelley's verse drama *Prometheus Unbound* (1820), 1.207. For the name Demogorgon, see note on "Minatory." In Shelley's drama, Demogorgon is the ruler of all the gods who finally relents and releases Prometheus. In ll. 15–19, Spica is the brightest star in the constellation Virgo; Procyon is the principal star in the constellation Canis Minor; Betelgeuse is a first-magnitude red star in the constellation Orion; Rutilicus is a variable star in the constellation Hercules; Alderamin is a star in the constellation Cepheus; Rigel is a double star in the constellation Orion; Bellatrix is a second-magnitude star in the constellation Orion; Aludra, Mirzam, and Phurud are all third-magnitude stars in the constellation Canis Major; Fomalhaut is the brightest star in the constellation Piscis Australis; Saiph is a third-magnitude star in Orion; Achernar is the brightest star in the constellation Eridanus. For Altair (l. 16), see note on "The Absence of the Muse." For Canopus (l. 19), see note on "Cleopatra."

[6] **Despondency.** MS (JHLS).

[7] **The Flight of the Seraphim.** MS (JHLS).

[8] **For Iris.** MS (JHLS). Written 18 April 1923. CAS has written "fragment" at the bottom of the ms. Iris, in Greek myth, is the goddess of the rainbow and the sister of the Harpies. CAS, however, appears to be referring to a woman of his acquaintance (see *SU* 231). "Mytelene" (l. 8) is CAS's misspelling of Mytilene, the chief city on the island of Lesbos. For another version, see "To Iris" (p. 655).

[9] **Haunting.** MS (JHLS). The ms. is dated 12 December 1912. In l. 11, CAS has initially written "menace of infinities" but then crossed it out, substituting nothing in its place.

[10] **The Milky Way.** MS (JHLS).

[11] **Night** (Twilight dim and gray,). In *SZ*.

[12] **The Night Wind.** MS (JHLS).

[13] No-Man's-Land. MS (JHLS). CAS has written "unfinished" at the bottom of the ms. The epigraph is from "The Wharf of Dreams," in *The Man with the Hoe and Other Poems* (New York: Doubleday & McClure, 1899), p. 64, by Edwin Markham (1852–1940), a colleague of Bierce and GS. GS considered the poem one of the greatest sonnets ever written, a judgment with which CAS apparently did not agree (see *SU* 38–39).

[14] Ode on Matter. MS (JHLS). Written 1912. Unfinished. See also "Ode to Matter" (p. 19).

[15] The Regained Past. MS (JHLS [fragment]).

[16] The Saturnienne. MS (JHLS). The relation of this poem to "The Saturnienne" (p. 280) is unclear.

[17] Sonnets of the Desert. MS (JHLS).

[18] The Temptation (In the close and clinging night,) MS (JHLS). For Lilith (l. 1), see note on "The Tears of Lilith."

[19] To a Comet. MS (JHLS).

[20] To Iris ("Nymph of the harvest-coloured hair"). MS (JHLS). A variant version of "For Iris" (p. 648). It is not clear which version was written first.

[21] To Iris ("Hidden within thy heart . . ."). MS (JHLS).

[22] To the Sun (Thou most august and everlasting one). MS (JHLS).

[23] The Vampire Night (The darkness falls like some great, silent doom,). MS (JHLS). Evidently an attempt to rewrite "The Vampire Night" (p. 53).

[24] Inscription by CAS in Genevieve Sully's copy of *A Wine of Wizardry*. Written c. 1927–1929.

[25] MS (JHLS). CAS has written "Fragment" at the bottom of the ms. For Circe (l. 3), see note on "Belated Love."

[26] MS (JHLS). This and the following two fragments were found in a series of aphorisms typed on the back of "Isle of the Shipwrecked."

[27] MS (JHLS).

[28] MS (JHLS).

[29] MS (JHLS). CAS has written "fragment" at the bottom of the ms.

[30] MS (JHLS). Found on the back of the ms. of "Simile" (Truth is a soundless gong).

[31] MS (JHLS). In **SP*. The epigraph for the section of *SP* subtitled "Incantations" (never published as a book). For "Hesperidean" (l. 2), see note on

"Song (from *The Fugitives*)." The ms. reads: "A spell to raise the vast auroras furled / Within the vaults of future skies, / And moons that were; to exorcise / This monstrous spectre called the world."

[32] MS (JHLS). In **SP* (as a translation of "Christophe des Laurières"). The epigraph for the section of *SP* subtitled "The Jasmine Girdle" (never published as a book). For Antares (l. 2), see note on "The Star-Treader."

[33] MS (JHLS).

[34] MS (JHLS).

[35] The epigraph to the section "Translations and Paraphrases" of *SP*, as by Christophe des Laurières.

[36] MS (JHLS).

[37] MS (JHLS).

[38] MS (JHLS).

[39] MS (JHLS).

[40] MS (JHLS).

[41] MS (JHLS).

[42] MS (JHLS). Labeled as p. 2 on the ms. At the end there are 20 additional lines, crossed out.

[43] MS (JHLS). Proteus is, in Homer's *Odyssey* (4.351f.), a sea-god capable of changing his shape at will.

[44] MS (JHLS). At the end of the ms., CAS has written "unfinished." Neoplatonism (l. 3) is a school of philosophy fostered by Plotinus and his disciples beginning in the third century C.E., which sought to meld the ideas of Plato, Aristotle, the Stoics, and other ancient thinkers into a phosophical and religious synthesis. Ovid (l. 3) (P. Ovidius Naso, 43 B.C.E.–17 C.E.) influenced CAS with such works as the *Metamorphoses* and the *Ars Amatoria*. "Spencer" (l. 4) refers to British positivist philosopher Herbert Spencer (1820–1903), whose densely technical style CAS apparently did not favor.

[45] MS (JHLS). Carol Smith has added a note: "Copied 10/67."

[46] MS (JHLS).

[47] MS (JHLS). Probably written c. 1910.

[48] MS (JHLS).

[49] MS (JHLS).

[50] MS (JHLS). Labeled as p. 2 on the ms.

[51] MS (JHLS). Labeled as p. 2 on the ms.

[52] MS (JHLS). The lines seem to have some relation to fragment 108.

[53] MS (JHLS).

[54] MS (JHLS).

[55] MS (JHLS).

[56] MS (JHLS). CAS has appended the note: "(Fragment)."

[57] MS (JHLS).

[58] MS (JHLS). The ms. is dated 6 June 1925. Croesus (l. 4) was the last king of Lydia (560?–546 B.C.E.) and reputed to be fabulously wealthy. For Asmodai (l. 6), see note on "Interrogation."

[59] MS (JHLS).

[60] MS (JHLS).

[61] MS (JHLS).

[62] MS (JHLS).

[63] MS JHLS). CAS has appended the note: "Fragment."

[64] MS (JHLS).

[65] MS (JHLS). For Cypris (l. 4), see note on "Dedication: To Carol." For Apollo (l. 4), see note on "The Masque of Forsaken Gods."

[66] MS (JHLS). The ms. is written on an envelope postmarked 15 July 1948. For Moloch (l. 1), see note on "Some Blind Eidolon."

[67] MS (JHLS).

[68] MS (JHLS).

[79] MS (JHLS). A complete sonnet, lacking a title; probably written c. 1910.

[70] MS (JHLS). The ms is dated 25 May 1912.

[71] *BB* 51.

[72] *BB* 77. For Cimmerian (l. 4), see note on "Ode on Imagination."

[73] *BB* 87.

[74] *BB* 90.

[75] *BB* 91. For Persephone (l. 2), see note on "On Re-reading Baudelaire."

[76] *BB* 94.

[77] *BB* 95.

[78] *BB* 96.

[79] *BB* 98. Xiphias (l. 2) is a modern constellation equivalent to Dorado.

[80] *BB* 103. Yoros and Ayair (l. 2) are CAS's inventions.

[81] *BB* 104.

[82] *BB* 106.

[83] BB 107.

[84] *BB* 108.

[85] *BB* 111.

[86] *BB* 115.

[87] *BB* 116.

[88] *BB* 119.

[89] *BB* 122.

[90] *BB* 124.

[91] *BB* 127.

[92] *BB* 128.

[93] *BB* 142.

[94] *BB* 145.

[95] *BB* 147.

[96] *BB* 157.

[97] *BB* 158.

[98] *BB* 178.

[99] *BB* 185.

[100] Broceliande. *BB* 186. Brocéliande is the medieval name for Paimpont forest, near Rennes in Brittany. It was the setting for a number of tales of Arthurian legend. After the first five lines, the item appears to devolve into prose.

[101] *BB* 191.

[102] *BB* 197.

[103] *BB* 198. A haiku.

[104] *BB* 199.

[105] *BB* 201.

[106] *BB* 202. Acheron (l. 2) and Phlegethon (l. 5) are rivers in the Greek underworld.

[107] *BB* 203. A slight variant is found in *BB* 92.

[108] Twilight Pilgrimage. *BB* 206. Cf. fragment 52.

[109] *BB* 218.

[110] *BB* 219.

[111] *BB* 221.

[112] *BB* 222. For "Devachanic," see note on "Enchanted Mirrors."

[113] *BB* 227.

[114] *BB* 228.

[115] *BB* V:9.

[116] *BB* V:10.

[117] *BB* V:11.

[118] *SS* VB:3. Fragments 118–21 comprise items left out of *BB*.

[119] *SS* VB:4. In *EOD*. Written c. 1918.

[120] *SS* A:1. Vixeela is a character in the story "The Theft of the Thirty-nine Girdles" (written 1953–57; *Saturn Science Fiction and Fantasy*, March 1958). The various fragments may have been intended as epigraphs to the story. The fragment beginning "Thy name, an invocation, calls to light" also exists in JHLS under the title "Elegy for Vixeela."

[121] *SS* A:4. Written c. 1954–61.

[122] MSs (JHLS).

[123] Ode to Antares. Included in the story "The Monster of the Prophecy" (written 3 December 1929). *WT* 19, No. 1 (January 1932): 11. In *OST*. For Antares, see note on "The Star-Treader."

[124] The Song of Xeethra. MS (JHLS). Designed as an epigraph to the story "The Dark Eidolon" (written 23 December 1932). *WT* 25, No. 1 (January 1935): 93. In *OST*. Xeethra is a shepherd later featured in the story "Xeethra" (written February–March 1934; *WT*, December 1934). Thasaidon (l. 1) is the Lord of the Underworld in the realm of Zothique.

[125] Song of the Galley Slaves. MS (JHLS). Designed as an epigraph to the story "Necromancy in Naat" (written 1934/35). *WT* 28, No. 1 (July 1936): 2. In **LW*. Written 6 February 1935. Naat is a region in CAS's realm of Zothique.

[126] Song of King Hoaraph's Bowmen. MS (JHLS). Designed as an epigraph to the story "The Black Abbot of Puthuum" (written 1935–36). *WT* 27, No. 3 (March 1936): 308. In **GL. WT*, March 1936). The tale is set in CAS's realm of Zothique.

[127] Ludar's Litany to Thasaidon (Black Lord of bale and fear, master of all confusion!). The epigraph to the story "The Death of Ilalotha" (written 16 March 1937). *WT* 30, No. 3 (September 1937): 323. In **OST*. The story is part of CAS's Zothique cycle. Thasaidon is the Lord of the Underworld.

[128] from Ludar's Litany to Thasaidon (Lord of the sultry, red parterres). The epigraph to the story "The Garden of Adompha" (written 31 July 1937). *WT* 31, No. 4 (April 1938): 393. In **GL*.

Appendix

The Abalone Song. San Francisco: Grabhorn Press for Albert Bender, 1937. (Three fugitive stanzas by unknown authors, as transcribed by DSF, are also provided.) The poem was largely written (or at least begun) by GS, but a number of GS's colleagues later added stanzas to it; CAS is reputed to have contributed some stanzas, but it is not known which ones.

Song. See notes above to "The Song of Aviol" under "The Fugitives.

Voices. MS (*AH; JHLS). The poem is signed "José Velasco (trans. By Clark Ashton Smith)." No Spanish-language poet of this name has been identified. The poem likely is by CAS himself.

Index of Titles

Index of First Lines

CPSIA information can be obtained
at www.ICGtesting.com
Printed in the USA
BVHW01s1651160718
520822BV00011B/30/P